SOLOMON
ISLANDS

BUSINESS LAW HANDBOOK

International Business Publications, USA
Washington, DC, USA- Solomon Islands

SOLOMON ISLANDS

BUSINESS LAW HANDBOOK

Editorial content: International Business Publications, USA

Editor-in-Chief:	**Dr. Igor S. Oleynik**
Editor:	**Natasha Alexander**
Managing Editor:	**Karl Cherepanya**

Published by: International Business Publications, USA
P.O.Box 15343, Washington, DC 20003
Phone: (202) 546-2103, Fax: (202) 546-3275.
E-mail: rusric@erols.com

UPDATED ANNUALLY

We express our sincere gratitude to all government agencies and international organizations which provided information and other materials for this handbook

Databases & Information: International Business Publications, USA
Cover Design: International Business Publications, USA

2006 Updated Reprint International Business Publications, USA
ISBN 0-7397-4661-8

For customer service and information, please contact:
in the USA: **International Business Publications, USA**
P.O.Box 15343, Washington, DC 20003
Phone: (202) 546-2103, Fax: (202) 546-3275.
E-mail: rusric@erols.com

Printed in the USA

SOLOMON
ISLANDS

BUSINESS LAW HANDBOOK

TABLE OF CONTENTS

STRATEGIC AND DEVELOPMENT PROFILES

Background:	The UK established a protectorate over the Solomon Islands in the 1890s. Some of the most bitter fighting of World War II occurred on these islands. Self-government was achieved in 1976 and independence two years later. Ethnic violence, government malfeasance, and endemic crime have undermined stability and civil society.

GEOGRAPHY

Location:	Oceania, group of islands in the South Pacific Ocean, east of Papua New Guinea
Geographic coordinates:	8 00 S, 159 00 E
Map references:	Oceania
Area:	total: 28,450 sq km water: 910 sq km land: 27,540 sq km
Area - comparative:	slightly smaller than Maryland
Land boundaries:	0 km
Coastline:	5,313 km
Maritime claims:	measured from claimed archipelagic baselines territorial sea: 12 NM exclusive economic zone: 200 NM continental shelf: 200 NM
Climate:	tropical monsoon; few extremes of temperature and weather
Terrain:	mostly rugged mountains with some low coral atolls
Elevation extremes:	lowest point: Pacific Ocean 0 m highest point: Mount Makarakomburu 2,447 m
Natural resources:	fish, forests, gold, bauxite, phosphates, lead, zinc, nickel
Land use:	arable land: 1.5% permanent crops: 0.64% other: 97.86% (1998 est.)

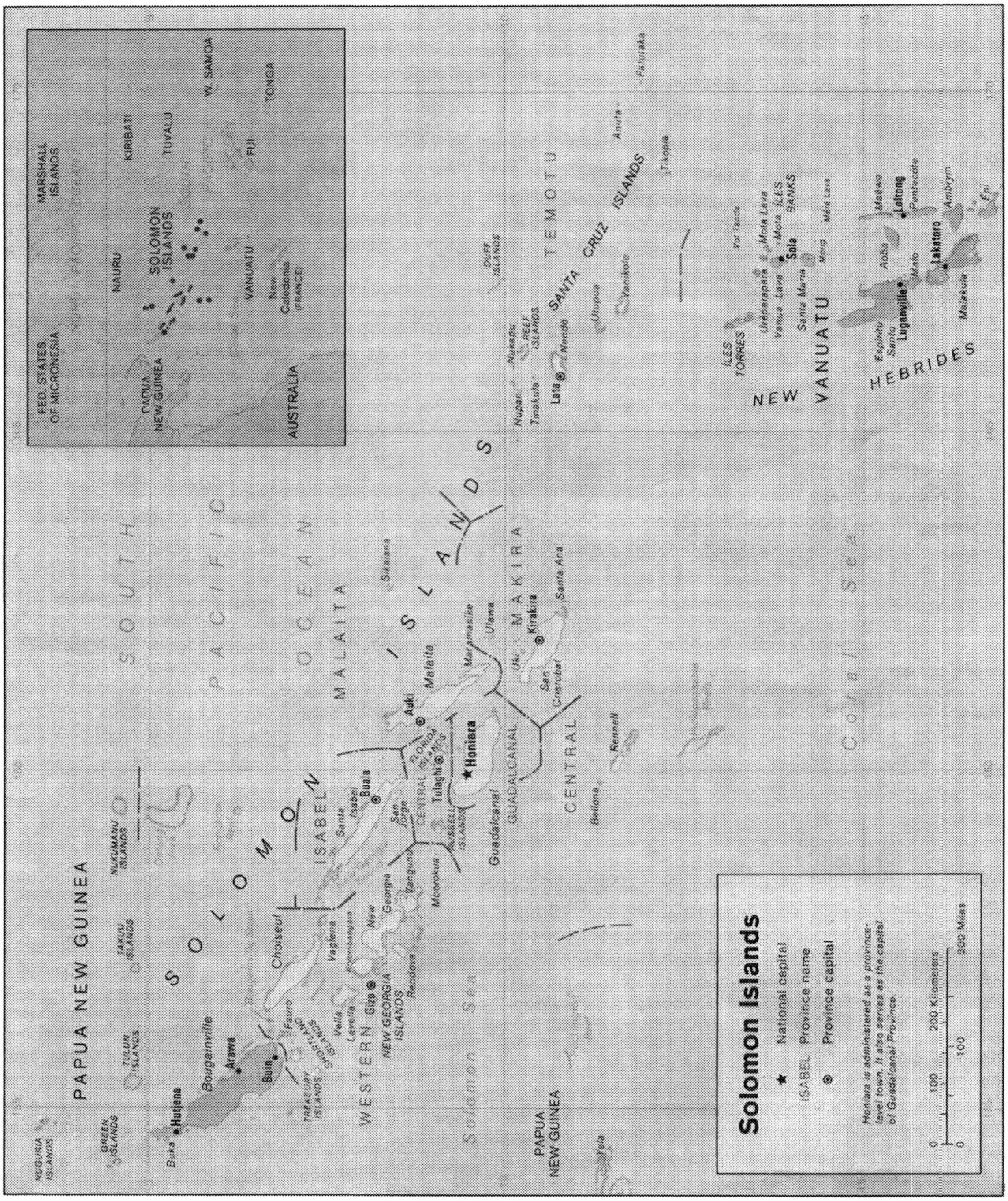
Solomon Islands
National capital
ISABEL Province name
Province capital
PAPUA NEW GUINEA
SOLOMON ISLANDS
SOUTH PACIFIC OCEAN
Solomon Sea
Coral Sea
WESTERN
ISABEL
MALAITA
CENTRAL
GUADALCANAL
MAKIRA
TEMOTU
SANTA CRUZ ISLANDS
VANUATU
NEW HEBRIDES
Honiara
Auki
Buala
Gizo
Tulaghi
Kirakira
Lata
Bougainville
Choiseul
Malaita
Guadalcanal
San Cristobal
Rennell
Bellona
AUSTRALIA

Natural hazards:	typhoons, but rarely destructive; geologically active region with frequent earth tremors; volcanic activity
Environment - current issues:	deforestation; soil erosion; many of the surrounding coral reefs are dead or dying
Environment - international agreements:	party to: Biodiversity, Climate Change, Desertification, Environmental Modification, Law of the Sea, Marine Dumping, Marine Life Conservation, Ozone Layer Protection, Whaling signed, but not ratified: Climate Change-Kyoto Protocol
Geography - note:	strategic location on sea routes between the South Pacific Ocean, the Solomon Sea, and the Coral Sea

PEOPLE

Population:	494,786 (July 2002 est.)
Age structure:	0-14 years: 43.4% (male 109,339; female 105,170) 15-64 years: 53.5% (male 134,125; female 130,804) 65 years and over: 3.1% (male 7,467; female 7,881) (2002 est.)
Population growth rate:	2.91% (2002 est.)
Birth rate:	33.26 births/1,000 population (2002 est.)
Death rate:	4.19 deaths/1,000 population (2002 est.)
Net migration rate:	0 migrant(s)/1,000 population (2002 est.)
Sex ratio:	at birth: 1.05 male(s)/female under 15 years: 1.04 male(s)/female 15-64 years: 1.03 male(s)/female 65 years and over: 0.95 male(s)/female total population: 1.03 male(s)/female (2002 est.)
Infant mortality rate:	23.68 deaths/1,000 live births (2002 est.)
Life expectancy at birth:	total population: 71.82 years female: 74.39 years (2002 est.) male: 69.38 years
Total fertility rate:	4.5 children born/woman (2002 est.)
Nationality:	noun: Solomon Islander(s) adjective: Solomon Islander
Ethnic groups:	Melanesian 93%, Polynesian 4%, Micronesian 1.5%, European 0.8%,

	Chinese 0.3%, other 0.4%
Religions:	Anglican 45%, Roman Catholic 18%, United (Methodist/Presbyterian) 12%, Baptist 9%, Seventh-Day Adventist 7%, other Protestant 5%, indigenous beliefs 4%
Languages:	Melanesian pidgin in much of the country is lingua franca; English is official but spoken by only 1%-2% of the population note: 120 indigenous languages
Literacy:	definition: NA total population: NA% male: NA% female: NA%

GOVERNMENT

Country name:	conventional long form: none conventional short form: Solomon Islands former: British Solomon Islands
Government type:	parliamentary democracy tending toward anarchy
Capital:	Honiara
Administrative divisions:	9 provinces and 1 capital territory*; Central, Choiseul (Lauru), Guadalcanal, Honiara*, Isabel, Makira, Malaita, Rennell/Bellona, Temotu, Western
Independence	7 July 1978 (from UK)
National holiday:	Independence Day, 7 July (1978)
Constitution:	7 July 1978
Legal system:	English common law, which is widely disregarded
Suffrage:	21 years of age; universal
Executive branch:	chief of state: Queen ELIZABETH II (since 6 February 1952), represented by Governor General Sir John LAPLI (since NA 1999) elections: none; the monarch is hereditary; governor general appointed by the monarch on the advice of Parliament for up to five years; following legislative elections, the leader of the majority party or the leader of a majority coalition is usually elected prime minister by Parliament; deputy prime minister appointed by the governor general on the advice of the prime minister from among the members of Parliament cabinet: Cabinet consists of 20 members appointed by the governor general on the advice of the prime minister from among the members of Parliament head of government: Prime Minister Allan KEMAKEZA (since 17 December 2001); Deputy Prime Minister Snyder RINI (since 17

	December 2001)
Legislative branch:	unicameral National Parliament (50 seats; members elected from single-member constituencies by popular vote to serve four-year terms) election results: percent of vote by party - PAP 40%, SIACC 40%, PPP 20%; seats by party - PAP 16, SIACC 13, PPP 2, SILP 1, independents 18 elections: last held 5 December 2001 (next to be held by December 2005)
Judicial branch:	Court of Appeal
Political parties and leaders:	Association of Independents [Snyder RINI]; People's Alliance Party or PAP [Allan KEMAKEZA]; People's Progressive Party or PPP [Mannaseh Damukana SOGAVARE]; Solomon Islands Alliance for Change Coalition or SIACC [Bartholomew ULUFA'ALU]; Solomon Islands Labor Party or SILP [Joses TUHANUKU] note: in general, Solomon Islands politics is characterized by fluid coalitions
International organization participation:	ACP, AsDB, C, ESCAP, FAO, G-77, IBRD, ICAO, ICRM, IDA, IFAD, IFC, IFRCS, ILO, IMF, IMO, IOC, ITU, Sparteca, SPC, SPF, UN, UNCTAD, UNESCO, UPU, WFTU, WHO, WMO, WTrO
Diplomatic representation in the US:	chief of mission: Ambassador (vacant); Charge d'Affaires Jeremiah MANELE chancery: 800 Second Avenue, Suite 400L, New York, NY 10017 telephone: [1] (212) 599-6192, 6193 FAX: [1] (212) 661-8925
Diplomatic representation from the US:	the US does not have an embassy in Solomon Islands (embassy closed July 1993); the ambassador to Papua New Guinea is accredited to the Solomon Islands
Flag description:	divided diagonally by a thin yellow stripe from the lower hoist-side corner; the upper triangle (hoist side) is blue with five white five-pointed stars arranged in an X pattern; the lower triangle is green

ECONOMY

Economy - overview:	The bulk of the population depends on agriculture, fishing, and forestry for at least part of their livelihood. Most manufactured goods and petroleum products must be imported. The islands are rich in undeveloped mineral resources such as lead, zinc, nickel, and gold. However, severe ethnic violence, the closing of key business enterprises, and an empty government treasury have led to serious economic disarray, indeed near collapse. Tanker deliveries of crucial fuel supplies (including those for electrical generation) have become sporadic due to the government's inability to pay and attacks against ships. Telecommunications are threatened by the nonpayment of bills

	and by the lack of technical and maintenance staff many of whom have left the country.
GDP:	purchasing power parity - $800 million (2001 est.)
GDP - real growth rate:	-10% (2001 est.)
GDP - per capita:	purchasing power parity - $1,700 (2001 est.)
GDP - composition by sector:	agriculture: 42% industry: 11% services: 47% (2000 est.)
Household income or consumption by percentage share:	lowest 10%: NA% highest 10%: NA%
Inflation rate (consumer prices):	7.9% (2001 est.)
Labor force:	26,842
Labor force - by occupation:	agriculture 75%, industry 5%, services 20% (2000 est.)
Budget:	revenues: $38 million expenditures: $NA, including capital expenditures of $NA
Industries:	fish (tuna), mining, timber
Electricity - production:	32 million kWh (2000)
Electricity - production by source:	fossil fuel: 100% hydro: 0% other: 0% (2000) nuclear: 0%
Electricity - consumption:	29.76 million kWh (2000)
Electricity - exports:	0 kWh (2000)
Electricity - imports:	0 kWh (2000)
Agriculture - products:	cocoa, beans, coconuts, palm kernels, rice, potatoes, vegetables, fruit; cattle, pigs; timber; fish
Exports:	$165 million (f.o.b., 1999 est.)
Exports - commodities:	timber, fish, copra, palm oil, cocoa
Exports - partners:	Japan 22%, China 15%, Philippines 13%, South Korea 12%, UK 12%, Thailand 5% (2000)
Imports:	$152 million (f.o.b., 1999 est.)
Imports - commodities:	plant and equipment, manufactured goods, food and live animals, fuels, chemicals
Imports -	Australia 27%, Singapore 25%, NZ 5.5%, Japan 5.3%, US 5.1%

partners:	(2000)
Debt - external:	$137 million (2001 est.)
Economic aid - recipient:	$28 million mainly from Japan, Australia, China, and NZ (2001 est.)
Currency:	Solomon Islands dollar (SBD)
Currency code:	SBD
Exchange rates:	Solomon Islands dollars per US dollar - 5.3728 (December 2001), 5.0889 (2000), 4.8381 (1999), 4.8156 (1998), 3.7169 (1997)
Fiscal year:	calendar year

COMMUNICATIONS

Telephones - main lines in use:	8,000 (1997)
Telephones - mobile cellular:	658 (1997)
Telephone system:	general assessment: NA domestic: NA international: satellite earth station - 1 Intelsat (Pacific Ocean)
Radio broadcast stations:	AM 3, FM 0, shortwave 0 (1998)
Radios:	57,000 (1997)
Television broadcast stations:	0 (1997)
Televisions:	3,000 (1997)
Internet country code:	.sb
Internet Service Providers (ISPs):	1 (2000)
Internet users:	3,000 (2000)

TRANSPORTATION

Railways:	0 km
Highways:	total: 1,360 km paved: 34 km unpaved: 1,326 km (includes about 800 km of private plantation roads) (1996 est.)
Waterways:	none
Ports and harbors:	Aola Bay, Honiara, Lofung, Noro, Viru Harbor, Yandina

Merchant marine:	none (2002 est.)
Airports:	31
Airports - with paved runways:	total: 2 1,524 to 2,437 m: 1 914 to 1,523 m: 1
Airports - with unpaved runways:	total: 29 1,524 to 2,437 m: 1 914 to 1,523 m: 9 under 914 m: 19

MILITARY

Military branches:	no regular military forces; Solomon Islands National Reconnaissance and Surveillance Force; Royal Solomon Islands Police (RSIP)
Disputes - international:	none

IMPORTANT INFORMATION FOR UNDERSTANDING SOLOMON ISLANDS

OFFICIAL NAME: Solomon Islands

GEOGRAPHY

Area: *Land*--27,556 sq. km. (11,599 sq. mi.). Archipelago--725,197 sq. km. (280,000 sq. mi.).
Cities: *Capital*--Honiara (on the island of Guadalcanal), pop. 30,000. Other towns--Gizo, Auki, Kirakira.
Terrain: Mountainous islands.
Climate: Tropical monsoon.

This island nation is situated between latitudes 5s to 12 S and longitudes 155 E to 170 E. The capital, Honiara, is approximately 2,500 km north east of Sydney, Australia; 3,900 km north west of Wellington, New Zealand: 1,400 km east of Port Moresby, Papua New Guinea and 5,900 km east of Jakarta, Indonesia. The Solomon Islands archipelago stretches over 1,0OO km and comprises a total land area of approximately 28,000 square km with six main islands: Guadacanal on which the capital Honiara is located, Malaita, Choiseul, New Georgia, San Cristobal and Santa Isabel: as well as hundreds of smaller islands.

The Solomon Islands form an archipelago in the Southwest Pacific about 1,900 kilometers (1,200 mi.) northeast of Australia. With terrain ranging from ruggedly mountainous islands to low-lying coral atolls, the Solomons stretch in a 1,450-kilometer (900 mi.) chain southeast from Papua New Guinea across the Coral Sea to Vanuatu.

The main islands of Choiseul, New Georgia, Santa Isabel, Guadalcanal, Malaita, and Makira have rainforested mountain ranges of mainly volcanic origin, deep narrow valleys, and coastal belts lined with coconut palms and ringed by reefs. The smaller islands are atolls and raised coral reefs, often spectacularly beautiful. The Solomon Islands region is geologically active, and earth tremors are frequent.

The islands' ocean-equatorial climate is extremely humid throughout the year, with a mean temperature of 27° C (80° F) and few extremes of temperature or weather. June through August is the cooler period. Though seasons are not pronounced, the northwesterly winds of November through April bring more frequent rainfall and occasional squalls or cyclones. The annual rainfall is about 305 centimeters (120 in.).

More than 90% of the islands is forested. The coastal strips are sheltered by mangrove and coconut trees. Luxuriant rainforest covers the interiors of the large islands. Soil quality ranges from extremely rich volcanic to relatively infertile limestone. More than 230 varieties of orchids and other tropical flowers brighten the landscape.

Climate

The Solomon enjoy a remarkably stable weather pattern. The daily temperature range is usually 21 to 30 degrees Celsius with the average humidity at 71%. Annual rainfall normally exceeds 3,000 mm with the monsoonal wet season occurring between November and March. However: significant rainfall of about 200 mm can be expected each month. April to October are relatively dryer and less humid.

PEOPLE

The Solomon Islanders comprise diverse cultures, languages, and customs. Of its 496,000 persons, 93.3% are Melanesian, 4% Polynesian, and 1.5% Micronesian. In addition, small numbers of Europeans and Chinese are registered. About 120 vernaculars are spoken.

Most people reside in small, widely dispersed settlements along the coasts. Sixty percent live in localities with fewer than 200 persons, and only 10% reside in urban areas.

The capital city of Honiara, situated on Guadalcanal, the largest island, has more than 30,000 inhabitants. The other principal towns are Gizo, Auki, and Kirakira.

Most Solomon Islanders are Christian, with the Anglican, Roman Catholic, South Seas Evangelical, and Seventh-day Adventist faiths predominating. About 5% of the population maintain traditional beliefs.

The chief characteristics of the traditional Melanesian social structure are:

- The practice of subsistence economy;
- The recognition of bonds of kinship, with important obligations extending beyond the immediate family group;
- Generally egalitarian relationships, emphasizing acquired rather than inherited status; and
- A strong attachment of the people to the land.

Most Solomon Islanders maintain this traditional social structure and find their roots in village life.

The total population is 354,000 composed of mostly young healthy Melanesians with smaller groups of Polynesians, Micronesians and Asians. The growth rate is 3.5% per annum. The population is cheerful and friendly with an increasingly well educated work force.

The Language

A rich mixture of languages exists throughout Solomon Islands. English and Solomon Pidgin English are the most common and the dominant languages used in commerce and everyday life.

Since gaining independence in 1978, Solomon Islands has developed into a vigorous and stable parliamentary democracy under which free enterprise has been given strong support. The Solomons has consistently welcomed foreign investment which provides significant nett benefits to the Solomon Islands people and its economy.

HISTORY

Although little prehistory of the Solomon Islands is known, material excavated on Santa Ana, Guadalcanal, and Gawa indicates that a hunter-gatherer people lived on the larger islands as early as 1000 B.C. Some Solomon Islanders are descendants of Neolithic, Austronesian-speaking peoples who migrated somewhat later to the Pacific Islands from Southeast Asia.

The European discoverer of the Solomons was the Spanish explorer Alvaro de Mendana Y Neyra, who set out from Peru in 1567 to seek the legendary Isles of Solomon. British mariner Philip Carteret, entered Solomon waters in 1767. In the years that followed, visits by explorers were more frequent.

Missionaries began visiting the Solomons in the mid-1800s. They made little progress at first, however, because "blackbirding"--the often brutal recruitment of laborers for the sugar plantations in Queensland and Fiji--led to a series of reprisals and massacres. The evils of the labor trade prompted the United Kingdom to declare a protectorate over the southern Solomons in 1893. In 1898 and 1899, more outlying islands were added to the protectorate; in 1900 the remainder of the archipelago, an area previously under German jurisdiction, was transferred to British administration. Under the protectorate, missionaries settled in the Solomons, converting most of the population to Christianity.

In the early 20th century, several British and Australian firms began largescale coconut planting. Economic growth was slow, however, and the islanders benefited little. With the outbreak of World War II, most planters and traders were evacuated to Australia, and most cultivation ceased.

From May 1942, when the Battle of the Coral Sea was fought, until December 1943, the Solomons were almost constantly a scene of combat. Although U.S. forces landed on Guadalcanal virtually unopposed in August 1942, they were soon engaged in a bloody fight for control of the islands' airstrip, which the U.S. forces named Henderson Field. One of the most furious sea battles ever fought took place off Savo Island, near Guadalcanal, also in August 1942. Before the Japanese completely withdrew from Guadalcanal in February 1943, more than 7,000 Americans and 21,000 Japanese died. By December 1943, the Allies were in command of the entire Solomon chain.

POSTWAR DEVELOPMENTS

Following the end of World War II, the British colonial government returned. The capital was moved from Tulagi to Honiara to take advantage of the infrastructure left behind by the U.S. military. A native movement known as the Marching Rule defied government authority. There was much disorder until some of the leaders were jailed in late 1948. Throughout the 1950s, other indigenous dissident groups appeared and disappeared without gaining strength.

In 1960, an advisory council of Solomon Islanders was superseded by a legislative council, and an executive council was created as the protectorate's policymaking body. The council was given progressively more authority.

In 1974, a new constitution was adopted establishing a parliamentary democracy and ministerial system of government. In mid-1975, the name Solomon Islands officially replaced that of British Solomon Islands Protectorate. On January 2, 1976, the Solomons became self-governing, and independence followed on July 7, 1978.

GOVERNMENT

The Solomon Islands is a parliamentary democracy within the Commonwealth, with a unicameral Parliament and a ministerial system of government. The British monarch is represented by a governor general, chosen by the Parliament for a 5-year term. The national Parliament has 50 members, elected for 4-year terms. However, Parliament may be dissolved by majority vote of its members before the completion of its term. Parliamentary representation is based on single-member constituencies. Suffrage is universal for citizens over age 18. The prime minister, elected by Parliament, chooses the other members of the cabinet. Each ministry is headed by a Cabinet member, who is assisted by a permanent secretary, a career public servant, who directs the staff of the ministry.

For local government, the country is divided into 10 administrative areas, of which nine are provinces administered by elected provincial assemblies, and the 10th is the town of Honiara, administered by the Honiara Town Council.

Land ownership is reserved for Solomon Islanders. At the time of independence, citizenship was granted to all persons whose parents are or were both British protected persons and members of a group, tribe, or line indigenous to the Solomon Islands. The law provides that resident expatriates, such as the Chinese and Kiribati, may obtain citizenship through naturalization. Land generally is still held on a family or village basis and may be handed down from mother or father according to local custom. The islanders are reluctant to provide land for nontraditional economic undertakings, and this has resulted in continual disputes over land ownership.

No military forces are maintained by the Solomon Islands, although the police force of nearly 500 includes a border protection element. The police also have responsibility for fire service, disaster relief, and maritime surveillance. The police force is headed by a commissioner, appointed by the Governor General and responsible to the prime minister.

POLITICAL CONDITIONS

Solomon Islands governments are characterized by weak political parties and highly unstable parliamentary coalitions. They are subject to frequent votes of no confidence, and government leadership changes frequently as a result. Cabinet changes are common.

The first post-independence government was elected in August 1980. Prime Minister Peter Kenilorea was head of government until September 1981, when he was succeeded by Solomon Mamaloni as the result of a realignment within the parliamentary coalitions. Following the November 1984 elections, Kenilorea was again elected Prime Minister, to be replaced in 1986 by his former deputy Ezekiel Alebua following shifts within the parliamentary coalitions. The next election, held in early 1989, returned Solomon Mamaloni as Prime Minister. Francis Billy Hilly was elected Prime Minister following the national elections in June 1993, and headed the government until November 1994 when a shift in parliamentary loyalties brought Solomon Mamaloni back to power.

The national election of August 6, 1997 resulted in Bartholomew Ulufa'alu's election as Prime Minister, heading a coalition government, which christened itself the Solomon Islands Alliance for Change. In June 2002, an insurrection mounted by militants from the island of Malaita resulted in the brief detention of Ulufa'alu and his subsequent forced resignation. Manasseh Sogavare, leader of the People's Progressive Party, was chosen

Prime Minister by a loose coalition of parties. New elections in December 2001 brought Sir Allan Kemakeza into the Prime Minister's chair with the support of a coalition of parties. Bartholomew Ulufa'alu is currently Leader of the Opposition.

PRINCIPAL GOVERNMENT OFFICIALS

Governor General--John Lapli
Prime Minister--Allan Kemakeza
Minister for Foreign Affairs--Nollen Levi

The Solomon Islands mission to the United Nations is located at 800 Second Avenue, Suite 400L, New York, NY 10017 (tel: 212-599-6192/93; fax: 212-661-8925).

International Relations

The Solomons has diplomatic representations in Australia, New Zealand, the United Kingdom, the European Economic Community, the United Nations, New York and Japan. Australia, New Zealand, the United Kingdom, Papua New Guinea, the European Economic Community and the Republic of China have diplomatic missions in Honiara. The Solomons is a member of the United Nations, the Convention of the European Community (LOME IV), the World Bank, Asian Development Bank and the IMF.

Socio-Cultural Notes

Land is a major complex issue and integral part of the Solomon Islands' way of life. It is generally communally owned by clans or lines. Title to land in Solomon Islands is either customary or registered. The Government recognises that all customary land is owned usually in a lineage group. Registered land has its ownership and boundaries recorded in a land registry in Honiara and these are guaranteed by law rather than by custom. The registered system is therefore attractive to investors, but permits to own a perpetual estate (freehold interest) in registered land are limited to indigenous Solomon Islanders. Non-Solomon Islanders, including expatriate Solomon Islands citizens, can only lease registered land. About 88% of land is customary and 12% registered.

The introduction of a cash economy into a subsistence economy is causing a number of substantial changes, but the Solomon Islands' way of life, in many ways, remains much the same as it has for hundreds of years. The majority of people continue to live a subsistence way of life, adhering to the extended family system.

The social structure of Solomon Islands is extremely diverse and complex, varying from island to island and even between villages and clans on the same island. Different customs, codes of behaviour, land tenure, leadership, traditional and contemporary religions, marriage, customs, tambus, compensation and other cultural practices exist throughout the nation.

Age-old customs shrouded in mythology, mystery, fear and respect are handed down from one generation to the next, allegedly from the ancestral spirits themselves, to form the cultural values to distinguish Solomon Islands. It is believed that the presence of the ancestors is still a reality, continuing to be revered and called upon in time of adversity. Custom stories, songs and dances commemorate great feasts, raids, harvests and other historic events of "time before".

Customs and traditions are still a major part of everyday life, even though somewhat minimised by factors such as Christianity, the drift of young people to urban centres and other contemporary influences.

The Solomon Islands' way of life has evolved over many generations and developed social and cultural strengths that have held communities and society together, generated social change and resisted and adapted foreign influences without social integration or disintegration. It is an egalitarian and communal society, sharing everything according to custom, with a hierarchy of chiefs, big men and village elders.

Personalities of the different island groups may vary as an result of environmental and other influences peculiar to them. For example, Western Solomons' people have been exposed to greater European influence, with traders, plantation owners, missionaries and timber companies establishing themselves there over the years more than in any other island group. Malaita people, on the other hand, have been more resistant to European influence, fiercely adhering to their customs and traditions. Malaitans also tend to be proud people.

Most Solomon Islanders wish to preserve their social and cultural strengths and to develop them alongside education, improved health and earning a cash income. Outside influences are considered desirable only where they enable social change to contribute to the well being of the people, society and country. It is difficult for an outsider to appreciate the depth of cultural values and traditions which are expressed through the customs of the people. While most Solomon Islanders do not expect outsiders to understand their customs and traditions, they do expect their visitor's respect and appreciation for the Solomon Islands' way of life.

While ancient traditions and customary practices have tended to slowly wane with the inevitable encroachment of modernity and sociodevelopment, the Solomon Islands has steadfastly maintained a vibrant and dynamic cultural way of life. Solomon Islanders are keenly aware of their special cultural heritage and traditional Pacific island environment.

They are determined to maintain and coexist their customary life in balance with the inherent changes of the modern world.

ECONOMY

GNP : $264.5 million.
Annual growth rate: Minus 24%.
Per capita income : $580.
Avg. inflation rate : 7.9%.
Natural resources: Forests, fish, agricultural land, marine products, gold.
Agriculture: *Products*--copra, cocoa, palm oil, palm kernels and subsistence crops of yams, taro, bananas, pineapple.
Industry: *Types*--fish canning, sawmilling, boats, rattan and wood furniture, fiberglass products, shell jewelry, tobacco, beer, clothing, soap, nails, handicrafts.
Trade (2000): *Exports*--$70 million (a 52% drop from 1999): fish, logs and timber, cocoa, copra. *Major markets*--Japan 39%, U.K. 23%, U.S. 2%. *Imports*--$94 million (an 11% drop from 1999): machinery and transport equipment, fuel, food and beverages. *Major suppliers*--Australia 34%, Japan 16%, New Zealand 9%.

Per capita GDP of $340 ranks Solomon Islands as a lesser developed nation. More than 75% of its labor force are engaged in subsistence farming and fishing. Until 1998, when world prices for tropical timber fell steeply, timber was Solomon Islands main export product, and, in recent years, Solomon Islands forests were dangerously overexploited. Other important cash crops and exports include copra and palm oil. In 1998 Ross Mining of Australia began producing gold at Gold Ridge on Guadalcanal. Minerals exploration in other areas continued. However in the wake of the ethnic violence in June 2000, exports of palm oil and gold ceased while exports of timber fell.

Exploitation of Solomon Islands rich fisheries offers the best prospect for further export and domestic economic expansion. However, a Japanese joint venture, Solomon Taiyo Ltd., which operated the only fish cannery in the country, closed in mid-2000 as a result of the ethnic disturbances. Though the plant has reopened under local management, the export of tuna has not resumed.

Tourism, particularly diving, is an important service industry for Solomon Islands. Growth in that industry is hampered, however, by lack of infrastructure, transportation limitations, and security concerns.

Solomon Islands was particularly hard hit by the Asian economic crisis even before the ethnic violence of June 2000. The Asian Development Bank estimates that the crash of the market for tropical timber reduced Solomon Island's GDP by between 15%-25%. About one-half of all jobs in the timber industry were lost. The government has said it will reform timber harvesting policies with the aim of resuming logging on a more sustainable basis.

Since 2000 the Government of Solomon Islands has become increasingly insolvent. It has exhausted its borrowing capacity; in 2001 the deficit reached 8% of GDP. It is unable to meet biweekly payrolls and has become extraordinarily dependent on funds from foreign aid accounts, which provided an estimated 50% of government expenditure in 2001. Principal aid donors are Australia, New Zealand, the European Union, Japan, and the Republic of China.

FOREIGN RELATIONS

Countries with diplomatic missions in the Solomon Islands are Australia, United Kingdom, New Zealand, Papua New Guinea, and Japan. The Solomon Islands also has diplomatic relations with the Republic of China, which has a resident representative in Honiara.

The U.S. Ambassador resident in Port Moresby, Papua New Guinea, also is accredited to Solomon Islands. The Solomon Islands' Permanent Representative to the United Nations also is accredited as its ambassador to the United States and Canada.

Relations with Papua New Guinea, which had become strained because of an influx of refugees from the Bougainville rebellion and attacks on the northern islands of the Solomon Islands by elements pursuing Bougainvillean rebels, have been repaired. A peace accord on Bougainville confirmed in 1998 has removed the armed threat, but refugee return has been slow.

Solomon Islands is a member of the United Nations, Commonwealth, South Pacific Commission, South Pacific Forum, International Monetary Fund, and the European Economic Community/African, Caribbean, Pacific Group (EEC/ACP)/(Lome Convention).

U.S.-SOLOMON ISLANDS RELATIONS

The United States and Solomon Islands established diplomatic relations following its independence on July 7, 1978. U.S. representation is handled by the U.S. Embassy at Port Moresby where the ambassador is resident. In recognition of the close ties forged between the United States and the people of the Solomon Islands during World War II, the U.S. Congress financed the construction of the Solomon Islands Parliament building. There are about 95 American citizens residing permanently in Solomon Islands.

The two nations belong to a variety of regional organizations, including the South Pacific Commission and the South Pacific Regional Environmental Program. The United States and Solomon Islands also cooperate under the U.S.-Pacific Islands multilateral Tuna Fisheries Treaty, under which the U.S. grants $18 million per year to Pacific island parties and the latter provide access to U.S. fishing vessels. A U.S. National Marine Fisheries Service Officer works with the South Pacific Forum Fisheries Agency in Honiara. The United States also supports efforts to protect biodiversity in the Solomon Islands. In addition to supporting the establishment of local conservation areas, the

United States supports the International Coral Reef Initiative aimed at protecting reefs in tropical nations such as Solomon Islands.

U.S. military forces, through the Pacific Theater Command in Honolulu, Hawaii, carry out annual bilateral meetings as well as smallscale exercises with the Solomon Islands Police Border Protection Force. The U.S. also provides appropriate military education and training courses to national security officials.

The U.S. Peace Corps suspended its program in June 2000 due to the ethnic violence and breakdown in governance. More than 70 volunteers, serving throughout the country in rural community development, education, environmental management, and youth programs, were evacuated.

U.S. trade with Solomon Islands is very limited. In 2001 U.S. exports to Solomon Islands were less than 5% of all exports, while Solomon Islands exports to the United States in that year were negligible.

PRINCIPAL U.S. EMBASSY OFFICIALS

Ambassador--Susan Jacobs (resident in Port Moresby, Papua New Guinea)

American Embassy Port Moresby is located on Douglas Street, Port Moresby, Papua New Guinea, P.O. Box 1492, Port Moresby (tel: (675) 321-1455; fax: (675) 321-3423).

SUSAN JACOBS AMBASSADOR, PAPUA NEW GUINEA

Term of Appointment: 10/20/2000 to present

Susan Jacobs, a career member of the Senior Foreign Service, was sworn in on October 20, 2000 as U.S. Ambassador to Papua New Guinea. She was nominated by President Bush on June 14, 2000 and confirmed by the U.S. Senate on June 9, 2000. Ambassador Jacobs occupied the position of Deputy Assistant Secretary for Global Affairs in the Bureau of Legislative Affairs in her most recent Washington assignment. She has previously served in Caracas, Tel Aviv, New Delhi and San Salvador as well as in the Department of State in the bureaus of Consular Affairs, International Organization Affairs, and Legislative Affairs. After completing an assignment as Consul General in Bucharest, she attended the Senior Seminar, an executive training program.

Ms. Jacobs received a B.A. in Political Science from the University of Michigan and later pursued graduate studies at Georgetown University and George Washington University. Her foreign languages are Spanish and Romanian.

Ms. Jacobs is married to Barry Jacobs, a retired Foreign Service Officer. They have three wonderful children and a spectacular granddaughter.

EU SOLOMON ISLANDS COOPERATION

Solomon Islands consists of 997 islands, and has a land area of 28,390 km2 and a population of about 500,000 with rapid population growth. With an estimated GDP per capita of around € 500 it ranks among the poorest of the Pacific Island countries. It is a Melanesian country with some 80 different languages. Some 85% of the population live in the rural areas with limited access to basic services.

POLITICAL SITUATION

From 1999 to mid-2003 Solomon Islands experienced a period of tensions and violence between the inhabitants of the two major islands, Guadalcanal and Malaita. An estimated 12,000 Malaitans and others left Guadalcanal. Estimates of the number of lives lost vary. One of the root causes of the conflict was poverty, as Malaitans felt compelled to leave their island in search of jobs and better opportunities in Guadalcanal. The Government found it increasingly difficult to maintain law and order, the economic and financial situation continued to decline and in early 2003 Solomon Islands had several characteristics of a failed state. As early as 2000 the democratically elected Prime Minister Ulufa'alu had to resign under duress.

In April 2003 Prime Minister Kemakeza requested assistance from Australia. The response was a multi-nation intervention, called Regional Assistance Mission to Solomon Islands (RAMSI), under the auspices of the Pacific Islands Forum and with the endorsement of Solomon Islands' Cabinet and Parliament. RAMSI arrived in Solomon Islands on 24 July 2003 with a police force, backed by military, from different Pacific countries, and included the deployment of approximately 50 economic and financial experts in line positions of key ministries, such as finance, customs and justice. RAMSI is led by Australia.

RAMSI's aims include restoring law and order, stabilising the budget, achieving longer-term economic reforms, rebuilding the government apparatus (in order to create an enabling environment for private sector development), and assisting in the delivery of social and public services to the people. The results of the first 2 ½ years have been positive, notably with law and order re-established, rapid financial stabilisation and the economy turning around, albeit from a very depressed state, and the country is unlikely to meet the majority of the Millennium Development Goals by 2015. The RAMSI intervention was assessed by a so-called Eminent Persons Group EPG) from the Pacific Forum, chaired by Fiji's Minister of Foreign Affairs in mid-2005. The EPG made a series of recommendations regarding RAMSI, which were endorsed by the Government. Solomon Islands is also one of 10 case studies included in the OECD-DAC analysis of how to optimise support to and cooperation with fragile countries.

The tensions undermined the standing of all levels of Government, and there has been demand in several provinces for further decentralisation and even independence. A draft constitution foreseeing a federal republic has been under consideration for some time. Prime Minister Kemakeza obtained a unanimous decision in parliament in favour of RAMSI, and has since sought to preserve a large consensus for his restoration and reform policies. Melanesian countries normally have fluid political systems, but Solomon

Islands has known a considerable degree of political stability under the present Government, apart from the fact that a number of ministers have been sacked and others arrested, mostly related to governance issues.

General elections are foreseen for March/April 2006. Solomon Islands has invited international observers.

ECONOMIC SITUATION

Solomon Islands is classified as an LDC in the Cotonou Agreement. In 2005 the country recorded steady but relatively modest growth on the basis of high rates of log exports, an improved situation in the agricultural sector and donor inflows. The economy is still rebounding from its depressed state during the tensions. For 2006 the real growth rate is projected at up to 5%, as a gold mine is expected to reopen. However, as Solomon Islands has to import all of its oil, a continued rise in oil prices would influence the growth prospects.

Furthermore the high dependence on the forestry sector is a major weakness, as current logging rates are unsustainable and it can be foreseen that revenue streams and exports from forestry sector will soon start to diminish. Consequently the current pattern of growth cannot continue in the medium-term.

In addition, as per capita income is still only two-thirds of its pre-conflict level, and as the country has an annual population growth of 2.8 per cent, it will take about 20 years at present economic growth rates before Solomon Islanders reach the level of income they had before the tensions.

Inflation is close to 10% p.a.; currency reserves suffice for some 6 months of imports; the Solomon dollar has been quite steady vis-a-vis the US dollar since 2003, but has depreciated against the Euro; the budget is fully funded, while the debt situation is serious, but turning around.

THE REGIONAL AND SUB-REGIONAL FRAMEWORKS

Solomon Islands is a member of the Pacific Forum which was established in 1971 reflecting a desire of the independent countries in the region (including Australia and New Zealand) to address common economic and political issues from a regional perspective. There is an annual gathering of the Heads of Government. The Forum is supported by the Forum Secretariat and a number of specialised agencies, such as the Forum Fisheries Agency (based in Solomon Islands), the South Pacific Applied Geosciences Commission (SOPAC), and the University of the South Pacific (USP). Solomon Islands is also a member of the Commonwealth, and a founding member of the Melanesian Spearhead Group, a sub-regional trade agreement.

RELATIONS WITH THE EU

Solomon Islands gained independence from the United Kingdom in 1978. The Head of State is Queen Elisabeth II, and the country still maintains close links with the United

Kingdom.
The EC is represented in Solomon Islands by a small Delegation which is attached to the Delegation in Papua New Guinea.
Negotiations regarding an Economic Partnership Agreement between the Pacific ACP countries and the EU continue. The EU and Solomon Islands have also negotiated a bilateral fisheries agreement, which is expected to be approved in early 2006.
Traditionally, about 5% of Solomon Islands' exports are directed to the EU, mainly the UK. Imports from EU countries are around 4 % of total.
Solomon Islands has benefited considerably from Pacific regional programmes, in particular for the Forum Fisheries Agency. The EIB and the CDE also cooperate with the country.
The United Kingdom has a High Commission in Solomon Islands, and Solomon Islands has an embassy in Brussels. There is an EC Delegation in Honiara.

COUNTRY STRATEGY

The CSP was formally signed on 21 May 2001, with sustainable rural development and community development as the focal sector.

The National Indicative Programme (NIP) consists of two envelopes. The A envelope is € 6.7 M and the B envelope is € 7.8 M, of which € 7.25 M has been allocated to compensate export losses under the FLEX system. The balance of the B-envelope (€ 550,000) remains available for unforeseen events. In addition to the NIP the Solomon Islands has been a major recipient of funds under the STABEX instrument.

PRIORITIES FOR CO-OPERATION

The focal sector of the 9 th EDF is "Sustainable Rural Development and Community Development" with a micro-projects programme and a coming capacity building and institutional strengthening programme as the key elements.
The STABEX 1998 resources (€ 42.7 M) have been allocated to transport, agriculture, forestry and rural development. Implementation has begun under the rural development component.

The Framework of Mutual Obligations of STABEX 1999 with an original budget of € 22 M focuses on the education sector. The remaining funds will be spent according to the provisions of the tripartite Memorandum of Understanding signed on 7 June 2004 between the Government, NZAID and the EC. The Government is committed to allocating at least 22% of its budget to education.

MID-TERM REVIEW

A mid-term review of the strategy and implementation of programmes and projects was carried out in 2004. In spite of the difficulties experienced by Solomon Islands during the tensions cooperation was deemed satisfactory, and it was decided to maintain the country strategy for Solomon Islands as well as the funding earmarked for cooperation with Solomon Islands. The review reflected that Solomon Islands is in a challenging post-conflict situation, and secondly that its security situation as well as public financial management improved markedly following the arrival of the regional assistance mission in July 2003.

9th EDF Financial Data
For the 9 th EDF the status was as follows at 30/11/2005 :

	Allocations	Commitments
Envelope A + transfers from earlier EDFs	13,345,091	53.0%
Envelope B	7,800,000	0%
Total	21,145,091	33.45%

TRAVEL AND BUSINESS INFORMATION

The U.S. Department of State's Consular Information Program provides Consular Information Sheets, Travel Warnings, and Public Announcements.

Consular Information Sheets exist for all countries and include information on entry requirements, currency regulations, health conditions, areas of instability, crime and security, political disturbances, and the addresses of the U.S. posts in the country.

Travel Warnings are issued when the State Department recommends that Americans avoid travel to a certain country.

Public Announcements are issued as a means to disseminate information quickly about terrorist threats and other relatively short-term conditions overseas which pose significant risks to the security of American travelers. Free copies of this information are available by calling the Bureau of Consular Affairs at 202-647-5225 or via the fax-on-demand system: 202-647-3000. Consular Information Sheets and Travel Warnings also are available on the Consular Affairs Internet home page: http://travel.state.gov. Consular Affairs Tips for Travelers publication series, which contain information on obtaining passports and planning a safe trip abroad are on the internet and hard copies can be purchased from the Superintendent of Documents, U.S. Government Printing Office, telephone: 202-512-1800; fax 202-512-2250.

Emergency information concerning Americans traveling abroad may be obtained from the Office of Overseas Citizens Services at (202) 647-5225. For after-hours emergencies, Sundays and holidays, call 202-647-4000.

Passport information can be obtained by calling the National Passport Information Center's automated system ($.35 per minute) or live operators 8 a.m. to 8 p.m. (EST) Monday-Friday ($1.05 per minute). The number is 1-900-225-5674 (TDD: 1-900-225-

7778). Major credit card users (for a flat rate of $4.95) may call 1-888-362-8668 (TDD: 1-888-498-3648). It also is available on the internet.

Travelers can check the latest health information with the U.S. Centers for Disease Control and Prevention in Atlanta, Georgia. A hotline at 877-FYI-TRIP (877-394-8747) and a web site at http://www.cdc.gov/travel/index.htm give the most recent health advisories, immunization recommendations or requirements, and advice on food and drinking water safety for regions and countries. A booklet entitled Health Information for International Travel (HHS publication number CDC-95-8280) is available from the U.S. Government Printing Office, Washington, DC 20402, tel. (202) 512-1800.

Information on travel conditions, visa requirements, currency and customs regulations, legal holidays, and other items of interest to travelers also may be obtained before your departure from a country's embassy and/or consulates in the U.S. (for this country, see "Principal Government Officials" listing in this publication).

U.S. citizens who are long-term visitors or traveling in dangerous areas are encouraged to register at the U.S. embassy upon arrival in a country (see "Principal U.S. Embassy Officials" listing in this publication). This may help family members contact you in case of an emergency.

IMPORTANT LAWS AND REGULATIONS AFFECTING BUSINESS

CHRONOLOGICAL INDEX OF ALL SOLOMON ISLANDS SINCE 1996

ACTS 1996

1. Solomon Islands Visitors Bureau Act 1996

2. Solomon Islands Postal Corporation Act 1996

4. Pure Food Act 1996

5. Television (Amendment) Act 1996

6. Mines and Minerals (Amendment) Act 1996

7. Debit Tax (Repeal) Act 1996

8. 1995 Supplementary Appropriation Act 1996

9. 1996 Supplementary Appropriation Act 1996

10. Investment (Amendment) Act 1996

11. 1997 Appropriation Act 1996

12. Income Tax (Amendment) Act 1996

13. Income Tax (Amendment) (No. 2) Act 1996

ACTS 1997

1.1997 Supplementary Appropriation Act 1997

2. Citizenship (Amendment) Act 1997

3. National Parliament Electoral Provisions (Amendment) Act 1997

4. Mamara-Tasivarongomavo Development Agreement Act 1997

5. Pharmacy Practitioners Act 1997

6. Nursing Council (Amendment) Act 1997

7. Provincial Government Act 1997

ACTS 1998

1. Islanders Divorce (Amendment) Act 1998
2. Income Tax (Amendment) Act 1998
3. Financial Institutions Act 1998
4. 1998 SUPPLEMENTARY APPROPRIATION ACT 1998 [MISSING]
5. Shipping Act 1998
6. Fisheries Act 1998
7. Passports (Amendment) Act 1998
8. Environment Act 1998
9. Immigration (Amendment) Act 1998
10. Wildlife Protection and Management Act 1998
11. 1998 Supplementary Appropriation Act 1998
12. 1999 Appropriation Act 1998

ACTS 1999

1. Leadership Code (Further Provisions) Act 1999
2. Honiara City Act 1999
3. Forests Act 1999
4. 1999 Supplementary Appropriation Act 1999
5. Conversion of Statutory Bodies to Companies Act 1999
6. Customs and Excise (Amendment) Act 1999
7. Divestment of Government Assets or Services Act 1999
8. Trade Disputes (Amendment) Act 1999

9. Deportation (Amendment) Act 1999

10. 1999 Supplementary Appropriation (No. 2) Act 1999

11. Financial Institutions (Amendment) Act 1999

12. Prisons (Amendment) Act 1999

13. Civil Aviation (Amendment) Act 1999

14. Income Tax (Amendment) Act 1999

ACTS 2000

1. Prescription of Ministers (Amendment) Act 2000

2. Firearms and Ammunition (Amendment) Act 2000

3. 1999 Supplementary Appropriation (No. 3) Act 2000

4. 2000 Supplementary Appropriation Act 2000

5. 2000 Supplementary Appropriation (No. 2) (Variation of Head of Expenditure) Act 2000

6. Forest Rescurces and Timber Utilisation (Amendment) Act 2000

7. Customs Recognition Act 2000

8. Amnesty Act 2000

ACTS 2001

1. Essential Services (Amendment) Act 2001

2. Constitution (Amendment) Act 2001

3. Amnesty Act 2001

4. 2001 Appropriation Act 2001

5. National Parliament Electoral Provisions (Amendment) Act 2001 [**successfully challenged in the High Court prior to the 2001 election and never enforced.*]

ACTS 2002

1. Provincial Government (Special Provisions) Act 2002

2. Customs and Excise (Amendment) Act 2002

3. 2002 Appropriation Act 2002

4. Mutual Assistance in Criminal Matters Act 2002

5. Money Laundering and Proceeds of Crime Act 2002

ACTS 2003

1. Facilitation of International Assistance Act 2003

2. Legal Practitioners (Amendment) Act 2003

3. Crown Proceedings (Amendment) Act 2003

4. 2004 Appropriation Act

5. 2000 Supplementary Appropriation (No 3) Act 2003

6. 2001 Supplementary Appropriation Act 2003

7. 2002 Supplementary Appropriation Act 2003

ACTS 2004

1 Sales Tax (Amendment) Act 2004

2 Prescription of Judges (High Court) (Amendment) Act 2004

3 2003 Supplementary Appropriation Act 2004

4 Adoption Act 2004

5 2004 Supplementary Appropriation (No 2) Act 2004

THE CUSTOMS AND EXCISE (AMENDMENT) ACT 1999

(NO. 6 OF 1999)

Passed by the National Parliament this twenty-second day of June 1999.
Assented to in Her Majesty's name and on Her Majesty's behalf this seventh day of September 1999.

Date of commencement: see section 1.

AN ACT TO AMEND THE CUSTOMS AND EXCISE ACT (CAP. 121).

ENACTED by the National Parliament of Solomon Islands.

Short title and date of commencement.

1. This Act may be cited as the Customs and Excise (Amendment) Act, 1999, and shall come into operation on such date as the Minister may appoint by notice published in the Gazette.

Insertion of new sections 212A, 212B and 212C in Cap. 121.

2. The Customs and Excise Act is hereby amended by inserting therein immediately after section 212, the following new sections 212A, 2128 and 212C respectively -

"**Penalty for loss of revenue due to false statement**

212A. (1) Subject to section 212C, where a person makes in respect of any goods a statement to an officer, for a purpose in connection with the operation of this Act -

(a) that is false or misleading in a material particular; or

(b) omits any matter or thing without which the statement is misleading in a material particular: and

(c) the duty properly payable by the person on those goods exceeds the duty that would have been payable by the person if the duty was assessed or determined on the basis that the statement was not false or misleading, as the case may be,

the person is liable to pay additional duty as prescribed in subsection (2).

(2) The Comptroller may within twelve months after the statement was made by notice in writing, require the owner of the goods (not being a person who is to be treated as the owner of the goods by reason off being an agent of the owner) to pay, within a period of ninety days after service of the notice, a penalty equal to twice the amount of the excess.

(3) The notice may be served on the owner of the goods or on the agent of the owner.

(4) If an amount required to be paid in accordance with subsection (2) within a period of ninety days is not so paid it becomes, upon the expiration of that period, a debt due to the Government and may be recovered in a court of competent jurisdiction.

(5) Where a person in respect of whom a demand for the payment of penalty in respect of any particular goods has been made under

subsection (2) makes application to a court for review of the decision as to the amount of duty payable on those goods -

(a) the period commencing on the making of that application and ending on the final determination of the amount of duty by the court shall not be taken into account in computing the period of ninety days referred to in subsections (2) and (4): and

(b) if it is determined, or ultimately determined, that the duty, or any part of the duty, demanded in respect of those goods is not payable, the demand for penalty shall thereupon be treated as if it were, and had always been, a demand for such amount, if any, as would be appropriate under subsection (2) having regard to the determination of the court.

(6) Where the Comptroller serves a notice under subsection (2) in relation to a statement made, or an omission from a statement made, by a person, proceedings shall not be instituted under any other provision of this Act against that person in relation to that statement or omission.

Remission of penalty.

212B. (1) Where a penalty is payable under section 212A as a result of a statement, or an omission from a statement, the Comptroller may, on the basis of a written application made to the Comptroller within thirty days after the Comptroller served the notice under section 212A (2) in relation to the statement or the omission from the statement, by the person liable to pay the penalty, remit the whole or any part of that penalty.

(2) Within thirty days after receiving an application for remission of penalty the Comptroller shall inform the applicant of the Comptroller's decision in relation to the application.

(3) Where the Comptroller fails to inform the applicant of the decision within thirty days after receiving the application, the Comptroller shall be taken to have decided not to remit the penalty.

(4) In considering an application under subsection (1) to remit the whole or a part of a penalty in respect of a statement or omission made by the applicant or by an agent of the applicant, the Comptroller shall have regard only to the following matters -

(a) whether the applicant or the applicant's agent, as the case requires, had voluntarily admitted that the statement was, or was as a result of the omission, false or misleading;

(b) the risk to the revenue occasioned by such a statement or omission;

(c) the capacity of the applicant or of the applicant's agent, as the case requires, to avoid making such a statement or omission and the extent to which that capacity was exercised;

(d) the history of the applicant or of the applicant's agent, as the case requires, in relation to the making of statements or omissions giving rise to convictions under this Act or to liability for penalty under section 212A.

(5) Where a decision of a court on an application for review of a decision taken under section 212A will result in a lesser amount of duty being payable than the amount demanded or in no duty being payable, the Comptroller shall remit any penalty paid or payable under section 212A to the extent necessary to give affect to the decision of the court.

Section 212A not to apply in certain cases.

212C. (1) Where the owner of any goods or the agent of the owner is uncertain whether any particular information included in a statement made in respect of those goods might be regarded as false or misleading in a material particular, that owner or agent may, by writing included in the statement, specify that information as information of which the owner or agent is uncertain and set out the reasons for that uncertainty, and, where the owner or agent does so, no penalty shall be imposed under section 212A in relation to that information.

(2) Where the owner of any goods or the agent of the owner is uncertain whether, by reason of the omission of particular information from statement made in respect of those goods, that statement might be regarded as misleading in a material particular, that owner or agent may, by writing included in the statement, specify the information that has been omitted and set out the reason for uncertainty concerning the effect of its omission, and, where the owner or agent does so, no penalty shall be imposed under section 212A in relation to that information."

THE FINANCIAL INSTITUTIONS ACT 1998

ARRANGEMENT OF SECTIONS

Section:

PART I
PRELIMINARY

PART II
LICENSING OF FINANCIAL INSTITUTIONS

PART III
PRUDENTIAL SUPERVISION

PART IV
RESTRICTIONS ON BUSINESS

PART V
CONTROL OVER LICENSED FINANCIAL INSTITUTIONS

PART VI
MISCELLANEOUS

PART I
PRELIMINARY

Short title and commencement.

1. This Act maybe cited as the Financial Institutions Act, 1998, and shall come into force on such date as the Minister may appoint by notice published in the Gazette.

Interpretation.

2. (1) In this Act unless the contrary intention appears, the expression-

"accounting and internal control system" include procedures and practices applicable to electronic data processing (hereinafter referred to as "EDP");

"accounts", "books", "vouchers", "minutes", "documents" or "records" include those kept in a computer, magnetic tape or any other storage device used in electronic data processing by a financial institution or by any EDP service or a financial institution;

"affiliate" means a company wherein another company's share holding is at least twenty percent but more than fifty percent of the outstanding voting stock or where that other company has the power to exercise influence over the policies of management of the company;

"bank" means any financial institution whose operations include the acceptance of deposits of money withdrawable or transferable by cheque or other means of payment transfer;

"banking business" means-

(a) the business of accepting deposits of money from the public or members thereof, withdrawable or payable upon demand or after a fixed period or after notice, or any similar operation through the frequent sales or placement of bonds, certificates, notes or other securities, and the use of such funds, either in whole or in part, for loans or investments for the account and at the risk of the person doing such business; and

(b) any other activity recognised by the Central Bank as customary banking practice which a licensed financial institution engaging in the activities described in paragraph (a), or any related activity which the Central Bank may consider appropriate;

"body corporate" means a company incorporated in Solomon Islands or elsewhere under any law of the time being in force relating to the formation and registration of companies, or a corporation established in the Solomon Islands or elsewhere under any Act;

"Central Bank" means the Central Bank of Solomon Islands established under the Central Bank of Solomon Islands Act;

Act No. 4 of 1976

"Court" means the High Court of Solomon Islands;

"credit institution" means any financial institution other than a bank;

"director" means an individual who exercises management and policy making functions at the highest level of an organisation and occupies the position of director by whatever name called, and includes a person who is a member of the board of directors, committee council or other governing body, howsoever of a body corporate;

"EDP service" refers to any person providing or maintaining electronic data processing service to a financial institution and includes an EDP division within the financial institution, and an EDP division within a subsidiary or affiliate of the financial institution, or any independent EDP service bureau;

"financial institution" means any body corporate doing banking business:

Provided, that for the purposes of this Act, unless the context otherwise requires, all offices and branches of a financial institution in Solomon Islands shall be deemed to be one financial institution;

"foreign financial institution" means a financial institution incorporated or established outside Solomon Islands and recognised as such under the laws of the country in which it was incorporated or established;

"licensed financial institution" means a financial institution licensed under the provisions of this Act;

"manager" includes any person for the time being in charge of the principal office in Solomon Islands of any financial institution;

"Minister" means the Minister responsible for finance;

"officer' includes a director, manager or secretary;

"subsidiary" means a company in which another company owns more than fifty per cent of the outstanding voting stock; and

"voting stock" means any stock, share or other entitlement which carries with it the right for the holder thereof whether personally or through a nominee to vote at any general meeting of the institution in respect of which it has been issued.

(2) A person shall be deemed to be carrying on banking business if he advertises for or solicits deposits of money, or offers to sell or place bonds, certificates, notes or other securities and uses or intends to use the funds so required, either in whole or part, for advances, investments or in any other operation either authorised by law or by customary banking practice for the account and at the risk of the person placing such advertisement.

PART II
LICENSING OF FINANCIAL INSTITUTIONS

Unlicensed financial institutions prohibited.

3. (1) No person other than a company incorporated under the Companies Act or established abroad, or a body corporate established in Solomon Islands by an Act of Parliament shall be eligible to apply for a licence under this Act to engage in the business of banking in Solomon Islands.

Cap. 66.

(2) A person commits an offence under this Act, who not being licensed as a financial institution-

(a) carries on banking business, whether on his own account, in partnership or otherwise; or

(b) purports to be licensed or otherwise entitled to carry on banking business; or

(c) takes or uses any name, title or description implying or likely to lead the public to believe that he is licensed or otherwise entitled to carry on banking business; or

(d) makes any representation to be a financial institution on any letter-head, notice, or advertisement or in any other manner.

(3) Where the Central Bank has reason to believe that any person is contravening the provisions of subsection (1) it may cause an examination of the books, accounts and records of such person to find out if that is the case.

(4) Any person who refuses to make available for examination such books, accounts and records requested by the Central Bank for purposes of subsection (3) shall be guilty of an offence.

(5) A person holding funds which he has obtained in contravention of subsection (1) shall repay such funds as directed by the Central Bank.

(6) Any person who is convicted of an offence under this section shall be liable to a fine not exceeding three thousand dollars for each day during which the offence continues or to imprisonment not exceeding three years or to both such fine and imprisonment.

(7) No company which has as part of its name or description the words "Bank", "Banking", "Savings" or "Savings and Loan" shall be incorporated or registered in Solomon Islands without the prior approval of the Central Bank. Where approval is granted under this section, such approval shall only be for the purpose of making an application under section 5 and does not confer or imply any enforceable right in respect of the grant of a licence.

Existing financial institutions deemed licensed.

4. (1) Notwithstanding the provisions of any other Act or law, the financial institutions specified in the Schedule shall-

(a) be deemed to be licensed under section 5 on the coming into force of this Act;

(b) be issued a licence accordingly; and

(c) be subject to this Act.

(2) Any financial institution specified in the Schedule which is, on the coming into force of this Act, in contravention of any provision of this Act, shall rectify such contravention

within six months of the coming into force of this Act. Details of such contravention shall be sent to the Central Bank within one month of the coming into force of this Act.

Licensing of financial institutions.

5. (1) Any company desirous of commencing banking business in Solomon Islands after the commencement of this Act shall, before commencing such business, apply for and obtain a licence to do so.

(2) An application for a licence under this section shall be made in writing to the Central Bank in such form as shall be specified by the Central Bank and shall be accompanied by such fee as may be specified.

(3) Every company that makes an application under this section shall furnish to the Central Bank such information, and such documents, authenticated in such manner as the Central Bank may specify, as may be required by the Central Bank to assist it to consider the application. The Central Bank may conduct such investigations as it deems necessary in regard to such application.

(4) Any person who knowingly furnishes any information or document which is false or misleading in any material particular in connection with an application under this Act is guilty of an offence and is liable on conviction to a fine not exceeding one hundred and fifty thousand dollars or to imprisonment not exceeding three years or to both such fine and imprisonment.

(5) In considering an application, the Central Bank shall have regard to the economic advantage of Solomon Islands, the need for and the viability of the financial institution proposed, its ownership spread, the financial capacity, history and qualifications of the applicant, promoters, substantial shareholders and management, their character and experience, the proposed financial institution's accounting, risk management and internal control systems, the adequacy and the structure of its capital and the business activities it intends to undertake.

(6) Where the applicant is a foreign financial institution, the Central Bank shall in addition to the matters specified in subsection (5) have regard to-

(a) the institution's international reputation;

(b) the ownership spread of the institution or of its holding company;

(c) the relevant law and regulatory requirement relating to the licensing and supervision of financial institutions in its country of incorporation;

and shall require-

(i) written information from the supervisory authority in the applicant's country of incorporation that the supervisory authority has no objection to the proposal to carry on banking business in Solomon Islands;

(ii) written confirmation that the applicant would provide support as necessary to its branch, subsidiary or affiliate in Solomon Islands; and

(iii) details of the programme of training the applicant would adopt in order to place Solomon Islands citizens in management positions in its operations in Solomon Islands.

(7) Within four months after receipt of an application under this section, and all other additional relevant information and documents it may require, the Central Bank shall-

(a) issue to the applicant a licence to carry on banking business subject to such terms and conditions as may be specified in the licence; or

(b) inform the applicant that its application is refused.

(8) A licence issued under this Act cannot be assigned or transferred and any purported transfer or assignment shall be null and void.

(9) The Central Bank may impose new or additional conditions on a licence issued pursuant to this Act, or vary or remove any conditions already imposed. Before taking such action, the Central Bank shall, by notice in writing to the licensed financial institution concerned, inform it of the changes proposed and afford it an opportunity to make submissions in writing to the Central Bank in this regard no later than fourteen days from the date of the notice. The Central Bank shall take into account any such submissions received in deciding whether or not to proceed with the changes.

(10) Every licensed financial institution shall pay such annual fee as may be determined by the Central Bank from time to time, on such basis as the Minister may approve. The prescribed annual fee shall be paid upon the granting of a licence and not later than the fifteenth day of January of every succeeding year. The annual fee shall be considered as a debt due to the Bank and any licensed financial institution which fails to pay the fee by the due date shall be liable to a surcharge equivalent to one hundred per cent of the prescribed fee. All fees and surcharges received under this subsection shall be paid by the Central Bank to the Treasury on account of the Consolidated Fund.

Revocation of licence.

6. (1) The Central Bank may revoke a licence issued under this Act-

(a) if the licensee-

(i) requests revocation of the licence;

(ii) was licensed on the basis of materially false or misleading information or documents;

(iii) fails to commence business within the time period prescribed by the Central Bank;

(iv) ceases to carry on banking business in Solomon Islands;

(v) contravenes the terms and conditions of its licence or the provisions of this Act; or

(vi) is subject to voluntary or involuntary winding-up proceedings or has a receiver appointed; or

(b) in the circumstances specified in section 17.

(2) Where the Central Bank intends to revoke the licence in any of the circumstances specified under subsection (1)(a), the Central Bank shall give the licensee notice in writing of that intention and shall afford the licensee the opportunity to submit to the Central Bank, within fourteen days of the date of the notice, reasons why the licence should not be revoked. The Central Bank shall take into account any such submissions in deciding whether or not to proceed with the revocation.

(3) The revocation of a licence in the circumstances specified in subsection (1)(a)(ii) shall not prejudice any other action which may be initiated under section 5(4).

Minimum capital of a financial institution.

7. (1) Every financial institution licensed under this Act shall maintain-

(a) if incorporated in Solomon Islands, paid-up capital and unimpaired reserves; and

(b) if incorporated abroad, assigned capital,

in such minimum proportion in relation to its assets, liabilities or risk exposures, and in such amount, as the Central Bank may in its absolute discretion specify from time to time.

(2) The Central Bank may in its absolute discretion specify the minimum amount of paid-up or assigned capital required by a financial institution for the issue of a licence under section 5.

(3) The Central Bank may in its absolute discretion specify different requirements for different financial institutions or classes of financial institutions.

(4) The minimum amount of paid-up capital or assigned capital which may be specified under subsections (1) and (2) is-

(a) in the case of a credit institution, not less than one million dollars; and

(b) in the case of a bank, not less than five million dollars.

(5) The computation and form of the capital required to be held under subsections (1) and (2) shall be determined by the Central Bank after consultation with the financial institution concerned.

(6) (a) No licensed financial institution shall declare or pay any dividend or make any other transfer from profits or reserves if such payment or transfer would contravene the provisions of this section or any specification made thereunder.

(b) No licensed financial institution incorporated in Solomon Islands shall pay any dividend on its shares or make any other transfer from profits and no licensed financial institution incorporated outside Solomon Islands shall remit any profits outside Solomon Islands until all its capitalised expenditure including preliminary expenses, organisation expenses, share selling commission, brokerage and amounts of losses incurred (not represented by tangible assets), has been completely written off.

PART III
PRUDENTIAL SUPERVISION

Prudential supervision.

8. (1) In the prudential supervision of licensed financial institutions and in determining whether or not a licensed financial institution carries on its business in a prudent manner, the Central Bank shall have regard to the following-

(a) capital adequacy in relation to the size and nature of the business;

(b) asset concentration and risk exposure;

(c) separation of banking business from other business and from other interests of any person owning or controlling the licensed financial institution;

(d) adequacy of liquidity in relation to liabilities;

(e) asset quality and adequacy of provisions for losses;

(f) internal controls, risk management accounting systems; and

(g) such other matters as the Central Bank considers relevant.

(2) The Central Bank may require a licensed financial institution to submit within a prescribed time and in a prescribed form such periodic returns and other information as it considers necessary for the purposes of this Act.

(3) The Central Bank may require any licensed financial institution to submit a certificate from its external auditor verifying the accuracy or any return or information furnished under subsection (2).

(4) The Central Bank may in its absolute discretion impose upon any licensed financial institution and upon any director or officer of the institution administrative fines for-

(a) failure to submit or for wilfully delaying the submission of any required return or information, or for wilfully submitting any false or inaccurate return or information required under subsection (2);

(b) failure to submit the certificate of the external auditor, if required in accordance with subsection (3); or

(c) failure to comply with a directive issued under section 16.

(5) (a) The administrative fines shall be in amounts as may be determined by the Central Bank to be appropriate but in no case may exceed ten thousand dollars for each violation or where the violation is a continuing one, may not exceed three thousand dollars for every day during which the violation continues, and shall take into consideration the surrounding circumstances, such as the nature and gravity of the violation. An administrative fine imposed shall be a civil debt and if not paid may be enforced by action in the Court.

(b) A licensed financial institution or any director or officer of that institution on whom an administrative fine is imposed may within fourteen days of the date of the notification of such fine, submit reasons to the Central Bank why such fine should not be imposed. After consideration of such submission the Central Bank may confirm, vary or rescind the fine.

External auditor and annual accounts.

9. (1) Every licensed financial institution shall, subject to the approval of the Central Bank, appoint annually one or more persons (whether as individuals or as members from time to time of any firm or firms) to be external auditors of the licensed financial institution.

(2) The duties of the external auditor shall include making a report upon the annual balance sheet and profit and loss account of the licensed financial institution and its subsidiaries in relation to the following matters-

(a) whether they have obtained all the information and explanations which to the best of their knowledge and belief were necessary for the purposes of their audit;

(b) whether, in their opinion, proper books of account have been kept by the licensed financial institution, so far as appears from their examination of those books, and proper returns adequate for the purposes of their audit have been received from branches not visited by them;

(c) whether the licensed financial institution's balance sheet and (unless it is framed as a consolidated profit and loss account) profit and loss account dealt with by the report are in agreement with the books of account and returns;

(d) whether, in their opinion and to the best of their information and according to the explanations given to them, the said accounts give a true and fair view-

(i) in the case of the balance sheet, of the state of the licensed financial institution's affairs as at the end of its financial year; and

(ii) in the case of the profit and loss accounts, of the profit or loss for its financial year;

(e) in the case of a licensed financial institution submitting group accounts as required by the Central Bank, whether in their opinion, the group accounts have been properly prepared as to give a true and fair view of the state of affairs and profit or loss of the licensed financial institution and its subsidiaries dealt with thereby; and

(f) in any case in which the external auditor has called for explanation or information from the officers or agents of the licensed financial institution and its subsidiaries whether it is satisfactory.

(3) Every licensed financial institution shall, within three months after the close of its financial year or such further period as the Central Bank may approve, submit to the Bank a copy of its audited annual balance sheet and profit and loss statement together with any notes thereon and a copy of the report of the external auditor made pursuant to subsection (2).

(4) In the case of a licensed financial institution incorporated in Solomon Islands, the report of the external auditor under subsection (2) shall be tabled together with the report of the directors of the licensed financial institution at the annual meeting of shareholders and copies of that report shall be sent to the Central Bank.

(5) Every director and every manager of a licensed financial institution which contravenes the provisions of subsection (4) shall be liable to an administrative fine

imposed by the Central Bank in accordance with section 8 (5).

(6) If a licensed financial institution fails to appoint an external auditor under subsection (1), or, at any time, fails to fill a vacancy for such external auditor, the Central Bank may appoint an external auditor and shall fix the remuneration to be paid by that institution to that external auditor.

(7) No person having an interest in any financial institution otherwise than as a depositor, and no director, employee or agent of any licensed financial institution shall be eligible for appointment as an external auditor for that institution; and any person appointed as external auditor to any licensed financial institution who subsequently acquires such interest or becomes a director, employee or agent of that institution shall cease to be external auditor thereof.

(8) (a) It shall be the duty of the external auditor to report immediately to the Central Bank information relating to the affairs of a licensed financial institution obtained in the course of an audit, if he is of the opinion that-

(i) the financial institution is insolvent or is likely to become insolvent or is likely to be unable to meet its obligations or is in serious financial difficulties;

(ii) a criminal offence involving fraud or dishonesty has been committed;

(iii) serious irregularities have occurred, including irregularities that jeopardise the interest of depositors and creditors;

(iv) losses have been incurred which substantially reduce the capital funds of the financial institution; or

(v) the financial institution is unable to confirm that the claims of creditors are still covered by the financial institution's assets.

(b) The external auditor may be required to discuss the audit directly with the Central Bank or be requested to provide additional information regarding the audit.

(9) The external auditor shall, before disclosing any information to the Central Bank under subsection (8), take reasonable steps to inform the licensed financial institution of the intention to disclose the information and the nature of such information, and of the intention to discuss the audit with the Central Bank.

(10) The Central Bank may, by notice in writing to a licensed financial institution, require it to supply the Central Bank with a report, prepared by its external auditor or other person nominated by the Central Bank, on such matters as the Central Bank may

determine which may include an opinion on asset quality, adequacy of provisions for losses, and the adequacy of the accounting and control systems.

(11) No civil, criminal or disciplinary proceedings shall lie against any external auditor arising from the disclosure in good faith of information to the Central Bank pursuant to this section.

(12) In the case of a licensed financial institution incorporated outside Solomon Islands, the provisions of subsections (1), (2), (3), (6), (7), (8), (9), (10), and (11) shall be applicable in respect to its operations in Solomon Islands; and a copy of the audited accounts shall be sent to the Central Bank.

Publication of financial statements.

10. (1) Not later than four months after the close of each financial year of each licensed financial institution, or such longer period as the Central Bank may in any particular case permit, the financial institution shall publish in a national publication specified by the Central Bank, and exhibit thereafter in a conspicuous position in each of its offices and branches in Solomon Islands copies of its audited balance sheet, and profit and loss account and the full and correct names of the directors of the financial institution.

(2) Any licensed financial institution which contravenes this section shall be guilty of an offence and liable on conviction to a fine not exceeding ten thousand dollars.

On-site examination.

11. (1) The Central Bank may, under conditions of confidentiality, initiate on-site examinations of the accounts and affairs of any licensed financial institution and any of its branches, agencies or offices. Such examinations may be conducted by Central Bank officers or by other persons designated as examiners by the Central Bank, (hereinafter referred to as "examiners".)

(2) A licensed financial institution under examination shall make available for the inspection of the examiners all cash and securities of the institution and all accounts, books, vouchers, minutes and any documents or records that are relevant to its business as may be required, within the time specified by the examiners.

(3) The examiners may make copies of and take away for further scrutiny, any papers or electronically stored data they require.

(4) An on-site examination may extend to any of the subsidiaries and affiliates of a licensed financial institution. Accordingly, the provisions of subsections (2) and (3) shall apply in the conduct of any examination of that institution's subsidiary or affiliate.

PART IV
RESTRICTIONS ON BUSINESS

Restrictions on advances, credit facilities and guarantees.

12. (1) A licensed financial institution together with it subsidiaries shall not, in respect of its Solomon Islands operations and, in the case of any such licensed financial institution which is incorporated in Solomon islands, also in respect of its overseas operations-

(a) make to any person, firm, corporation or company, or to any group of companies or of persons which group is under the control or influence of one and the same person, any advance or credit facility, or give any financial guarantee or incur any other exposure or liability on behalf of that person, firm, corporation, company or group so that the total value of that advances, credit facilities, financial guarantees and other exposures or liabilities in respect of that person, firm, corporation, company or group is at any time more than twenty-five per cent of that licensed financial institution's total capital as determined by the Central Bank:

Provided that this paragraph shall not apply to transactions between banks or between the branches of a bank, or the purchase of telegraphic transfers, or to the purchase of bills of exchange or documents of title to goods, where the holder of those bills or documents is entitled to payment outside Solomon Islands for exports from Solomon Islands, or to advances made against those transfers, bills or documents; or to any advance or credit facility made to or guaranteed by the Government of Solomon Islands;

(b) make any advances or credit facility against the security of its own shares;

(c) (i) grant to any of its directors or shareholders any advance, credit facility or guarantee unless granted on substantially the same terms, including interest rates and security, as those prevailing at the time for comparable transactions by the financial institution with members of the general public;

(ii)make or permit to be outstanding unsecured advances or unsecured credit facilities of an aggregate amount in excess of ten thousand dollars or of one per cent of the sum of the paid-up capital and published reserves of the licensed financial institution, whichever is the greater, or give any financial guarantees in excess of that amount without security, or incur any other liability in excess of that amount without security-

(A) to or on behalf of any one of its directors, whether the advances, facilities, guarantee or other liabilities are obtained by or on account of the director jointly or severally;

(B) to or on behalf of any firm, partnership or private company in which it, or any one or more of its directors is interested as director, partner, manager or agent, or to or on behalf of any individual, firm, partnership or private company of whom or of which any one or more of its directors is a guarantor.

For the purpose of this sub-paragraph, a private company shall have the meaning ascribed by the, Companies Act, and a director shall include a wife, husband, father, mother, son or daughter of a director, and persons who stand in a "wantok" relationship to a director;

Cap. 66

(d) make or permit to be outstanding to its officers and employees unsecured advances or unsecured credit facilities which, in aggregate amount for any one officer or employee, exceed one year's emolument of the officer or employee.

(2) For the purposes of paragraph (a) of subsection (1) -

(a) "control or influence of one and the same person" shall mean that the person holds and has the power to vote a minimum of fifty-one per cent of the voting shares or stock of the borrower, firm, corporation or company or a group of companies or of persons:

Provided that, the foregoing notwithstanding, a preponderance of evidence may prove "control or influence" if it can be shown that the person exercises a factual control in the policies of the borrower, firm, corporation or company or any group of companies or of persons.

(b) total capital in relation to a financial institution incorporated outside Solomon Islands shall be the sum of the global consolidated issue paid-up capital and published reserves of that licensed financial institution.

(3) In any or all of paragraphs (c) and (d) of subsection (1) the expression "unsecured advances or unsecured credit facilities" means advances or credit facilities made without security, or, in respect of any advance or credit facility made with security, any part, which at any time exceeds four-fifths of the market value or in the case of non-marketed securities a valuation by the Central Bank of the assets constituting that security.

(4) Any financial institution specified in the Schedule which is in contravention of this section at the time this Act comes into force, shall within three months of such time submit a statement thereof to the Central Bank and shall rectify such contravention within eighteen months of such time, or such further period as the Central Bank may allow.

Prohibited activities.

13. (1) A licensed financial institution shall not, in respect of its Solomon Islands operations, and in the case of any such licensed financial institution which is incorporated in Solomon Islands, also in respect of its overseas operations-

(a) engage in any business other than the business specified in the licence;

(b) engage, whether on its own account or on a commission basis, in the wholesale or retail trade, including the import or export trade, or otherwise, have a direct interest in any commercial, agricultural, industrial or other undertaking, except as permitted under paragraph (d) of this subsection and except insofar as may be necessary with respect to such interest as a licensed financial institution may acquire in the course of the satisfaction of debts due to it; but all such interests shall be disposed of within such period of time as may be determined by the Central Bank;

(c) acquire a subsidiary company, or operate via a subsidiary company, or permit a subsidiary company to operate or carry on business in any capacity, without the written approval of the Central Bank;

(d) acquire or hold to an aggregate value exceeding twenty-five per cent of that licensed financial institution's total capital as determined by the Central Bank, any part of the share capital of any financial, commercial, agricultural, industrial, or other undertaking except such share holding as a licensed financial institution may acquire in the course of the satisfaction of debts due to it; but any such shareholding shall, however be disposed of within such period of time as may be determined by the central Bank:

Provided that this paragraph shall not apply to-

(i) any shareholding, approved in writing by the Central Bank, in a subsidiary financial institution or in a subsidiary company formed by a licensed financial institution for execution of nominee, executor or trustee functions or other functions incidental to banking business; and

(ii) the acquisition and disposal of shares as a trustee or nominee, or the purchase and sale of shares upon the order and for the count of a customer;

(e) purchase, acquire or lease real property, except as may be necessary, for the purpose of conducting its business or housing its staff or providing amenities for its staff, having regard to any reasonable requirements for future expansion of its business or staff, but, in the event of any debt due to a licensed financial institution which is secured upon any real or other property of the debtor becoming endangered, the licensed financial institution may acquire such property; but any such property shall be resold within a period of time as may be determined by the Central Bank.

(2) For the purposes of paragraph (b) of subsection (1)-

(i) total capital in relation to a licensed financial institution incorporated outside Solomon Islands shall be the sum of the global consolidated issued paid-up capital and published reserves of that licensed financial institution;

(ii) shareholding acquired or held by a licensed financial institution shall include share capital acquired or held by any subsidiary or subsidiaries of the said financial institution, whether or not the subsidiary or subsidiaries are licensed under this Act.

(3) Except with the consent, in writing, of the Central Bank no financial institution incorporated in Solomon Islands shall open a new branch, agency or office in any place outside Solomon Islands.

(4) No licensed financial institution shall open or close a branch in Solomon Islands without first notifying the Central Bank of its intention to do so.

(5) (a) Every director and every manager of a licensed financial institution, which contravenes the provisions of any or all of paragraphs (a), (b), (c), (d) and (e) of subsection (1) or subsection (3) shall be liable to an administrative fine not exceeding three thousand dollars for every day during which the contravention continues, such administrative fine to be imposed by the Central Bank as provided for under section 8 (5).

(b) Any person liable to an administrative fine in terms of paragraph (a) shall have a good defence if he proves that the contravention was committed without his consent or connivance and that he exercised all such diligence to prevent the commission of the contravention as he ought to have exercised having regard to his position in the financial institution in respect of which the contravention was committed.

(6) The restriction contained in paragraph (d) of subsection (1) shall not apply, where a licensed financial institution or a subsidiary or subsidiaries of a licensed financial institution acquires or holds any part of the share capital of any company or companies under an underwriting or sub-underwriting contract for a period not exceeding three months, or such other period as the Central Bank may approve in writing in any particular case.

Persons debarred from management.

14. (1) Any person -

(a) who has been a director of, or directly concerned in the management of, a financial institution in Solomon Islands or elsewhere which has had its licence revoked or has been wound up by a court; or

(b) who has been sentenced by a court in any country to a term of imprisonment for an offence involving dishonesty and has not received a full pardon for that offence; or

(c) who is or becomes bankrupt, suspends payment to or compounds with his creditors,

shall not without the express authorisation of the Central Bank act or continue to act as a director, manager, secretary or other employee, of any financial institution.

(2) The Central Bank may in its absolute discretion, impose upon any person who contravenes the provisions of subsection (1) an administrative fine as provided for under section 8(5).

PART V
CONTROL OVER LICENSED FINANCIAL INSTITUTIONS

Assets of licensed financial institutions.

15. In the event of a licensed financial institution becoming unable to meet its obligations or suspending payment or in the case of a licensed financial institution incorporated outside Solomon Islands, in the event of its liquidation, bankruptcy or dissolution in its country of incorporation for whatever reason, the assets of the licensed financial institution in Solomon Islands shall be available to meet the licensed financial institution's deposit liabilities in Solomon Islands in priority to all other liabilities of the licensed financial institution, which priority the Central Bank shall be empowered to protect and preserve.

Unsound or unsafe practices.

16. (1) Where the Central Bank is of the opinion, either as a result of an inspection carried out pursuant to section 11 or otherwise, that a licensed financial institution-

(a) is following unsound or unsafe practices in the conduct of its business that are likely to jeopardise its obligations to its depositors or other creditors, or adversely affect the operation or stability of the financial system; or

(b) has contravened or failed to company with the terms and conditions of its licence or the provisions of this Act, the Central Bank may issue a directive to such licensed financial institution to-

(i) cease and desist from such practice, contravention or non-compliance; and

(ii) take such action (including action to replace or strengthen management) as may be specified in the directive to correct the conditions resulting from such practice, contravention or non-compliance.

Enforcement.

17. (1) Where-

(a) a licensed financial institution informs the Central Bank that it is insolvent, is likely to become so, or is likely to be unable to pay its obligations; or

(b) if in the opinion of the Central Bank, or if an external audit or an on-site examination shows that a licensed financial institution-

(i) is carrying on its business in a manner that is detrimental to the interests of its depositors, creditors or the public; or

(ii) is likely to be unable to meet its obligations when they fall due,

the Central Bank shall exercise one or more of the powers specified in subsection (2).

(2) The powers referred to in subsection (1) are-

(a) to direct the licensed financial institution to take whatever action in relation to its business as the Central Bank may specify;

(b) to appoint a qualified person to advise the licensed financial institution on the proper conduct of its business;

(c) to direct the licensed financial institution to pay such remuneration to a person appointed under paragraph (b) of this subsection, as may be fixed by the Central Bank;

(d) to revoke the licensed financial institution's licence; or

(e) to present a Petition to the Court for the winding up of the licensed financial institution.

(3) Where an advisor is appointed under subsection (2)(b) the licensed financial institution shall afford the advisor access to its books, accounts and documents and shall give such information and facilities as necessary to enable him to carry out his duties.

Court supervised management.

18. (1) If the Central Bank considers that it is proper to take control of and manage the banking business of a licensed financial institution in order to protect the stability of the financial system, the interest of depositors or in the public interest, it may apply to the Court for any order under this section.

(2) The Court may, if it considers that in the circumstances of the case it is appropriate that the Central Bank or its nominee be appointed to take control of and manage the banking business of a licensed financial institution, make any or all of the following orders-

(a) that the Central Bank or a person nominated by the Central Bank and approved by the Court, be appointed as Court Appointed Manager, to take control of the banking business of a licensed financial institution;

(b) that the Court Appointed Manager shall have such powers and authority as the Court specifies, including the following-

(i) power to carry on or cease to carry on, or sell the business of the financial institution and in so doing, to have and exercise all the powers, rights and authorities necessary to do so;

(ii) such of the powers of a liquidator under the Companies Act as are specified by the Court;

Cap. 66

(c) that any subsidiary of the licensed financial institution be subject to control and management under this section in like manner to the licensed financial institution;

(d) any order in relation to the licensed financial institution that the Court would be able to make in relation to a company that is in liquidation under the Companies Act, including-

(i) a moratorium on actions or enforcement action against the licensed financial institution on such terms as the Court considers appropriate; or

(ii) prohibition against the removal or disposal of assets except with the consent of the Court Appointed Manager; or

(e) that the Court Appointed Manager be entitled to apply to the Court in the case to seek directions.

(3) If a licensed financial institution that is subject to management and control under this section is incorporated outside Solomon Islands, this section applies to the operations of the licensed financial institution in Solomon Islands and to its property, rights, assets and liabilities relating to its business in Solomon Islands.

(4) If a licensed financial institution or subsidiary that becomes subject to management and control under this section is already in liquidation or receivership-

(a) the liquidation or receivership shall cease; and

(b) the person appointed as liquidator or receiver shall be discharged;

Provided that if the control and management of the licensed financial institution or subsidiary under this section is terminated, the Court may order that the liquidation or receivership shall be revised, upon such terms as the Court may specify.

(5) The Court, on the application of the Central Bank or of its own motion, may terminate the appointment of a person as Court Appointed Manager, for any reason, including the resignation of that person.

(6) A licensed financial institution or subsidiary shall cease to be subject to control and management under this section if-

(a) the Court, on the application of the Central Bank, so orders; or

(b) the Central Bank presents a petition for the winding up of the licensed financial institution.

(7) In the exercise of its powers, the Court Appointed Manager shall have regard to -

(a) the need to avoid significant damage to the financial system; and

(b) the preservation, subject to paragraph (a), of the position of creditors and the maintenance of the ranking of claims of creditors, provided that depositors shall receive priority ahead of other creditors.

(8) A Court Appointed Manager shall comply with any written directions of the Central Bank relating to the exercise of his powers under this Act unless-

(a) such directions conflict with any order of the Court; or

(b) the Central Bank is the Court Appointed Manager.

(9) A Court Appointed Manager, and any employee, director or assistant thereof, shall not incur any personal liability by virtue of the exercise, in good faith, of any power or duty under this Act.

(10) An application to the Court under subsection (1) shall be by notice of motion and thereafter the form of the proceedings shall be as directed by the Court.

Liquidation proceedings.

19. Notwithstanding anything to the contrary contained in the Companies Act-

Cap. 66.

(a) no licensed financial institution shall be wound up without the prior approval of the Central Bank;

(b) the Registrar of Companies shall be the liquidator in any proceedings in Solomon Islands for the winding up of a licensed financial institution except in the case of a members' voluntary winding up of such institution wherein the Registrar may be the liquidator;

(c) the Court may, in the proceedings for the winding up of a licensed financial institution, dispense with any meetings of creditors or contributors or with the appointment of a committee of inspection if it considers that no object will be served thereby sufficient to justify the delay and expense; and

(d) the Court shall presume the amounts shown in the books of the licensed financial institution as standing to the credit of depositors are proved without requiring further proof from the depositors concerned unless the liquidator shows that there is reason for doubting any particular entry.

Misleading or obstructive conduct an offence.

20. Any director, officer, employee, former officer or former employee of a licensed financial institution or of the EDP Servicer of that licensed financial institution, who-

(a) with intent to deceive -

(i) makes or provides any false or misleading statement, report, return, document or information;

(ii) makes or provides any false or misleading entry in any book or record;

(iii) omits an entry or alters or conceals an entry in any book or record;

(iv) conceals or destroys any information, book, voucher, record, report, return, minutes or document, relating to the accounts, transactions, affairs or business of the financial institution; or

(b) obstructs or endeavours to obstruct-

(i) the proper performance by an external auditor of his duties;

(ii) an on-site examination of the licensed financial institution (or any branch, agency, office, subsidiary or affiliate of that institution) by an examiner appointed by the Central Bank; or

(iii) the proper performance by an advisor or Court Appointed Manager of his duties,

commits an offence and shall be liable, on conviction to a fine not exceeding one hundred thousand dollars or to imprisonment for a term not exceeding five years or to both such fine and imprisonment.

Identification of transactors.

21. (1) Any director, manager or other officer concerned in the management of a financial institution who makes or authorises, or permits to be made or authorised by any officer of the financial institution any transaction-

(a) without taking or causing to be taken all reasonable steps to establish the true identity of the persons concerned in the transaction;

(b) when he or the officer concerned doubts or has reason to doubt the authenticity of documents and the truth of written or oral statements material to the transaction; or

(c) when he or the officer concerned knows or has reason to suspect that any of the funds involved in the transaction have been obtained by any party as the direct or indirect result of activity that is illegal inside or outside Solomon Islands,

is guilty of an offence and is liable on conviction to a fine of twenty thousand dollars or imprisonment for one year or both.

(2) No director, manager or other officer concerned in the management of a financial institution who discloses in good faith to a police officer any information regarding any customer or transaction which he believes to be connected to illegal activity, shall incur any liability as a result of such disclosure.

PART VI
MISCELLANEOUS

Notice of changes.

22. (1) When any alteration is made in the memorandum or articles of association of a licensed financial institution or in any other instruments whereunder that institution was incorporated, the institution shall forthwith give to the Central Bank full particulars, in writing, of such alteration, verified by a statutory declaration made by a director of the institution.

(2) In respect of any application made to the Court under section 24 of the Companies Act proposing a compromise or arrangement that involves a licensed financial institution, the Central Bank shall-

Cap. 66

(a) be served with a notice of every meeting ordered by the Court and also a statement explaining the effect of the compromise or arrangement as provided under the Companies Act; and

(b) be eligible to attend and be considered competent to participate and to give advice in any meeting of which such notice is given.

(3) A licensed financial institution shall consult with, and obtain the approval of the Central Bank before making any arrangement or entering into any agreement for the purchase or acquisition of the business of any other financial institution in Solomon Islands, or elsewhere in the case of a financial institution incorporated in Solomon Islands.

(4) Any licensed financial institution which acts in contravention of this section commits an offence and is liable on conviction to a fine not exceeding twenty thousand dollars.

Transfer of control.

23. (1) Any event specified in subsection (2) that may result in a transfer of control of a licensed financial institution incorporated in Solomon Islands shall be subject to the written approval of the Central Bank before implementation.

(2) For the purposes of subsection (1), the following events are hereby specified -

(a) any agreed sale, transfer or other disposition whatsoever of a licensed financial institution's share capital or issue or allotment of any new share capital;

(b) any proposed compromise or arrangement that involves a licensed financial institution for which an application has been made to the Court pursuant to the provisions of the Companies Act and where the proposed compromise or arrangement is for the purposes of or in connection with a scheme for the reconstruction or amalgamation of that institution; or

Cap. 66

(c) any other event or scheme the effect of which transfers, directly or indirectly, the ownership or the powers exercisable over the voting stock of a licensed financial institution.

(3) For the purpose of this section, "transfer of control" refers to any event specified in subsection (2) that results in a person acquiring ownership or exercising power over twenty per cent or more of the voting stock of a licensed financial institution.

(4) No licensed financial institution incorporated in Solomon Islands shall effect a reduction of its issued share capital without prior notice to the Central Bank.

(5) Any licensed financial institution or any person who acts in contravention of this section commits an offence and is liable on conviction to a fine not exceeding thirty thousand dollars and any purported transfer may be declared null and void.

Use of the word "bank" and name restriction.

24. (1) Every licensed bank shall use as part of its name description or title the word "bank" or one or more of its derivatives.

(2) No institution other than an institution established under an Act of Parliament in Solomon Islands or a bank licensed under this Act shall use the word "bank" or any of its derivatives in any language or any other word that indicates that such institution may be undertaking or carrying on the business of a banking or make any representation to such effect in any billhead, letter, paper, notice or advertisement or by any other means whatsoever.

(3) Notwithstanding subsection (2) the Central Bank may approve the use of the word "bank" where that word is included in the name of a foreign financial institution which is permitted by the Central Bank to establish a representative office in Solomon Islands.

(4) No bank shall be granted or continue to hold a licence under a name which so

closely resembles the name of an existing bank that it is likely, in the opinion of the Central Bank, to mislead the public.

(5) No licensed financial institution shall change its name or use a name other than under which it was licensed unless the written consent of the Central Bank is obtained.

(6) Nothing in this section shall apply to an association of banks or bank employees, formed for the protection of their common interests.

Bank holidays.

25. (1) If the Central Bank considers it necessary or expedient in the public interest, it may by order declare any day a non-business day for financial institutions.

(2) Without prejudice to subsection (1), the Central Bank may in the event of hurricane, earthquake or other natural disaster declare in such manner as it considers appropriate any day a non-business day for financial institutions, which declaration may relate to any part of or to the whole of Solomon Islands.

(3) Any day declared to be a non-business day under this section shall be regarded as a bank holiday for the purposes of the Bills of Exchange Act.

Act of 1882 (45 and 46 Vict.)

Retention of cheques, etc. for seven years.

26. (1) All cheques and bank drafts in the possession of a licensed financial institution on which they are drawn and all bills of exchange or promissory notes in the possession of a licensed financial institution and made payable at the institution shall be retained by that institution until the expiration of the period of seven years from the date thereof in the case of documents payable on demand or from the due date thereof in the case of all other documents.

(2) This section shall apply to cheques, drafts, bills and notes received by a financial institution either before or after the coming into force of this Act.

(3) No document to which this section refers shall be destroyed under the implied authority thereof at any time after a demand for the delivery of the document has been made to the licensed financial institution by the person entitled thereto.

(4) It shall be sufficient compliance with the duty to retain imposed by subsection (1), if a copy of the document has been made by the financial institution on microfilm, microfiche, tape, disc, or electronic or photographic storage media, and is retained by the licensed financial institution for the same period as that document is required to be retained pursuant to subsection (1).

(5) Notwithstanding subsection (4), no document shall be destroyed under the authority thereof at any time within two years after the date thereof in the case of documents payable on demand or from the due date thereof in the case of all other documents.

(6) Notwithstanding the provisions of any other Act or law, a copy of a document made pursuant to this section shall be admissible as evidence in any legal proceedings to the same extent as the document of which it is a copy would have been admissible.

Prohibition of receipt of commission by staff, etc.

27. Any director or employee of a licensed financial institution who asks for or receives, consents or agrees to receive, any gift, commission, emolument, service, gratuity, money, property or thing of value for his own personal benefit or advantage or that of any of his relatives for procuring or endeavouring to procure for any person any advance, loan, financial guarantee or credit facility from that financial institution, or the purchase or discount of any draft, note, cheque, bill of exchange or other obligation by that financial institution, or for permitting any person to overdraw any account with the financial institution shall be guilty of an offence and shall be liable to a fine of five thousand dollars or to a term of imprisonment not exceeding six months.

Non-compliance with the Act an offence.

28. (1) Any director or officer concerned in the management of any licensed financial institution who -

(a) fails to comply with the requirements of Act or any of the regulations, notices or directives issued under this Act; or

(b) aids or abets or counsels or procures any person to commit an offence under this Act,

commits an offence and shall be liable on conviction to a fine not exceeding ten thousand dollars or to a term of imprisonment not exceeding one year or to both such fine and imprisonment.

(2) Any person who commits an offence or any individual responsible for any offence against this Act or any of the regulations, notices or directives issued under this Act for which no penalty is expressly provided in this Act is liable upon conviction to a fine not exceeding fifty thousand dollars or to a term of imprisonment not exceeding three years or to both such fine and imprisonment and if the offence is a continuing one, to a further fine not exceeding two thousand dollars for every day during which the offence continues.

Prohibition on disclosure.

29. (1) Any statement or return or information provided by a licensed financial institution or obtained from a licensed financial institution by an examiner, advisor or Court Appointed Manager shall be regarded as confidential. The Central Bank and any of its directors, officers, employees or any individual or person designated by the Central Bank under the provisions of this Act shall not disclose any information relevant to the affairs or condition of any licensed financial institution or any of its clients acquired in the performance of his duties except-

(a) for the purpose of the performance of his duties or the exercise of his functions;

(b) when lawfully required to do so by any court, or in connection with any proceedings for an offence against this Act;

(c) with the consent of the person to whom the information relates;

(d) to the extent that the information is available under any other Act or in a public document;

(e) in aggregated or summary form, in such a manner as to prevent any information disclosed from being identified by any person as relating to a particular person; or

(f) in confidence to a supervisory authority in any other country for the purposes of the exercise of functions corresponding to or similar to those conferred on the Central Bank under this Act, if the Central Bank is reasonably satisfied that the recipient of the information will maintain confidentiality.

(2) Any person who contravenes this section commits an offence and shall be liable on conviction to a fine not exceeding thirty thousand dollars or to a term of imprisonment not exceeding two years or to both such fine and imprisonment.

Exclusion from liability.

30. Neither the Central Bank nor any director, officer, employee of the Central Bank or person duly appointed or authorised by the Central Bank shall incur any liability as a result of anything done in good faith in the exercise of any power or the performance of any duty under this Act.

Consent of Director of public Prosecutions.

31. No prosecution in respect of any offence under this Act shall be instituted except by or with the consent of the Director of Public Prosecutions.

Non-application to credit unions, etc.

32. (1) Subject to the provisions of subsection (2), this Act shall not apply to -

(a) a credit union within the meaning of the Credit Unions Act;

Act No. 1 of 1986. Cap 73

(b) a co-operative society within the meaning of the Co-operative Societies Act.

(2) Notwithstanding the provisions of subsection (1), the Minister may, by order, apply any provision of this Act to a credit union or a co-operative society, if the Minister is satisfied upon a finding by the Central Bank, that a credit union or a co-operative society is accepting deposits or granting loans aggregating to one hundred thousand dollars at any one time.

Unclaimed moneys.

33. (1) Every licensed financial institution shall, within sixty days after the end of each financial year, publish in a national publication specified by the Central Bank a statement showing all accounts payable by the financial institution in Solomon Islands in respect of which during a period of ten years, or any longer period as the case may be, no transaction has taken place and no statement of account has been requested or acknowledged by the creditor.

(2) Every statement published under subsection (1) shall require the person to whom the account is payable or his legal or personal representative, as the case may be, to submit a claim to the licensed financial institution within three months from the date of publication in a national publication.

(3) When any of the sums included in the statement published under subsection (1) remains unclaimed for a period of three months after publication of the statement in a national publication, such sums, after deduction of the costs of publication, shall be paid to the Central Bank which shall credit such sums into the Consolidated Fund.

(4) Subject to subsection (5), a licensed financial institution is, upon payment to the Central Bank of any sums due under this section, discharged from further liability in respect of that amount.

(5) Where unclaimed moneys have been paid into the Consolidated Fund under this section and the Minister is satisfied that, but for subsection (4), a person would be paid those unclaimed moneys by the licensed financial institution (or, if that financial institution is no longer carrying on banking business, by a licensed financial institution to which the business of the first-mentioned licensed financial institution has been sold or disposed of), those unclaimed moneys shall be paid to that licensed financial institution, which shall thereupon pay those moneys to that person, and those unclaimed moneys shall be a charge upon the Consolidated Fund which is hereby, to the extent necessary, appropriated for the purpose.

Application of the Act.

34. (1) The provisions of any other Act or any law that may be inconsistent with the provisions of this Act shall be read subject to or modified by the provisions of this Act. Nothing in this Act shall exempt a licensed financial institution from the provisions of the Companies Act, save that where there is any conflict between the provisions of this Act and the provisions of the Companies Act, this Act shall prevail.

Cap. 66

(2) The Minister, after consultation with the Central Bank, may, by order, apply any provision of this Act to the Development Bank of Solomon Islands, Home Finance Corporation and Solomon Islands National Provident Fund which shall each for the purpose of such provision be deemed to be a licensed financial institution.

Regulations.

35. The Central Bank may with the approval of the Minister make regulations in accordance with the provisions of this Act.

Repeal.

36. The Banking Act 1976 is hereby repealed.

Act No. 20 of 1976.

SCHEDULE
(Section 4)

Australia and New Zealand Banking Group Limited
Australian Guarantee Corporation (SI) Limited
National Bank of Solomon Islands
Westpac Banking Corporation.

FINANCIAL INSTITUTIONS (AMENDMENT) ACT 1999

Passed by the National Parliament this thirtieth day of November 1999.
Assented to in Her Majesty's name and on Her Majesty's behalf this tenth day of December 1999.
Date of commencement: date of publication in the Gazette.
AN ACT TO Amend the Financial Institutions Act 1998.
ENACTED by the National Parliament of Solomon Islands.

ARRANGEMENT OF SECTIONS

SECTION:

Short title.

1. This Act may be cited as the Financial Institutions (Amendment) Act 1999.

Amendment of section 2 Act No. 3 of 1998.

2. Section 2 of the Financial Institutions Act 1998 (hereinafter referred to as the "principal Act") is hereby amended in the following respects –

(a) in subsection (1) –

(i) in paragraph (b) of the definition of "banking business", by inserting the words "may additionally be authorised to engage in by the Central Bank" after the words "paragraph (a),";

(ii) by deleting the words "EDP service" occurring immediately after the definition of "director", and substituting therefor the words "EDP Servicer";

(iii) by inserting immediately after the definition of "officer", the following new definition –

"pyramid selling scheme" means a scheme which constitutes primarily an opportunity for participants to sell an investment opportunity to other participants in the scheme; and which is or is likely to be unfair to many of the participants in the scheme in that -

(a) the financial rewards of many of those participants are dependent on the recruitment of additional participants (whether or not at successively lower levels); and
(b) the number of additional participants that must be recruited to produce reasonable financial rewards to participants in the scheme is not attainable or is not likely to be attainable, by many of the participants in the scheme;'; and

(b) in subsection (2) by deleting the words "such advertisement." and substituting therefor the words "such advertisement; or advertises, promotes or operates a pyramid selling scheme.".

Amendment of section 3.

3. Section 3 of the principal Act is hereby amended in the following respects –

(a) by deleting subsection (1) and substituting therefor the following new subsection –

> "(1) No person shall carry on banking business in Solomon Islands unless such person is a financial institution licensed under this Act."; and

(b) in subsection (7) by inserting the words "or establishing a representative office in Solomon Islands pursuant to section 24(3)" after the words "section 5".

Amendment of section 5.

4. Section 5 of the principal Act is hereby amended in the following respects –

(a) in subsection (1) by deleting the word "company" and substituting therefor the word "person";

(b) by nserting immediately after subsection ('07 the following new subsection. –

> "(1A) No person other than a body corporate shall be issued with a license to carry on banking business pursuant to this Act.";

(c) in subsection (3) by deleting the word "company" and substituting therefor the word "person";

(d) by inserting immediately after subsection (7), the following new subsection –

> "(7A) A license shall not be issued pursuant to paragraph (a) of sub-section (7) unless the Central Bank is satisfied in respect of the matters set out in subsection (5) and, where the applicant is a foreign financial institution, the matters set out in subsection (6)"; and

(e) in subsection (10) by adding, the words "and as prescribed by regulations" after the word "approve".

Amendment of section 9.

5. Paragraph (v) of subsection (8)(a) of section 9 of Amendment of the principal Act is hereby amended by deleting the words "the financial institution is unable" and substituting therefor the words "he is unable".

Amendment of section 16.

6. Paragraph (b) of subsection (1) of section 16 of Amendment of the principal Act is hereby amended by deleting the word "company" and substituting therefor the word "comply".

Amendment of section 18.

7. The proviso to subsection (4) of section 18 of the principal Act is hereby amended by deleting the word "revised" and substituting therefor the word "revived".

Amendment of section 24.

8. Subsection (2) of section 24 of the principal Act is hereby amended by inserting the words 'with the word "bank" (or its derivative) in its title' after the words "Solomon Islands".

Amendment of section 27.

9. Section 27 of the principal Act is hereby amended by inserting the words "on conviction" after the word "liable".

Amendment of schedule.

10. The Schedule to the principal Act is hereby amended in the following respects –

(a) by deleting the words "Australian Guarantee Corporation (SI) Limited" and substituting therefor the words "A.G.C. Finance (SI) Limited"; and

(b) by addling the word "Limited" after the words "National Bank of Solomon Islands".

THE INCOME TAX (AMENDMENT) ACT 1996

Shirt title and commencement.

1. This Act may be cited as the Income Tax (Amendment) Act, 1996, and shall come into operation on such date as the Minister may appoint by Notice published in the Gazette.

Amendment of section 2 of Cap 61.

2. Section 2 of the Income Tax Act (hereinafter referred to as the "principal Act") is hereby amended in the following respects -

(a) by inserting therein in proper alphabetical sequence the following new definitions-

"approved mining company" means a company that -

(a) is authorised to carry out mining under a mineral licence acquired under the Mines and Minerals Act; or
Act No. 3 of 1990

(b) has entered into a mining agreement with the Government in accordance with the provisions of section 30(6) of the Mines and Minerals Act;

"special benefits" mean benefits or incentives granted to an approved mining company.";

(b) by inserting therein immediately after subsection (3) the following new subsection as subsection (4) -

"(4) Unless the context otherwise requires, where any expression defined in paragraph 1 of the Twelfth Schedule appears in any provisions of this Act, such expression shall in relation to an approved mining company have the same meaning assigned to it in the aforesaid Schedule."

Insertion of new section 4A

3. The principal Act is hereby amended by inserting therein immediately after section 4 the following new section as section 4A-

"Income derived from foreign currency chargeable to tax in Solomon Islands.

4A. (1) Subject to the provisions of subsection (2), any income derived from moneys retained outside Solomon Islands by an approved mining company for the purposes of meeting foreign currency requirements for procuring supplies and services in connection with mining operations shall be deemed to be income derived in Solomon Islands and chargeable to tax.

(2) In computing the income chargeable to tax under the provisions of subsection (1), the tax paid on such income in any foreign country shall not be creditable against income tax or any other tax in Solomon Islands but shall be deductible."

Insertion of new section 11H and 11I

4. The principal Act is hereby amended by inserting therein immediately after section 11G the following new sections as sections 11H and 11I respectively -

"Tax credit for expenditure incurred in approved infrastructure development of an approved mining company.

11H. (1) Where pursuant to a relevant agreement, an approved mining company has, in any tax year incurred expenditure in the construction of an approved infrastructure development scheme approved by the Government as provided for in the relevant agreement the amount of such expenditure not exceeding such amount as specified in the relevant agreement shall be allowed to the approved mining company as a tax credit against the income tax due and payable under this Act by the approved mining company in respect of that tax year provided that -

(a) no other allowance deduction or tax credit under this Act shall be granted to the approved mining company in respect of such expenditure in that or any other tax year; and

(b) the tax credit for any tax year shall not exceed the amount of income tax payable for that tax year; and provided further that, where the relevant agreement so provides, in relation to any tax year during the period specified in the relevant agreement, such expenditure not exceeding the amount specified in the relevant agreement shall be allowed to the approved mining company as a tax credit against the income tax due and payable under this Act by the approved mining company in respect of that tax year and the tax credit in respect of such tax year to the extent that such tax credit exceeds the amount of income tax payable in such tax year may be carried forward to the immediately succeeding tax year.

(2) For the purposes of subsection (1) "infrastructure development scheme" means a scheme for the development of such infrastructure (other than infrastructure relating to or required by the mining operations carried out by the approved mining company pursuant to the relevant agreement) and in such locality or area in Solomon Islands as approved by the Government.

Certain restrictions on special benefits granted to approved mining companies.

11I. An approved mining company shall not be eligible or qualified for exemptions granted to a foreign investor under sections 11A, 11B, 11C, 11D and 11F of this Act."

Amendment of section 14.

5. Subsection (2) of section 14 of the principal Act is hereby amended by inserting at the end therein the following new paragraphs as paragraphs (o) and (p) respectively -

"(o) the costs incurred in any tax year in respect of rehabilitation and reclamation by an approved mining company in accordance with the relevant agreement shall be deductible in such tax year and shall be debited to the provision for rehabilitation and reclamation costs made in accordance with the relevant agreement in relation to the mining operations by the approved mining company. Where at the end of the mining operations the aforesaid financial provision and the income of the approved mining company is insufficient to meet the rehabilitation and reclamation costs incurred by the approved mining company in accordance with the relevant agreement, any loss resulting therefrom may be carried back and recovered out of the income for the period not exceeding five years commencing from the year when the mining operations cease.

(p) operating and other costs and expenses reasonably incurred by the approved mining company to carry out mining operations including any tax, royalty, charge, duty or other levy (excluding income tax and additional profits tax) payable in Solomon Islands by the approved mining company."

Amendment of section 32.

6. Section 32 of the principal Act is hereby amended by inserting therein the following new subsection as subsection (3) -

"(3) Notwithstanding the provisions of subsections (1) and (2), the tax upon the chargeable income of an approved mining company shall for any tax year be charged at the rate of thirty-five cents in the dollar for every dollar of such chargeable income."

Insertion of new section 32C.

7. The principal Act is hereby amended by inserting therein immediately after section 32B the following new section as section 32C -

"**Additional profits tax.**

32C. Subject to and in accordance with the provisions of the Twelfth Schedule, an additional profits tax shall be payable by an approved mining company as set forth in the Twelfth Schedule."

Amendment of First Schedule.

8. The First Schedule to the principal Act is hereby amended by adding at the end thereof the following new paragraph -

> "**36.** The Minister may by order exempt fees derived from mining operations by expatriate contractors engaged by or on behalf of an approved mining company subject to such conditions as may be specified by the Minister."

Amendment of Second Schedule.

9. The Second Schedule to the principal Act is hereby amended by inserting at the end of Part III the following new paragraph as paragraph 12A -

> "**Certain deductions in respect of an approved mining company.**
>
> **12A.** In computing the gains and profits of mining company, for any tax year -
>
> > (a) interest paid by an approved mining company on a loan to finance its mining operations in accordance with the relevant agreement shall be deductible provided that -
> >
> > (i) the rate of interest on the loan does not exceed a rate based upon an arm's length competitive third party transaction at the time the loan was made; and
> >
> > (ii) only to the extent that the ratio of loan capital to paid up equity does not exceed 3:1 or such other ratio as the Commissioner may permit;
> >
> > (b) (i) exploration and development expenditure incurred prior to the date of commencement of commercial production by an approved mining company; and
> >
> > (ii) where a relevant agreement so provides, exploration and development expenditure on the approved expansion of the mining project in accordance with the relevant agreement incurred by an approved mining company,
> >
> > shall be deductible annually at such rate as the Commissioner may permit:
> >
> > Provided that such exploration and development expenditure that is incurred by an affiliate of the approved mining company in accordance with the relevant agreement prior to the date of incorporation of the

approved mining company and as may be approved by the Commissioner shall be deemed for the purpose of this subparagraph to have been incurred by the approved mining company; and

(c) subject to paragraph (b), exploration and development expenditure incurred by an approved mining company after the date of commencement of commercial production shall be deductible at the rates set forth in Part III of this Schedule."

Amendment of Seventh Schedule.

10. The Seventh Schedule to the principal Act is hereby amended by inserting at the end thereof the following -

"(xi) interest paid on borrowings made overseas or from non-resident companies by an approved mining company, and where the relevant agreement so provides by an affiliate company of the approved mining company in relation to the mining operation as approved by the Commissioner shall be at the rate provided in subparagraph (1) or such reduced rate as the Minister may provide by order;

(xii) gross payments made to non-Solomon Islands contractors or sub-contractors by an approved mining company and where the relevant agreement so provides by an affiliate company of the approved mining company in relation to the mining operation as approved by the Commissioner for services performed shall be at the rate of seven cents in every dollar; and

(xiii) no withholding tax shall be payable by an approved mining company on any dividend and, where a relevant agreement so provides, payable by an affiliate company of the approved mining company on any dividend in respect of the income derived from the mining operations of the approved mining company paid to a non-resident person to such extent the Minister may provide by Order."

Insertion new Twelfth Schedule.

11. The principal Act is hereby amended by inserting at the end thereof the following new Schedule as the Twelfth Schedule -

"TWELFTH SCHEDULE
(Section 32C)

Interpretation.

1. In this Schedule, unless the context otherwise requires -

"affiliate company" in relation to an approved mining company means any person, firm or company, directly or indirectly, controlling, controlled by or under common control with the approved mining company;

"date of commencement of commercial production" means the date when the production of minerals from the mining lease for sale commences or such other date as specified in the relevant agreement;

"development expenditure" means expenditure incurred, whether directly or indirectly, in or in connection with the carrying out of development operations in or in connection with the mineral licence area, including expenditure incurred in respect of -

(a) the acquisition of -

(i) machinery, implements, utensils and other articles used for purposes of production, treatment and processing;
(ii) furniture, tools and equipment used in offices and export terminals, vehicles, motorised rolling equipment, aircraft, fire and security stations, water and sewage plants, power plants and other works in connection with development operations;

(b) the leasing of fixed and mobile plant, buildings and structures;

(c) labour, fuel, haulage, and related costs in connection with and construction of mine facilities and other works in connection with development operations;

(d) the advancement of training and education of Solomon Islands citizens at institutions approved by the Ministry of Education and the provision of educational and scientific materials and equipment;

(e) charges, fees or rent for, or in respect of, land or buildings occupied for purposes of carrying out development operations;

(f) preparation of feasibility studies and applications for requisite approvals and consents and related costs;

(g) the general and administrative expenditure directly connected with development operations;

(h) the restoration of the mineral licence area, or any part thereof, after cessation of development operations in such area to the extent to which such expenditure has been incurred by virtue of any term and condition of the mining lease or the relevant agreement relating to safety or the prevention of pollution;

(i) customs duty and goods tax in respect of the importation for use in or in connection with development operations in the mineral licence area of plant, machinery, equipment, spare parts, materials, supplies or consumable items to be used in or in connection with such development operations; and

(j) such items of expenditure included as development expenditure in a relevant agreement as the Commissioner determines appropriate and by Order specifies;

"development operations" means operations relating to the development and construction of the mine under a mining lease, and includes development operations for the approved expansion of the mining project under the mining lease in accordance with the relevant agreement;

"exploration expenditure" means expenditure incurred, whether directly or indirectly, by an approved mining company in or in connection with the carrying out of prospecting operations in the mineral licence area, including expenditure relating to such operations incurred in respect of -

(a) the acquisition of machinery, implements, utensils and other articles employed in such operations;

(b) labour, fuel, haulage, supplies, materials and repairs and related costs in connection with a survey or study or other prospecting operations;

(c) the advancement of training and education of Solomon Islands citizens at institutions approved by the Ministry of Education and the provision of educational and scientific material and equipment;

(d) charges, fees or rent including tenement fees and compensation for access to land for, or in respect, of land or buildings occupied for purposes of carrying out prospecting operations;

(e) the general and administrative expenditure directly connected with prospecting operations;

(f) the restoration of the mineral licence area, or any part thereof, after cessation of prospecting operations in the area to the extent to which such expenditure has been incurred by virtue of any term and condition of the prospecting licence or the relevant agreement relating to safety or the prevention of pollution;

(g) customs duty and goods tax in respect of the importation for use in or, in connection with prospecting operations in the mineral licence area, of plant, machinery, equipment, spare parts, materials, supplies or consumable items used in or in connection with such prospecting operations; and

(h) such items of expenditure included as exploration expenditure in a relevant agreement as the Commissioner determines appropriate and by Order specifies;

"general and administrative expenditure" means expenditure incurred on general administration and management primarily and principally related to mining operations in or in connection with the mineral licence area, comprising and limited to -

(a) expenditure related to office, field office and general administration in Solomon Islands, including supervisory, legal, accounting and employee relations services (excluding commissions paid to intermediaries by the approved mining company); and

(b) an annual overhead charge for services rendered outside Solomon Islands and not otherwise deducted under any other head of expenditure under this Act, for managing mining operations and for staff advice and assistance including financial, legal, accounting and employee relations services, provided that -

(i) for the period from the date on which the relevant agreement takes effect until the date on which a mining lease under the agreement is granted to the approved mining company, or such other date as specified in the relevant agreement, such annual charge

shall be the approved mining company's verifiable reasonable expenditure as approved by the Commissioner and allowable as deduction in the computation of taxable income under this Act; and
(ii) for the period commencing from the date on which the mining lease is granted to the approved mining company, or such other date as specified in the relevant agreement, the charge shall be at an amount or rate agreed between the parties to the relevant agreement and specified in the feasibility study approved with the grant of the mining lease;

"gross income" means total income as defined in this Act and shall in relation in this Act and shall in relation to an approved mining company that derives assessable income from mining operations, include any amount received or receivable in the tax year by the approved mining company, including proceeds under a policy of insurance of otherwise, in respect of the loss or destruction of minerals obtained by it from mining operations carried out by it and any interest or amount in the nature of interest or any other amount received or receivable by it in the tax year from or in connection with mining operations carried out by it.

"mineral licence" means a prospecting licence or a mining lease or both;

"mining operations" means prospecting operations, development operations and production operations and includes all other operations incidental thereto carried out by an approved mining company pursuant to a mineral license;

"net cash receipts" in relation to a mining lease in a tax year, means the result denominated in such foreign currency as specified in the relevant agreement which may be a negative amount, that is obtained by aggregating the gross income of the approved mining company from mining operations for that tax year and subtracting therefrom the sum of -

(i) income tax on taxable income from mining operations paid by the approved mining company in that tax year; and

(ii) subject to paragraphs 2, 3 and 4, all exploration, development and production expenditures incurred by the approved mining company in that tax year in relation to mining operations but excluding amounts in respect of interest and other financing charges on loans raised by the approved mining company for mining operations carried out by it;

"production expenditure" means expenditure incurred in production operations by the approved mining company and which, is allowed as a deduction in the determination of taxable income under this Act;

"production operations" means operations carried out under the mining lease other than development operations;

"prospecting operations" means operations carried out under a prospecting licence other than development operations;

"relevant agreement" means an agreement between the government and the approved mining company relating to a mineral licence; and

"tax Year" means .a calendar year or any other period of twelve months as specified in the relevant agreement.

Allowable expenditure.

2. (1) The expenditures described in subparagraphs (2) to (9) shall be classified under the headings exploration expenditure, development expenditure, production expenditure and general and administrative expenditure in accordance with the definitions of these terms sets out in paragraph 1 and, subject to the provisions of this Schedule shall be allowable deductions in the computation of net cash receipts for the purposes of calculation of additional profits tax.

(2) Surface rights expenditure cover all expenditure directly attributable to the acquisition, renewal or relinquishment of surface rights acquired and maintained in force for the mineral area.

"prospecting operations" means operations carried out under a prospecting licence other than development operations;

(3) Labour and related expenditure -

(a) gross salaries and wages, including bonuses of approved mining company's employees directly and necessarily engaged in the mining operations, irrespective of the location of such employees, provided that in the case of those employees, only a portion of whose time is wholly dedicated to the mining operations, only that pro rata portion of applicable salaries and wages will be allowable;

(b) cost relating to the approved mining company of established plans for employees' group life insurance, hospitalisation, company pension, retirement and other benefits of a life nature customarily granted to the approved mining company's employees and the approved mining company's expenditure regarding holiday, vacation, sickness and disability payments applicable to the salaries and wages chargeable under clause (a) shall be allowed at actual cost, provided, however, that such total expenditure shall not exceed twenty-five per cent of the approved mining company's total labour expenditure under clause (a);

(c) expenditure or contributions made pursuant to assessment or obligations imposed under the laws of Solomon Islands which are applicable to the approved mining company's expenditure on salaries and wages chargeable under clause (a);

(d) reasonable travel and personal expenditure of employees of the approved mining company, including those made for travel and relocation of the expatriate employees assigned to Solomon Islands.

(4) The expenditure incurred in respect of transportation of employees, equipment, materials and supplies necessary for the conduct of mining operations.

(5) Charges for services -

(a) the expenditure incurred under contracts for technical and other services entered into by the approved mining company for the mining operations, made with third parties other than affiliated companies of the approved mining company are deductible, provided that the prices paid by the approved mining company are no higher than those generally charged by other international or domestic suppliers for comparable work and services;

(b) in the case of services rendered to the mining operations by an affiliated company of the approved mining company the charges shall be based on the expenditure incurred without including any profits and shall be competitive. The charges shall be no higher than the most favourable prices charged by the affiliated company to third parties for comparable services under similar terms and conditions elsewhere. The approved mining company shall, if requested by the Commissioner, specify the amount of the charges which constitutes an allocated proportion of the general material, management, technical and other expenditure of the affiliated company, and the amount which is the direct cost incurred in respect of providing the services concerned. If required by the Commissioner certified evidence regarding the basis of prices charged shall be obtained by the approved mining company from the auditors of the affiliated company;

(c) in the event that the prices and charges referred to in clauses (a) and (b) are shown to be uncompetitive then the Commissioner may under this Schedule disallow as a deduction such portion of the prices and charges as he deems fit.

(6) For services rendered to the mining operations through the use of property exclusively owned by the approved mining company, the accounts shall be charged at rates not exceeding those prevailing in the region which reflect the cost of ownership and operation of such property or at rates to be agreed.

(7) Material and equipment -

(a) Material and equipment held as inventory shall only be charged to the accounts of the mining operations when such material is removed from the inventory and used in the mining operations;

(b) in the case of defective material or equipment, any adjustment received by the approved mining company from the suppliers or manufacturers or their agents shall be credited to the accounts of the mining operations;

(c) Value of material charged to the account of the mining operations -

(i) except as otherwise provided in subclause (ii) below, material purchased by the approved mining company for use in the mining operations shall be valued to include invoice price less trade and cash discounts, if any, purchase and procurement fees plus freight and forwarding charges between point of supply and point of shipment, freight to port of destination, insurance. taxes, custom duties, consular fees, other items chargeable against imported material and, where applicable handling and transportation costs from point of importation to warehouse or operating site, and its costs shall not exceed those currently prevailing in normal arms length transactions on the open market;

(ii) material purchased from or sold to affiliated companies of the approved mining company or transferred to or from activities of the approved mining company other than operations -

(aa) in the case of new material (hereinafter referred to as "condition A) ,"shall be valued at the current price which shall not exceed the price prevailing in normal arms length transactions on the open market;
(bb) in the case of used material which is in sound and serviceable condition and is suitable for re-use without reconditioning (hereinafter referred to as "condition B),"shall be priced at not more than seventy-five per cent of the current price of the above mentioned new materials;
(cc) in the case of used material which cannot be classified as condition B, but which, after reconditioning, is further serviceable for the original function as good second hand condition B material or is serviceable for original function, but substantially not suitable for reconditioning (hereinafter referred to as "condition C)," shall be priced at not more than fifty per cent of the current price of the new material referred to above as condition A;

(iii) the cost of reconditioning shall be charged to the reconditioned material, provided that the condition C material value plus the cost of reconditioning does not exceed the value of condition B material. Material which cannot be classified as condition B or condition C shall be priced at a value commensurate with its use.

(iv) when the use of material is temporary and its service to the mining operations does not justify the reduction in price in relation to materials referred to above as conditions B and C such material shall be priced on a basis that will result in a net charge to the accounts of the mining operations consistent with the value of the service rendered.

(8) insurance premiums and expenditure incurred for insurance in respect of mining operations pursuant to a relevant agreement shall be

deductible, provided that where such insurance is wholly or partly placed with an affiliated company of the approved mining company such premiums and expenditure shall be deductible only to the extent generally charged by competitive insurance companies other than an affiliated company of the taxpayer. Expenditure and losses incurred as a consequence of events which are, and in so far as, not made good by insurance shall be deductible, provided that any expenditure or loss caused by wilful misconduct or negligence of the approved mining company shall not be deductible.

(9) Expenditure incurred by, the approved mining company in training of its employees who are nationals of Solomon Islands engaged in the mining operations and such other training as is required under a relevant agreement shall be deductible.

(10) For the purposes of calculation of additional profits tax, general and administrative expenditure shall be deductible. Such expenditure shall be allocated to and form part of exploration expenditure, development expenditure and production. expenditure incurred in each tax year in proportion to the amount of exploration expenditure, development expenditure and production expenditure incurred in such tax year, or in such other equitable and consistent manner as determined by the Commissioner.

Expenditure not deductible.

3. The following expenditure shall not be deductible in the computation of net cash receipts for the purposes of calculating additional profits tax -

(a) interest and any other financing charges or fees incurred on loans raised by the approved mining company;

(b) expenditure incurred on the marketing or transportation of minerals produced by the approved mining company beyond the delivery point designated in the relevant agreement;

(c) costs incurred by- the approved mining company in obtaining and maintaining a bank guarantee and performance guarantee required under a relevant agreement (and any other amounts spent on indemnities with regard to non-fulfilment of contractual obligations thereunder);

(d) donations and contributions made by the approved mining company;

(e) expenditure incurred in relation to arbitration in respect of any dispute under a relevant agreement;

(f) fines and penalties imposed on the approved mining company by a court or tribunal;

(g) expenditure incurred by the approved mining company as a result of its wilful misconduct or negligence;

(h) any expenditure which by reference to international mining industry practices is excessive; and

(i) expenditure relating to the negotiation of a relevant agreement.

Other expenditure.

4. Other expenditure not covered or dealt with in paragraphs 2 and which is incurred by other expenditure the approved mining company for the necessary and proper conduct of the mining operations shall, for the purposes of this Schedule be deductible subject to the prior approval in writing of the Commissioner.

Additional profits tax.

5. (1) (a) An additional profits, tax shall be payable by an approved mining company in any tax year when the accumulated present value of net cash receipts, at the end of that tax year, calculated in accordance with the formula set out below, is a positive amount, at the rate of X per cent (X%) of that positive amount -

"A" = B(100% + R) + C, where

"A" = accumulated present value of net cash receipts at the end of the tax year for which the calculation is made;

"B" = accumulated present value of net cash receipts at the end of the preceding tax year;

"C" = net cash receipts for the tax year in respect of which the assessment of additional profits tax is made;

"R" = the accumulation rate specified in the relevant agreement with the approved mining company;

"X" = the rate of additional profits tax specified in the relevant agreement with the approved mining company,

provided that, where in any tax year the accumulated present value of the net cash receipts is a positive amount, such accumulated present value of the net cash receipts shall, for the purposes of determining the accumulated present value of the net cash receipts in respect of the immediately succeeding tax year, be deemed to be zero;.

(b) where, in relation to an approved mining company the relevant agreement so provides, the present value of net cash receipts shall be adjusted by applying the price index agreed in the relevant agreement in the manner set out therein.

(2) Where an approved mining company carries on mining operations on two or more areas that are the subject of two or more mining leases, this Schedule applies, in relation to the operations of the approved mining company on and in connection with each of the mining leases as if it were the only mining lease on which the approved mining company carries on mining operations.

(3) For the purposes of the application of this Schedule by virtue of subparagraph (2) in relation to an approved mining company in relation to a mining lease -

(a) any thing relating exclusively to any other mining lease on which the approved mining company carries on mining operations shall be disregarded; and

(b) amounts of expenditure (including expenditure on plant for use in operations on two or more of the mining leases on which the taxpayer carries on mining operations) or other amounts to which clause (a) does not apply shall be apportioned in such manner as the Commissioner may determine.

(4) The additional profits tax shall be payable within 90 days of the end of the tax year concerned. Interest on the amount of the additional profits tax payable in any tax year shall accrue as of the due date at the rate applicable under section 71 of the Act in relation to late payment of income tax (hereinafter called "Accrued Interest") and shall be payable

within 30 days of the notification issued by the Commissioner pursuant to subparagraph (5).

(5) The Commissioner shall notify the approved mining company of his assessment of additional profits tax and accrued interest for each tax year. If the amount of additional profits tax paid to the government is less or more than the amount of, the commissioner's assessment, the shortfall together with accrued interest thereon shall be promptly paid by the approved mining company or the excess, if any, subject to the Government's right to set off against such excess any sums due from the approved mining company in accordance with the relevant agreement shall be refunded to the approved mining company, as may be the case.

(6) The provisions of section 70(5), relating to advance payments of income tax shall apply, *mutatis mutandis*, to an approved mining company in relation to the payment of additional profits tax.

Miscellaneous income and credits.

6. The net proceeds received in connection with mining operations by the approved mining company shall be included as gross income of the approved mining company in the tax year received. Such net proceeds shall include, but not limited to, the following -

(a) the net proceeds of any insurance or claim in connection with the mining operations or any assets relating thereto where the costs of such insurance have been included as allowable expenditure under this Schedule;

(b) revenue received by the approved mining company from third parties or affiliated companies for the use of property or assets relating to the mining operations where the costs of such property or assets have been included as allowable expenditure under this Schedule;

(c) any adjustment received by the approver mining company from the suppliers or manufacturers or their agents in connection with defective material for use in the mining, operations where the costs of such material have been included as allowable expenditure under this Schedule;

(d) the cost of materials which have been included as allowable expenditure under this Schedule, where such materials are subsequently exported from Solomon Islands without being used in the mining operations;

(e) the proceeds from the sale or exchange by the approved mining company of plant or facilities from or in connection with the mineral licence area or, plant or facilities where the expenditure incurred on the acquisition thereof has been included as allowable expenditure under this Schedule;

(f) the proceeds from the sale or exchange by the approved mining company of any licence, lease or other right held by the approved mining company relating to the mining operations;

(g) the proceeds from the sale of any mining information which relates to the mineral licence area provided that expenditure incurred in respect of the acquisition of such information has been included as allowable expenditure under this Schedule.

(h) the proceeds derived from the sale or licence of any intellectual property developed in the course of the mining operations.

Duplication of charges and credits

7. Notwithstanding any provision of this Schedule, where any expenditure is allowed or any credit given under any provision of this Schedule there shall be no duplication of that allowance or the credit under any other provision of this Act.

Additional profits tax statements.

8. (1) The approved mining company shall prepare profits tax statements with respect to each tax year an additional profits tax statement containing the following information -

(a) the value of net cash receipts for the tax year. identifying separately each of the categories of gross income and allowable deductions provided for under this Act;

(b) the appropriate value of the price index for the tax year;

(c) the accumulated present value of the net cash receipts for the tax year;

(d) the amount of additional profits tax payable for the tax year.

(2) The information required in subparagraph (1) shall be presented in sufficient detail so as to enable the Commissioner to verify the timing and amount of additional profits tax payment.

(3) The Commissioner may require the submission of additional profits tax statements more frequently than annually or at such intervals as specified in the relevant agreement.

(4) The additional profits tax statement for each tax year shall be submitted to the Commissioner not later than sixty days after the end of such tax year.

(5) The approved mining company shall submit to the Commissioner such records, returns and information relating to the approved mining company's liability to additional profits tax as may be prescribed or required by the Commissioner."

THE MINES AND MINERALS (AMENDMENT) ACT 1996

AN ACT To Amend the Mines and Mineral Act 1990.

ENACTED by the National Parliament of Solomon Islands.

Short title and Commencement

1. This Act may be cited as the Mines and Minerals (Amendment) Act, 1996, and shall come into operation on such date as the Minister may appoint by notice published in the Gazette.

Amendment of section 3 of Act No. 3 of 1990.

2. Section 3 of the Mines and Minerals Act 1990 (hereinafter referred to as the "principal Act") is hereby amended by inserting therein immediately after the definition of "mineral" the following new definition -

""mineral licence" means a prospecting licence or mining lease or both;".

Amendment of section 30.

3. Section 30 of the principal Act is hereby amended by inserting therein immediately after subsection (5) the following new subsections as subsections (6) and (7) respectively -

"(6) Where an agreement has been negotiated pursuant to subsections (3) and (4), the Minister may on behalf of the Government enter into an agreement with the negotiating parties.

(7)The Minister may establish appropriate modalities to coordinate and procedures the issue and grant, subject to the relevant law, by the relevant agencies of requisite licences, permits, orders d notices to the holder of a mining lease to enable him to conduct activities and operations under his mining lease."

Amendment of Section 43.

4. Section 43 of the principal Act is hereby amended the following respects -

(a) by renumbering the existing section as subsection thereof; and

(b) by adding immediately after the subsection renumbered the following as subsection (2) thereof -

"(2) Subject to the provisions of this Act and to any other law relating to buildings, drainage, land, protection of the natural environment and the control of natural water supplies, including river waters, the mining company shall have the exclusive right to mine on or under the area covered by its mining lease for the minerals specified in the mining lease and to remove or dispose of any such mineral as its own property upon extraction of the mineral from the mineral or body mined under the mining lease."

Amendment of section 45.

5. Section 45 of the principal Act is hereby amended in the following respects -

(a) by adding at the end of subsection (3) the words "or, where the relevant mining agreement provides for the valuation of the mineral, in accordance with the relevant mining agreement.";

(b) by deleting subsection (4) and substituting therefor the following new subsection -

"(4) For the purposes of this section a special fund to be known as the Mining Royalty Special Fund is hereby established in accordance with section 100 of the Constitution and all royalties paid in pursuance of this section shall be credited to the Fund so established and the Minister may from the fund , so established authorise payment, not exceeding one hundred per cent to be paid to the owner of the land from or under which the minerals are obtained and to such other beneficiaries as may be determined by the Minister.";

(c) by inserting immediately after subsection (4) the following as subsection (5) -

"(5) The Minister may by regulations prescribe -

(a) the manner and procedure for the making of payments to the Fund and payments out of the Fund to the beneficiaries referred to in subsection (4);

(b) the maintenance of a separate account in respect of each holder of a mining lease or building materials permit;

(c) the division of any account referred to in paragraph (b) to sub-accounts in respect of the owners and beneficiaries referred to in subsection (4);

(d) the manner and procedure for the control and management of the Fund and the accounts referred to in paragraphs (b) and (c); and

(e) such other terms and conditions as may be necessary for the proper administration of the Fund and the accounts".

Insertion of new sections 49A, 49B, 49C, 49D and 49E

6. The principal Act is hereby amended by inserting immediately after section 49, the following new sections as sections 49A, 49B, 49C, 49D and 49E respectively -

"**Grant of special site right.**

49A. (1) Subject to the provisions of this Act and to any terms and conditions not inconsistent therewith that he may think fit, the Director may grant a special site right to the holder of a mineral licence.

(2) An application for a special site right shall be in the prescribed form and shall be accompanied by the prescribed fees, together with a deposit as may be prescribed.

(3) Special site rights may be granted for such purposes, for such period and in such manner as may be prescribed, in respect of the following acts or things -

(a) the construction and use of passageways other than roads;

(b) water rights;

(c) installation of machinery;

(d) disposal of earth and tailings; and

(e) installation of furnaces:

Provided that -

(i) the Director may issue special site rights for such other purposes in respect of water or land as may, in his opinion, be necessary or advisable for the conduct of prospecting or mining operations or for any other purposes connected with mining;

(ii) water rights for the generation of electric power shall not be granted under this section unless such electric power is to be used by the holder of the mineral licence for the purpose of prospect or mining operations conducted under such licence;

(iii) nothing in this Act shall affect the right of any person to divert water under a permit issued under the provisions of the River Waters Act.
Cap 96

(4) Land which is the subject of a special site right shall not exceed dimensions as may be prescribed.

(5) A special site right may be extended by renewal for such periods as the Director may determine.

(6) The Director shall notify the Registrar of Titles of every grant, renewal, surrender, determination or variation of the term or area of a special site right and shall furnish the requisite details for the purpose of noting the grant, renewal, surrender, determination or variation.

Road access licence.

49B. (1) No person shall, in the exercise of any rights conferred on him under this Act, construct any road on or over any land not being the subject of a mineral licence held by him without first obtaining a road access licence empowering him to do so:

Provided that the holder of the mineral licence shall have the right of access for himself, his servants and agents to and from a licence area and for that purpose may pass without hindrance over any unimproved land.

(2) Subject to the provisions of this Act and to any terms and conditions not inconsistent therewith that he may think fit, the Director may with the concurrence of the Commissioner of Lands, grant a road access licence to the holder of a mineral licence.

(3) A road access licence shall authorise the holder, his servants and agents, with or without vehicles, to pass over the land the subject of such licence and to construct the roads thereon.

(4) Every application for a road access licence shall be in the prescribed form and shall be accompanied by the prescribed fees together with a deposit as may be prescribed.

(5) A road access licence may be granted for such period as may be prescribed and may be renewed for such periods as the Director may determine.

(6) The Director may require the applicant for a road access licence to adjust the plans and makings in respect of any proposed road as he considers reasonable bearing in mind the convenience of all parties that may be affected by the road.

(7) All rights under any road access licence conferred upon the holder of a mining licence under this Act shall expire when such licence is terminated or abandoned for any reason whatsoever and thereupon the holder shall, if required by the owner or occupier, restore the surface of the land to its former state so far as is practicable, and the provisions of sections 25(3) and 34 shall apply in relation to determination of compensation for damages:

Provided that the holder of any other mineral licence in the same vicinity who wishes to use such road may apply for a road access licence over the whole or any part of the land, the subject of the expiring licence, and if such licence is granted the obligations of the holder of the expiring road access licence under this subsection shall cease in respect of the land, the subject of the licence so granted.

(8) The holder of a road access licence shall not hinder or prevent any other person from passing over the land the subject of that licence:

Provided that -

(a) where any person uses such road in such manner as to do appreciable damage thereto or to enhance substantially the cost of upkeep thereof, the holder of the licence may require him to contribute to the cost of making good such damage or to the cost of upkeep; and

(b) where any person uses such road in such manner as to interfere materially with the free use and enjoyment thereof by the holder of the mineral licence, the holder of the licence may require him to limit his use of the road so as to remove such interference.

(9) If any dispute arises in connection with damage, upkeep or interference under subsection (8), any person affected by such dispute may lodge a complaint with the Director who shall decide the matter at issue.

(10) If any mineral licence is granted in respect of any part of the land, the subject of a road access licence, the holder of such licence may require, the holder of the road access licence to deviate the road, and the cost of such deviation shall be borne by the holder of such other mineral licence:

Provided that prior approval of the Director is required for such deviation, and if he approves the deviation the Director shall amend the road access licence accordingly.

(11) The Director shall notify the Registrar of Titles of every grant, renewal, surrender, determination and variation of the term or area of a road access licence and shall furnish the requisite details for the purpose of noting that grant, renewal, surrender, determination or variation.

Payment into Court.

49C. (1) Where any compensation or surface rent is payable or ordered to be paid under this Act and the identity of the person or persons entitled to such compensation is not known, or is in doubt or is disputed, the compensation or rent may be paid where it does not exceed one thousand dollars into a Magistrate's Court, and in all other cases into the High Court.

(2) Upon being so paid the compensation or rent shall be presumed to have been paid to the person or persons thereto entitled. and such presumption shall not be questioned in any proceedings whatsoever.

(3) Any person claiming to be entitled to payment of the whole or any part of compensation or rent so paid into court may, within twelve years of the payment into court, make application to the court for the payment to him of the compensation or part thereof.

(4) The Court may of its own motion or upon application by a claimant, order the whole or part of any sum paid into court under this section, to be paid to any person or persons.

(5) Where any compensation or rent paid into court under this section has not been paid out within twelve years, it shall be credited to and form part of the Consolidated Fund.

Director may suspend and cancel.

49D. If, in any case where the holder of a mineral licence is required to pay rent or other compensation under this Act, payment is in arrears or the amount deposited is insufficient, the Director may suspend such mineral licence until the amount payable has been paid and until such holder has deposited with him such further sums as may be demanded as security for further payments, and, if such payment and deposit is not made within such time as the Director may consider reasonable, the mineral licence may be cancelled in accordance with the provisions of section 71.

Restoration of the land.

49E. (1) Where the surface of the land, the subject of a mineral licence has been disturbed by prospecting or mining operations during the term of the licence, the Director may order the holder thereof to restore the surface of the land. Such requirements of restoration shall be embodied in an appendix to such mineral licence before issue or thereafter by due service of such order.

(2) Where any mineral licence is terminated or abandoned for any reason whatsoever, the person whose mineral licence has been terminated or abandoned shall, not later than thirty days from the date of termination of the mineral licence, fill up all shafts, pits, holes and other excavations or when the Director so permits, in an appropriate case, otherwise secure them in a permanent manner to the satisfaction of the Director so as to prevent persons or livestock inadvertently entering therein, and shall within such period furnish a certificate to the Director that he has complied with the provisions of this section as to the fencing or filling up of shafts, pits, holes and other excavations and the removal of posts:

Provided that no such person shall be liable for filling up or securing any excavations made by other persons on the land, the subject of his mineral licence, prior to the grant thereof, if, on application for the mineral licence, he has shown on the plans submitted with his application, the position of these excavations in relation to the boundaries of the land, or if he submits within a period of one month from the date of grant of the mineral licence, a plan showing the position of such excavations.

(3) If any person whose mineral licence has been terminated or abandoned neglects to fill up or secure any excavations or to notify the Director in accordance with subsection (2) within the prescribed time, the Director shall have the right to cause such excavations to be filled up may charge such person such sum as the Director considers reasonable, and such charge shall be a lawful deduction from any amount deposited by such person with the Director under this Act and may be recovered as a civil debt at the suit of the Director:

Provided that such filling up or securing by the Director and the payment of such charge shall not exempt such person from his liability under this Act or any other law for his failure to fill up or secure such excavations.

(4) Where a mineral licence is renewed in respect of a reduced area only, subsections (2) and (3) shall apply to the land not included in such renewal.

(5) This section shall be in addition to and not in derogation of any other provision of this Act."

Insertion of new section 71A.

7. The principal Act is hereby amended immediately after section 71 the following new section 71A:

"**Force majeure.**

71A. (1) Subject to a mining agreement entered into with the holder of a mineral licence where the holder of such licence is prevented from carrying out his operations under the mineral licence due to *force majeure*, the period during which the *force majeure* event subsisted shall be added on to the term of the mineral licence.

(2) In this section -

"mineral licence" includes a prospecting licence deemed to be granted under section 81(2).

"*force majeure*' means any cause beyond the reasonable control of the holder of the mineral licence prescribed in the mining agreement as constituting *force majeure*; and

"mining agreement" means the agreement entered into by the Minister with the holder of a mineral licence pursuant to section 30(6)."

THE INVESTMENT ACT 1990

Passed by the National Parliament this twenty-second day of November 1990

This printed impression has been carefully compared by me wth the Bill passed by Parliament and found by me to be a true and correct copy of the said Bill.

J. M. Tuhaika Clerk to the National Parliament

Assented to in Her Majesty's name and on Her Majesty's behalf this sixth day of December 1990.

G.G-D. Lepping Governor-General

Date of commencement: see section I

AN ACT to Repeal the Foreign Investment Act 19984 and to make other provisions in lieu thereof, for the promotion of local and foreign investment.

ENACTED by the National Parliament of Solomon Islands

THE INVESTMENT ACT 1990

ARRANGEMENT OF SECTIONS

Section:

1. This Act may be cited as the Investment Act 1990, and shall come into operation on such date as the Minister may appoint by notice published in the Gazette

short title and commencement

2. In this Act, unless the context otherwise requires -

Interpretation

"approved enterprise" means an investment approved by the Board under sections 5, 6, 7 or 8;
"Board" means the Investment Board established under section 3;
"foreign investment" means an industrial, commercial, business or service undertaking carried on by a foreign investor;
"foreign investor" means a person who is not a citizen of Solomon Islands and includes -
(a) a body corporate or any other organisation established in Solomon Islands, in which a foreign investor holds the whole or any part of the equity or ownership in the capital;
(b) a branch in Solomon Islands of a body corporate or any other business organisation not established in Solomon Islands;

Caps 61 and 58

"incentives" means the benefits that an approved enterprise may qualify for under the Income Tax Act ,the Customs and Excise Act and other relevant or qualifying Acts; "
"investor" means any person or company including a foreign investor;
"Minister" means the Minister for the time being charged with responsibilty for investment in Solomon Islands;
"prescribed undertaking" means any industrial, commercial, business or service undertaking in operation in Solomon Islands on the date of commencement of this Act;
"relevant or qualifying Act" means any, law under which an investor may qualify for the grant of incentives or exemptions;
"technology or external agreement" means an agreement involving payments in foreign currency for royalty or any professional services provided.

3.(1) The Investment Board established under the Foreign Investment Act 1984, (repealed by this Act) shall continue to function as the Investment Board until a new Board is appointed under the provisions of this Act.

Constitution of the Board and its secretariat.

(2)The Board appointed under the provisions of this Act shall consist of the Minister as chairman and such other members being not less than six nor more than eight appointed by the Minister with the approval of Cabinet.
(3) The quorum for a meeting of the Board shall be one half of the number of members, one of whom shall be the chairman or his designate, who shall in addition to an original vote have a casting vote in case the voting is equal.

(4) The Board shall meet when the chairman requires but in any event not less than once in every three months.
(5) The Investment Division of the Ministry dealing with investment for the time being shall act as the secretariat to the Board.
(6) The Chief Officer of the Investment Division shall be the secretary of the Board who shall maintain the records of the preceedings of the Board and all other such records and data as may be required by the Board or chairman.

Functions of the Board

4.The functions of the Board shall be -

- (a) to approve any foreign investment in Solomon Islands in terms of this Act;
- (b) to approve any technology or external agreements;
- (c) to approve any application for the grant of incentives under any relevant or qualifying Act;
- (d) to co-ordinate with relevant Ministries, Provincial Governments, Honiara Town Council and other Government Agencies in order to facilitate the obtaining of approval for proposed investment;
- (e) to issue certificates of approval to approved investors;
- (f) to monitor compliance with the terms and conditions of any approval granted under this Act and other relevant or qualifying Acts; and
- (g) to review and advise the Government on policies and procedures relating to the promotion and regulation of investments, whether local or foreign and matters connected therewith.

Approval of application for foreign investment

5. (1) On receipt of an investment application from a foreign investor, the Board shall give notice of the application to the appropriate Ministries, the relevant Provincial Governments or the Honiara Town Council, as the case may be, and seek their approval in respect of the investment application
(2) On receipt of confirmation from the appropriate Ministries, the relevant Provincial Governments or the Honiara Town Council, as the case may be, that the investment proposal complies with the requirements of the relevant or qualifying laws, the Board may approve such investment proposal as an approved enterprise and grant the investor a certificate of approval.

Foreign investor to register With Board and possess certificate of approval

6. Subject to the provisions of section 20, from and after the commencement of this Act no foreign investor shall engage in any investment in Solomon islands, unless the foreign investor is registered with the Board and is in possession of a certificate of approval in terms of this Act.

7. (1) Any investor may make application in the prescribed form to the Board for the grant of incentives in respect of any proposed or existing investment or enterprise. — Application for incentives by investor

(2) Where the Board receives an application referred to in subsection (1), the Board shall give notice of the application to the appropriate Ministries and Government Agencies and seek their approval in respect of the investment or enterprise.

(3) On receipt of confirmation from the appropriate Ministries and Government Agencies that the investment or enterprise is approved as it complies with the requirements of the relevant or qualifying Acts, the Board may approve such investment or enterprise as an approved enterprise.

(4) Where the investment or enterprise does not qualify for incentives in terms of any relevant or qualifying Acts, the Board shall inform the applicant accordingly.

(5) On receipt of approval from the Board, the approved enterprise shall be entitled to the agreed incentives provided for under the Income Tax, the Customs and Excise Act and other relevant or qualifying Acts. — Caps 61 and 58

8. Any prescribed undertaking may apply to the Board for the grant of incentives in the manner provided under section 7 and the provisions of section 7 shall mutatis mutandis apply in relation to the application. — Prescribed undertaking may make application

9. (1) No approved enterprise shall be entitled to more than one tax exemption or other incentives within the agreed period, in respect of any particular investment or undertaking, so however, that any such approved enterprise may make application for a further tax exemption period provided - — Further tax exemption period or additional incentives subject to certain restrictions

(a) a substantial additional investment is proposed; and

(b) the approved enterprise has satisfied the conditions stipulated in relation to its original investment.

(2) Where the Board is satisfied that an approved enterprise referred to in subsection (I) has satisfied the conditions stipulated in its original investment and that the additional investment is of a kind that would be of benefit to Solomon Islands, it may recommend to the Commissioner of Inland Revenue and the Controller of Customs and Excise, as the case may require, to grant the approved enterprise further tax exemptions not exceeding a period of five years, and other incentives it may qualify for in terms of the investment.

10. (1) In approving an application under sections 5,7 8, or 9, the Board shall satisfy itself - — Criteria for approval of investment or incentives

(a) that the investment would further the economic development of, or be of benefit to Solomon Islands;

(b) that citizens of Solontion Islands would be employed, except where the employment of foreign nationals is necessarv and that trainina would be provided to citizens of

Solomon Islands at technical, skilled and managerial levels;
(c) that local raw materials and supplies would be used as far as practicable;
(d) that the enterprise or investment has or may have the potential to promote exports or to substitute imports;
(e) of the extent to which the proposed investment would be dispersed in the provinces; and
(f) of the extent and capacity to transfer technology.
(2) Where the application referred to in subsection (1) is in respect of a foreign investment, the Board shall in addition to the conditions specified in that subsection, have particular regard to -
(a) the maximum and minimum total capital investment and the percentage of foreign investment in the equity or ownership in the capital of the approved enterprise or investment; and
(b) the value of such assets where the investment is in the form of tangible assets, other than foreign currency.

Foreign investment within approved period

11. If any approved foreign investment is not made within the approved period or such extended period as the Board may permit on the application of the foreign investor or enteprise, the certificate of approval granted under the provisions of this Act shall be deemed to have been terminated.

Registers

12. The Board shall maintain a register of approved enterprises which shall be in such form and contain such particulars as the Minister may specify.

Approval of Board required to vary investment

13. (1) Except with the approval of the Board, no approved enterprise shall -
(a) acquire any interest in or take over any other enterprise; or
(b) diversify into any other non-related activity, unless otherwise specified in the certificate of approval.
(2) Where the approved enterprise is a foreign investment, such investment or enterprise in addition to complying with the requirements of subsection (1) shall not, except with the prior approval of the Board -
(a) increase its approved percentage of foreign investment;or
(b) alter or change its majority shareholdings.
(3) Where an approved enterprise seeks approval from the Board to effect any change mentioned in subsections (1) or (2), the Board shall not unreasonably withhold such approval.

Guarantees

14. Subject to current Exchange Control Regulations, a foreign investor shall be entitled in respect of an approved enterprise to transfer out of Solomon Islands in foreign currency at the prevailing official rate of exchange and after payment of taxes, if any -
(a) the proceeds of sale of all or any part of the approved

enterprise;
(b) the dividends in case of a body corporate and profits in other cases from the approved enterprise.

15. (1) Where any approved enterprise fails to comply with the provisions of this Act or the provision of the certificate of approval, the Board may -
(a) direct the respective ministries to withdraw, alter or disallow any or all incentives granted; or
(b) withdraw the certificate of approval.
(2) Before taking any action under subsection (1), the approved enterprise shall be informed in writing of the nature of the contravention or non-compliance and be afforded an adequate opportunity to represent its case, and the Board may, if it thinks fit permit an opportunity for the contravention or non-compliance to be corrected.

Board may direct any approval to be withdrawn

16. The Minister may by order prescribe fees for applications, certificates of approval and other charges.

Minister to prescribe fees. etc.

17. (1) The Minister may, in consultation with the Board, make regulations for the purposes of carrying this Act into effect, and in particular, without prejudice to the generality of the foregoing with respect to any of the following matters -
(a) prescribe charges for anything required to be done by the Board;
(b) prescribe forms for application, certificates or any other documents to be issued;
(c) prescribe the procedure to be followed in forwarding an application under this Act; or
(d) prescribe any matter which may be or is required to be prescribed under the provisions of this Act.
(2) Regulations made under subsection (1) of this section may make different provisions for different classes or categories of investments.

Regulations

18. The provisions of this Act shall be supplementary to, but not derogation of any other Act.

Provisions supplementary to provisions in any other Act.

19. No investor shall enter into any technology or other external agreement in relation to any investment without the prior approval of the Board.

Technology and any other external agreements.

20. (1) The Foreign Investment Act 1984, (hereinafter referred to as the "repealed Act") is hereby repealed.
(2) Notwithstanding such repeal from and after the date of coming into operation of this Act -
(a) any certificate of approval granted under the repealed Act shall continue to be valid on such terms and conditions of approval for the period stipulated therein;

(b) a foreign investor shall be entitled to enjoy any investment guarantee approved under the repealed Act for such approved period; and
(c) any foreign investor as defined in this Act, who is operating any enterprise without approval or registration under the repealed Act shall hereinafter be required to obtain approval from the Board and such approval shall not be unreasonably withheld.

INVESTMENT CHAPTER 142

ARRANGEMENT OF SECTIONS

SECTION

CHAPTER 142
INVESTMENT

AN ACT TO MAKE PROVISIONS FOR THE PROMOTION OF LOCAL AND FOREIGN INVESTMENT.

[*18th January 1991*]
14 of 1990

Short title

1. This Act may be cited as the Investment Act.

Interpretation

2. In this Act, unless the context otherwise requires—

"approved enterprise" means an investment approved by the Board under sections 5, 6, 7 or 8;

"Board" means the Investment Board established under section 3;

"foreign investment" means an industrial, commercial, business or service undertaking carried on by a foreign investor;

"foreign investor" means a person who is not a citizen of Solomon Islands and includes—

(a) a body corporate or any other organisation established in Solomon Islands, in which a foreign investor holds the whole or any part of the equity or ownership in the capital;

(b) a branch in Solomon Islands of a body corporate or any other business organisation not established in Solomon Islands;

"incentives" means the benefits that an approved enterprise may qualify for under the Income Tax Act, the Customs and Excise Act and other relevant or qualifying Acts;
Cap. 123
Cap. 121

"investor" means any person or company including a foreign investor;

"Minister" means the Minister for the time being charged with responsibility for investment in Solomon Islands;

"prescribed undertaking" means any industrial, commercial, business or service undertaking in operation in Solomon Islands on the date of commencement of this Act;

"relevant or qualifying Act" means any law under which an investor may qualify for the grant of incentives or exemptions;

"technology or external agreement" means an agreement involving payments in foreign currency for royalty or any professional services provided.

Constitution of the Board and its secretariat

3. (1) The Investment Board established under the Foreign Investment Act 1984, (repealed by this Act) shall continue to function as the Investment Board until a new Board is appointed under the provisions of this Act.

(2) The Board appointed under the provisions of this Act shall consist of the Minister as Chairman and such other members being not less than six nor more than eight appointed by the Minister with the approval of Cabinet.

(3) The quorum for a meeting of the Board shall be one half of the number of members, one of whom shall be the Chairman or his designate, who shall in addition to an original vote have a casting vote in case the voting is equal.

(4) The Board shall meet when the Chairman requires but in any event not less than once in every three months.

(5) The Investment Division of the Ministry dealing with investment for the time being shall act as the secretariat to the Board.

(6) The Chief Officer of the Investment Division shall be the Secretary of the Board who shall maintain the records of the proceedings of the Board and all other such records and data as may be required by the Board or Chairman.

Functions of the Board

4. The functions of the Board shall be –

(a) to approve any foreign investment in Solomon Islands in terms of this Act;

(b) to approve any technology or external agreements;

(c) to approve any application for the grant of incentives under any relevant or qualifying Act;

(d) to co-ordinate with relevant Ministries, Provincial Governments, Honiara Town Council and other Government Agencies in order to facilitate the obtaining of approval for proposed investment;

(e) to issue certificates of approval to approved investors;

(f) to monitor compliance with the terms and conditions of any approval granted under this Act and other relevant or qualifying Acts; and

(g) to review and advise the Government on policies and procedures relating to the promotion and regulation of investments, whether local or foreign and matters connected therewith.

Approval of application for foreign investment

5. (1) On receipt of an investment application from a foreign investor, the Board shall give notice of the application to the appropriate Ministries, the relevant Provincial Governments or the Honiara Town Council, as the case may be, and seek their approval in respect of the investment application.

(2) On receipt of confirmation from the appropriate Ministries, the relevant Provincial Governments or the Honiara Town Council, as the case may be, that the investment proposal complies with the requirements of the relevant or qualifying laws, the Board may approve such investment proposal as an approved enterprise and grant the investor a certificate of approval.

Foreign investor to register with Board and possess certificate of approval

6. Subject to the provisions of section 20, from and after the commencement of this Act no foreign investor shall engage in any investment in Solomon Islands, unless the foreign investor is registered with the Board and is in possession of a certificate of approval in terms of this Act.

Application for incentives by investor

7. (1) Any investor may make application in the prescribed form to the Board for the grant of incentives in respect of any proposed or existing investment or enterprise.

(2) Where the Board receives an application referred to in subsection (1), the Board shall give notice of the application to the appropriate Ministries and Government Agencies and seek their approval in respect of the investment or enterprise.

(3) On receipt of confirmation from the appropriate Ministries and Government Agencies that the investment or enterprise is approved as it complies with the requirements of the relevant or qualifying Acts, the Board may approve such investment or enterprise as an approved enterprise.

(4) Where the investment or enterprise does not qualify for incentives in terms of any relevant or qualifying Acts, the Board shall inform the applicant accordingly.

(5) On receipt of approval from the Board, the approved enterprise shall be entitled to the agreed incentives provided for under the Income Tax Act, the Customs and Excise Act and other relevant or qualifying Acts.

Cap. 123
Cap. 121

Prescribed undertaking may make application

8. Any prescribed undertaking may apply to the Board for the grant of incentives in the manner provided under section 7 and the provisions of section 7 shall mutatis mutandis apply in relation to the application.

Further tax exemption period or additional incentives subject to certain restrictions

9. (1) No approved enterprise shall be entitled to more than one tax exemption or other incentives within the agreed period, in respect of any particular investment or undertaking, so however, that any such approved enterprise may make application for a further tax exemption period provided—

(a) a substantial additional investment is proposed; and

(b) the approved enterprise has satisfied the conditions stipulated in relation to its original investment.

(2) Where the Board is satisfied that an approved enterprise referred to in subsection (1) has satisfied the conditions stipulated in its original investment and that the additional investment is of a kind that would be of benefit to Solomon Islands, it may recommend to the Commissioner of Inland Revenue and the Comptroller of Customs and Excise, as the case may require, to grant the approved enterprise further tax exemptions not exceeding a period of five years, and other incentives it may qualify for in terms of the investment.

Criteria for approval of investment or incentives

10. (1) In approving an application under sections 5, 7, 8, or 9, the Board shall satisfy itself—

(a) that the investment would further the economic development of, or be of benefit to Solomon Islands;

(b) that citizens of Solomon Islands would be employed, except where the employment of foreign nationals is necessary and that training would be provided to citizens of Solomon Islands at technical, skilled and managerial levels;

(c) that local raw materials and supplies would be used as far as practicable;

(d) that the enterprise or investment has or may have the potential to promote exports or to substitute imports;

(e) of the extent to which the proposed investment would be dispersed in the provinces; and

(f) of the extent and capacity to transfer technology.

(2) Where the application referred to in subsection (1) is in respect of a foreign investment, the Board shall in addition to the conditions specified in that subsection, have particular regard to –

(a) the maximum and minimum total capital investment and the percentage of foreign investment in the equity or ownership in the capital of the approved enterprise or investment; and

(b) the value of such assets where the investment is in the form of tangible assets, other than foreign currency.

Foreign investment within approved period

11. If any approved foreign investment is not made within the approved period or such extended period as the Board may permit on the application of the foreign investor or enterprise, the certificate of approval granted under the provisions of this Act shall be deemed to have been terminated.

Registers

12. The Board shall maintain a register of approved enterprises which shall be in such form and contain such particulars as the Minister may specify.

Approval of Board required to vary investment

13. (1) Except with the approval of the Board, no approved enterprise shall -

(a) acquire any interest in or take over any other enterprise; or

(b) diversify into any other non-related activity, unless otherwise specified in the certificate of approval.

(2) Where the approved enterprise is a foreign investment, such investment or enterprise in addition to complying with the requirements of subsection (1) shall not, except with the prior approval of the Board –

(a) increase its approved percentage of foreign investment; or

(b) alter or change its majority shareholdings.

(3) Where an approved enterprise seeks approval from the Board to effect any change mentioned in subsections (1) or (2), the Board shall not unreasonably withhold such approval.

Guarantees

14. Subject to current Exchange Control Regulations, a foreign investor shall be entitled in respect of an approved enterprise to transfer out of Solomon Islands in foreign currency at the prevailing official rate of exchange and after payment of taxes, if any -

(a) the proceeds of sale of all or any part of the approved enterprise;

(b) the dividends in case of a body corporate and profits in other cases from the approved enterprise.

Board may direct any approval to be withdrawn

15. (1) Where any approved enterprise fails to comply with the provisions of this Act or the provisions of the certificate of approval, the Board may -

(a) direct the respective Ministries to withdraw, alter or disallow any or all incentives granted; or

(b) withdraw the certificate of approval.

(2) Before taking any action under subsection (1), the approved enterprise shall be informed in writing of the nature of the contravention or non-compliance and be afforded an adequate opportunity to represent its case, and the Board may, if it thinks fit permit an opportunity for the contravention or non-compliance to be corrected.

Minister to prescribe fees, etc

16. The Minister may by order prescribe fees for applications, certificates of approval and other charges.

Regulations

17. (1) The Minister may, in consultation with the Board, make regulations for the purposes of carrying this Act into effect, and in particular, without prejudice to the generality of the foregoing with respect to any of the following matters -

(a) prescribe charges for anything required to be done by the Board;

(b) prescribe forms for application, certificates or any other documents to be issued;

(c) prescribe the procedure to be followed in forwarding an application under this Act; or

(d) prescribe any matter which may be or is required to be prescribed under the provisions of this Act.

(2) Regulations made under subsection (1) may make different provisions for different classes or categories of investments.

Provisions supplementary to provisions in any other Act

18. The provisions of this Act shall be supplementary to, but not in derogation of any other Act.

Technology and any other external agreements

19. No investor shall enter into any technology or other external agreement in relation to any investment without the prior approval of the Board.

Transitional and savings

20. (1) The Foreign Investment Act, 1984 (hereinafter referred to as the "repealed Act") is hereby repealed.

(2) Notwithstanding such repeal from and after the date of coming into operation of this Act—

(a) any certificate of approval granted under the repealed Act shall continue to be valid on such terms and conditions of approval for the period stipulated therein;

(b) a foreign investor shall be entitled to enjoy any investment guarantee approved under the repealed Act for such approved period; and

(c) any foreign investor as defined in this Act, who is operating any enterprise without approval or registration under the repealed Act shall hereafter be required to obtain approval from the Board and such approval shall not be unreasonably withheld.

THE INVESTMENT (AMENDMENT) ACT 1996

ARRANGEMENT OF SECTIONS

Section.

Short title and commencement.

1. This Act may be cited as the Investment (Amendment) Act, 1996 and shall come into operation on such date as the Minister may appoint by notice published in the Gazette.

Amendment of section 2 of Act No. 14 of 1990.

2. Section 2 of the Investment Act (hereinafter referred to as the "principal Act") is hereby amended as follows -

(a) by deleting the definition of "foreign investment" and substituting therefor the following new definition -

"foreign investment" means any industrial, commercial, business or service undertaking carried on by a foreign investor in Solomon Islands and includes any such undertaking which -

(a) does not have its central management or control in Solomon;

(b) has its voting power controlled by a person who is not a citizen of Solomon Islands;

(c) is incorporated or established by or under any law outside Solomon Islands;

(d) is an enterprise in which a joint venture is established;

(e) has the voting power held, controlled or value of shares beneficially owned by persons who are not citizens of Solomon Islands; or

(f) is carried on in the name of an agent, associate, nominee or a person closely connected with a foreign investor. For the purposes of this sub-paragraph, a person is closely connected with a foreign investor, where the Board in its opinion considers that such persons are substantially identical or that the ultimate controlling interest is owned or deemed to be owned by the foreign investor; and"

(b) by deleting the definition of "technology or external agreement" and substituting therefor the following new definition -

""technology or external agreement" means an agreement which involves payments in local or foreign currency for royalty or professional services and includes licensed rights over specific processes, formulae or manufacturing technology (patent or unpatented), knowledge and expertise necessary for the setting up of plant, building, and provisions of various assistance and supporting services which may be in the form of agreements of joint venture, technical, assistance know how, licence, patent and trade marks, sales commissions, turn-key contracts, contracts to build, operate and transfer or management."

Repeal and replacement of section 5.

3. Section 5 of the principal Act is hereby repealed and the following new section substituted therefor -

"Approval of application for foreign investment.

5. (1) On receipt of an investment application from a foreign investor and on being satisfied that the proposal would be beneficial or would further the economic development of Solomon Islands, the Board shall give notice of such application to the appropriate ministries and the provincial government within whose area the proposed investment scheme is to be operative.

(2) Any government ministry or provincial government affected by a proposed investment scheme shall, within the prescribed time and in the prescribed manner, submit to the Board any objectives or representations, which it may desire to make in respect of the proposal.

(3) Where any notice is given under subsection (1), the appropriate ministry and provincial government shall comply with such notice within the time specified in the notice and forward to the Board their objections or representations with a statement of particulars in regard to the consultations held, if any, with persons interested or whose interests are likely to be affected.

(4) Where the appropriate ministry or the provincial government does not respond within the time specified in the notice, the Board, where it deems that the proposal satisfies the criteria specified in section 10, may enter into direct consultations with the parties whose interests are likely to be affected.

(5) The Board may, when approving an investment proposal take into consideration any objections or representations made to it in pursuance of this section and shall afford the persons or bodies making such objections or representations an opportunity to be heard.

(6) Upon the approval of an investment proposal under this section, the Board shall issue to such investor a certificate of approval on such terms and conditions as it deems fit to impose.

(7) In this section the reference to "provincial government" includes the Honiara Town Council, area assembly or other area declared to be a town for the purposes of the Local Government Act.".
Cap. 14

Amendment of section 6.

4. Section 6 of the principal Act is hereby amended as follows -

(a) by renumbering the existing subsection (1) thereof; and

(b) by adding thereto immediately after the subsection so renumbered the following as subsections (2), (3), (4) and (5) respectively -

"(2) Where the Board is of the opinion that any investment or undertaking carried on by a person who is not a citizen of Solomon Islands is in breach of the provisions of this Act, it may by notice in writing call upon such person to show cause within a specified period, why the investment or undertaking should not be declared a foreign investment.

(3) If, after considering any representations made by such person referred to in subsection (2), the Board is of the opinion that such investment or undertaking-

(a) qualifies for foreign investment status, it shall require such person to comply with the requirements of this Act;

(b) does not qualify for foreign investment status it shall require such person to cease operations and advise the Director of Immigration and the Commissioner of Labour to take measures to withdraw the permits issued to such person.

(4) A person aggrieved by any action taken under subsection (3) may appeal to the High Court which may make such order as it deems fit in the circumstances.

(5) Any foreign investor who is in breach of the provisions of this section shall be liable on conviction to a fine not exceeding fifty thousand dollars or in default of payment to imprisonment for two years."

Insertion of new section 6A.

5. The principal Act is hereby amended by inserting therein immediately after section 6 the following new section as section 6A-

"Grant of work permits, visa, etc.

6A. No foreign investor shall be granted any work permit, visa or other document enabling him or an expatriate employee of such foreign investor to engage in any form of investment or undertaking in Solomon Islands unless such investor has been granted a certificate of approval by the Board."

Insertion of new section 8A.

6. The principal Act is hereby amended by inserting therein immediately after section 8 the following new section as section 8A-

"Application of incentives in respect of mining enterprise.

8A. (1) Notwithstanding the provisions of sections 7 and 9, where a foreign investor has entered into an agreement with the Government of Solomon Islands, in relation to a mining enterprise or any other large scale investment, such foreign investor or mining enterprise shall, subject to the relevant law, only be entitled to the incentives granted pursuant to the agreement and not the incentives provided for in sections 7 or 9.

(2) In this section "mining enterprise" means any operation for exploration, prospecting or extraction of minerals within the meaning of the Mines and Minerals Act.
Act No. 3 of 1990.

Amendment of section 9.

7. Subsection (1) of section 9 of the principal Act is hereby amended in the following respects -

(a) by deleting the word "and" which appears at the end of paragraph (a);

(b) by deleting the full stop that appears at the end of paragraph (b) and substituting therefor a semi-colon and the word "and"; and

(c) by adding immediately after paragraph (b) the following new paragraph as paragraph (c) thereof -

"(c) a part of the profits earned is reinvested in the particular investment or undertaking as specified in the certificate of approval or as otherwise specified by the Board."

Repeal and replacement of section 10.

8. Section 10 of the principal Act is hereby repealed and the following new section substituted therefor -

"Criteria for investment approval.

10. (1) In approving application under sections 5, 7, 8 or 9, the Board shall take into consideration -

(a) the extent to which the investment would further the economic development of, or be of benefit to the economy of Solomon Islands;

(b) the number of citizens of Solomon Islands that would be employed and the training such persons employed are likely to receive;

(c) the number of foreign citizens likely to be employed, (such employment being permitted only where nationals of Solomon Islands do not possess the necessary skills);

(d) the amount of local raw materials and supplies to be used;

(e) the capacity or potential of the enterprise or investment to promote exports or substitute imports;

(f) the extent to which the proposed investment would be dispersed in the provinces;

(g) the extent and capacity to transfer technology;

(h) the extent and capacity to which the investment would benefit or provide for related or ancillary services; and

(i) the total paid-up capital in the investment and the loan financing arrangements.

(2) Where the application referred to in subsection (1) is in respect of a foreign investment, the Board shall in addition to the conditions specified in subsection (1), have particular regard to -

(a) the maximum and minimum total capital investment and the percentage of foreign capital (emanating from external sources) in the equity or ownership in the capital of the approved enterprise of investment;

(b) the value of such assets where the investment is in the form of tangible assets, other than foreign currency; and

(c) the extent of direct investment in the form of foreign currency or exchange."

Insertion of new section 10A

9. The principal Act is hereby amended by inserting therein immediately after section 10 the following new section as section 10A -

"Deposit in foreign currency or exchange.

10A. (1) Where approval is granted to a foreign investor making an application under section 5, the Board may where it considers appropriate direct that the granting of the certificate of approval is subject to the deposit by the foreign investor of a specified sum in foreign currency or exchange with any commercial bank of Solomon Islands, which moneys the foreign investor is required to expend or disburse in Solomon Islands for the purposes for which approval is granted.

(2) The specified sum referred to in subsection (1) shall be determined by the Board in accordance with regulations made by the Minister".

Repel and replacement of section 11.

10. Section 11 of the principal Act is hereby repealed under following new section substituted therefor -

"Revocation of approval in certain cases.

11. (1) Where the Board is satisfied that in respect of any approved foreign investment or additional investment there is failure to commence or operate such foreign investment or undertaking as approved, the Board may by notice in writing require the investor to establish to the satisfaction of the Board in writing within such period a the notice shall specify that such failure is due to circumstances beyond the control of such investor and that there is a reasonable prospect of commencing the original investment within a reasonable time. If the Board does not receive, within the period referred to in this subsection, written information which is satisfactory to it, the Board may, if it thinks it expedient so to do, revoke the approval granted.

(2) Where the Board is satisfied that in respect in any application for foreign investment any representations made in connection with the application were false in any material particular or were made in intent to deceive or were otherwise not made in good faith and that such representations substantially influenced the grant of approval, the Board may revoke the approval so granted."

Amendment of section 13

11. Section 13 of the principal Act is hereby amended in the following respects-

(a) in subsection (2)-

(i) by deleting the word "or" that appears at the end of paragraph (a) thereof;

(ii) by deleting the full stops that appear at the end of paragraph (b) and substituting therefor a semi-colon and inserting the word "or" immediately thereafter; and

(iii) by adding immediately after paragraph (b), the following paragraph as paragraph (c)-

"(c) dispose of the entity or ownership during the tax exemption period;" and

(b) by adding immediately after subsection (3) the following new subsections as subsections (4), (5), (6) and (7) respectively-

"(4) Any transfer of shareholding in a company or other change of ownership which has the effect of substantially changing the identity of the foreign investor is deemed to be a transfer contrary to subsection (2) and shall render the approval invalid.

(5) Where a foreign investor transfers or otherwise disposes of a certificate of approval granted under this Act, all concessions or benefits enjoyed or to which such approved foreign investor was entitled shall cease as of the date of such transfer or disposition and the Minister shall by notice published in the Gazette make a declaration to the effect that the certificate of approval granted in respect of the particular investment is cancelled.

(6) Any foreign investor who is aggrieved by a decision made under this section, may within 30 days of the publication of such notice in the Gazette appeal to the Minister in writing stating full particulars of the nature of the transfer, change of ownership or other disposition.

(7) The onus of proving that the nature of the transfer or disposition does not alter or substantially change the identity of the original foreign investor is on the person appealing."

Insertion of new section 13A.

12. The principal Act is hereby amended by inserting therein immediately after section 13 the following new section as section 13A -

"Restrictions on the acquisition of interests in land.

13A. No foreign investor shall purchase or acquire any perpetual estate or fixed term estate in any land in Solomon Islands unless -

(a) the purchase or the acquisition of such interest is for the purpose of carrying out the approved foreign investment or solely for residential purposes of such foreign investor or his employees; and

(b) the payment for the acquisition of such estate is made through external funds or foreign currency paid into any commercial bank of Solomon Islands."

Amendment of section 17.

13. Subsection (1) of section 17 of the principal Act is hereby amended in the following respects -

(a) by renumbering paragraph (d) as paragraph (e) thereof; and

(b) by inserting immediately before the paragraph so renumbered the following as paragraph (d) thereof -

"(d) prescribe or specify the sector or activities which are open or closed to foreign investment and activities which are open to foreign investment in partnership with an individual or an enterprise owned by citizens of Solomon Islands;".

Insertion of new section 21.

14. The principal Act is hereby amended by inserting after section 20, the following new section as section 21-

"Penalty.

21. Where a person is in breach of any provisions of this Act, for which no penalty has been prescribed, such person shall be liable on conviction to a fine not exceeding fifty thousand dollars or to imprisonment for a term not exceeding two years or to both such fine and imprisonment."

THE MONEY LAUNDERING AND PROCEEDS OF CRIME ACT 2002

PART I
PRELIMINARY

Short title and commencement

1. This Act may he cited as the Money Laundering and Proceeds of Crime Act, 2002 and shall come into operation on such date as the Minister may appoint by Notice published in the Gazette.

Interpretation

2. (1) In this Act, unless the context otherwise requires-

"account" means any facility or arrangement by which a financial institution or cash dealer does any one or more of the following:-

(i) accepts deposits of currency;

(ii) allows withdrawals of currency or transfers into or out of the Account;

(iii) pays cheques or payment orders drawn on a financial institution or cash dealer by, or collects cheques or payment orders on behalf of, a person;

(iv) supplies a facility or arrangement for a safety deposit box;

"appeal" includes proceedings by way of discharging or setting aside a judgment, and an application for a new trial or for stay of execution;

"authorised officer" means a person designated by the Minister as an authorised officer for the purposes of this Act;

"Cash dealer" means-

(i) a person who carries on a business of an insurer, an insurance intermediary, a securities dealer or a futures broker;

(ii) a person who carries on a business of dealing in billion, of issuing, selling or redeeming travellers' cheques, money orders or, similar instruments or of collecting, holding and delivering cash as part of a business of providing payroll services;

(iii) an operator of a casino or lottery; or

(iv) a trustee, cr manager of a unit trust;

"Commission" means the Anti-Money Laundering Commission established under section 11;

"Court" means the High Court of Solomon Islands;

"currency" means the coin and paper money of Solomon Islands or of a foreign country that is designated as legal tender which is customarily used and accepted as a medium of exchange in the country of issue;

"defendant" means a person charged with a serious offence, whether or not he has been convicted of the offence, and includes in the case of proceedings for a restraining order under section 55, a person who is about to be charged with a serious offence;

"document" means any record of information, and includes -

(i) anything on which there is writing;

(ii) anything on which there are marks, figures, symbols, or perforations having meaning for persons qualified to interpret them;

(iii) anything from which sounds, images or writings can be produced, with or without the aid of anything else; or

(iv) a map, plan, drawing, photograph or similar thing;

"financial institution" has the meaning assigned thereto in the Financial Institutions Act;
(Act No. 3 of 1998)

"gift" includes any transfer of property by a person to another person directly or indirectly-

(i) after the commission of a serious crime by the first person;
(ii) for a consideration the value of which is significantly less than the value of the consideration provided by the first person; and
(iii) to the extent of the difference between the market value of the property transferred and the consideration provided by the transferee;

"interest" in relation to property, means-

(i) a legal or equitable estate or interest in the property; or

(ii) a right, power or privilege in connection with the property;

"proceedings" means any procedure conducted by or under the supervision of a judge or judicial officer however described in relation to any alleged or proven offence, or property derived from such offence, includes an inquiry, investigation, or preliminary or final determination of facts;

"proceeds of crime" means any property derived or realised directly or indirectly from a serious offence and includes, on a proportional basis, property into which any property derived or realised directly from the offence was later successively converted, transformed or intermingled, as well as income, capital or other economic gains rived or realised from such property at any time since the offence;

"property" means currency and all other real or personal property of every description, whether situated in Solomon Islands or elsewhere and whether tangible or intangible, and includes an interest in any such property;

"property of or in the possession or control of any person " includes any gift made by that person;

(i) any property held by a defendant; or

(ii) any property held by a person to whom a defendant has directly or indirectly made a gift within the meaning assigned thereto in this Act;

"serious offence" means an offence against a provision of -

(i) any law in Solomon Islands, for which the maximum penalty is imprisonment or other deprivation of liberty for a period of not less than twelve months; or

(ii) a law of a foreign State, in relation to acts or omissions, which had they occurred in Solomon Islands would have constituted an offence for which the maximum penalty is imprisonment or other deprivation of liberty of not less than twelve months;

"unit trust" means any arrangement made for the purpose of having the effect of providing, for a person having funds available for investment, facilities for the participation by the person as a beneficiary under a trust, in any profits or income arising from the acquisition, holding, management or disposal of any property pursuant to the trust.

(2) A reference in this Act to the law of-

(a) Solomon Islands; or

(b) any foreign State,

includes a reference to a written law or unwritten law of, or in force in, any part of Solomon Islands or that foreign State, as the case may be.

Meaning of charge in relation to a serious offence

3. Any reference in this Act to a person being charged or about to be charged with a serious offence is a reference to a procedure, however described, in Solomon Islands or elsewhere, by which criminal proceedings may be commenced.

Meaning of conviction in relation to a serious offence

4. For the purposes of this Act, a person shall be taken to be convicted of a serious offence if the person is convicted, whether summarily or on indictment, for the offence.

Meaning of quashing of convictions

5. For the purposes of this Act, a person's conviction for a serious offence shall be taken to be quashed in any case if the conviction is quashed or set aside.

Meaning of value of property, etc.

6. (1) Subject to subsections (2) and (3), for the purposes of this Act the value of property (other than cash) in relation to any person holding the property is-

(a) its market value, or

(b) where any other person holds an interest in the property-

(i) the market value of the first-mentioned person's beneficial interest in the property; less

(ii) the amount required to discharge any encumbrance (other than a charging order) on that interest.

(2) Subject to section 8(2), references in this Act to the value, at any time referred to in subsection (3) as "the material time", of a gift, or of any payment or reward, are references to

(a) the value of the gift, payment or reward to the recipient when he received it, adjusted to take account of any subsequent changes in the value of money; or

(b) where subsection (3) applies, the value there mentioned,

whichever is the greater.

(3) Subject to section 8(2), if at the material time the recipient holds -

(a) the property which he received (not being cash); or

(b) property which, in whole or part, directly or indirectly represents, in the recipient's hands, the property which he received,

the value referred to in subsection (2)(b) is the value to him at the material time of the property mentioned in subsection (2)(a) or as the case may be, subsection (2)(b) so far as it represents the property which he received, but disregarding in either case any changing order.

Meaning of dealing with property

7. For the purposes of this Act, dealing with property held by any person includes, without prejudice to the generality of the expression -

(a) where the property is a debt owed to that person, making a payment to any person in reduction or full settlement of the amount of the debt;

(b) making or receiving a gift of the property; or

(c) removing the property from Solomon Islands.

Meaning of gift

8. (1) A transfer of property amounts to a gift within the meaning of this Act if -

(a) it was made by the defendant at any time after the commission of the serious offence, or if more than one, the earliest of the offences, to which the proceedings for the time being relate; and

(b) the Court considers it appropriate in all the circumstances to take the gift into account.

(2) For the purposes of this Act -

(a) the circumstances in which the defendant is to be treated as making a gift include those where he transfers property to another person directly or indirectly, for a consideration the value of which is significantly less than the value of the consideration provided by the defendant; and

(b) in those circumstances, the provisions of sections 6(2) and (3) shall apply, as if the defendant had made a gift of such proportionate share in the property as the difference between the values referred to in paragraph (a) bears, to the -value of the consideration provided by the defendant.

Meaning of deriving a benefit

9. A reference to a benefit derived or obtained by or otherwise accruing to a person includes a reference to a benefit derived or obtained by, or otherwise accruing to, another person at the request or direction of the first person.

Meaning of benefiting from the proceeds of a serious offence

10. For the purposes of this Act -

(a) a person is deemed to have benefited from an offence if the person has at any time after the commencement of this Act received any payment or other reward in connection with, or derived any pecuniary advantage from, the commission of a serious offence whether committed by that person or another person;

(b) a person's proceeds of a serious offence are-

(i) any payments or other rewards received by the person in connection with; and

(ii) any pecuniary advantage derived by the person at any time from,

the commission of the offence received or derived after the commencement of this Act; and

(c) the value of a person's proceeds of a serious offence is the aggregate of the values of the payments, rewards or pecuniary advantages received by him in connection with, or derived by him from, the commission of the offence.

PART II
MONEY LAUNDERING

Anti-Money Laundering commission and its functions

11. (1) The Anti-Money Laundering Commission shall consist of-

(a) the Attorney-General or his representative as Chairman;

(b) the Commissioner of police or his representative;

(c) the Secretary, Minister of Finance or his representative;

(d) the Governor of the Central Bank or his representative; and

(e) such other technical experts appointed by the Minister on the recommendation of the Commission as it deems necessary in dealing with a particular transaction or investigation.

(2) The Commission -

(a) shall receive reports of suspicious transactions issued by financial institutions and cash dealers pursuant to section 14(1);

(b) shall send any such report to the appropriate law enforcement authorities, if having considered the report, the Commission also has reasonable grounds to suspect that the transaction is suspicious;

(c) may enter the premises of any financial institution or cash dealer during ordinary business hours to inspect any record kept pursuant to section 14(1), and ask any question relating to such record, make notes and take copies of the whole or any part of the record;

(d) shall send to the appropriate law enforcement authorities, any information derived from an inspection carried out pursuant to paragraph (c), if it gives the Commission reasonable grounds to suspect that a transaction involves proceeds of crime;

(e) may instruct any financial institution or cash dealer to take such steps as may be appropriate to facilitate any investigation anticipated by the Commission;

(f) may compile statistics and disseminate information within Solomon Islands or elsewhere, make recommendations arising out of any information received, issue guidelines to financial institutions and advise the Minister of Finance;

(g) shall create training requirements and provide such training for any financial institution in respect of transactions record-keeping and reporting obligations provided for in sections 13(1) and 14(1);

(h) may consult with any relevant person, institution or organisation for the purpose of exercising its power or duties under paragraphs (c), (f) or (g);

(i) shall not conduct any investigation into money laundering, other than for the purpose of ensuring compliance by a financial institution with the provisions of this Part.

Financial institutions and cash dealers to verify customer's identity

12. (1) A financial institution reasonable measures to satisfy itself as to applicant seeking to enter into a business relationship with it, or to carry out a transaction or series of transactions applicant to produce an official record establishing the true identity of the applicant, such as a birth certificate, passport or other official means of identification, and in the case of a body corporate, a certificate of incorporation together with a copy of the latest annual return submitted to the Registrar of Companies in terms of the Companies Act.
Cap. 175

(2) Where an applicant requests a financial institution or cash dealer to enter into -

(a) a continuing business; or

(b) in the absence of such a relationship, any transaction,

the institution or cash dealer shall take reasonable measures to establish whether the person is acting on behalf of another person.

(3) If it appears to a financial institution or cash dealer that an applicant requesting it to enter into any transaction, whether or not in the course of a continuing business relationship, is acting on behalf of another person, the institution or cash dealer shall take reasonable measures to establish the true identity of any person on whose behalf or for whose ultimate benefit the applicant may be acting in the proposed transaction, whether as trustee, nominee, agent or otherwise.

(4) In determining what constitutes reasonable measures for the purpose of subsection (1) or (3), regard shall be had to all the circumstances of the case, and in particular as -

(a) to whether the applicant is a person based or incorporated in a country, in which there are in force provisions applicable to it to prevent the use of the financial system for the purpose of money laundering; and

(b) to custom and practice as may from time to time be current in the relevant field of business.

(5) Nothing in this section shall require the production of any evidence of identity where -

(a) the applicant is itself a financial institution or a cash dealer to which this Act applies; or

(b) there is a transaction or a series of transactions taking place in the course of a business relationship, in respect of which the applicant has already produced satisfactory evidence of identity.

Financial institutions and cash dealers to establish and maintain customer records

13. (1) A financial institution or cash dealer shall establish and maintain-

(a) records of all transactions exceeding such amount of currency or its equivalent in foreign currency as may be specified from time to time by the Minister of Finance, carried out by it, in accordance with the requirements of subsection (3); and

(b) where evidence of a person's identity is obtained in accordance with section 12, a record that indicates the nature of the evidence obtained, and which comprises either a copy of the evidence or such information as would enable a copy of it to be obtained.

(2) Customer accounts of a financial institution or cash dealer shall be kept in the true name of the account holder.

(3) Records required under subsection (1)(a) shall contain particulars sufficient to identify -

(a) the name, address and occupation (or where appropriate business or principal activity) of each person:-

(i) conducting the transaction; or

(ii) if known, on whose behalf the transaction is being conducted,

as well as the method used by the financial institution or cash dealer to verify the identity of each such person;

(b) the nature and date of the transaction;

(c) the type and amount of currency involved;

(d) the type and identifying number of any account with the financial institutions or cash dealer involved in the transaction;

(e) the name of the drawer of the instrument, the name of the institution on which it was drawn, the name of the payee (if any), the amount and data of the instrument, the number (if any) of the instrument and details of any endorsements appearing on the instrument, if the transaction involves a negotiable instrument other than currency; and

(f) the name and address of the financial institution or cash dealer, and of the officer, employee or agent of the financial institution or cash dealer who prepared the report.

(4) Records required under subsection (1) shall be kept by the financial institution for a period of at least five years from the date the relevant business or transaction was completed.

Financial institutions and cash dealers to report suspicious transactions

14. (1) Whenever a financial institution or cash dealer is a party to a transaction and has reasonable grounds to suspect that information that it has concerning the transaction may be relevant to the investigation or prosecution of a person for a serious offence, it shall as soon as possible but not later than three working days after forming that suspicion and whenever possible before the transaction is carried out-

(a) take reasonable measures to ascertain the purpose of the transaction, the origin and ultimate destination of the funds involved, and the identity and address of any ultimate beneficiary;

(b) prepare a. report of the transaction in accordance with subsection (2); and

(c) communicate the information contained therein to the Commission in writing or in such other form as the Minister of Finance may from time to time approve.

(2) A report required by subsection (1) shall -

(a) contain particulars of the matters specified in subsection (1) (a) and in section 12(1);

(b) contain a statement of the grounds on which the financial institution or cash dealer holds the suspicion; and

(c) be signed or otherwise authenticated by the financial institution or cash dealer.

(3) A financial institution or a cash dealer which has reported a suspicious transaction in accordance with this Part shall, if requested to do so by the Commission, give such further information as it has in relation to the transaction.

Financial institutions and cash dealers to establish and maintain internal reporting procedures

15. A financial institution or a cash dealer shall establish and maintain internal reporting procedures to-

(a) identify persons to whom an employee is to report any information which comes to the employee's attention in the course of employment, and which gives rise to knowledge or suspicion by the employee that another person is engaged in money laundering;

(b) enable any person identified in accordance with paragraph (a) to have reasonable access to information that may be relevant in determining whether sufficient basis exists to report the matter pursuant to section 14(1); and

(c) require the identified person to report the matter pursuant to section 14(1), in the event that he determines that sufficient basis exists.

Further preventive measures by financial institutions and cash dealers

16. A financial institution or cash dealer shall establish and maintain internal reporting procedures to -

(a) take appropriate measures for the purpose of making employees aware of the laws of Solomon Islands relating to money laundering, and related policies established and maintained by it pursuant to this Act; and

(b) provide its employees with appropriate training in the recognition and handling of money laundering transactions.

Money-laundering offences

17. (1) A person commits the offence of money laundering if the person -

(a) acquires, possesses or uses property, knowing; or having reason to believe that it is derived directly or indirectly from acts or omissions -

(i) in Solomon Islands which constitute an offence against any law of Solomon Islands punishable by imprisonment for not less than twelve months;

(ii) outside Solomon Islands which, had they occurred in Solomon Islands, would have constituted an offence against the law of Solomon Islands arid punishable by imprisonment for not less than twelve months;

(b) renders assistance to another person for -

(i) the conversion or transfer of property derived directly or indirectly from those acts or omissions, with the aim of concealing or disguising the illicit origin of that property, or of aiding any person involved in the commission of the offence to evade the legal consequences thereof; or

(ii) concealing or disguising the true nature, origin, location, disposition, movement or ownership of the property derived directly or indirectly from those acts or omissions.

(2) Any person who is guilty of an offence under this section shall on conviction be liable to -

(a) in the case of an individual, to a fine not exceeding one hundred and fifty thousand dollars or to imprisonment for a term not exceeding ten years or to both such fine and imprisonment; or

(b) in the case of a body corporate, to a fine not exceeding two hundred thousand dollars.

Related offences

18. (1) A person shall not open or operate an account with a financial institution or a cash dealer in a false name.

(2) A person who contravenes subsection (1) shall be guilty of an offence and on conviction be liable -

(a) in the case of an individual, to a fine not exceeding one hundred thousand dollars or to imprisonment not exceeding ten years or to both such fine and imprisonment; or

(b) in the case of a body corporate, to a fine not exceeding two hundred thousand dollars.

(3) A financial institution or cash dealer who fails to comply with any requirement of this Part for which no penalty is specified commits an offence; and shall on conviction be liable -

(a) in the case of an individual, to a fine not exceeding two hundred and fifty thousand dollars or to imprisonment not exceeding ten years or to both such fine and imprisonment; or

(b) in the case of a body corporate, to a fine not exceeding five hundred thousand dollars.

(4) In determining whether a person has complied with any requirement of subsection (1) the Court shall have regard to all the circumstances of the case, including such custom and practice as may from time to time be current in the relevant trade, business, profession or employment, and may take account of any relevant guidance adopted and approved by a public authority exercising public interest supervisory functions in relation to the financial institution or cash dealer, or any other body that regulates or is representative of the trade, business, profession or employment carried on by that person.

(5) Any person who discloses to another person any information of a report being prepared under section 14 or other information or matter likely to prejudice any investigation of an offence or possible offence of money laundering shall be guilty of an offence and liable on conviction to a fine not exceeding one thousand dollars or to imprisonment for or a term not exceeding one month.

(6) In proceedings for an offence against subsection (5), it is a defence to prove that the person did not know or have reasonable grounds to suspect that the disclosure was likely to prejudice any investigation of an offence or possible offence of money laundering under section 17.

Seizure and detention of suspicious imports or exports of currency

19. (1) An authorised officer may seize and, in accordance with this section detain, any currency which is being imported into or exported from Solomon Islands, if -

(a) the amount is more than the prescribed sum; and

(b) he has reasonable grounds for suspecting that it is -

(i) property derived from a money laundering offence; or

(ii) intended by any person for use in the commission of a money-laundering offence.

(2) Currency detained under subsection (1) shall not be detained for more than seventy two hours after seizure, unless a magistrate orders its continued detention for a period not exceeding three months from the date of seizure, upon being satisfied that -

(a) there are reasonable grounds for the suspicion referred to in subsection (1)(b); and

(b) its continued detention is justified while -

(i) its origin or derivation is further investigated; or

(ii) consideration is given to the institution in Solomon Islands or elsewhere of criminal proceedings against any person for an offence with which the currency is connected.

(3) A magistrate may subsequently order continued detention of the currency if satisfied of the matters mentioned in subsection (2), so however, that the total period of detention shall not exceed two years, from the date of the order made under that subsection.

(4) Subject to subsection (5), currency detained under this section may be released in whole or in part to the person on whose behalf it was imported or exported -

(a) by order of a magistrate that its continued detention is no longer justified, upon application by or on behalf of that person and after considering any views of the Director of Public Prosecutions to the contrary; or

(b) by an authorised officer, if satisfied that its continued detention is no longer justified.

(5) No currency detained under this section shall be released whereof -

(a) an application is made under Part III for the purpose -

(i) the confiscation of the whole or any part of the currency; or

(ii) its restraint pending determination of its liability to confiscation; or

(b) proceedings are instituted in Solomon Islands or elsewhere against any person for an offence with which the currency is connected,

unless and until the proceedings relating to the relevant application or the proceedings for the offence, as the case may be, have been concluded.

Commission's power to obtain search warrant.

20. (1) The Commission or any police officer may obtain apply to the Magistrate's Court for a warrant to enter any premises belonging to or in the possession or control of a financial institution, cash dealer, or any officer or employee thereof, and to search the premises and remove any document, material or other thing therein for the purposes of the investigation, as ordered by the Court and specified in the warrant.

(2) The Court shall grant the application if it is satisfied that there are reasonable grounds to believe that -

(a) the financial institution or cash dealer has failed to keep a transaction record, or report a suspicious transaction, as required by this Act; or

(b) an officer or employee of a financial institution or cash dealer is committing, has committed or is about to commit an offence of money laundering.

Property tracking and monitoring Orders

21. For the purpose of determining whether any property belongs to or is in the possession or under the control of any person, the Commission or a police officer may, upon application to the Court obtain an order -

(a) that any document relevant to -

(i) identifying, locating or quantifying any such property; or

(ii) identifying or locating any document necessary for the transfer of any such property,

belonging to, or in the possession or control of that person be delivered forthwith to the Commission or the police officer; or

(b) that the financial institution or cash dealer forthwith produce to the Commission or the police officer all information obtained about any transaction conducted by or for that person during such period before or after the order as the Court directs.

Orders to enforce compliance with obligations under this Part

22. (1) The Commission or any police officer may, upon application to the Court, after satisfying the Court that a financial institution or cash dealer has failed to comply with any obligation provided for under sections 12, 13, 14, 15 or 16, obtain an order against all or any officers or employees of the institution or dealer in such terms as the Court deems necessary, in order to enforce compliance with such obligation.

(2) In granting the order pursuant to subsection (1), the Court may order that should the financial institution or cash dealer fail without reasonable excuse to comply with all or

any provisions of the order, such institution, dealer, officer or employee shall pay a financial penalty in the sun and in the manner directed by the Court.

Secrecy obligations over-ridden

23. The provisions of this Act shall have effect notwithstanding any obligations as to secrecy or other restriction on disclosure or information imposed by law or otherwise.

Immunity where suspicious transaction reported

24. No action, suit or other proceedings shall lie against any financial institution or cash dealer, or any officer, employee or other representative of the institution acting in the ordinary course of the person's employment or representation, in relation to any action taken in good faith by that institution or person pursuant to section 14(1).

Immunity where official powers or functions exercised in good faith

25. No suit, prosecution or other legal proceedings shall lie against the Government or any officer or other person in respect of anything done by or on behalf of that person, with due diligence and in good faith in the exercise of any power or the performance of any function under this Act or any regulation made thereunder.

Restitution of restrained property

26. Where an investigation has commenced against a person for a serious offence, property was restrained under this Act in relation to that offence, and any of the following occurs -

(a) the person is not charged in Solomon Islands with the serious offence;

(b) the person is charged with a serious offence in Solomon Islands, but not convicted of that offence; or

(c) a conviction for that serious offence in Solomon Islands is taken to be quashed and no conviction for such an offence substituted,

the Court shall order restitution of the restrained property.

Damages

27. Nothing in this Act affects the right of a person whose property has been restrained to seek the payment of damages, either actual or punitive, in cases where it is alleged that the action involved any abuse of process.

PART III
CONFISCATION
Division 1 - Confiscation and Pecuniary Penalty Orders

Application for confiscation order or pecuniary penalty order

28. (1) Where a person is convicted of a serious offence, the Director of Public Prosecutions may, not later than six months after the conviction, apply to the Court for one or both of the following orders -

(a) a confiscation order against property that is tainted property in respect of the offence;

(b) a pecuniary penalty order against the person in respect of benefits derived by the person from the commission of the offence.

(2) An application under subsection (1) may be made in respect of one or more than one offence.

(3) Where an application under this section is finally determined, no further application for a confiscation order or a pecuniary penalty order may be made in respect of the offence for which the person was convicted without the leave of the Court. The Court shall not give such leave unless it is satisfied that-

(a) the property or benefit to which the new application relates was identified after the previous application was determined;

(b) necessary evidence became available after the previous application was determined; or

(c) it is in the interest of justice that a new application be made.

Notice of application

29. (1) Where the Director of Public Prosecutions applies for a confiscation order against property in respect of the person's conviction of a serious offence -

(a) the Director of Public Prosecutions shall give not less than fourteen days written notice of the application to the person and to any other person who the Director of Public Prosecutions has reason to believe may have an interest in the property;

(b) the person and any other person who claims an interest in the property may appear and adduce evidence at the hearing of the application; and

(c) the Court may, at any time before the final determination of the application, direct the Director of Public Prosecutions to -

(i) give notice of the application to any person who, in the opinion of the Court, appears to have an interest in the property; and

(ii) publish in the Gazette or a newspaper published and circulating in Solomon Islands, a notice of the application.

(2) Where the Director of Public Prosecutions applies for a pecuniary penalty order against a person -

(a) the Director of Public Prosecutions shall give the person not less than fourteen days notice of the application; and

(b) the person may appear and adduce evidence at the hearing of the application.

Amendment of application

30. (1) The Court hearing the application under section 28(1) may, before the final determination of the application, and on the application of the Director of Public Prosecutions, amend the application to include any other property or benefit, as the case may be, upon being satisfied that-

(a) the property or benefit was not reasonably capable of identification when the application was made; or

(b) necessary evidence became available only after the application was originally made.

(2) Where the Director of Public Prosecutions applies to amend an application for a confiscation order and the amendment would have the effect of including additional property in the application for confiscation, he shall give not less than fourteen days written notice of the application to amend to any person who he has a reason to believe may have an interest in the property to be included in the application for a confiscation order.

(3) Any person who claims an interest in the property to be included in the application for a confiscation order may appear and adduce evidence at the hearing of the application to amend.

(4) Where the Director of Public Prosecutions applies to amend an application for a pecuniary penalty order against a person and the effect of the amendment would be to include an additional benefit in the application he shall give the person not less than fourteen days written notice of the application to amend.

Procedure on application

31. (1) Where an application is made to the Court for a confiscation order or a pecuniary penalty order in respect of a person's conviction of a serious offence, the Court may, in determining the application, have regard to the transcript of any proceedings against the person for the offence.

(2) Where an application is made for a confiscation order or a pecuniary penalty order to the Court before which the person was convicted, and the Court has not, when the application is made, passed sentence on the person for the offence, the Court may, if it is satisfied that it is reasonable to do so in all the circumstances, defer passing sentence until it has determined the application for the order.

Procedure for *in rem* confiscation order where person dies or absconds

32. (1) Where -

(a) an information has been laid alleging the commission of the offence by a person; and

(b) a warrant for the arrest of the person has been issued in relation to that information,

the Director of Public Prosecutions may apply to the Court for a confiscation order in respect of any tainted property if the defendant has died or absconded.

(2) For the purposes of subsection (1), the person is deemed to have absconded if reasonable attempts to arrest the person pursuant to the warrant have been unsuccessful during the period of six months commencing on the day the warrant was issued, and the person shall be deemed to have so absconded on the last day of that period.

(3) Where the Director of Public Prosecutions applies under this section for a confiscation order against any tainted property the Court shall, before hearing the application -

(a) require notice of the application to be given to any person who, in the opinion of the Court, appears to have an interest in the property; and

(b) direct notice of the application to be published in the Gazette and in a newspaper published and circulating in Solomon Islands containing such particulars and for so long as the Court may require.

Confiscation order on conviction

33. (1) Where, upon application by the Director of Public Prosecutions, the Court is satisfied that property is tainted property in respect of a serious offence for which a person has been convicted, the Court may order that specified property be confiscated.

(2) In determining whether property is tainted property the Court may infer, in the absence of evidence to the contrary -

(a) that the property was used in or in connection with the commission of the offence if it was in the person's possession at the time of, or immediately after the commission of the offence for which the person was convicted; or

(b) that the property was derived, obtained or realised as a result of the commission of the offence if it was acquired by the person before, during or within a reasonable time after the period of the commission of the offence for which the person was convicted, and the Court is satisfied that the income of that person from sources unrelated to criminal activity of that person cannot reasonably account for the acquisition of that property.

(3) Where the Court orders that property, other than money, be confiscated, the Court shall specify in the order the amount that it considers to be the value of the property at the time when the order is made.

(4) In considering whether a confiscation order should be made under subsection (1) the Court shall have regard to -

(a) the rights and interests, if any, of third parties in the property;

(b) the gravity of the offence concerned;

(c) any hardship that may reasonably be expected to be caused to any person by the operation of the order; and

(d) the use that is ordinarily made of the property, or the use to which the property was intended to be put.

(5) Where the Court makes a confiscation order, the Court may give such directions as are necessary or convenient for giving effect to the order.

Effect of confiscation

34. (1) Subject to subsection (2), where the Court makes a confiscation order against any property, the property vests absolutely in the Government of Solomon Islands by virtue of the order.

(2) Where property ordered to be confiscated is registrable property -

(a) the property vests in the Government of Solomon Islands in equity but does not vest in the Government of Solomon Islands at law until the applicable registration requirements have been complied with;

(b) the Government of Solomon Islands is entitled to be registered as owner of the property; and

(c) the Director of Public Prosecutions has power on behalf of the Government of Solomon Islands to do or authorise the doing of anything necessary or convenient to obtain the registration of the Government of Solomon Islands as owner, including the execution of any instrument to be executed by a person transferring an interest in property of that kind.

(3) Where the Court makes a confiscation order against property -

(a) the property shall not, except with the leave of the Court and in accordance with any directions of the Court, be disposed of, or otherwise dealt with, by or on behalf of the Government of Solomon Islands before the relevant appeal date; and

(b) if, after the relevant appeal date, the order has not been discharged, the property may be disposed of and the proceeds applied or otherwise dealt with in accordance with the direction of the Permanent Secretary, Ministry of Finance.

(4) In this section -

"registrable property" means property the title to which is passed by registration in accordance with the provisions of the Land and Titles Act; *Cap. 133*

"relevant appeal date" used in relation to a confiscation order made in consequence of a person's conviction of a serious offence means -

(a) the date on which the period allowed by rules of court for the lodging of an appeal against a person's conviction or for the lodging of an appeal against the making of a confiscation order expires without an appeal having been lodged, whichever is the later, or

(b) where an appeal against a person's conviction or against the making of a confiscation order is lodged, the date on which the appeal lapses in accordance with the rules of court or is finally determined, whichever is the later.

Voidable transfers

35. The Court may -

(a) before making a confiscation order; and

(b) in the case of property in respect of which a restraining order was made, where the order was served in accordance with section 59,

set aside any conveyance or transfer of the property that occurred after the seizure of the property or the service of the restraining order, unless the conveyance or transfer was made for valuable consideration to a person acting in good faith and without notice.

Protection of third parties

36. (1) Where an application is made for a confiscation order against property, a person who claims an interest in the property may apply to the Court, before the confiscation order is made for an order under subsection (2).

(2) If a person applies to the Court for an order under this section in respect of property and the Court is satisfied on a balance of probabilities -

(a) that the person was not in any way involved in the commission of the offence; and

(b) where the person acquired the interest during or after the commission of the offence, that he acquired the interest -

(i) for sufficient consideration; and

(ii) without knowing, and in circumstances such as not to arouse a reasonable suspicion, that the property was, at the time he acquired it, property that was tainted property,

the Court shall make an order declaring the nature, extent and value at the time the order is made of the person's interest.

(3) Subject to subsection (4), where a confiscation order has already been made directing the confiscation of property, a person who claims an interest in the property may, before the end of the period of twelve months commencing on the day on which the confiscation order is made, apply under this subsection to the Court for an order under subsection (2).

(4) A person who -

(a) had knowledge of the application for the confiscation order before the order was made; or

(b) appeared at the hearing of that application,

shall not be permitted to make an application under subsection (3), except with leave of the Court.

(5) A person who makes an application under subsection (1) or (3) shall give not less than fourteen days written notice of the making of the application to the Director of Public Prosecutions, who shall be a party to any proceedings in the application.

(6) Any person exercising the powers conferred on the Court by section 67 shall, on application by any person who has obtained an order under subsection (2), and where the period allowed by the rules of court with respect to the making of an appeal has expired and any appeal from that order has been determined -

(a) direct that the property or part thereof to which the interest of the applicant relates, be returned to the applicant; or

(b) direct that an amount equal to the value of the interest of the applicant, as declared in the order, be paid to the applicant.

Discharge of confiscation order on quashing of conviction

37. (1) Where the Court makes a confiscation order against property in reliance on a person's conviction of a serious offence and the conviction is subsequently quashed the quashing of the conviction discharges the order.

(2) Where a confiscation order against property is discharged as provided for in subsection (1) or by the Court of Appeal hearing an appeal against the making of the order, any person who claims to have an interest in the property immediately before the making of the confiscation order may apply to the Commissioner of Lands in writing for the transfer of the interest to the person.

(3) On receipt of an application under subsection (2) the Commissioner of Lands shall-

(a) if the interest is vested in the Government of Solomon Islands, give directions that the property or part thereof to which the interest of the applicant relates be transferred to the person; or

(b) in any other case, direct that there be payable to the person an amount equal to the value of the interest as at the time the order is made.

(4) In the exercise of his powers under this section, and section 36(6), the Commissioner

of Lands shall have the power to do or authorise the doing of anything necessary or convenient to effect the transfer or return of the property, including the execution of any instrument and the making of any application for the registration of an interest in the property on any appropriate register.

Payment instead of a confiscation order

38. Where the Court is satisfied that a confiscation order should be made in respect of the property of a person convicted of a serious offence, but that the property or any part thereof or interest therein cannot be made subject to such an order and, in particular -

(a) cannot, on the exercise of due diligence be located;

(b) has been transferred to a third party in circumstances which do not give rise to a. reasonable inference, that the title or interest was transferred for the purpose of avoiding the confiscation of the property;

(c) is located outside Solomon Islands;

(d) has been substantially diminished in value or rendered worthless; or

(e) has been co-mingled with other property that cannot be divided without difficulty,

the Court may, instead or ordering the property or part thereof or interest therein to be confiscated, order the person to pay to the Government of Solomon Islands an amount equal to the value of the property, part or interest.

Application of procedure for enforcing fines

39. Where the Court orders a person to pay an amount under section 38, that amount shall be treated as if it were a fine imposed upon him in respect of a conviction for a serious offence, and the Court shall -

(a) notwithstanding anything contained in any other Act, impose in default of the payment of that amount, a teen of imprisonment of two years; or

(b) direct that the term of imprisonment imposed pursuant to paragraph (a) be served consecutively to any other form of imprisonment imposed on that person, or that the person is then serving.

Confiscation where a person dies or absconds

40. (1) Subject to section 32(3), where an application is made to the Court under section 32(1) for a confiscation order against any tainted property in consequence of a person having died or absconded in connection with a serious offence and the Court is satisfied that -

(a) any property is tainted property in respect of the offence;

(b) proceedings in respect of a serious offence committed in relation to that property were commenced; and

(c) the accused charged with the offence referred to in paragraph (b) has died or absconded,

the Court may order that the property or such property as is specified by the Court in the order be confiscated.

(2) The provisions of sections 33, 34, 35 and 36 shall apply with such modifications as are necessary to give effect to this section.

Division 2 - Pecuniary Penalty Orders

Pecuniary penalty order on conviction

41. (1) Subject to this section, where the Director of on conviction public Prosecutions applies to the Court for a pecuniary penalty order against a person in respect of that person's conviction for a serious offence the Court shall, if it is satisfied that the person has benefited from that offence, order him to pay to the Government of Solomon Islands an amount equal to the value of his benefit from the offence or such lesser amount as the Court certifies in accordance with section 44(2) to be the amount that might be realised at the time the pecuniary penalty order is made.

(2) The Court shall assess the value of the benefits derived by a person from the commission of an offence in accordance with sections 42, 43, 44 and 45.

(3) The Court shall not make a pecuniary penalty order under this section -

(a) until the period allowed by the rules of court for the lodging of an appeal against conviction has expired without such appeal having been lodged; or

(b) where an appeal against conviction has been lodged, until the appeal lapses in accordance with the rules of court or is finally determined, whichever is the later date.

Rules determining benefit and assessing value

42. (1) Where a person obtains property as the result of, or in connection with the commission of a serious offence, his benefit is the value of the property so obtained.

(2) Where a person derived an advantage as a result of or in connection with the commission of a serious offence, his advantage shall be deemed to be a sum of money equal to the value of the advantage so derived.

(3) The Court in determining whether a person has benefited from the commission of a serious offence or from that offence taken together with other serious offences shall, unless the contrary is proved, deem -

(a) all property appearing to the Court to be -

(i) held by the person on the day on which the application is made; and

(ii) all property appearing to the Court to be held by the person at any time -

(A) within the period between the day the serious offence, or the earliest serious offence, was committed and the day on which the application is made; or

(B) within the period of six years immediately before the day on which the application is made, whichever is the longer,

to be property that carne into the possession or under the control of the person by reason of the commission of that serious offence or those serious offences for which the person was convicted;

(b) any expenditure by the person since the beginning of that period to be expenditure met out of payments received by him as a result of, or in connection with, the commission of that serious offence or those serious offences; and

(c) any property received or deemed to have been received by the person at any time as a result of, or in connection with the commission by him of that serious offence or those serious offences as property received by him free of any interest therein.

(4) Where a pecuniary penalty order has been previously made against a person, in assessing the value of any benefit derived by him from the commission of the serious offence, the Court shall leave out of account any benefits that are shown to the Court to have been taken into account in determining the amount to be recovered under that order.

(5) If evidence is given at the hearing of the application that the value of the person's property at any time after the commission of the serious offence exceeded the value of the person's property before the commission of the offence then the Court shall, subject to subsection (6) treat the value of the benefit as being not less than the amount of that excess.

(6) If, after evidence of the kind referred to in subsection (5) is given, the person satisfies

the Court that the whole or part of the excess was due to causes unrelated to the commission of the serious offence, subsection (5) does not apply to the excess or, as the case may be, that part.

Statements relating to benefits from commission of serious offences

43. (1) Where -

(a) a person has been convicted of a serious offence and the Director of Public Prosecutions tenders to the Court a statement as to any matters relevant to -

(i) determining whether the person has benefited from the offence or any other serious offence of which he is convicted in the same proceedings or which is taken into account in determining his sentence; or

(ii) an assessment of the value of the person's benefit from the offence or any other serious offence of which he is convicted in the same proceedings or which is taken into account; and

(b) the person accepts to any extent an allegation in the statement,

the Court may, for the purposes of so determining or making that assessment, treat the acceptance, as conclusive of the matters to which it relates.

(5) An allegation may be accepted of a matter indicated for the purposes of this section, either -

(a) orally before the Court; or

(b) in writing, in accordance with rules of court.

(6) An acceptance by a person under this section that he received any benefits from the commission of a serious offence is admissible in any proceedings for any offence.

Amount recovered under pecuniary penalty order

44. (1) Subject to subsection (2), the amount to be recovered in the person's case under a pecuniary penalty order shall be the amount which the Court assesses to be the value of the person's benefit from the serious offence, or if more than one, all the offences in respect of which the order may be made.

(2) Where the Court is satisfied as to any matter relevant for determining the amount which might be realised at the time the pecuniary penalty order is made (whether by acceptance under section 43 or otherwise), the Court may issue a certificate giving the

Court's opinion as to the matters concerned, and shall do so if satisfied that the amount that might be realised at the time the pecuniary penalty order is made is less than the amount that the Court assesses to be the value of the person's benefit from the offence, or if more than one, all the offences in respect of which the pecuniary penalty order may be made.

Variation of pecuniary penalty order

45. Where -

(a) the Court makes a pecuniary penalty order against a person in relation to a serious offence;

(b) in calculating the amount of the pecuniary penalty order, the Court took into account a confiscation order of the property or a proposed confiscation order in respect of property; and

(c) an appeal against confiscation or a confiscation order is allowed, or the proceedings from the proposed confiscation order terminate without the proposed confiscation order being made;

the Director of Public Prosecutions may apply to the Court for a variation of the pecuniary penalty order to increase the amount of the order by the value of the property not so confiscated and the Court may, if it considers it appropriate to do so, vary the order accordingly.

Lifting the corporate veil

46. (1) In assessing the value of benefits derived by a person from the commission of a serious offence, the Court may treat as property of the person any property that, in the opinion of the Court, is subject to the effective control of the .person, whether or not he has-

(a) any legal or equitable interest in the property; or

(b) any right, power or privilege in connection with the property.

(2) Without prejudice to the generality of subsection (1), the Court may have regard to -

(a) shareholdings in, debentures over or directorships in any company that has an interest, whether direct or indirect, in the property, and for this purpose the Court may order the investigation and inspection of the books of a named company;

(b) any trust that has any relationship to the property;

(c) any relationship whatsoever between the, persons having an interest in the, property or in companies of the kind referred to in paragraph (a) or trust of the -kind referred to in paragraph (b), and any other persons.

(3) Where the Director of Public Prosecutions makes an application for an order under subsection (3) that property is available to satisfy a pecuniary penalty order against a person.

(a) the Director of Public Prosecutions shall give written notice of the application to the person and to any person who the Director of Public Prosecutions has reason to believe may have an interest in the property; and

(b) a person and any person who claims an interest in the property may appear and adduce evidence at the hearing.

Enforcement of pecuniary penalty orders

47. Where the Court orders a person to pay an amount under a pecuniary penalty order, the provisions of section 39 shall apply with such modifications as the Court may determine for the purpose of empowering the Court to impose a term of imprisonment on a person in default of compliance by him with a pecuniary penalty order.

Discharge of pecuniary orders

48. A pecuniary penalty order is discharged -

(a) if the conviction of the serious offence or offences in reliance on which the order was made is or is taken to be quashed and no conviction for the offence or offences is substituted;

(b) if the order is quashed on appeal; or

(c) on the satisfaction of the order by payment of the amount due under the order.

Division 3 - Control of Property

Powers to search for and seizure of tainted property

49. (1) A police officer may -

(a) search a person for tainted property;

(b) enter upon land or upon or into premises and search the land or premises for tainted property; and

(c) in either case, seize any property found in the course of the search that the police officer believes, on reasonable grounds to be tainted property,

provided that the search or seizure is made -

(i) with the consent of the person or the occupier of the land or premises as the case may be; or

(ii) under warrant issued under section 50.

(2) Where a police officer searches a person under this Division, he may also search -

(a) the clothing that is being worn by the person; and

(b) any property in, or apparently in, the person's immediate control.

Search warrants in relation to tainted property

50. (1) Where a police officer has reasonable grounds for suspecting that there is, or may be within the next seventy-two hours, tainted property of a particular kind -

(a) on a person;

(b) in the clothing that is being worn by a person;

(c) otherwise in a person's immediate control; or

(d) upon land or upon or in any premises,

the police officer may lay before a magistrate an information on oath setting out those grounds and apply for the issue of a warrant to search the person, the land or the premises as the case may be, for tainted property of that kind.

(2) Where an application is made under subsection (1) for a warrant to search a person, land or premises, the magistrate may, subject to subsection (4) issue a warrant authorising a police officer (whether or not named in the warrant) with such assistance and by suet] force as is necessary and reasonable -

(a) to search the person for tainted property of that kind;

(b) to enter upon the land or in or upon any premises and to search the land or premises for tainted property of that kind; and

(c) to seize property found in the course of the search that the police officer believes on reasonable grounds to be tainted property of that kind.

(3) A warrant may be issued under subsection (2) in relation to tainted property, whether or not an information has been laid in respect of the relevant offence.

(4) A magistrate shall not issue a warrant under subsection (2) unless, where an information has not been laid in respect of the relevant offence at the time when the application for the warrant is made, the magistrate is satisfied that -

(a) an information will be laid in respect of the relevant offence within forty-eight hours; and

(b) the property is tainted property.

(5) A warrant issued under this section shall state -

(a) the purpose for which it is issued, including a reference to the nature of the relevant offence;

(b) a description of the kind of property authorised to be seized;

(c) a time at which the warrant ceases to be in force; and

(d) whether entry is authorised to be made at any time of the day or night or during specified hours.

(6) If during the course of searching under a warrant issued under this section, a police officer finds -

(a) property that the police officer believes on reasonable grounds to be tainted property either of a type not specified in the warrant or tainted property in relation to another serious offence; or

(b) any thing the police officer believes on reasonable grounds may afford evidence as to the commission of a serious offence,

the police officer may seize that property or thing and the warrant shall be deemed to authorise such seizure.

Searches in emergencies

51. (1) Where, a police officer suspects on reasonable grounds that -

(a) particular property is tainted property;

(b) it is necessary to exercise the power of search and seizure in order to prevent the concealment, loss or destruction of the property; and

(c) the circumstances are so urgent that they require immediate exercise of the power without the authority of a warrant or the order of a court,

the police officer may -

(i) search a person;

(ii) enter upon land, or upon or into premises and search for the property; and

(iii) if property is found, seize the property.

(2) If during the course of a search conducted under this section, a police officer finds -

(a) property that the police officer believes on reasonable grounds to be tainted property; or

(b) anything the police officer believes on reasonable grounds may afford evidence as to the commission of a criminal offence,

the police officer may seize that property or thing.

Record of property seized

52. A police officer who seizes property under section 50 or section 51 shall detain the property seized, taking reasonable care to ensure that the property is preserved.

Return of seized property

53. (1) Where property has been seized under section 50 or section 51 (otherwise than because it may afford evidence of the commission of an offence), a person who claims an interest in the property may apply to the Court for an order that the property be returned to the person.

(2) Where a person makes an application under subsection (1) and the Court is satisfied that -

(a) the person is entitled to possession of the property;

(b) the property is not tainted property; and

(c) the person in respect of whose conviction, charging or proposed charging the seizure of the property was made has no interest in the property,

the Court shall order the return of the property to the person.

Search for and seizure of tainted property in relation to foreign offences

54. Where a foreign State requests assistance to locate seize property suspected to be tainted property in respect of an offence within its jurisdiction, the provisions of sections, 50 and 51 *mutatis mutandis* provided that the Attorney-General has, under section 4 of the Mutual Assistance in Criminal Matters Act, 2002, authorised the giving of assistance to the foreign State.

Division 4 - Restraining Orders

Application for restraining orders

55. (1.) The Director of Public Prosecutions may apply to the Court for a restraining order against any realisable property held by the defendant or specified realisable property held by a person other than the defendant.

(2) An application for a restraining order may be made *ex parte* and shall be in writing and be accompanied by an affidavit stating:-

(a) where the defendant has been convicted of a serious offence, the serious offence for which he was convicted, the date of the conviction, the Court before which the conviction was obtained and whether an appeal has been lodged against the conviction;

(b) where the defendant has not been convicted of a serious offence, the serious offence for which he is charged or about to be charged and the grounds for believing that the defendant committed the offence;

(c) a description of the property in respect of which the restraining order is sought;

(d) the name and address of the person who is believed to be in possession of the property;

(e) the grounds for the belief that the property is tainted property in relation to the offence;

(f) the grounds for the belief that the defendant derived a benefit directly or indirectly from the commission of the offence;

(g) where the application seeks a restraining order against property of a person other than the defendant, the grounds for the belief that the property is tainted property in relation to the offence and is subject to the effective control of the defendant; and

(h) the grounds for the belief that a confiscation order or a pecuniary penalty order may be or is likely to be made under this Part in respect of the property.

Restraining orders

56. (1) Subject to this section, where the Director of Public Prosecutions applies to the Court for a retraining order against property and the Court is satisfied that:-

(a) the defendant has been convicted of a serious offence, or has been charged or is about to be charged with a serious offence;

(b) where the defendant has not been convicted of a serious offence, there are reasonable grounds for believing that the defendant committed the offence;

(c) there is reasonable cause to believe that the property is tainted property in relation to an offence, or that the defendant derived a benefit directly or indirectly from the commission of the offence;

(d) where the application seeks a restraining order against property of a person other than the defendant, there are reasonable grounds for believing that the property is tainted property in relation to an offence and that the property is subject to the effective control of the defendant; or

(e) there are reasonable grounds for believing that a confiscation order or a pecuniary penalty order is likely to be made under this Part in respect of the property,

the Court may make an order prohibiting the defendant or any person from disposing of, or otherwise dealing with, the property or such part thereof or interest therein as is specified in the order, except in such manner as may be specified in the order.

(2) Where an order has been made under subsection (1) the Court may at the request of the Director of Public Prosecutions, if satisfied that the circumstances so require -

(a) direct the Registrar of the court or such other person as the Court may appoint, to take custody of the property or such part thereof as is specified in the order and to manage or otherwise deal with all or any part of the property in accordance with the directions of the Court; and

(b) require any person having possession of the property to give possession thereof to the Registrar of the Court or to the person appointed under paragraph (a) to take custody and control of the property.

(3) An order under subsection (1) may be made subject to such conditions as the Court thinks fit and, without limiting the generality of this subsection, may make provision for meeting out of the property or a specified part of the property, any or all of the following -

(a) the person's reasonable living expenses (including the reasonable living expenses of the person's dependants, if any) and reasonable business expenses;

(b) the person's reasonable expenses in defending the criminal charge and any proceedings under this Division; and

(c) any specified debt incurred by the person in good faith.

(4) In determining whether there are reasonable grounds for believing that property is subject to the effective control of the defendant, the Court may have regard to the matters referred to in section 46.

(5) Where the Registrar of the court or other person appointed under subsection (2) is given a direction in relation to any property, he may apply to the Court for directions on any question respecting the management or preservation of the property under his control.

(6) An application under section 55 shall be served on all persons interested in the application or such of them as the Court thinks expedient and all such persons shall have the right to appear at the hearing and be heard.

(7) When the application is made under section 55(1) on the basis that a person is about to be charged, any order made by the Court shall lapse if the person is not charged within reasonable time.

Undertaking by the Government of Solomon Islands

57. (1) Before making an order under section 56(1), the Court may require the Director of Public Prosecutions on behalf the Government of Solomon Islands to give such undertakings as the Court considers appropriate with respect to the payment of damages or costs, or both, in relation to the making and execution of the order.

(2) For the purposes of this section, the Director of Public Prosecutions may give such undertakings with respect to the payment of damages or costs or both as are required by the Court.

Notice of application for restraining order

58. Before making a restraining order the Court may require notice to be given to, and may hear, any person who, in the opinion of the Court, appears to have an interest in the property, unless the Court is of the opinion that giving such notice before making the order would result in the disappearance, dissipation or reduction in value of the property.

Service of restraining order

59. A copy of a restraining order shall be served on a person affected by the order in such manner as the Court directs or as may be prescribed by rules of court.

Registration of restraining order

60. (1) A. copy of a restraining, order which affects lands in Solomon Islands shall be registered with the Commissioner of Lands.

(2) A restraining order is of no effect with respect to registered land unless it is registered as a charge, under the Land and Titles Act.

Cap 133

(3) Where particulars of a restraining order are registered under the Land and Titles Act, a person who subsequently deals with the property shall, for the purposes of section 61 be deemed to have notice of the order at the time of the dealing.

Contravention of restraining order

61. (1) A person who knowingly contravenes a restraining order by disposing of or otherwise dealing with property that is subject to the restraining order commits an offence and shall upon conviction be liable -

(a) in the case of an individual, to a fine not exceeding five thousand dollars or to imprisonment for a term not exceeding two years or to both such fine and imprisonment; or

(b) in the case of a body corporate, to a fine not exceeding twenty-five thousand dollars.

(2) Where a restraining order is made against property and the. property is disposed of, or otherwise dealt with, in contravention of the restraining order, and the disposition or dealing was not for, sufficient consideration or not in favour of a person who acted in good faith and without notice, the Director of Public Prosecutions may apply to the Court that made the restraining order for an order that the disposition or dealing be set aside.

(3) Where the Director of Public Prosecutions makes an application under subsection (2) in relation to a disposition or dealing, the Court may -

(a) set aside the disposing or dealing as from the day on which the disposition or dealing took place; or

(b) set aside the disposition or dealing as from the day of the order under this subsection and declare the respective rights of any persons who acquired interest in the property on, or after the day on which the disposition or dealing took place, and before the day of the order under this subsection.

Duration of restraining Order

62. A restraining order remains in force until -

(a) it is discharged, revoked or varied;

(b) the period of six months from the date on which it is made or such later time as the Court may determine;

(c) a confiscation order or a pecuniary penalty order, as the case may be, is made in respect of property which is the subject of the order.

Review of restraining order

63. (1) A person who has an interest in property in respect of which a restraining order was made, may at any time, apply to the Court for an order under subsection (4).

(2) An application under subsection (1) shall not be heard by the Court unless the applicant has given to the Director of Public Prosecutions at least three working days notice in writing of the application.

(3) The Court may require notice of the application to be given to, and may hear, any person who in the opinion of the Court appears to have an interest in the property.

(4) On an application under subsection (1), the Court may revoke or vary the order or make the order subject to such conditions as the Court thinks fit. For the purposes of this subsection the Court may -

(a) require the applicant to enter into recognisances; or

(b) vary the order to permit the payment of reasonable living expenses to the applicant, including his dependants, if any, and reasonable legal or business expenses of the applicant.

(5) An order under subsection (4) may only be made if the Court is satisfied that -

(a) the applicant is the lawful owner to the property or is entitled to lawful possession thereof, and appears to be innocent of any complicity, in the commission of a serious offence or of any collusion in relation to such offence; and

(b) the property will no longer be required for the purposes of any investigation or as evidence in any proceedings.

Extension of restraining order

64. (1) The Director of Public Prosecutions may apply to the Court that made it restraining order for an extension of the period of the operation of the order.

(2) Where the Director of Public Prosecutions makes an application under subsection (1), the Court may extend the operation of a restraining order for a specified period, if it is satisfied that a confiscation order may be made in respect of the property or part thereof or that a pecuniary penalty order may be made against the person.

Division 5 - Realisation of Property

Realisation of property

65. (1) Where:-

(a) a pecuniary penalty order is made;

(b) the order is not subject to appeal; and

(c) the order is not discharged,

the Court may on application by the Attorney-General, exercise the powers conferred upon the Court by this section.

(2) The Court may appoint a receiver in respect of realisable property.

(3) The Court may empower a receiver appointed under subsection (2) to take possession of any realisable property subject to such conditions or exceptions as may be specified by the Court.

(4) The Court may order any person having possession of realisable property to give possession of it to any such receiver.

(5) The Court may empower any such receiver to realise any realisable property in such manner as the Court may direct.

(6) The Court may order any person holding an interest in realisable property to make such payment to the receiver in respect of any beneficial interest held by the defendant

or has the case may be, the recipient of a gift within the meaning of this Act as the Court may direct, and the Court may, on the payment being made, by order transfer, grant or extinguish any interest in the property.

(7) The Court shall not, in respect of any property, exercise the powers conferred by subsection (3, (4), (5) or (6), unless a reasonable opportunity has been given for persons holding any interest in the property to make representation to the Court.

Application of proceeds of realisation and other sums

66. (1) Subject to subsection (2), the following; property in the hands of a receiver appointed under section 56 or 65 that is to say:-

(a) the proceeds of they realisation of any property under section 65; and

(b) any other sums, being property held by the defendant,

shall, after such payments, if any, as the Court may direct have been made out of those sums, be payable to the Registrar of the Court and be applied on the defendant's behalf towards the satisfaction of the pecuniary penalty order in the manner provided by subsection (3).

(2) If, after the amount payable under the confiscation order has been fully paid, any such sums remain in the hands of such a receiver, the receiver shall distribute the sums remaining -

(a) among such of those persons who held property which has been realised under this Part; and

(b) in such proportions,

as the Court may direct, after giving a reasonable opportunity for those persons to make representations to the Court.

(3) Property received by the Registrar of the Court on account of an amount payable under a confiscation order shall be applied as follows:-

(a) if received by him from a receiver under subsection (1), it shall first be applied in payment of the receiver's remuneration and expenses; and

(b) the balance shall be paid or, as the case may be, transferred, to the Government of Solomon Islands for the use of prevention of drug abuse or drug or alcoholic related diseases.

Exercise of powers by Court and receivers

67. (1) The following provisions of this section apply to the powers conferred on the Court by sections 56, 63, 64 and 65 or on a Receiver appointed under section 56(2) or section 65(2)

(2) Subject to the following provisions of this section, the powers shall be exercised with a view to making available for satisfying the pecuniary penalty order or, as the case may be, any pecuniary, penalty order that may be made in the defendant's case, the value for the time being of realisable property held by any person by the realisation of such property.

(3) In the case of realisable property held by a person to whom the defendant has directly or indirectly made a gift within the meaning of this Act, the powers shall be exercised with a view to realising no more than the value for the time being of the gift.

(4) The powers shall be exercised with the view to allowing any person other than the defendant or the recipient of any such gift to retain or recover the value of any property held by him.

(5) An order may be, made or other action taken in respect of the debt owed by Solomon Islands.

(6) In exercising these powers, no account shall be taken of any obligations of the defendant or of the recipient of any such gift which conflict with the obligation to satisfy the confiscation order.

Application of this Part in bankruptcy or winding up

68. (1) Where a person who holds realisable property is adjudged bankrupt:

(a) property for the time being subject to a restraining order made before the order adjudging him bankrupt; and

(b) any proceeds of property realised by virtue of section 65(5) or (6) for the time being in the hands of a person appointed under section 56(2) or 65(2),

is excluded from the property of the bankrupt for the purposes of the Bankruptcy Act.

Cap 3

(2) Where a person has been adjudged bankrupt the powers conferred on the Court by sections 56 and 65 or on a person appointed under section 56(2) or 65(2) shall not be exercised into property of the time being comprised in the property of the bankrupt for the purposes of the Bankruptcy Act.

(3) Where in the case of a debtor, a receiver stands appointed under section 75 of the Bankruptcy the debtor is subject to a restraint order under that Act, the powers conferred on the receiver not apply to property for the time being subject or, a receiver stands ct and any property of or for the purposes of y virtue of that Act do to such restraint order.

(4) Where a person is adjudged bankrupt and has directly or indirectly made a gift within the meaning of this Act -

(a) no order shall be made in pursuance of the provision of the Bankruptcy Act in respect of the making of the gift at any time when the person has been charged with a serious offence and the proceedings have not been concluded by the acquittal of the defendant or proceedings, or when property of the person to whom the gift was made is subject to a restraint order or a charging order made under or for the purposes of that Act.; and

(b) any order made in pursuance of the provisions of the Bankruptcy Act after the conclusion of the proceedings shall take into account any realisation under this Part of property held by the person to whom the gift was made.

Winding up of company holding realisable property

69. (1) Where realisable property is held by a company and an order for the winding up of made or a resolution has been passed by the company for its voluntary or any provisional winding up, the functions of the liquidator shall not be exercisable in relation to:

(a) property for the time being subject to a restraining order made before the relevant time; or

(b) any proceeds of property realised by virtue of section 65(5) or (6) for the time being in the hands of a person appointed under section 56(2) or 65(2),

but there shall be payable out of such property any expenses (including the remuneration of the liquidator or provisional liquidator) properly incurred in the winding up in respect of the property.

(2) Where, in the case of a company, such an order has been made or such a resolution has been passed, the powers conferred on the Court by section 56 or 65 shall not be exercised in relation to any realisable property held by the company in relation to which the functions of the liquidator are exercisable -

(a) so as to inhibit him from exercising those functions for the purpose of distributing any property held by the company to the company's creditors; or

(b) so as to prevent the payment out of any property of expenses (including the remuneration of the liquidator or any provisional liquidator) properly incurred in the winding up in respect of the property.

(3) Subsection (2) does not affect the enforcement of charging order: -

(a) made before the relevant time; or

(b) on property which was subject to a restraining order at the relevant time.

(4) Nothing in the Companies Act shall be taken a restricting, or enabling the restriction of, the exercise of the power conferred on the Court by section 56 or 65.

Cap 175

(5) In this section -

(a) "company" means any company within the meaning of the Companies Act;

(b) "liquidator" includes any person appointed t the office of liquidator (whether provisionally or otherwise) under the Companies Act; and

(c) "relevant time" means

(i) where no order for the winding up of the company has been made, the time of the passing of the resolution for voluntary winding up;

(ii) where such an order has, been made and before the presentation of the petition for the winding up of the com any by the Court, such a resolution had been passed by the company, the time of the passing of the resolution; and

(iii) in any other case where such an order has been made, the time of making of the order.

Division 6 - Production Orders and other Information Gathering Powers

Production orders

70. (1) Where a person has convicted of a serious offence and a police officer has reasonable grounds for suspecting that any person has possession or control of -

(a) a document relevant t or quantifying property of the person locating a document necessary for the such person; or

(b) a document relevant to identifying, locating or quantifying tainted property in relation to the offence, or to identifying or locating a document necessary for the transfer of tainted property in relation to the offence,

the police officer may apply *ex parte* and in writing to a judge in chambers for an order against the person suspected of having possession or control of a document of the kind referred. The application shall be supported by an affidavit.

(2) The judge may, if he considers there are reasonable grounds for so doing, make an order that the person produce to a police officer, at a time and place specified in the order, any documents of the kind referred to in subsection (1), provided that an order under this subsection may not require the production of bankers books.

(3) A police officer to whom documents are produced may -

(a) inspect the documents;

(b) make copies of the documents; or

(c) retain the documents for so long as is reasonably necessary for the purposes of this Act.

(4) Where a police officer restrains documents produced to him, he shall make a copy of the documents available to the person who produced them.

(5) A person is not entitled to refuse to produce documents ordered to be produced under this section on the ground that -

(a) the document might tend to incriminate the person or make the person liable to a penalty; or

(b) the production of the document would be in breach of an obligation (whether imposed by law or otherwise) of the person not to disclose the existence or contents of the document.

Evidential value of information

71. (1) Where a person produces a document pursuant to an order under this section, the production of the document, or any information, document or thing obtained as a direct or indirect consequence of the production of the document, is not admissible against the person in any criminal proceedings except proceedings under section 72.

(2) For the purposes of subsection (1), proceedings on an application for a restraining order, a confiscation order or a pecuniary penalty order are not criminal proceedings.

Failure to comply with a production order

72. Where a person is required by a production order to produce a document to a police officer, the person is guilty of an offence against this section if he -

(a) contravenes the order without reasonable cause; or

(b) in purported compliance with the order, produces or makes available a document known to the person to be false or misleading in a material particular and does not so indicate to the police officer and provide to the police officer any correct information of which the person is in possession, and shall on conviction be liable-

(i) in the case of an individual, to a fine not exceeding one thousand dollars or to imprisonment for a term not exceeding one year or to both such fine and imprisonment; or

(ii) in the case of a body corporate, to a fine not exceeding two thousand dollars.

Production orders in relation to foreign offences

73. Where a foreign State requests assistance to locate or seize property suspected to be tainted in respect of an offence within its jurisdiction, the provisions of section 69 apply *mutatis mutandis* provided that the Attorney-General has, under section 4(2) of the Mutual Assistance in Criminal Matters Act, 2002, authorised the giving of assistance to the foreign State.

Power to search for and seize documents relevant to locating property

74. A police officer may:-

(a) enter upon land or into premises;

(b) search the land or premises for any document of the type described in section 70(1); and

(c) seize any document found in the course of that search that the police officer believes, on reasonable grounds, to be a relevant document in relation to a serious offence,

provided that the entry, search and seizure is made within the content of the occupier of the land or the premises, or under warrant issued under section 75.

Search warrant for location of documents relevant to locating property

75. (1) Where -

(a) a person has been charged or convicted of a serious offence; or

(b) the police officer has reasonable grounds for suspecting that there is, or may be within the next seventy-two hours, upon any land or upon or in any premises, a document of the type described in section 70(1) in relation to the offence,

the police officer may make application supported by information on oath to a magistrate for a search warrant in respect of that land or those premises.

(2) Where an application is made under subsection (1) for a warrant to search land or premises, the magistrate may, subject to subsection (4) issue a warrant authorising a police officer (whether or not named in the warrant), with such assistance and by such force as is necessary and reasonable -

(a) to enter upon the land or in or upon any premises and to search the land or premises for property of that kind; and

(b) to seize property found in the course of the search that the police officer believes on reasonable grounds to be property of that kind.

(3) A magistrate shall not issue a warrant under subsection (2) unless he is satisfied that -

(a) a production order has been given in respect of the document and has not been complied with;

(b) a production order in respect of the document would be unlikely to be effective;

(c) the investigation for the purposes of which the search warrant is being sought might be seriously prejudiced if the police officer does not gain immediate access to the document without any notice to any person; or

(d) the document involved cannot be identified or described with sufficient particularity to enable a production order to be obtained.

(4) A warrant issued under this section shall state -

(a) the purpose for which it is issued, including a reference to the nature of the relevant offence;

(b) a description of the kind of documents authorised to be seized;

(c) a time at which the warrant ceases to be in force; and

(d) whether entry is authorised to be made at any time of the day or night or during specified hours.

(5) If during the course of searching under a warrant issued under this section, a police officer finds -

(a) a document of the type described in section 70(1) that the police believes on reasonable grounds to relate to the relevant offence, or to another serious offence; or

(b) any thing the police officer believes on reasonable grounds may afford evidence as to the commission of a serious offence,

the police officer may seize that property or thing and the warrant shall be deemed to authorise such seizure.

Search warrants in relation to foreign offences

76. Where a foreign State requests assistance to locate or seize property suspected to be tainted property in respect of an offence within its jurisdiction, the provisions of section 75 apply *mutatis mutandis*, provided that the Attorney-General has, under section 4(2) of the Mutual Assistance in Criminal Matters Act 2002, authorised the giving of assistance to the foreign State.

Monitoring orders

77. (1) The Director of Public Prosecutions or a police officer may apply, *ex parte* and in writing to a judge for an order (in this section called a "(monitoring order)" directing a financial institution to give information to a police officer. An application under this subsection shall be supported by an affidavit.

(2) A monitoring order shall -

(a) direct a financial institution to disclose information obtained by the institution about transactions conducted through an account held by a particular person with the institutions;

(b) not have retrospective effect; and

(c) only apply for a period of a maximum of three months from the date of making.

(3) A judge shall not issue a monitoring order unless he is satisfied that there are reasonable grounds for suspecting that the person in respect of whose account the order is sought -

(a) has committed or was involved in the commission, or is about to commit or be involved in the commission of a serious offence; or

(b) has benefited directly or indirectly, or is about to benefit directly or indirectly from the commission of a serious offence.

(4) A monitoring order shall specify -

(a) the name or names in which the account is believed to be held; and

(b) the class of information that the institution is required to give.

(5) Where a financial institution, which has been given notice of a monitoring order, knowingly-

(a) contravenes the order; or

(b) provides false or misleading information in purported compliance with the order,

the institution commits an offence against this subsection and shall on conviction be liable:-

(i) in the case of an individual, to a fine not exceeding one thousand dollars or to imprisonment for a term not exceeding one year or to both such fine and imprisonment; or

(ii) in the case of a body corporate, to a fine not exceeding five thousand dollar.

Monitoring orders not to be disclosed

78. (1) A financial institution that is, or has been subject to a monitoring order shall not disclose the existence or operation of the order to any person except to -

(a) an officer or agent of the institution for the purpose of ensuring compliance with the order;

(b) a legal practitioner for the purpose of obtaining legal advice or representation in respect of the order; or

(c) a police officer authorised in writing to receive the information.

(2) A person who contravenes subsection (1) shall be guilty of an offence and on conviction be liable -

(a) in the case of an individual, to a fine not exceeding one thousand dollars or to imprisonment for a term not exceeding one year or to both such fine and imprisonment; or

(b) in the case of a body corporate, to a fine not exceeding five thousand dollars.

(3) A person described in subsection (1)(a), (b) or (c) shall not disclose the existence or operation of a monitoring order except to another such person, and may do so only for the purposes of the performance of the person's duties or functions.

(4) A person who contravenes subsection (3) shall be guilty of an offence and shall on conviction be liable to a fine not exceeding one thousand dollars or to imprisonment for a term not exceeding one year or to both such fine and imprisonment.

(5) Nothing in this section prevents the disclosure of information concerning a monitoring order for the purpose of or in connection with legal proceedings or in the course of proceedings before a court, provided that nothing in this section shall be construed as requiring a legal practitioner to disclose to any court the existence or operation of a monitoring order.

Regulation

79. The Minister may make regulations, not inconsistent with this Act, for or with respect to any matter that by this Act is required or permitted to be prescribed or that is necessary or convenient.

THE FISHERIES ACT 1998

PART I PRELIMINARY

Short title and commencement.

1. (1) This Act may be cited as the Fisheries Act, 1998, and shall subject to subsection (2), come into operation on such date as the Minister may appoint by notice published in the Gazette.

(2) Section 6 shall come into operation on such other date as the Minister may appoint by notice published in the Gazette.

Interpretation.

2. In this Act, unless the context otherwise, requires -

"access agreement" means an agreement entered into under section 15;

"administrator" means a Pacific Island State, a competent regional fisheries agency, or an official of such Pacific Island State or competent regional fisheries agency designated to administer a regional access agreement entered into under section 15;

"aquatic organism" means an aquatic plant or animal whether living or dead, and includes an amphibious animal;

"authorised officer" means a fisheries officer, a police officer, and includes any other public officer or provincial government officer or a person declared under section 36 to be an authorised officer for the purposes of this Act;

"automatic locations communicator" means a Forum Fisheries Agency approved device placed on a fishing vessel that transmits either in conjunction with another device or devices or independently information relating to the position, fishing and such other activities of the vessel as may be required under this Act;

"canoe" means any craft which is less than twenty feet in length and moved by one or more paddles;

"commercial fishing" means fishing for the purpose of selling all or some of the fish caught;

"commercial sport fishing operation" means the operation for hire or other profit of a vessel for sport fishing;

"Council," means the Fisheries Advisory Council established under section 5;

"customary fishing rights holder" in respect of any area with in Solomon Islands waters means such person or persons as may be authorised under customary law to give an behalf of the owners of customary fishing rights permission to fish;

"Director" means the Director of Fisheries appointed pursuant to section 36;

"driftnet" means a gillnet or other net or a combination of nets which is more than 2.5 kilometres in length the purpose of which is to enmesh, entrap or entangle fish by drifting on the surface of or in the water;

"driftnet fishing activities" means-

(a) catching, taking or harvesting fish with the use of a driftnet;

(b) attempting to catch, take or harvest fish with the use of a driftnet;

(c) engaging in, any other activity which can reasonably be expected to result in the catching, taking or, harvesting of fish with the use of a driftnet, including searching for and locating fish to be taken by that method;

(d) any operations at sea in support of, or in preparation for any activity described in this definition, including operations of placing, searching for or recovering fish with aggregating devices or associated electronic equipment such as radio beacons;

(e) aircraft use, relating, to the activities described in this definition, except for flights in emergencies involving the health or safety of crew members of safety of a vessel;

(f) transporting, transhipping and processing any driftnet catch, and co-operation in the provision of food, fuel and other supplies for vessels equipped for or engaged in driftnet fishing;

"fish" includes any aquatic animal, whether piscine or not and the eggs thereof and includes shell fish;

"fishing" means -

(a) searching for, catching, taking or harvesting fish;

(b) attempting to search for, catch, take or harvest fish;

(c) engaging in any other activity which can reasonably be expected to result in the locating, catching, taking or harvesting fish;

(d) placing, searching for or recovering fish aggregating devices or associated electronic equipment such as radio beacons;

(e) any operations at sea directly in support of, or in preparation for any activity described in this definition; or

(f) aircraft use, relating to the activities described in this definition except for flights in emergencies involving the health or safety of crew members or the safety of the vessel;

"fishery" means one or more stocks of fish or other aquatic organisms or fishing operations based on such stocks which can be treated as a unit for purposes of conservation and management;

"fish aggregating device" means a man-made floating device intended for the purpose of aggregating fish, and includes a natural floating object on which a device has been placed to facilitate its location;

"fishing gear" means any equipment, implement or other thing that may be used in the act of fishing, and includes diving gear, fishing net, rope, pole, line, float, hook, boom, power block or winch, boat, dinghy, helicopter or aeroplane that may be used;

"fishing licence" means any licence issued under section 14 or 16;

"fisheries management area" in respect of reef or inshore fisheries means an area that can be treated as a unit for purposes of conservation and management, and may encompass areas, including reef area subject to customary fishing rights, extending beyond the waters of a single province;

"fisheries officer" means a fisheries officer not below the rank of assistant fisheries officer appointed under the provisions of this Act or by provincial Ordinance;

"fish processing establishment" means any land, jetty, premises, vessel or other place on or in which fish or other aquatic organisms are processed but does not include any place in which fish or other aquatic organisms are processed exclusively for sale by retail to the public or for consumption on the premises, or any fishing vessel on which fish or other aquatic organisms which have been caught from such fishing vessels are only gutted, salted, iced, chilled or frozen for the purpose of preserving such fish or other aquatic organisms;

"fish product" means a product of fish processing;

"fishing vessel" means any boat, ship or other craft which is used for, equipped to be used for, or of a type used for commercial fishing;

"foreign fishing vessel" means a fishing vessel other than a local fishing vessel;

"Fund" means the Fisheries Management and Development Fund established under section 6;

"licensing officer" means a fisheries officer to whom the power to issue licences under this Act has been delegated by the Minister or the Director under section 60, and includes the Principal Licensing Officer;

"local company" means a company incorporated under the laws of Solomon Islands and having its principal place of business in Solomon Islands;

"local fishing vessel" means a fishing vessel -

(a) wholly owned by the Government of Solomon Islands or by a public corporation or statutory body by or under the laws of Solomon Islands;

(b) wholly owned by one or more natural persons who are citizens of Solomon Islands; or

(c) wholly owned by a local company, but does not include any fishing vessel registered in a country outside Solomon Islands;

"locally based foreign fishing vessel" means a foreign fishing vessel which is based in Solomon Islands and lands all its catch in Solomon Islands and operate under a joint venture arrangement in Solomon Islands which is approved by the Government of Solomon Islands or under arrangements whereby the operator of the vessel is participating in shore based development;

"Minister" means the Minister for the time being assigned responsibility for the administration of fisheries;

"operate" in relation to a fish processing establishment, means to own or be in charge of the fish processing establishment, and, where the fish processing establishment is a vessel, means to be the master, owner or charterer thereof;

"operator" means any person who is in charge of, responsible for the operations of, directs or controls a fishing vessel, including the owner, charterer and master;

"Pacific Island State" means a party to the South Pacific Forum Fisheries Agency Convention 1979;

"Pacific Island State Officer" means any officer authorised under a Treaty to which Solomon Islands is a party to enforce Solomon Islands fisheries laws;

"processing" in relation to fish or other aquatic organism, includes preserving or preparing fish or other aquatic organisms by any method,

"provincial waters" means waters within the area of each province as defined in section 3 of the Provincial Government Act 1997;

Act No. 7 of 1997

"regional access agreement" means an agreement between a number of Pacific Island States, including Solomon Islands, and a state other than a Pacific Island State providing for fishing by vessels of that State within Solomon Islands waters or agreement between a number of Pacific Island States including Solomon Islands providing for fishing by vessels of those States in Solomon Islands waters;

"regional fishing licence" means a regional fishing licence issued in respect of a foreign fishing vessel by an administrator under a regional access agreement;

"related activities" in relation to fishing means -

(a) transhipping fish or other aquatic organisms to or from any vessel;

(b) storing, processing or transporting fish or other aquatic organisms taken from Solomon Islands waters;

(c) refuelling or supplying fishing vessels or performing other activities in support of fishing operations; or

(d) attempting or preparing to do any of the above activities;

"Solomon Islands waters" means waters within the fishery limits of Solomon Islands and the exclusive economic zone, territorial sea, archipelagic waters and internal waters as defined in the Delimitation of Marine Waters Act 1978;

Act No. 32 of 1978

"sport fishing" means fishing for the purpose of recreation or competition;

"test fishing operations" means fishing operations approved as such by the Minister under section 18; and

"vessel monitoring system" means the system employed by the Pacific Island States and co-ordinated by the Forum Fisheries Agency to monitor the position and activities of fishing vessels for the purposes of the effective management of fisheries.

PART II
FISHERIES ADMINISTRATION, MANAGEMENT, CONSERVATION AND REGULATION OF FISHING

Management and development of fisheries.

3. (1) For the purposes of this Act the Minister shall exercise in relation to fisheries such powers and functions as provided under this Act.

(2) The objective of Fisheries management and development in Solomon Island shall be to ensure the long-term conservation and the sustainable utilisation of the fishery resources of Solomon Islands for the benefit of the people of Solomon Islands.

Fisheries conservation and management principles.

4. In exercising his powers under this Act, the Minister shall have regard to -

(a) the principle that Solomon Islands fisheries resources shall be managed, developed and conserved so as to ensure through proper conservation and management measures that the maintenance of those resources are not endangered by over-exploitation and are utilised at a level that shall ensure their optimum sustainable yield;

(b) the principle that the marine biodiversity, coastal and aquatic environments of Solomon Islands shall be protected and managed in a sustainable manner;

(c) the application of the precautionary approach to the conservation, management and exploitation of fisheries resources in order to protect the fisheries resources and preserve the marine environment;

(d) the sustainable utilisation of Solomon Islands fisheries resources so as to achieve economic growth, human resource development, employment creation and a sound ecological balance, consistent with its national development objectives;

(e) principle of sustainable yields and allowable catch which may be supported or adopted nationally or internationally from time to time;

(f) any relevant international obligations or bilateral or multilateral agreements which Solomon Islands is a party to, or applicable rules of international law relating to the exercise of jurisdiction by Solomon Islands within its waters;

(g) any customary rights of customary rights holders over or in relation to any area within Solomon Islands waters; and

(h) any fisheries management and development plans made in accordance with this Act.

Fisheries Advisory Council and functions.

5. (1) There is hereby established a Fisheries Advisory Council which shall advise the Minister on such matters relating to the conservation, protection and development of fisheries in Solomon Islands and such other matters as the Minister may from time to time require.

(2) The provisions of the Schedule shall have effect with respect to the constitution and operation of the Council or otherwise in relation thereto.

(3) Without prejudice to the generality of subsection (1), the Council shall advise the Minister on the following; matters, -

(a) fisheries management and development plans prepared under section 7;

(b) proposals for fisheries development and research projects, to be funded under the Fisheries Management and Development Fund provided for under, section 6; and

(c) such other matters as may be referred to it by the Minister or any Provincial Executive.

Fisheries Management and Development Fund.

6. (1) There is hereby established a Fisheries Management and Development Fund for the management and development of fisheries in Solomon Islands which shall be deemed a Special Fund in terms of section 100(2) of the Constitution.

(2) There shall be paid into the Fund -

(a) fifty per cent of the revenue derived from foreign fishing vessel licence fees and other charges in respect of foreign fishing vessels provided for under section 25;

(b) fifty per cent of the revenue derived from penalties for offences against this Act, or from compounding of offences under this Act;

(c) such moneys as may be appropriated to the Fund by Parliament; and

(d) such moneys as may be donated to the Fund by any person, country or organisation.

(3) Moneys may be expended from the Fund for all or any of the following purposes -

(a) projects for the development of small-scale commercial fisheries in provincial waters;

(b) research into the impact of bait fishing and other large-scale commercial and subsistence fisheries in provincial waters; and

(c) assistance to provincial governments in the preparation and implementation of fisheries management and development plans under section 7.

(4) Expenditure from the Fund shall be approved by the Minister on the recommendation of the Council.

Fisheries management and development plans.

7. (1) The Director shall prepare and keep under review a management and development plan, in accordance with this section, of fisheries in Solomon Islands waters (outside the jurisdiction of provincial waters) including fisheries of highly migratory species.

(2) Each provincial government shall prepare and keep under review a plan for the management and development of fisheries in its provincial waters other than fisheries of highly migratory species.

(3) Where fisheries or fisheries management areas are shared by two or more provinces, the relevant provincial governments shall consult with each other regarding the management and development of the fisheries or fisheries management areas.

(4) Where fisheries or fisheries management areas extend beyond the waters of a single province but are not shared with another province, the province concerned shall consult with the Director regarding the management and development of the fisheries or fisheries management areas concerned.

(5) Where the Director or relevant provincials government is of the opinion that the situation with respect to a single fishery or fishery management area is such as to require special consideration, in respect of fisheries management or development including specification of specific licensing programmes or limitations of catch or effort, special provisions maybe made for such fishery or fishery management area within the framework of a plan under subsection (1) or (2) or as a supplement to that plan.

(6) The Director shall, where practicable, provide such assistance to provincial, governments in the preparation and review, of fisheries management and development plans under this section as the provincial governments may require.

(7) A provincial government shall, in preparing any fisheries management and development plan under subsection (2) consult with the Director where the interests of commercial fisheries outside provincial waters are likely to be affected by the implementation of the plan.

(8) Any fisheries management and development plan or modification thereof prepared under this section may, and in the case of a plan prepared under subsection (1) or a plan which has been the subject of consultation under subsection (6) or (7) shall, be referred to the Council for its consideration.

(9) Subject to subsection (3) any fisheries management and development plan or modification thereof prepared under subsection (8) shall be referred together with the advice of the Council to the relevant provincial government for its approval and adoption.

(10) Subject to subsection (3), any fisheries management and development plan or modification thereof prepared under subsection (2) shall be referred together with the advice of the Council to the Minister for approval and adoption.

(11) Where following consultations under subsections (6) and (7), and consideration by the Council, the relevant provincial government and the Director are unable to agree on the contents of the fisheries management and development plan in question and either the provincial government or the Director considers that the matter is likely to have a significant effect on essential interests of the provincial government concerned or on the commercial fisheries of Solomon Islands, the matter shall be referred to the Minister for decision.

Contents etc. of fisheries management and development plans.

8. (1) A fisheries management and development plan shall *inter alia-*

(a) identify the fishery and its characteristics, including its current state of exploitation;

(b) specify the objectives to be achieved in the management of the fishery;

(c) specify the management and development strategies to be adopted for the fishery, and the limitations, if any, to be applied to the issue of licences in respect of the fishery;

(d) identify any possible adverse environmental effects of the operation of fishing activities in the fishery, together with proposals for the management of those effects;

(e) specify the information and other data required to be given or reported for effective management and development; and

(f) take into account any relevant traditional fishing methods or principles.

(2) The Director shall during the preparation of a fisheries management and development plan, consult as appropriate with -

(a) other government departments and agencies, including provincial governments, area councils, bodies and authorities, affected by the plan;

(b) any customary groups or private organisations or similar bodies affected by the plan; and

(c) where practicable, the appropriate fisheries management authorities of other states in the region with a view to ensuring the harmonisation of their respective management and development plans.

Responsibilities of provincial governments.

9. Subject to sections 3 and 7, each provincial government shall be responsible for the proper management and development of the reef, inshore, and freshwater fisheries within its provincial waters.

Power of Provincial Assemblies to make Ordinances.

10. (1) Subject to the provisions of the Provincial Government Act each Provincial Assembly may make Ordinances not inconsistent with this Act or any regulations made under this Act, for the regulation of fisheries within its provincial waters.
Act No. 7 of 1997.

(2) The Provincial Executive of a province may appoint by notice published in the Gazette an authorised officer for the purposes of enforcing the provisions of this Act in that province.

(3) Ordinances made under this section may provide for any or all of the following -

(a) measures for the development of fisheries in provincial waters and the approval of fisheries development projects;

(b) the registration or recording of customary fishing rights, their boundaries and the persons or groups of persons entitled under those rights;

(c) open or closed seasons for fishing for all or any species of fish or other aquatic organisms in all or any areas of provincial waters based on scientific advice;

(d) the closure of areas in which fishing for all or any species of fish or other aquatic organisms may be prohibited;

(e) prescribing the minimum mesh sizes for nets employed, and minimum species sizes for all or any species of fish or other aquatic organisms caught and retained or collected in all or any fisheries management areas in provincial waters;

(f) prescribing the number of fishing vessels, the types of fishing gear employed in any fishery or fishery management area in provincial waters;

(g) prohibiting specified methods of fishing that are harmful to fisheries and the environment, or the use of specified types of fishing gear in provincial waters;

(h) the establishment and protection of marine reserves;

(i) regulating and prohibiting the destruction of mangroves;

(j) subject to subsection (4), authorising the use of specified natural poisons indigenous to Solomon Islands for fishing in, any specified area or areas of provincial waters;

(k) prescribing penalties for offences against any Ordinance or by-law made under this section, not exceeding two thousand dollars for an offence against any Ordinance and one thousand dollars for an offence against a by-law.

(4) No authorisation shall be given under subsection (3)(j) unless the Provincial Assembly has determined that the use of the natural poison to be authorised is a customary practice in the area in which such poison is intended to be used and that the continued use of such poison will not significantly impair the ecology of such area.

(5) Any Ordinance adopted under this section shall be notified forthwith to the Minister responsible for provincial government and shall not come into force until it has been approved by that Minister in consultation with the Minister responsible for fisheries.

Application of the precautionary approach.

11. (1) The precautionary approach shall be applied to the conservation, management and exploitation of the fisheries resources in order to protect the fisheries resources and preserve the marine environment.

(2) The Minister may make regulations for the implementation of the precautionary approach to fisheries management.

Customary fishing rights.

12. (1) Commercial fishing in waters subject to customary fishing rights may be carried out subject to such rights.

(2) Any person fishing in waters subject to customary fishing rights with or from a fishing vessel which is required to be licensed under section 14 or 16, shall be presumed, until the contrary is proved, to be fishing commercially.

(3) When it is proved that customary fishing rights have been breached the court may order compensation to be paid to the customary fishing rights holders.

(4) Any person who fails to comply with an order made under subsection (3) shall be guilty of an offence and be liable to pay in addition to compensation ordered under subsection (3) a further fine not exceeding five hundred dollars or imprisonment of six months.

Licensing Guidelines.

13. (1) The Director shall, in consultation with the Council, draw up Licensing Guidelines for endorsement by the Minister in relation to -

(a) the fisheries for which commercial fishing licences may be issued;

(b) the methods of fishing, types and quantity of equipment, including use of vessel monitoring systems, that may be used in relation to each fishery;

(c) the sustainable yields, allowable levels of fishing and total allowable catches in respect of any fishery;

(d) quotas of the numbers and kinds of licences that may be issued, overall and to any operator, in relation to specified fisheries, methods of fishing, related activities and similar matters;

(e) the economic viability of various kinds of fishing operations and related activities, both current and proposed, and the effects of that viability on the setting of quotas;

(f) priorities to be observed in the granting of all or any class of licence;

(g) the persons or classes of persons who may apply for commercial fishing or related activities; and

(h) any other matters relating to the granting of licences for fishing or a related activity.

(2) In preparing the Licensing Guidelines, the Director shall have regard to any fisheries management and development plan made in accordance with section 7.

(3) The Licensing Guidelines made under this section, and any amendments to or revisions thereof -

(a) shall comprise the primary statement of national policy in respect of the licensing of fishing and related activities;

(b) may contain directives and prohibitions, consistent with the provisions of this Act, which shall be observed by all persons and bodies responsible for the administration of this Act; and

(c) shall come into effect upon receiving endorsement by the Minister.

Local fishing vessel licences.

14. (1) No local fishing vessel shall be used for commercial fishing or related activities in Solomon Islands waters without a valid licence issued under this section in respect of that vessel.

(2) Subject to any regulations made under section 59, subsection (1) shall not apply to a canoe -

(a) powered solely by paddle or sail; or

(b) owned by a customary fishing rights holder or a person or persons customarily entitled to fish in waters subject to customary fishing rights.

(3) An application for a local fishing vessel licence shall be made in the prescribed form to the Director.

(4) Subject to subsection (5), the Director may issue a local fishing vessel licence in the

prescribed form.

(5) An application for a local fishing licence may be refused on any of the following grounds-

(a) that it would be detrimental to the proper management and conservation of the fisheries and other aquatic organisms of Solomon Islands to grant the licence, taking into account the contents of any applicable fisheries management and development plan;

(b) that the Director has reason to believe that the applicant may not comply with the conditions of the licence; or

(c) such other grounds as may be specified in this Act or any regulations made under this Act.

(6) No licence shall be issued in respect of a local fishing vessel which is a vessel to which section 57 of the Shipping Act, 1998 applies unless that vessel has a valid safety certificate issued under section 64 of that Act, or, if no such certificate is required, unless the vessel complies with any safety standards prescribed under section 59 of this Act.

Act No. 5 of 1998.

(7) No licence issued under this section in respect of any local fishing vessel shall be valid for fishing in any provincial waters unless the licence has been endorsed in the prescribed manner by the relevant provincial government:

Provided that where a licence has been issued to a local fishing vessel in respect of bait fishing operations on established bait grounds under a written agreement with customary fishing rights holders, endorsement of the licence shall not be unreasonably refused or delayed by the provincial government concerned.

(8) Where a local fishing vessel is used in contravention of subsection (1), the master, operator; owner and charterer shall each be liable to a fine not exceeding two thousand dollars.

(9) Where a local fishing vessel in respect of which a licence has been issued under this section is used in contravention of any condition of that licence, or is used for fishing in provincial waters without the endorsement of the relevant provincial government under subsection (7) or contrary to the terms of that endorsement, the master, operator, owner and charterer shall each be guilty of an offence and shall be liable to a fine not exceeding one hundred thousand dollars.

Access agreements.

15. (1) The Minister may with the approval of the Cabinet -

(a) enter into agreements with other States on a bilateral or regional basis providing for the allocation of fishing rights in the waters of those States to Solomon Islands fishing vessels; and

(b) enter into agreements with other States and with associations representing foreign fishing vessel owners or charterers, on a bilateral or regional basis, providing for the allocation of fishing rights in Solomon Islands waters to vessels from those States or associations.

(2) Any agreement entered into under subsection (1)(b) shall include a provision establishing the responsibility of the foreign State or association to take all necessary measures to ensure compliance by its vessels with the terms and conditions of the agreement and with the laws relating to fishing in Solomon Islands waters.

(3) For the purposes of this section and section 16 the term "State" shall include any regional organisation to which the power to negotiate access agreements has been delegated by the member countries of that regional organisation.

Foreign fishing vessel licences.

16. (1) Subject to subsection (2), no foreign fishing vessel shall be used for fishing or related activities in Solomon Islands waters without-

(a) a valid foreign vessel licence under this section; or

(b) a regional fishing licence issued in accordance with an arrangement or agreement entered into under section 15.

(2) Subsection (1) shall not apply to any foreign fishing vessel used solely for fisheries research or survey operations.

(3) Any foreign vessel fishing by means of fishing gear other than a hand line or rod and line shall be deemed not to be fishing for sport.

(4) An application for a foreign fishing vessel licence shall be made in the prescribed form to the Director.

(5) An application for a regional fishing licence shall be made, in the prescribed form, to the competent regional agency authorised to issue regional fishing licences under section 21.

(6) Subject to subsection (7) the Director may issue a foreign fishing vessel licence in respect of any foreign fishing vessel authorising that vessel to be used in such areas of Solomon Islands waters for such fishing or related activities as may be prescribed in the licence.

(7) Subject to subsection (8), no foreign fishing vessel licence shall be issued in respect of any foreign fishing vessel unless there is in force with the Government of the flag State of the vessel or with an association of which the owner or charterer is a member, an access agreement to which the Government of Solomon Islands is a party.

(8) A licence maybe issued in respect of-

(a) a foreign fishing vessel for test fishing operations; or

(b) a locally based foreign fishing vessel,

notwithstanding the absence of an access agreement otherwise required under subsection (7).

(9) No licence issued under this section in respect of any foreign fishing vessel shall be valid for fishing in any provincial waters unless the licence has been endorsed in the prescribed manner by the relevant provincial government.

(10) In issuing a licence under this section the Director shall take into account Solomon Islands obligations under bilateral or multilateral treaties relating to fisheries.

(11) Where a foreign fishing vessel is used in contravention of subsection (1), the master, owner or charterer shall each be guilty of an offence and shall each be liable to a fine not exceeding one million dollars.

(12) Where a foreign fishing vessel is in breach of any conditions of its licence or has contravened the provisions of subsection (9) the operator shall on conviction be liable to a fine not exceeding one million dollars and such foreign fishing vessel shall have its licence revoked.

Licence not to relieve vessel, master or crew of obligations under other laws.

17. No licence issued under this Act shall relieve any foreign fishing vessel or its owner, charterer, master or crew of any obligation or requirement imposed by laws of Solomon Islands concerning navigation, customs, immigration, health or other matters.

Test fishing operations.

18. (1) The Minister may, by notice published in the Gazette, approve as test fishing operations, any fishing operations carried out by foreign fishing vessels in Solomon Islands for a limited period of time for the purpose of testing the feasibility of commercial fishing operations with the view to the establishment of locally based fishery operations.

(2) Where the test fishing operations are to be carried out wholly, or in part in provincial waters the Minister shall consult with the provincial government or governments concerned prior to approving such operations under this section.

(3) Any approval given by the Minister under this section shall not relieve the operator of

the vessel from the licensing requirements of section 16.

(4) Any fish caught during the course of approved test fishing operations shall be disposed of in accordance with the conditions of the fishing licence.

Fisheries research and survey operations.

19. (1) The Minister may, on the submission of a satisfactory research or survey plan in consultation with the Director, authorise any vessel or person to undertake fisheries research or survey operations in Solomon Islands waters.

(2) No authorisation shall be granted in respect of fisheries research or survey operations to be carried out in provincial waters without the agreement of the relevant provincial government.

(3) The Minister shall in writing set out such conditions as he deems fit in respect of any authorisation granted under subsection (1).

(4) Any person who undertakes or assists in any fisheries research or survey fishing operations in Solomon Islands waters -

(a) without authorisation under subsection (1); or

(b) in contravention of any condition or conditions attached to the authorisation under subsection (3),

shall be guilty of an offence and shall on conviction be liable to a fine not exceeding two thousand dollars or sentenced to imprisonment for a period not exceeding six months.

Stowage of fishing gear by foreign fishing vessels.

20. (1) All fishing gear on board a foreign fishing vessel in Solomon Islands waters shall be stowed in such a manner that it is not readily available for use for fishing.

(2) Subsection (l) shall not apply -

(a) to a foreign fishing vessel that is in an area of Solomon Islands waters in which it is licensed to fish in accordance with a fishing licence issued under section 16 or a regional fishing licence, or in which it is authorised to undertake fisheries research or survey operations under section 19, or commercial sport fishing operations under section 23; or

(b) to handlines on board a foreign vessel used solely for sport fishing:

Provided, however, that the provisions of this subsection shall apply in the case of foreign fishing vessels transiting in a closed area.

(3) Where a foreign fishing vessel contravenes subsection (1), the master, owner and charterer shall each be guilty of an offence and shall each be liable to a fine not exceeding five hundred thousand dollars.

Power to enter into regional agreements.

21. (1) The Minister may with the approval of the Cabinet enter into arrangements or agreements with Pacific Island states or any distant water fishing nation or with any competent regional fisheries agency, providing agreements for –

(a) the harmonisation of licensing procedures and conditions in respect of foreign fishing vessels and the maintenance of a regional register of foreign fishing vessels;

(b) the designation of an administrator in respect of any regional access agreement, the issuance by the administrator of regional fishing licences under any regional access agreement and the conditions under which such regional fishing licences may be issued by the administrator;

(c) the taking of joint or harmonised enforcement measures in respect of foreign fishing vessels contravening fisheries laws in the region; or

(d) the establishment of regional fisheries organisations or arrangements for the conservation and management of highly migratory species and associated species.

(2) For the purpose of giving effect to any arrangement or agreement entered into under this section, the minister may by order.

(a) exempt any foreign fishing vessel holding a valid regional fishing licence from any provision of this Act or any regulations made under this Act as may be inconsistent with the requirements imposed under any regional access agreement or which imposed requirements also imposed by such regional access agreement;

(b) prescribe the conditions to be observed by operators of foreign fishing vessels exempted under paragraph (a) while fishing or navigating in Solomon Islands waters;

(c) provide that where any foreign fishing vessel is used in contravention of any of the conditions prescribed under paragraph (b), the master, owner and charterer shall each be guilty of an offence and provide for a penalty of a fine not exceeding one million dollars for such offence; and

(d) provide that on conviction of the master, owner or charterer for an offence against an order made under this subsection, the court may also order the forfeiture to the Government of the fishing vessel and any fish, fishing gear, cargo and stores found therein or thereon.

(3) Any order, made under subsection (2) shall be subject to negative resolution of Parliament.

Sport fishing by foreign vessels.

22. (1) No foreign vessel shall be used for sport fishing in waters subject to customary fishing rights without the agreement of the customary fishing rights holder.

(2) Any person who contravenes subsection (1) shall be liable to a fine not exceeding one hundred thousand dollars.

Commercial sport fishing by foreign vessels.

23. (1) Subject to subsection (2) the Minister may in consultation with the Director on the submission of a satisfactory proposal in writing, authorise any foreign fishing vessel to undertake commercial sport fishing operations in Solomon Islands waters for such period of time as he may specify in the authorisation.

(2) No authorisation shall be granted in respect of commercial sport fishing operations to be carried out in provincial waters without the agreement of the relevant provincial government.

(3) The Minister may prescribe such conditions as he deems fit to any authorisation granted under subsection (1).

(4) Any person who undertakes or assists in any commercial sport fishing operations in Solomon Islands waters without the authorisation of the Minister or in contravention of any condition or conditions attached to the authorisation shall be guilty of an offence and shall be liable to a fine not exceeding one hundred thousand dollars.

Fishing licences.

24. (1) Every fishing licence shall be in the prescribed form and shall be subject to such general conditions as may be prescribed and to special conditions as may be specified under subsection (2).

(2) The Director, with the approval of the Minister, may prescribe in any fishing vessel licence such special conditions as he may think fit, including conditions relating to -

(a) the type and method of fishing or related activity authorised;

(b) the areas within which such fishing or related activities are authorised; and

(c) the target species and amount of fish authorised to be taken including any restriction on by-catch.

(4) The Director, with the approval of the Minister, may, from time to time, where he is satisfied that it is expedient for the proper management of fisheries, vary any special conditions prescribed in any fishing licence.

(5) Where the Director varies any special conditions prescribed in any fishing licence he shall notify the licence holder of such variation as soon as practicable.

Fees.

25. (1) Subject to subsections (2) and (3) there shall be payable -

(a) in respect of every fishing licence, every endorsement of a fishing licence under section 16 and every authorisation issued under section 23, such fees as may be prescribed by the Minister; and

(b) in the case of foreign fishing vessel licences such other charges as may be provided for in any access agreement or as the Minister may otherwise determine.

(2) No fee shall be payable for a fishing licence or endorsement of a licence under section 14(7) issued or made in respect of a canoe operating solely within the waters of a single province.

(3) Where a licence has been issued to a local fishing vessel in respect of baitfishing operations on established bait grounds under a written agreement with customary fishing rights holders, no fee shall be payable in respect of the endorsement of the licence by the provincial government concerned other than costs incurred in respect of such endorsement.

(4) Subsection (2) shall not restrict the powers of a Provincial Assembly under section 10 to make Ordinances for the licensing of canoes operating within the waters of the provinces and for the payment of a fee for any such licence.

Validity of licences.

26. (1) A licence issued under this Act unless earlier cancelled or suspended in accordance with section 27, shall be valid for such period not exceeding twelve months as may be specified in the licence.

(2) Where a vessel licensed as a local fishing vessel becomes a foreign fishing vessel that licence shall automatically terminate.

(3) The validity of a licence issued to a foreign fishing vessel shall not extend beyond that validity of any applicable access agreement and charter agreement.

(4) No licence issued under this Act shall be transferred, sold or disposed of in any way whatsoever except with the written approval of the Director and any transfer, sale or disposal of a licence without the Director's approval shall render such licence invalid.

Cancellation suspension of licences.

27. (1) The Director may cancel or suspend a fishing licence on any of the following grounds-

(a) where the Director, is satisfied that the vessel in respect of which the licence has been issued has been used in contravention of this Act or any other applicable law, any other condition of the licence or in breach of any applicable access agreement;

(b) where be is required to do so in accordance with the provisions of any agreement or arrangement enter into under section 15; or

(c) such other grounds as may be prescribed for purposes of fisheries management and conservation.

(2) Where a fishing licence has been cancelled or suspended under subsection (1), notification of the cancellation or suspension shall be given to the person to whom the licence was issued.

(3) Where a fishing licence has been cancelled or suspended on any of the grounds specified in subsection (1)(c) a proportion of any fee paid for the fishing licence representing the unexpired period of that licence or the period of suspension, as the case may be, shall be reimbursed to the licensee at his request.

Notification of suspension or cancellation.

28. (1) Any notification given under section 24(5) or section 27(2) shall be in writing except as otherwise specified in subsection (2).

(2) In the case of a foreign fishing vessel, a notification referred to in subsection (1) may be in writing or by telex, radio or such other form as the Director deems appropriate.

Appeals.

29. Any person aggrieved by -

(a) the refusal of the Director to issue or renew a licence under this Act other than a licence issued in respect of a foreign fishing vessel under any powers delegated to the Director under section 60; or

(b) the cancellation or suspension of a licence under this Act, may, within thirty days of the receipt of notification of that decision, appeal to the Minister.

Fishing with explosives, etc.

30. (1) Subject to any Provincial Ordinance made under section 10 (3), any person who -

(a) permits to be used, uses or attempts to use any explosive, poison or other noxious substance, for the purpose of killing, stunning, disabling or catching fish or in any way rendering fish more easily caught; or

(b) carries or has in his possession or control any explosive, poison or other noxious substance in circumstances which raise a reasonable presumption that such explosive, poison or other noxious substance is intended to be used for any of the aforesaid purposes,

shall be guilty of an offence, and liable to a fine not exceeding one thousand dollars.

(2) Any explosive, poison or other noxious substance found on board any fishing vessel or a canoe shall be presumed, unless the contrary is proved to be intended for the purpose referred to in subsection (1).

(3) Any person who, knowing or having reasonable cause to believe that any fish has been taken in contravention of the provisions of this section without lawful excuse receives or is found in possession of such fish, shall be guilty of an offence and liable to a fine of one thousand dollars or twelve months imprisonment.

(4) Where the circumstances of such receipt or possession raise a reasonable presumption that the fish is intended for the purpose of sale, trade, or profit, such person is liable to a fine not exceeding one thousand dollars or twelve months imprisonment.

(5) Far the purposes of this section, a certificate as to the cause and manner of death or injury of any person signed by the Chief Medical Officer or such other person as may be in charge of medical services in any province, or in the case of the alleged use of explosives, by the Director or by any person authorised by him in writing, shall be accepted as prima facie evidence in a court without proof of the signature of the person appearing to have signed the certificate or his official capacity.

(6) The defendant to proceedings brought under this section is entitled to fourteen days notice in writing of the prosecution's intention to introduce a certificate under subsection (4) as evidence in any court proceedings.

Aquaculture operations.

31. (1) No person shall set up or operate any aquaculture operations without the written permission of the Director and in accordance with such conditions as he may specify.

(2) Conditions specified by the Director under the preceding subsection may relate to the location of the aquaculture facilities and the operation of those facilities, the prevention of the spread of communicable fish diseases, the inspection of aquaculture sites and the provision of statistical information.

(3) Any person who contravenes the provisions of subsection (1) shall be guilty of an offence and shall be liable on conviction to a fine not exceeding one hundred thousand dollars.

Import and export of live fish, etc.

32. (1) No person shall import or export any live fish into or from Solomon Islands without the written permission of the Director.

(2) The Director may, before granting any permission under this section require that an assessment be carried out at the expense of the person seeking to import or export the live fish -

(a) in the case of imports, of the possible effects of the release of such fish into the wild;

(b) in the case of exports, of the potential impact of the harvesting and export of the fish on the fisheries resources of Solomon Islands;

(c) on any matter, which the Director thinks appropriate.

(3) Any person who contravenes subsection (1) shall be guilty of an offence and liable to a fine not exceeding five hundred thousand dollars.

Driftnet fishing.

33. (1) Any person who within Solomon Islands waters engages or attempts to engage in any driftnet fishing activities shall be liable on conviction to a fine not exceeding two million dollars.

(2) Where any foreign or local fishing vessel within Solomon Islands waters engages or attempts to engage in any driftnet fishing activities, the operator, master, owner or charterer, if any, of such vessel shall be liable on conviction to a fine not exceeding two million dollars.

(3) No foreign or local fishing vessel which engages in any driftnet fishing activities may tranship, land or process the fish or have access to ports and port serving facilities.

(4) It is an offence for any fishing vessel to possess driftnets while licensed to fish in Solomon Islands waters. Any fishing vessel in possession of driftnets shall be liable to a fine of five hundred thousand dollars.

Fish processing establishments.

34. (1) The Principal Licensing Officer may on payment of the prescribed fee grant to any person a licence in the prescribed form to operate a fish processing establishment.

(2) The Principal Licensing Officer may on granting a licence under this section prescribe any conditions as he deems appropriate and such conditions shall be endorsed on the licence.

(3) Any person who operates or causes or allows to be operated any fish processing establishment without a valid licence granted under this section shall be guilty of an offence and liable to a fine not exceeding two hundred and fifty thousand dollars or to imprisonment for twelve months, or to both such fine and imprisonment.

Records.

35. (1) Any person engaged in fishing, fish processing, fish marketing or the export of fish or fish products shall keep such records and supply such information relating to such fishing, in such form as the Director may require.

(2) Any person who, without lawful cause, refuses to keep records or supply information as required under subsection (1) or who knowingly supplies false information shall be guilty of an offence and liable to a fine not exceeding one hundred thousand dollars.

PART III
ENFORCEMENT

Appointment of authorised officers.

36. (1) There shall be appointed a Director of Fisheries, a Principal Licensing Officer and such licensing officers, fisheries officers and other officers for carrying out the purposes and provisions of this Act.

(2) For the purposes of this Act, a fisheries observer appointed by the Director shall be deemed to be an authorised officer.

(3) Any appointment made under subsection (1) shall, if the person appointed is to be a public officer, be made in accordance with the Constitution but otherwise shall be made by the Minister.

(4) For the purposes of this Act any person appointed under this section shall be an authorised officer.

Powers of authorised officers.

37. (1) For the purposes of ascertaining whether there is or has been any contravention of the provisions of this Act any authorised officer shall have power to -

(a) at all reasonable hours enter any fish processing establishment and any premises other than premises use exclusively as a dwelling-house;

(b) stop, board and search:

(i) any foreign fishing vessel, within Solomon Islands waters;

(ii) any local fishing vessel, inside or outside Solomon Islands waters; or

(iii) any canoe in Solomon Islands waters which an authorised officer reasonably believes is being used in the commission of an offence under this Act;

(c) stop and search any vehicle transporting, or reasonably suspected of transporting, fish or fish products;

(d) make such examination, inspection and inquiry as may appear necessary to him concerning any premises, fish processing establishment, vessel or vehicle. In the exercise of these powers, the authorised officer may take samples of any fish, or fish products, found therein;

(e) require any person to produce his licence or his authority, if it appears to the authorised officer that such person is doing any act for which a licence or other authority is required under this Act and take copies of any such licence or other authority; and

(f) require any person to produce any log-book, record or other document required to be held by him under this Act or any regulations made under this Act, and take copies of such log-book, record or other document.

(2) A Pacific Island State Officer may, pursuant to any Treaty to which Solomon Islands is a party, exercise any of the powers described in subsection (1)(a), (b), (c), (d), (e) and (f), and where a Pacific Island State Officer exercises such a power, he is taken, for the purposes of this Act, to have exercised the power of an authorised officer.

Powers of authorised officers without a warrant.

38. (1) Where he has reasonable grounds for believing that an offence against the provisions of this Act has been committed, any authorised officer without a warrant, may -

(a) following hot pursuit as recognised by international law and commenced within the fishery limits, stop, board and search outside Solomon Islands waters any foreign fishing vessel which he believes has been used in the commission of that offence within Solomon Islands waters or in relation to which he believes such an offence has been committed and bring such vessel and all persons and things therein to a port within Solomon Islands waters;

(b) within Solomon Islands waters -

(i) arrest any person whom he believes has committed such an offence, and if the authorised officer making such arrest is not a police officer, he shall without unnecessary delay hand over such person to a police officer or in the absence of a police officer, shall take such person to the nearest police station;

(ii) in the case of an offence against section 16, 20, 22 or 30, seize any vessel (together with its fishing gear, stores and cargo), which he believes has been used in the commission of such offence or in respect of which he believes such offence has been committed;

(iii) seize any fish which be believes have been taken or fish products produced in the commission of such offence; and

(iv) seize any explosive, poison or other noxious substance which he believes has been used, carried, possessed or controlled in contravention of section 30.

(2) After a vessel has been stopped under the provisions of subsection (1)(a) any authorised officer may exercise concerning it or in relation to any fish or fish products therein any of the power; conferred by paragraphs (d) and (e) of subsection (1) of section 37.

(3) A written receipt shall be given for anything seized under subsection (1) by the authorised officer concerned to the person from whom the seizure is made.

(4) Any vessel seized under this section and the crew thereof shall be taken to the nearest or most convenient port and the vessel may be detained pending the outcome of any legal proceedings under this Act or its release on bond or other form of security under section 53.

Wilful obstruction, etc.

39. Any person who wilfully obstructs, assaults or threatens with violence an authorised officer in the exercise of any of his powers shall be guilty of an offence and liable to a fine not exceeding two hundred thousand dollars or to imprisonment for twelve months, or to both such fine and such imprisonment.

Failure to comply with lawful requirements.

40. Subject to section 42, any person who fails to comply with any lawful enquiry made by any authorised officer under this Act, shall be guilty of an offence and liable to a fine not exceeding fifty thousand dollars.

Failure to stop or facilitate boarding of foreign fishing vessel.

41. Subject to section 42, the master of any foreign fishing vessel within Solomon Islands waters or of any local fishing vessel inside or outside Solomon Islands waters which fails to stop as ordered or who fails to facilitate boarding of the vessel in accordance with this Act, shall be guilty of an offence and shall be liable to a fine not exceeding two hundred thousand dollars.

Defence to prosecution under section 40 or 41.

42. It shall be a defence to any prosecution under section 40 or 41 if it is proved that to have complied with the requirement or order would have placed the safety of the vessel or the lives of its crew in imminent danger.

Authored officers to declare identity.

43. Any authorised officer acting in the exercise of his powers under this Act shall, on demand, produce such document of identification or other evidence as may be reasonably sufficient to show that he is an authorised officer for the purposes of this Act.

Non-liability of authorised officers.

44. No authorised officer shall be personally liable in respect of any act done or omitted to be done by him in good faith in the execution or purported execution of his powers and duties under this Act.

Destroying of evidence.

45. Any person who, being on board any vessel being pursued or about to be boarded by any authorised officer, throws over board or destroys any fish, fishing gear, explosive, poison, noxious substance or any other thing whatsoever, with intent to avoid the seizure of such fish, fishing gear, explosive, poison, noxious substance or thing, or the detection of any offence under this Act, shall be guilty of an offence and liable to a fine not exceeding one hundred thousand dollars.

Power of forfeiture of fish, etc.

46. Where any person is convicted of an offence against this Act the Court may, in addition to any other penalty it may impose, order that any fish caught or fish product produced in the commission of such offence or the proceeds of sale of such fish or fish product, and any fishing gear, and in the case of an offence under section 16(1), 20(3), 30(1), 41 or 45, any vessel (together with its fishing gear, stores and cargo) used in the commission of such offence or in respect of which such offence has been committed, shall be disposed of in such manner as the Minister of Finance may direct.

Presumption.

47. Any fish found on board any fishing vessel used in the commission of an offence under this Act or in respect of which any such offence has been committed, shall, unless the contrary is proved, shall be presumed to have been caught in the commission of such offence.

Jurisdiction of the Courts.

48. Any offence against any of the provisions of this Act committed within Solomon Islands waters may be dealt with, and judicial proceedings taken, as if the offence has been committed in any place in Solomon Islands.

Compounding of offences.

49. (1) Subject to subsection (3) the Minister may, where he is satisfied that any person has committed an offence against this Act, compound such offence by accepting on behalf of the Government from such person a sum of money not exceeding the maximum fine specified for that offence.

(2) On compounding an offence under this section the Minister may order the release of any vessel or other article seized under section 38 or the proceeds of sale of any article under section 52 on such, conditions including the payment of such additional sump of money not exceeding the value of the vessel or other article seized, as he may think fit.

(3) Where the person who has committed the offence is no longer within Solomon Islands, the Minister may send written notice of his intention to compound the offence to the legal address of the person outside Solomon Islands

(4) No offence shall be compounded under this section unless the person who has committed the offence has expressed his willingness in the prescribed form that the offence be so dealt with, or in the case of a notification under subsection (3), if the person concerned notifies the Minister in writing that he does not wish the offence to be compounded, submits to the jurisdiction of the Courts of Solomon Islands and, where so required by the Court, files a satisfactory bond or other form of security in accordance with section 53.

(5) The compounding of an offence under this section shall be notified in writing to the appropriate Court under the signature of both parties, except that in the case of a compounding following a notification under subsection (3), the signature of the Minister alone will suff ce.

(6) In any proceedings brought against any person for an offence against this Act or any regulation made under this Act, it shall be a defence if such person proves that the offence with which he is charged has been compounded under this Act.

(7) The powers conferred on the Minister by subsection (1) may be exercised by the Director in respect of an offence involving the use of a local dishing vessel or an offence

committed by a citizen of Solomon Islands.

Certificate of evidence.

50. (1) The Minister, an authorised officer or a Pacific Island State officer may give evidence by way of certificate, including but not limited to, evidence that -

(a) a specified vessel was or was not on a specified date or dates, a vessel licensed under this Act;

(b) a specified person was or was not on a specified date or dates, the holder of any specified licence, authorisation or certificate of registration;

(c) an appended document is a true copy of the licence, authorisation or certificate of registration for a specified vessel or person;

(d) a particular location or area of water was on a specified date or dates within the fishery limits or within a closed, limited, restricted or in any other way a controlled area of Solomon Islands waters or an area of Solomon Islands waters subject to specified conditions;

(e) an appended chart shows the boundaries on a specified date or dates of Solomon Islands waters, closed or limited or zones delineated for any specified purpose;

(f) a particular item or piece of equipment is a fishing gear;

(g) the cause and manner of death or injury to any fish;

(h) an appended document is a true copy of an access agreement;

(i) a call sign, name or number is that of or allotted under any system of naming or numbering of vessels to a particular vessel;

(j) a specified vessel has good standing on the Regional Register, as evidenced by an appended certificate to that effect from the Director of the South Pacific Forum Fisheries Agency;

(k) a particular position or catch report, a copy of which is appended, was given in respect of a specific vessel;

(l) the date and time or period of time that a vessel was in a place or area;

(m) the place or area at which a vessel was located;

(n) a person was fishing or a vessel was used for fishing;

(o) that information appended is information received from an observer.

(2) A certificate given in evidence pursuant to subsection (1), is admissible and sufficient evidence of the facts referred to unless the contrary is proven.

Service and validity of certificates.

51. (1) Where a certificate is to be produced in judicial proceedings a copy of every certificate shall be given to a person charged with every offence three days before the date of the hearing.

(2) Where an owner, master, operator or charterer of a vessel is charged with an offence under this Act, and a certificate under section 50 cannot be served, then in that case, service is deemed to have been properly completed if a copy of the certificate is served upon the agents of the vessel.

(3) An omission from or mistake made in a certificate issued under section 50 does not render it invalid unless the Court considers the omission or mistake as material to any issue in the proceedings concerned, or the defendant is materially prejudiced.

(4) Where is any proceedings a certificate made under section 50 is produced to the Court, the prosecution is not obliged to call the maker of the certificate unless the Court otherwise directs.

Disposal of seized goods.

52. (1) Any fish, fish product or other article of a perishable nature seized or taken under the provisions of this Act may, on the direction of the Director, be sold and the net proceeds of the sale held pending the outcome of any prosecution brought under this Act, and if no such prosecution is brought such proceeds shall be paid to the owner of the fish, fish product or other article sold.

(2) Any fishing vessel, fishing gear, fish or fish product seized under section 38, or the proceeds of sale of any fish or fish product or other article under this section, which is not, ordered to be forfeited under section 46 shall be returned to its owner.

Release of vessel on bond, etc.

53. Where any fishing vessel, fishing gear, fish or fish product has been seized under section 38, the Court may, order its release on receipt of a satisfactory bond or other security from any person claiming such property, conditioned on such person -

(a) delivering such property to the Court upon the order of the Court, without any impairment of its value; or

(b) paying the monetary value of such property in accordance with an order or judgment of the Court.

Duties of the flag State.

54. (1) No foreign fishing vessel shall be licensed to fish in Solomon Islands waters unless the flag State of the vessel takes measures to enforce this Act and the terms and conditions of the licences issued under this Act.

(2) The measures to be taken by the flag State include -

(a) applying the terms and conditions of the licence;

(b) prohibiting fishing by vessels that are not licensed to fish in Solomon Islands waters;

(c) requiring vessels fishing in Solomon Islands waters to carry the licence at all times and to produce it on demand for inspection by an authorised officer;

(d) marking of fishing vessels and fishing gear for identification in accordance with the Food and Agriculture Organisation, the United Nations Standard Specifications for the Marking and Identification of Fishing Vessels;

(e) recording of and timely reporting of vessel position, catch of target and non-target species, fishing effort and other relevant fisheries data;

(f) verifying the catch of target and non-target species through observer programmes, inspection of such unloading reports, supervision of transhipment and monitoring of landed catches and market statistics; and

(g) monitoring, control and surveillance of fishing activities.

(3) The flag State shall ensure that the master and crew of its fishing vessels -

(a) accept and facilitate prompt and safe boarding by authorised officers;

(b) co-operate and assist in the inspection of the vessel;

(c) do not obstruct, intimidate or interfere with the performance by the authorised officers of their duties;

(d) permit the authorised officers to communicate with the authorities of the flag State;

(e) provide reasonable facilities, including food and accommodation to the authorised officers; and

(f) facilitate safe disembarkation by the authorised officers.

(4) The flag State shall appoint an agent who shall responsible for receiving and responding to any legal process.

Port state enforcement.

55. Any authorised officer may inspect the documents, fishing gear and catch, on board a foreign fishing vessel when such vessel is in port.

Illegal import of fish etc.

56. (1) Subject to subsection (3), a person who -

(a) on his own account, or as partner, agent or employee of another person, lands, imports, exports, transports, sells, receives, acquires or purchases; or

(b) causes or permits a person acting on his behalf, or uses a fishing vessel, to land, import, export, transport, sell, receive, acquire or purchase,

any fish taken, possessed, transported or sold contrary to the law of another State shall be guilty of an offence and shall be liable to a fine not exceeding one million dollars.

(2) This section does not apply to fish taken on the high seas contrary to the laws of another State where Solomon Islands does not recognise the jurisdiction of that State to extend to the high seas.

(3) Where there is an agreement with another State relating to an offence referred to in subsection (1)(b), the penalty provided by subsection (1), or any portion of it according to the terms of the agreement, shall, after all the costs and expenses have been deducted, be remitted to that State according to the terms of the agreement.

Vessel monitoring system.

57. (1) No foreign fishing vessel shall be licensed unless the operator of the vessel installs, maintains and operates a registered automatic locations communicator in accordance with such specifications as prescribed by the Forum Fisheries Agency.

(2) The operator of a foreign fishing vessel shall ensure that the automatic locations communicator is operational at all times while the vessel is in Solomon Islands waters.

(3) The operator of a foreign fishing vessel shall notify the Director of the breakdown of the automatic locations communicator. Where the automatic locations communicator has been reported to have broken down, the operator shall submit to the Director reports of the vessel's name, call sign, position (expressed in Latitude and Longitudes to minutes

of arc), and the date and time of the report at intervals of eight hours commencing from the time of notification of the failure of the automatic locations communicator.

(4) Any person who intentionally, recklessly or negligently destroys, damages, renders inoperative or otherwise interferes with any part of the automatic locations communicator shall be guilty of an offence and liable to fine not exceeding two hundred thousand dollars.

(5) Any person who intentionally, recklessly or negligently divulges information from the vessel monitoring system, to any person or persons not authorised to receive such information shall be guilty of an offence and liable to a fine not exceeding fifty thousand dollars.

PART IV
GENERAL

Compulsory acquisition of land.

58. Whenever it appears to the Minister that any land is required for the purpose of developing fisheries or fisheries industries in Solomon Islands he may make a declaration to that effect and that purpose shall be deemed to be a public purpose and the provisions of Division 2 of Part V of the Land and Titles Act (relating to the compulsory acquisition of land), shall apply in relation thereto.

Cap. 93.

Minister's power to make regulations.

59. (1) The Minister may make regulations as may seem to him expedient for carrying into effect the provisions of this Act, and, without prejudice to the generality of the forgoing, such regulations may provide for all or any of the following purposes -

(i) the training of fishermen;

(ii) the licensing, regulation and management of any fishery and the conservation of particular species of fish or other aquatic organisms;

(iii) extending the licensing requirements of section 14 to cover other canoes engaged in commercial fishing;

(iv) prescribing fisheries management conservation measures, including prescribed mesh size, gear standards, minimum and maximum species sizes, limitation on the amount of fish authorised to be caught by any vessel or person or from any fishery, closed season, closed areas, prohibited methods of fishing or fishing gear and schemes for limiting effort in all or any specified fisheries;

(v) prohibiting or regulating fishing for whales and other species of marine mammals;

(vi) the registration and licensing of fishermen and their fishing gear, including fixed nets, stakes, and weirs, and the registration of fishing vessels;

(vii) conditions and procedures to be observed by foreign fishing vessels while within Solomon Islands waters;

(viii) regulating the transiting of foreign fishing vessels through Solomon Islands waters, and the manner in which fishing gear is to be stowed, by both licensed and unlicensed foreign fishing vessels;

(ix) prescribing procedures to be followed by the masters of foreign and local fishing vessels to facilitate boarding and inspection by authorised officers;

(x) rewards to be paid to any person providing information on the operations of foreign fishing vessels leading to a conviction or compounding of an offence under this Act;

(xi) the implementation of any agreement or arrangement entered into under section 15 or 21 or the licensing and control of fish aggregating devices and for rights to fish aggregated by such devices;

(xii) the organisation and regulation of sport fishing;

(xiii) standards and other measures for the safety of local fishing vessels and fishermen;

(xiv) regulating the cultivation of seaweed and other aquatic organisms;

(xv) the licensing of fish farms and the regulation of the importation of live fish;

(xvi) the organisation and regulation of the marketing, and distribution of fish, other aquatic organisms and fish products;

(xvii) controlling the handling, landing and transportation of fish, other aquatic organisms and fish products;

(xviii) prohibiting or regulating the export of specified, species of fish, other aquatic organisms and fish, of other aquatic organism products and fish products;

(xix) methods and procedures to be adopted in relation to fish storage and processing;

(xx) substances and materials to be used in fish processing;

(xxi) the inspection of fish processing establishments and fish products;

(xxii) minimum standards in relation to the quality of fish or fish products;

(xxiii) methods of analysis of fish and fish products;

(xxiv) the grant of exemption to any class of vessels or fish processing establishments from all or any of the provisions of this Act;

(xxv) penalties for the contravention of any regulation made under this section, which may not exceed a fine of two hundred thousand dollars;

(xxvi) the implementation of the precautionary approach;

(xxvii) prescribing of fees for licences issued under this Act; and

(xxviii) any other matter authorised or required to be prescribed by this Act.

(2) Where, in the opinion of the Minister it would be appropriate to delay the promulgation of any regulations under this section until a meeting of the Council can be convened, the Minister may seek the advice of members of the Council through correspondence or other methods without convening a meeting of the Council.

Powers of delegation.

60.-(1) The Minister may, in writing, delegate any of the powers conferred on him under this Act, with the exception of the powers conferred by sections 54 and 59.

(2) The Director may, in writing, delegate any of the powers conferred on him under this Act, with the exception of the powers conferred by sections 27 and 32.

Repeal and savings.

61. (1) The Fisheries Act 1972, (hereinafter referred to as the "repealed Act") is hereby repealed.

Act No. 13 1972.

(2) Notwithstanding such repeal from and after the date of coming into operation of this Act -

(a) any licence granted under the repealed Act shall continue to be valid can such terms and conditions of approval for the period stipulated therein; and

(b) all regulations and orders made under the repealed Act and in force at the date of commencement of this Act shall subject to such modifications and adaptations as may be necessary to bring them into conformity with this Act continue until such time as new regulations or orders are made under this Act.

SCHEDULE
(Section 5(1))
THE FISHERIES ADVISORY COUNCIL

Appointment of members.

1. (1) The Council shall consist of not less than five nor more than seven members appointed by the Minister of whom one shall be appointed by the Minister to be the Chairman of the Council.

(2) The members of the Council shall be selected by the Minister from among persons appearing to him to have ability and experience in matters relating to fisheries.

Tenure of office.

2. A member of the Council shall, subject to the provisions of this Schedule, hold office for a period not exceeding three years, but such member shall be eligible for reappointment.

Temporary appointments.

3. Subject to paragraph 1(2), the Minister may appoint any person to act temporarily in place of the Chairman or a member of the Council in the case of the absence or inability to act of the Chairman or such member, as the case may be.

Resignation.

4. (1) Any member of the Council, other than the Chairman, may at any time resign his office by instrument in writing addressed to the Minister and transmitted through the Chairman and from the date of the receipt by the Minister of such instrument, such member shall cease to be a member of the Council.

(2) The Chairman may at any time resign his office by instrument in writing addressed to the Minister and such resignation shall take effect as from the date of the receipt of such instrument by the Minister.

Revocation of appointment.

5. The Minister may at any time revoke the appointment of the Chairman and of any member of the Council.

Publication.

6. The names of all members of the Council as first constituted and every change in the

membership thereof shall be published in the Gazette.

Remuneration.

7. The Chairman and other members of the Council or committees may be paid such remuneration whether by way of honorarium, fees, and such other allowances as the Minister may determine.

Appointment of committees.

8. The Council may in the discharge of its duties appoint committees comprising of members of the Council or non-members or both and may assign to them such functions as the Council may determine.

Information.

9. The Council may invite any person to furnish or provide information, explanations, advice or express an opinion at any of its meetings.

Procedure and meetings.

10. (1) The Council shall meet as often as may be Procedure and necessary or expedient for the transaction of its business, and such meetings shall be held at such places and times and on such days as the Council may determine.

(2) The Chairman may at any time call a special meeting to be held within seven days of a written request for that purpose addressed to him by any two members of the Council.

(3) The Chairman shall preside at all meetings of the Council at which he is present, and in his absence from any meeting the members present and constituting a quorum shall elect a Chairman from among their number to preside at that meeting.

(4) The quorum of the Council shall be three.

(5) The decisions of the Council shall be by a majority of votes and in addition to an original vote, the person presiding at a meeting shall have a casting vote in any case in which the voting is equal.

(6) Minutes in proper form of each meeting shall be kept.

(7) The validity of the proceedings of the Council shall not be affected by any vacancy amongst the members thereof or by any defect in the appointment of any member thereof.

(8) Subject to the provisions of this Schedule, the Council may regulate its own proceedings.

Disclosure of interest.

11. (1) Any member of the Council who, otherwise than as such member, is directly or indirectly interested in a contract made or entered into, or proposed to be made or entered into, by the Council, or in the subject matter of any proceedings before the Council shall as soon as practicable after the relevant facts have come to his knowledge, disclose the nature of his interest at a meeting of the Council.

(2) A disclosure under this paragraph shall be recorded in the minutes of the Council and the member -

(a) shall not take part after the disclosure in any deliberation or decision of the Council and relating to the contract or matter in question; and

(b) shall be disregarded for the purpose of forming a quorum of the Council for any such deliberation or decision.

Immunity from action.

12. No action, suit, prosecution or other proceedings shall be brought or instituted personally against any member of the Council in respect of any act done *bona fide* in pursuance or execution or intended execution of this Act.

Office of Chairman, etc, not public office.

13. The office of Chairman or member of the Council shall not be a public office for the purpose of Chapter XIII of the Constitution of Solomon Islands.

INVESTING SOLOMON ISLANDS: PRACTICAL INFORMATION

INVESTMENT CONSIDERATIONS

GOVERNMENT POLICY

The Solomon Islands' Government welcomes and encourages investors whose development proposals are compatible with its national aims and objectives in respect of the environment and social structure. In addition, the Government has developed a list of desired investment areas for potential investors. This can be obtained from the Investment Board.

The Government recognises the important role that overseas investment can play in broadening the country's economic base. The assessment process for overseas investment also pays particular attention to the impact of the proposal on:

- strengthening the technical and marketing expertise of the private sector;
- use of local raw materials;
- net export income;
- import cost savings; and
- employment and training, especially in regional areas.

RESTRICTIONS ON FOREIGN INVESTMENT

There are several sectors of the economy reserved for Solomon Islanders. To date, there has not been a strict application of this policy. At present, the new government is reviewing these sectors so these restrictions may be lifted in the near future.

REPATRIATION OF CAPITAL AND PROFITS

Approval for repatriation of funds is required under the Exchange Control Act 1976 and the Exchange Control Regulations 1977. The Central Bank of the Solomon Islands administers the exchange control policy and authorises commercial banks to deal and process applications for remittance of foreign exchange.

Exchange control approval is required on importation of capital; repatriation of capital; transfer of profits; dividends, interest and royalties; borrowing of overseas funds; repayment of interest or a loan to a non-resident lender; crediting of non-resident accounts; transfer of property, goods, right to I services etc to non-residents; operation and settlement of inter-company accounts; transfer overseas of sale proceeds of Solomon Islands assets; direct investment overseas and lending of Solomon Islands currency outside the Solomon Islands. Exchange control approval is also required for companies incorporated in the Solomon Islands to issue and register shares in the name of non-residents and to dispatch the scrip from the Solomon Islands.

TAXATION

Individuals
Tax is payable on total income less personal exemptions, with all individuals being taxed at the following rates:

Personal Income Tax Rates	
US$0 - US$2,915	11%
US$2,915 - US$5,829	23%
US$5,829 - US$11,658	35%
US$11,658 and above	40%

Note the above rates are calculated on USD selling rate to SBD$ of 0.1943
Company

Resident establishment:	30 percent
Non-resident establishment:	35 percent

Witholding Taxes
Withholding tax on dividends paid to non-residents by companies incorporated in the Solomons is 35 percent and 20 percent on dividends paid to residents. Gross dividends are a deductible expense of the paying company.

INVESTMENT PROTECTION

While investment protection is a priority, there are no formal laws or regulations in place to provide expropriation and compensation for foreign investments. A Trade Dispute Panel has been set up to hear and settle disputes. The Panel has been vested with the necessary powers under the law to settle disputes. All foreign investors in Solomon Islands are entitled to:

- repatriation of dividends on a current basis
- repatriation of capital, incorporated into their rights to sell their shares in a local operation
- access to and use ofthe country's stock of foreign reserves in accordance with the policies and procedures governing such use
- liberal and flexible levels of shareholding and directorships
- enjoy the benefits and rewards of all legitimate entrepreneurial efforts including payments for patents, technology, management, technical assistance as well as other special provisions
- work permits and residential permits for approved levels of foreign workers under conditions governing the granting of such permits
- all rights under the Solomon Islands constitution and before the law
- the settlement of disputes in accordance with intemationally agreed criteria and the laws of Solomon Island

INVESTMENT INCENTIVES

The Solomon Islands Investment Board is empowered by the Solomon Islands Investment Act to negotiate investment incentive packages tailored for individual proposals. The incentive package includes:

- up to 10 years tax free holiday;
- the capacity to carry forward losses (limited to five years only);
- depreciation on capital expenditure of 40% in the first year and 5% per annum thereafter for factory expansions (a special rate of 50% is allowed for tourist developments)
- double deduction for expenditure on apprenticeships and tertiary eduction;
- 150 percent deduction for cost of inter-province transport of raw materials;
- 150 percent deduction for export promotion expenditure;
- duty free entry for capital equipment and drawback on re-exported items;
- special additional incentives for tourism developments; and
- free movement of capital and profit remittances.

CONTACTS FOR FURTHER INFORMATION

Secretary
Foreign Investment Board
Department of Commerce, Employment and Tourism
PO Box G26
Honiara
SOLOMON ISLANDS
Tel: (677) 23 015/21 849/21 928
Fax: (677) 21 651/26 075

Manager
Foreign Exchange Department
Central Bank of Solomon Islands
PO Box 634
Honiara
SOLOMON ISLANDS
Tel: (677) 23 492/21 791
Fax: (677) 23 513

INVESTMENT AND BUSINESS CLIMATE

- stable political environment
- available low - cost labour

- presence of untapped natural resources
- friendly people and rich cultural diversity
- unique beauty and pollution - free water
- an abundance of biodiversity resources, the basis for growth & development
- foreign investors whose mission statements include environmental and social responsibilities are favoured by the Government.

[1] Politically and socially, Solomon Islands is a very stable and a safe destination for foreign investment. {refer to Government, General Information}
[2] The Government is committed to creating an economic climate which is conducive to investment. Functional and practical guidelines are being developed to provide for speedy and organized review and monitoring of foreign investment.
[3] New investments that will increase import substitution production and or increase export marketing are encouraged.
[4] The overriding objective of the Solomon Islands Government is to keep improving the decision - making process affecting investment applications and to provide services and assistance to foreign investors at a professional level.
[5] The Government encourages foreign investment in the private sector as the basis for growth and development.
[6] The Government welcomes investors whose development proposals are compatible with Solomon Islands national aims and objectives.

The Solomon Islands Government holds a firm belief that the private sector has the potential to provide the desired level of national economic growth. This belief is backed by the resilience of established companies and a growing number of Solomon Island entrepreneurs engaged in service and manufacturing industries, as well as small-scale export production.

INTERNATIONAL BUSINESS ENVIRONMENT

Major international finance, accounting and legal firms are already established in the Solomons. Satellite communications and frequent sea and air links to major markets ensure a solid business environment for investors.

LABOUR FORCE

Less than 20% of the population aged between 15 and 54 are currently engaged in paid full time employment. Most are seeking such employment.

The Solomon Islands Labour Force Policy clearly aims to promote the employment of Solomon Islanders and to control the level of foreign workers. All foreign workers require work permits.

SALARIES AND WAGES

Minimum wages and conditions are set by the Wages Advisory board under the Labour Act. The average monthly earnings for employed workers in 1993 was $51641.

A sample of average annual wage rates applicable on 1 January, 1993 is set out below. Pay rates are the same for male and female employees.

- Middle Management $516 -10.000
- Fitter and Turner $516 -10,000
- Clerical Worker $514 - 6,000
- Sales Person $514 - 6,000
- Agricultural Worker $512 - 4,000

The normal working week is 45 hours including a half day on Saturday. Four weeks paid holiday per annum is provided for full time employees.

EMPLOYER AND EMPLOYEE ORGANISATIONS

There are fourteen trade unions affiliated to the Solomon Islands Council of Trade Unions. The three major employer groups are:

- The Chinese Association;
- The Chamber of Commerce: and
- The Federation of Employers.

ESSENTIAL FACILITIES

Electricity
Diesel stations provide most of the power generated in the Solomons. 415/240 volt 50 cycle power is available in Guadacanal (Honiara and Lungga): New Georgia (Gizo, Noro and Munda): Santa Isabel (Duals): Malaita (Auki): Santa Cruz (Lata) and San Cristobal (Kira Kira). A mini hydro plant also operates at Malu'u on Malaita.
A standard tariff structure applies throughout the Solomon Islands. Currently domestic users are charged 5137.5 cents per KWh and commercial/industrial users 5155.5 cents per KWh. Tariff rates are reviewed quarterly and adjusted in line with oil price movements.Power generation and distribution is controlled by the Solomon Islands Electricity Authority.

Water
Water supply is controlled by the Ministry of Transport, Works and Utilities.
The Ministry supplies the first 10 metres of pipe from the mains free of charge, with the customer meeting the cost of installation for the remainder. In addition there is a $S1350 installation fee.
Domestic water rates are:

0 - 2,000 gallons	$2.60 - $3.90 (minimum)
2 001 - 8,000	$1.30 - $1.30
8 001 -19,000	$1.90 - $2.85
Above 19,000	$3.40 - $5.10

Industrial water rates are:

0-10,000 gallons	$15.00 - $22.50 (minimum)
10,001-20,000	$ 2.30 - $ 3.45
Above 20,000	$3.40 - $ 5.10

Sewerage and Disposal of Trade Effluent
Waste disposal is subject to individual arrangements.
As a rough guide, construction costs range from $512,300 per square metro for simple concrete slab and wood structures through to $513,000 per sq. metre for concrete and brick hotel type structures.

Roads
There are 2,900 km of sealed and unsealed roads in the Solomons. Hire cars are available on Guadacanal.

Sea Freight Services
International shipping services call at the major ports of Honiara, Noro and Yandina from Australia, New Zealand, Papua New Guinea and Singapore. An extensive network of inter-island shipping provides for smooth freight and passenger carriage to the smaller ports.
Solomons have direct shipping services to Australia, New Zealand and Papua New Guinea on Pacific Forum Lines with two sailings per month.
Honiara has a deep water berth, 120m long with a maximum depth of 9.2m alongside, capable of taking vessels up to 200m in length. In addition, there is an 85m wharf with a depth alongside of 3.4m and a barge ramp. Total warehouse space available is 54,000 square metres. Maximum forklift capacity is 32 ton. The port handles more than 300 ships per annum.

Noro Port on New Georgia has a wharf of 62m with a depth alongside of 14 m and is the main export port for canned fish. Covered transit storage of 500 5q. metres is available.
Yandina on the Russell Islands i5 the export port for Russell Islands Plantation Estates Limited. The wharf is 53m with a depth alongside of 6.4 m.

Air Services
International air services operate from the Henderson International Airport, Honiara.
Solomon Airlines, Qantas, Air Niugini and Air Nauru operate a total of 18 flights per week between the Solomons and Australia, New Zealand, Papua New Guinea, Tonga, Vanuatu, Fiji and Nauru.Solomon Airlines provides internal air transport to 22 airfields within the Solomons.

Telecommunications
Most major centres in the Solomons have international standard telecommunication facilities including IDD, Fax and Telex utilising a standard "B" earth station. Smaller centres are linked by either the domestic satellite service or VHF radio telephone.
Overseas service charges are set out below.

	Telephone per minute	Telex per minute

Australia	$S1 4.26	$SI 4.26
New Zealand/PNG/Fiji	$SI 4.46	$SI 4.46
Other Pacific Islands	$SI 5.41	$SI 5.41
Asia	$SI 8.5I	$SI 8.51
Rest	$SI 8.5I	$SI 8.5I

CENTRAL BANK OF SOLOMON ISLANDS

The Central Bank has responsibility for the Solomons' monetary system.

In managing foreign exchange, the basic principle applied is that all foreign exchange receipts become part of the official external reserves and that all foreign exchange payments are made by drawing on those reserves. The regulations are administered through the commercial banks who act as authorised dealers.

The financial aspects of trade in goods and services including forward exchange cover proceed with minimum interference. Capital transactions, borrowing remittances. etc. require specific Central Bank approval. Non-resident investors may not raise equity or long term capital from the Solomon Islands' banking system. Resident foreign investors may seek specific approval for such borrowing. Working capital is readily available.

Development Bank of Solomon Islands

The bank was established in 1987 as an independent statutory body to promote:

- Solomon Islanders' participation in economic development:
- rural development: and
- agri-processing, industrial activities and tertiary industries which might be expected to strengthen the economic independence of the Solomons.

Other Sources of Finance

The major commercial banks operating in the Solomons are Westpac Banking Corporation, The Australian and New Zealand Banking Group Limited and The National Bank of the Solomon Islands (major shareholder is Bank of Hawaii).
These banks pursue normal commercial banking practices in lending to the private sector.

GOVERNMENT POLICY

Industrial growth and development in Solomon Islands will continue to depend primarily on private sector reinvestment activity. In recognition of this, the Government continues to play a facilitating role in making the private sector more dynamic and growth-oriented.

It is the Government's expressed development policy to broaden the economic base of the country through diversified economic activities. In this regard, the Government recognises that private sector foreign investment can make enormous contributions to the achievement of this goal. With a strong belief in private capital investment, the

Government is committed to creating an economic climate which is conducive to private sector foreign investment.

The Solomons' Government is committed to pursuing policies aimed at achieving economic self reliance.

GOVERNMENT POLICY ON FOREIGN INVESTMENT

The Government of Solomon Islands places great emphasis on the encouragement of foreign investment in the private sector as the basis for growth and development. It also welcomes those investors whose development proposals are compatible with its national aims and objectives.

The net economic benefit of the proposed investment: Is the dominant consideration in assessing both the acceptability of an investment d the degree of assistance to be accorded. The assessment process will pay particular interest to impact of investment on;

- widening the productive base:
- strengthening the technical and marketing expertise of the private sector:
- generating either net export income or import cost savings: and
- providing employment and training, especially in regional areas.

In the medium term, the successful businesses within the Solomon Islands will be those that focus on import replacement.

GENEROUS INCENTIVES

Major incentive packages, tailored to the specific circumstances of the potential investor are available. Tax holidays of up to ten years are negotiable.
Income tax relief is often of paramount concern to a potential investor and is available in several forms under the Income Tax Act.
Benefits Include:

- Exemption from import duty on plant, machinery and equipment:
- Accelerated factory depreciation deduction:
- Double deduction for Bona-Fide sponsored apprentices:
- Double deduction for local and overseas training:
- No withholding tax on dividends arising and remitted during a ten year period plus a further period of five years up to a level of dividends that covers investment in the project:
- No withholding tax on interest paid to non-residents during a ten year period plus further period to a maximum of five years until the original project financial loans have been repaid.

Over and above this, the Government of Solomon Islands stands ready to consider proposals for:

Financial concessions under the Customs and Excise (Duties) (Amendments) Order 1991, including import and export (with re-export) duty exemptions and tariff protection: and

Assistance in such areas as obtaining suitable land tenure with related planning and design, infrastructure and communications support, staff recruiting and training and marketing.

In all cases, available concessions and incentives are essentially discretionary and, as such, must be specifically requested at the proposal stage when full details and reasons should be given.

Investment applications are evaluated according to the following criteria.

1. Priority will be given to projects that are net foreign exchange earners. If an applicant can adequately demonstrate that an export market is available for a product and provide evidence of links to that market, favourable consideration will be given.
2. Import substitution - priority will be given to projects that save hard currency, but cost, quality and quantity of the proposed import substitution will also be taken into account.
3. Special attention will be given to investments involving high levels of local value-added production using local primary products or other raw materials.
4. Positive consideration will be given to local value added production using imported raw materials that are not available locally.
5. Investments which involve high levels of local employment are located in low areas of employment and commercial or industrial activity will be given special consideration.
6. Only sound financial projects will be given support. Applicants are required to demonstrate adequate evidence of their ability to finance a project.
7. The overall net economic benefit in terms of duties, wages, tax revenues, foreign exchange earnings, multipliers and stimulative effects as well as social and environmental costs will be considered.
8. Favourable consideration will be given to projects that involve the transfer of technology training of local staff.

Generally, therefore, foreign investors will have to justify investment in terms of:
a) furthering economic development to the benefit of Solomon Islands:

b) employing citizens of Solomon Islands and training Solomon Islanders in technical and management skills:
c) using local raw materials, supplies and services:
d) potential for import substitution:
e) dispersal of investment to provinces: and
f) potential for technology transfer.
The Government is particularly encouraging the production of substitutes for imports by companies which can put together local manpower and raw materials in a basic processing operation. Ideally, this would involve some form of processing or manufacturing that would provide either import substitution or export opportunities.
The tax year follows the calendar year, although businesses may adopt an alternative accounting period. Returns of income are due within three months of balance date. Tax is payable within nine months of balance date.

INVESTMENT/POTENTIAL INVESTMENT SECTORS

FORESTRY

While the Government supports forestry sector investment, biodiversity, conservation and ecological preservation (replanting and cutting quotas) are major components in this sector's overall sustainable development strategy. Forests cover some 88% of the total land area of Solomon Islands, but only about 10% or 250,000 hectares are thought to be commercially workable. The forest products/timber sector is one of the backbones of the Solomon Islands' economic base. Although native timbers are abundant, commercial planting and reforestation are encouraged with a view to increasing the availability of raw timber for further local processing for both export and local consumption. Most of Solomon Islands timber is hard wood.

FAUNA

Solomon Islands has a unique biodiversity resources. The mammals of Solomon Islands include one of the world's richest diversity of bats and rats. The array of butterfly species are a great attraction.

BIRDS

Approximately 173 species of land birds live in the Solomon Islands. In fact Solomon Islands has the most diverse avifauna of all the Pacific Ocean Islands. Birds of Solomon Islands are by far the country's best - studied animal group. Because of its uniqueness and diversity, Solomon Islands avifauna should be regarded as being of international value and significance..

FLORA

Solomon Islands is rich in plant life. There is considerable scope for developing of herbal medicines and pharmaceutical products. Floristic products are an attraction for further development for both commercial and conservation purposes. Terresterial biodiversity is a potential investment sector but requires appropriate conservation and management planning.

FISHERIES & MARINE PRODUCTS

The Solomon Islands Economic Zone contains extremely rich ocean resources that are virtually untapped at present. For example, only half of the allowable catch of tuna fish is currently being exploited. Other areas of the fisheries sector which could see major developedment are deep sea and reef fishing as well as marine resource farming and breeding including aquaculture development of fish, prawns, crayfish, crabs, eels, clams and seaweed. There are opportunities for the development of commercial fisheries in Solomon Islands. Priority areas include tuna canning and processing, fish farming, and reef fish processing. Investment proposals for any of these activities will receive favourable consideration.

AGRICULTURE AND FOOD

The Solomon Islands is an agricultural country. Investments which have the objectives of commercial development to serve the growing population, increase the export earnings of the sector and provide for the material needs of food processing industries will receive favourable consideration. Henderson and Hancock (1988) identify 119 species of native plants that are important for food in the villages. 64 plant species are of agricultural value (crop protection, fencing and annual medicine).

SERVICE INDUSTRIES

Commercial banking, off-shore banking, insurance and other financial services are potential investment areas.

MINING

It is anticipated that by the end of the 1990s the majority of the world's gold will be sourced from the Pacific region. Current prospecting in the Solomon Islands reveals them to be rich in a variety of minerals including gold and bauxite and nickle. Use of the country's mineral resources including mining and processing greatly encouraged. Investment proposals for mineral prospecting and mining will receive favourable consideration. Prospecting for minerals and the actual mining of minerals are encouraged. Potential investors can contact the Solomon Islands Mission to the United Nations for more information and further consultation.

ENERGY

Use of available renewable energy sources is encouraged. Solar, wind and hydro power will become important sources of energy for urban and rural consumption.

TOURISM

1. adventure tourism

2. biodiversity tourism
3. cultural tourism

Hotel development with international standards will receive favourable consideration. Likewise, Island resorts development and eco - tourism will receive encouragement and support. Tourism related activities such as scuba diving, game fishing, fishing, cruise boats, etc, will also receive favorable consideration {ref ; }. The war relics from the Battle of Guadalcanal are a great attraction deserving appropriate investment.

TRANSPORTATION

With the large number of islands in the Solomon group there is room for the development of inter-province tourist and local passenger and freight shipping services. Construction and operation of vessels for such purposes as well as for export is highly desirable.

MANUFACTURING

Considerable opportunities exist in the manufacturing and processing industries. Priority is accorded to new investments that are import substitution oriented and export marketing oriented. Investments promoting the use of local or imported raw materials not available locally will also be encouraged. The abundance of tropical fruits such as pineapple, pawpaw, water melon, mango and guava provides attractive opportunities for investment.

TELECOMMUNICATIONS

The telecommunicatiions network has been upgraded and expanded extensively in the last five years and telephone connections are increasing at the rate of 30% per annum. The Solomon Telekom Company now maintains the best telecommunications facilities in the Pacific. Direct dial ISD and SID telephone, telex and facsimile services are readily available at competitive rates.

INVESTMENT/INCENTIVES

Investment incentives are expected to play a major role in shaping the pace and direction of the country's industrial development. The incentives will be applied with a degree of flexibility, for it is not possible to anticipate how far as possible the instruments to be relied upon will be sensitive and responsive to changing circumstances.

The regime of investment incentives will be streamlined and reoriented to induce import substitution activity, production for export markets and tourism development as means of reducing the country's dependence on imported manufactured goods and the export of primary products.

A well-defined regime of fiscal and other incentives will be made available to enterprises. These include:

- tax holiday
- investment allowance
- duty-free concessions
- training allowance
- market development allowance
- expansion allowance
- regional development allowance

INVESTMENT/RIGHTS OF FOREIGN INVESTORS

All foreign investors in Solomon Islands are entitled to

- repatriation of dividends on a current basis
- repatriation of capital, incorporated into their rights to sell their shares in a local operation
- access to and use of the country's stock of foreign reserves in accordance with the policies and procedures governing such use
- liberal and flexible levels of shareholding and directorships
- enjoy the benefits and rewards of all legitimate entrepreneurial efforts including payments for patents, technology, management, technical assistance as well as other special provisions.
- work permits and residential permits for approved levels of foreign workers under conditions governing the granting of such permits
- all rights under the Solomon Islands constitution and before the law
- the settlement of disputes in accordance with internationally agreed criteria and the laws of Solomon Islands

For further information or discussion of investment, please contact:

Permanent Secretary Ministry of Commerce, Employment and Trade P.O. Box G26 Honira Solomon Islands Telephone: (677) 22378	High Commissioner Solomon Islands High Commission 1st Floor JAA Building Unit 4/19 Napier Close Deakin P.O. Box 256 Deaking West ACT 2600

Fax: (677) 25084	Australia Telephone: (06) 282 7030 Fax: (06) 282 7040
The Ambassador Permanent Mission of Solomon Islands to the United Nations 820 Second Avenue, Suite 800B New York, New York 10017 Telephone: (212) 599 - 6192 Fax: (212) 661 - 8925 E-mail: simny@solomons.com	Solomon Islands Consul-General I Solomon Islands Consulate-General 97 Creek Street Brisbane, QLD 4000 Australia Telephone: (07) 221 - 7899 Fax: (07) 221 - 2296
Ambassador Solomon Islands Mission to the European Community Avenue de L'Yser, 13 Bte 3 1040 Bruxelles Belgium Telephone: (32 - 2) 732 - 70 . 85 Fax: (32 -2) 732 - 68 . 85	Honorary Consul Solomon Islands Honorary Consulate 19 Springfield Road London SW19 7AL United Kingdom Telephone: (44-181) 946 - 1744 Fax: (44-181) 946 - 1744
Foreign Investment Board Ministry of Commerce Industries & Employement P.O. Box G-26 Honiara, Solomon Islands Telephone: (677) 21849 Fax: (677) 21651	**Ministry of Commerce Employement & Trade** P.O. Box G-26 Honiara, Solomon Islands Telephone: (677) 21849 Fax: (677) 25084

SELECTED BUSINESS OPPORTUNITIES

Business Opportunities and Classifieds
Department of Commerce, Employment and Trade
PO Box G26, Honiara, Solomon Islands
Tel: (677)25095 Fax (677) 22808
Email : commerce@commerce.gov.sb
See also: Online Business Information Service

VAMATAKA Development Company wholly locally owned by indiginous resources owners.
We are interested in joint-venture with foreign Co. sharing basis of 50%:50%
We are interested in venturing into timbers, tourist, food processing, local farm produce for export such as pineapple, cassava, mangoes etc. We have abundant supply of timber resources of different variaties, fertile land and beautiful toursit sites.
For more information contact the Chairman of B.O.D
Martin Tolule
C/o: Email: commerce@commerce.gov.sb

TO WHOM IT MAY CONCERN: The following Dog tags are available for sale to anyone who would be interested.

BUSTER SHAW
34247708 T43
FARIE WHITKER
GEN DEL
WILDWOOD FLORIDA
WILLIAM CURTIN JR
T42 20143693 COD
JENSINE CURTIN
BL ELSNERE AVE.
50. PORTLAND, ME. B
GANNON WILLIAM DAVID
616 18 54
T-3-42
U.S.N.R

For more Information Please contact dept of Commerce:
Tel:+677 25095
Fax: +677 22808
C/o Email: commerce@commerce.gov.sb

SECURITY SERVICE:A local registered company by the name of PEACE MAKER PROTECTIVE HOLDINGS is looking for any interested individual or company who would be interested in establishing a joint venture partnership with the aim of providing security service to its clients. The company will be based in Honiara the capital of Solomon Islands.

For more information contact:
Director of Peace Maker Protective Holdings
PO Box 1785
Honiara
Solomon Islands
Tel: +677 21652
c/o Email: commerce@commerce.gov.sb

To Whom it may Concern: Investment Opportunity. Renbel Limited is an incorporated registered local company, having its office here in Honiara and a branch base at Lavagu Seaport on Rennell and Bellona Province. Renbel Ltd, is involved in the following marine products activities;

- Reef fish (frozen)
- crayfish, tail only (frozen)
- bech-ce-mer (dried)
- shark fins (dried)

We would like to invite any genuine foreign investors who would be interested in assisting in harvesting and maybe can provide a boat on a partnership basis with us.
For further details contact:
George Tuhaika
Managing Director
PO Box 592
Honiara
Tel: +677 25114
c/o Email: commerce@commerce.gov.sb

The following local is seeking investors to farm Oysters at Rarumana, Parara Island in the Western Province. The place is ideal for Oyster farm. Any interested parties should contact the Ministry of Commerce for further details.
The local farmer is also looking for potential buyers of seaweed with the Common Name: Euchema or Cottonii and Scientific Name: Kappaphycus sp.
Email: commerce@commerce.gov.sb
Fax: +677 22808
Posted 17th May 2004

Mangakiki Families Teak project was started in 2001. Total number of hectare planted which are 3 years old is 26/ha and planting still continue.
Land tenure system is customary but not disputed because the families own land. These families have acquired technique and knowledge how to manage and look after Teak plantation after the Solomon Islands Forestry Project Management has conducted a 2 days workshop at the Project location in March 2003 covering Teak nursery Silviculture of teak ect..
The project has an official committee with elected Office Bearers of a Chairman, Vice Chairman, Treasurer, Secretary and Committee members.
The project is interested in:

- 1. Buyers with funds for maintenance at the early stage of the plantation.
- 2. Buyers with genuine interest on harvesting proposals which can be negotiated.
- 3. Funding Agencies which can provide fund for forestry project or reforestation.

Project location: Mangakiki Village, West Guadalcanal 30Km from Honiara and can be reached by boat or by vehicle.
Enquiries should be addresses to:
Mr. Hillary Limanipiru
Chairman, Mangakiki Teak Committee
C/o Email: commerce@commerce.gov.sb
Posted 22nd March 2004
A teak farmer located on the Island of Choiseul is looking for any interested buyers of teak wood who can assist him in maintaining the plantation. The area contents 1000 trees of height 7m and covering an area of 5 hectares. Visits are welcome.
Email the Ministry of commerce for more details.

San Jorge Resources Development (SJRD) will be exporting Tubi a very durable Tropical Hard Wood. We have already been issued the Liscense to harvest.
Local Name: Tubi
Scientific name: Xanthostemon
Common name: Sp
We are looking for buyers, prices and size specifications.
As prohibited species, SJRD will be the only company issued to harvest this species in the Solomon Islands.
For more detailed information we can be contacted on email: dth8@hotmail.com or C/o Ministry of Commerce email:commerce@commerce.gov.sb

SOLOMON ISLANDS GOVERNMENT

PROGRAMME OF ACTION

POLICY, OBJECTIVES, STRATEGIES AND TARGETS 2002-2005

The National Coalition Government for Peace Unity and Restoration was formed on December 17, 2001, the date the Prime Minister was elected to the Office. The Government is fully mindful of its clear mandate from the electorate to chart a new direction for the country's Political and Constitutional Development. The mandate also embraces sustaining the Peace Process, restoration of Law and Order, and the reconstruction and revitalization of the nation's shattered Economy.
This programme is a people-oriented plan to advance Solomon Islands. Its formulation emanates from the manifesto and policy statements of the People's Alliance Party (PAP) and the Association of Independent Members of Parliament (AIMP), the two groups which make up the coalition. Hence, this document will form the basis for the formulation of the National Development Plan 2002 - 2005.

This plan of action will be guided by the five principles of:

- Re-direction;
- Reconstruction;

- Participation;
- Production;
- Distribution.

These principles will be advanced to serve the needs of the people of Solomon Islands. This plan of advance will lay the foundation for Solomon Islands to face the challenges and take advantage of the opportunities presented by the 21st century.

This programme carries the message of change. We have to accept changes as inevitable and effect necessary adjustments, however painful they may be. Hence, one of the cornerstones of this plan is Re-direction. This is fitting and proper. For the past twenty years we have been soul searching for the best system of decentralization that would augur National Unity that our people desire. The Government believes that we should no longer defer the inevitable. Therefore, the Government will put in motion major constitutional reforms to change the form and system of Government from the present unitary constitutional monarchy to a democratic Federal Republic within the Commonwealth of Nations.

In line with the principle of Re-direction the Government will embark on a revised economic restructuring and structural adjustments. This programme aims at right-sizing the Public Service and shift resources to advance a private sector-led growth in the economy. Furthermore, the Government intends to re-establish confidence in the Securities Market by refraining from domestic borrowing as well as servicing and settling the Nation's outstanding debts within a reasonable period.

In consonance with the principle of Reconstruction, the Government will take steps to consolidate and sustain thePeace Process and restore as well as maintain Law and Order in the country. Steps will also be taken to reconstruct the Nation's Social and Economic Infrastructure, halt the descending economic trend, stabilize and reverse it, and thereby attain economic recovery. In our efforts to embark on this difficult but worthwhile task, we will have to be progressive. We do not wish to build a community of consumers. Instead we will seek and accept outside assistance that is genuine and meaningful for our people.

This plan also maps out the course of action we will take. Like any other course of action, there are risks involved.That is the worth of the challenge at hand. These risks notwithstanding, I believe the time demands action - and action with a purpose. The greatest danger of all would be to do nothing. What we require is the political will, vision, determination, faith, hard work and human ingenuity to navigate the affairs of our nation safety and firmly in both calm and stormy seas.

My good people of Solomon Islands, I commend this Plan of Action to you. For us to succeed, we will need the co-operation, understanding and active participation of each and every citizen. Let us put the interest of others and the nation first before our own. Let us ask not what our country can do for us. Rather, let us ask what, together, we can do for our country - Solomon Islands.

………………………………………………………

Honourable Sir Allan Kemakeza
PRIME MINISTER

ACKNOWLEDMENT

The National Coalition Government acknowledges the effort, time and commitment of persons and organizations that have assisted in putting together the Government's Program of Action. Gratitude is due to the Office of the Prime Minister in providing funds to put this document together and the Solomon Islands Printers for printing and binding this volume. Special thanks are due to the Manager and the former Executive Secretary of the People's Alliance Party Office as well as assistance given by the Secretariat of the Association of Independent Members of Parliament (AIMP). Their inputs have been invaluable.

....

Sir George Lepping
(GCMG, MBE, KSt J)
Chairman of the Task Force

PART ONE MISSION STATEMENT

The National Coalition Government (NCG) comprising at its core elected MPs from the Peoples Alliance Party (PAP) and elected MPs from the Association of Independent Members Group (AIMG) assumed power when the country had reached its lowest. From the very beginning, there was little doubt that the sovereign mandate to lead the country was a heavy one. The weight and welter of such a mandate involves holding together the country when it had almost fall asunder. We thank God for His mercy and grace that had augur so well for us even at our lowest period in our National Life!
That aside, the NCG is committed to a Vision. This Vision is to offer Solomon Islanders hope and get hold of opportunities, however rare the latter come these days. NCG hopes to do this through the provision of Confident Political Leadership and the Reworking of the Shattered Economy. This is pusued in the hope that Solomon Islands will, once again, prosper as a united Nation of diverse Traditions and Cultures.
In pursuing this Vision, NCG is charged with a Mission. Acting on the Mercy, Guidance and Direction of the Almighty, energized with the Mandate from the people of Solomon Islands and embracing the Principles of Good and Responsible Governance, NCG strives in the earnest to fulfill the following Mission goals: Restore Law and Order so that Peace, Harmony and Investment Confidence return to Solomon Islands; Revive the Economy in order that Productivity, Growth and Prosperity are achieved; Reform the Political System to increase Peoples' Participation in decision-making and in so doing, strengthen Good Governance; and Reform the Government System in order to improve Efficiency, beef up Service Delivery and enlarge our Financial Capability.

In pursuing the above goals, the Government is cognizant of the need to continue with some of the ongoing programs and projects that had, hitherto fore, been pursued. In all these, fundamental adjustments have to be made in order to facilitate Sustainable Progress and ensure Prosperity

We invite and call on the Provincial Assemblies, Church Leaders, Leaders in the Public and Private Sectors, Village Leaders, Women Leaders and Youth Leaders and our Students to assist us work toward Peace and Harmony and to better the quality of life for all Solomon Islanders.

PART TWO CHALLENGES, PRINCIPLES & OBJECTIVES

INTRODUCTION

- The challenges facing the Government over the past ethnic conflict period are formidable. But with determination and political will are not unsolvable. Some of these challenges call for immediate attention whilst others can be addressed on a medium to long-term basis.
- Hence, whilst the Government is mindful of the diverse needs of the country, it is presented with a position where it has to set priorities to address urgent issues and simultaneously pay attention to medium and long term planning. Along with the afore-mentioned any established policy framework will have to control and monitor the distribution of limited resources to ensure the principles of fairness and equity are upheld.

IMMEDIATE CHALLENGES

- The Government will give priority attention to the following issues during its first year in office.
- Law and Order
    - The restoration of Law and Order and hence internal security is crucial if the peace process is to be sustained, public confidence and normalcy restored for the revitalization of the economy.
    - The Government will undertake these measures:
    - Set a date [31st.May 2002] for the return of illegal arms as required by the Amnesty Act;
    - Take appropriate measures to restore discipline in the Police Force;
    - Reduce the number of Special Constables to an affordable level required by the Police Force as stipulated in the TPA;
    - Strengthen the Police Force by continuing recruitment and training;
    - Ensure that all arms presently held by Police and Prison Service Officers are returned to the Armory and strictly keep a register of arms leaving the Armory for operational purposes;
    - Aggressively pursue disarming of those in possession of illegal firearms; ammunitions and weapons of war.
    - Arrest, detain and prosecute perpetrators of criminal activities.

PEACE PROCESS

The following will be undertaken:

- As soon as practicable reconvene Townsville Peace Agreement (TPA) review meetings between the parties to the agreement;
- Engage the Melanesian Brotherhood [Tasius] of the Church of Melanesia to assist in the retrieval of arms, ammunition and weapons of war;
- Prudently continue to pay reasonable compensation where proper and appropriate for properties lost as required by the TPA;
- Seek funding for the rehabilitation of ex-combatants in genuine cases;
- Implement the demobilization, reintegration and rehabilitation programs;

- Initiate dialogue with the discontented elements of the Isatabu Freedom Movement with a view to bringing them to accept and be involved in the Peace process.

FINANCE

The following will be undertaken:
Monetary Sector

- Re-establish confidence in the securities markets by servicing and settling outstanding debts;
- Refrain from domestic borrowing to prevent a crowding out of the private sector;
- Protect and ensure that the foreign exchange is maintained at a satisfactory level.

Fiscal Sector

- Broaden the taxation base;
- Strengthen collection of government revenue;
- Amend the Customs and Excise Act to vest the discretionary power of granting remissions in acommittee;
- Establish a cash flow unit in the Ministry;
- Reduce the government's expenditure on payroll and other payments;
- Maintain a creditable budget by ensuring its integrity;
- Privatise ICSI port folio companies where appropriate;
- Privatise the Development Bank of Solomon Islands (DBSI);
- Work on reviving these projects:
    - SIPL
    - Gold Ridge Mining

PRINCIPLES

The following are Principles which the Government has adopted as guidelines for the process of National Development and Nation-building:

- Continue to uphold the democratic principles of universal suffrage and the responsibility of executive authorities to elected bodies;
- Advance and uphold the principles of equality, social justice and the sharing of costs and benefits of the development of our resources;
- Respect and enhance human dignity and strengthen the building of our communal solidarity;
- Cherish and promote the different cultural traditions within Solomon Islands to achieve diversity in unity;
- Ensure active participation of our people in the governance of their affairs and provide within the framework of our national unity for the decentralization of power;
- Provide good leadership to encourage our people to be purposeful in the development of their resources and thereby be able to contribute to the building

up of Solomon Islands to be an inclusive society in line with our good, traditional and cultural norms and practices;
- Promote self-reliance as a means to encouraging our people to be productive in all spheres of development;and
- Encourage partnerships in development and adopt a gender-balanced approach in education and employment on the basis of just opportunity for all our people.

NATIONAL OBJECTIVES

The following National Objectives have been set by the Government:

- Consolidate and sustain the Peace Process and the restoration of Law and Order to ensure the nation attains peace, unity and harmony;
- Reconstruct the social and economic infrastructure, halt the current economic decline, stabilize and reverse it, thereby attain economic recovery;
- Downsizing the Public Service and shift resources towards private sector driven economic growth;
- Servicing and settling the nation's debts within reasonable time and maintain greater financial sustainability and stability;
- Foster a greater sense of National Unity and Identity;
- Promote better distribution of the benefits of development and ensure a healthy, to literate and a contended population;
- Achieve political stability and de-centralized decision making;
- Generate job opportunities for Solomon Islands growing population;
- Achieve higher economic growth, wealth and social well-being for all in Solomon Islands;
- Advance Solomon Islands for its existence in the 21st century; and
- Ensure Solomon Islands is properly governed.

PART THREE: PRIORITIES

The Government will give priority attention to the following issues during its first year in office.

RESTORATION OF LAW AND ORDER

- The restoration of Law and Order and hence internal security is crucial if the peace process is to be sustained;public confidence and normalcy should be restored to allow for the revitalization of the economy.
- The Government will undertake these measures:
  - Set a date for the return of illegal arms as required by the Amnesty Act;
  - Take appropriate measures to restore discipline in the Police Force;
  - Reduce the number of Special Constables to an affordable level required by the Police Force;
  - Strengthen the Police Force by continuing recruitment and training;
  - Ensure that all arms presently held by Police and Prison Service Officers are returned to the RSIPF Armory and strictly keep a register of arms leaving the RSIPF Armory for operational purposes;
  - Aggressively pursue disarming of those in possession of illegal firearms; ammunitions and weapons of war;

- Arrest, detain and prosecute perpetrators of criminal activities; and
- Implement the Amnesty Acts.

PEACE PROCESS

The following will be undertaken:

- As soon as practicable reconvene Townsville Peace Agreement (TPA) review meetings between the parties to the Agreement;
- Engage the Melanesian Brotherhood [Tasius] of the Church of Melanesia to assist in the retrieval of arms,ammunition and weapons of war;
- Prudently continue to pay reasonable compensation where proper and appropriate for lost properties as required by the TPA;
- Seek funding for the rehabilitation of ex-combatants where there are genuine cases;
- Implement the demobilization, reintegration and rehabilitation programs;
- Initiate and continue dialogue with the discontented elements of the Isatabu Freedom Movement [IFM] who were not parties to the TPA with a view to bringing them to accept and to be involved in the Peace process;
- Encourage women, youth, Churches, NGOs, Traditional Leaders and other members of the Civil Society to actively participate in the Peace Process; and
- Strengthen the Peace and Reconciliation Committee (PRC) to efficiently and effectively play its role in the Peace Process so as to advance National Reconciliation and Healing.

CONSTITUTIONAL, LEGISLATIVE, POLITICAL & STRUCTURAL REFORM:

- Neither centralization nor de-centralization guarantees complete national unity. This depends ultimately on the will of the people who make up the Nation- State. It is in this context that the desire of Provinces towards more autonomy in the form of Statehood cannot be ignored nor deferred for a later time. It is in the National Interest of Solomon Islands that a home-grown Federal System of Government which takes into serious consideration the unity, rights, wishes, security, prosperity, participation and pursuits of happiness of all the people in the Country can be encouraged, designed, established and progressively brought into operation as soon as practicable.
- Political stability is essential to the Nation's development and progress. The Government intends to take appropriate actions to remove any legal or administrative impediments to its political reform and progress. In the interest of developing the political party system it will also consider providing financial assistance to legallyestablished functioning political parties which meet certain required criteria, standards and code of conduct for leaders will also be drawn up and enforced.
- The following will be undertaken:
    - Appoint a Constitutional Council to rewrite the Constitution with the view to effect major constitutional reforms to change the system of Government from a Unitary Constitutional Monarchy to a sovereign democratic Federal Republic within the Commonwealth of Nations. This is

taking into account the report of the "State Government Task Force 2001";

- Reduce the number of Ministries to 10 whilst retaining 20 Political Heads of Departments;
- Establish a revised Economic and Structural Reform Program;
- Introduce a special Provincial Government Bill in Parliament to defer elections in dissolved Provincial Assemblies for one year in view of the Government's current financial difficulties;
- Introduce an amendment to the Customs and Excise Act which vests the discretionary power of granting remissions in a committee;
- Effect political reforms to ensure political stability by reforming the constitution to:
- Provide for a Political party with the majority after a general election to form the Government; and Cause elected MPs who switch party affiliations to automatically vacate their seats and bye-elections be held.

EDUCATION

Education is a right and all citizens should have access to it as a matter of right. In its resolve to revitalize the education sector in the post conflict period the Government will ensure that a minimum level of Education Services are restored and maintained. The Government will also undertake:

- Strengthen the Education Services for the populace making certain that all women and children have access to basic Education Services;
- Launch a program which include the rehabilitation of schools, Rural Training Centers, supply of school materials to new schools. This will be done in partnership with concerned groups including development partners;
- Review the education system with a view to doing away with elimination exams until Form 5. It should subsidize school fees until Form 6; and
- Adopt as a matter of policy the establishment of and support for Vocational Training Schools as a stream parallel to the academic stream.

HEALTH AND MEDICAL SERVICES

Access to proper health care is the right of every citizen. The Government subscribes to the conviction that "healthy people make a healthy nation". In its resolve to revitalize the health sector the Government will restore and maintain basic Health Services. The Government will also undertaken to:

- Strengthen the Health and Medical Services to make it certain all women and children have access to basic Health Services;
- Launch a program which include the rehabilitation of health centers and clinics, the provision of needed drugs and construction of new clinics. This program will be carried out with the active participation and partnership of parents, communities, NGOs and development partners;
- Convene a National Health Seminar to address all related health issues including HIV-AIDS 'epidemic' in the Asia-Pacific region;
- Work towards the general acceptance of the Primary Health Care Program to achieve the global aim of "Health for All" by the year 2005.

FINANCE

The following will be undertaken:
Monetary Sector

- Re-establish confidence in the securities markets by servicing and settling outstanding debts;
- Refrain from domestic borrowing to crowd out the private sector;
- Protect and ensure that the foreign exchange is maintained at a satisfactory level.

Fiscal Sector

- Broaden the taxation base;
- Strengthen collection of government revenue;
- Amend the Customs and Excise Act to vest discretionary power of growing remissions in a committee;
- Establish a cash flow unit in the Ministry;
- Reduce government's expenditure on payroll and other payments;
- Maintain a creditable budget by ensuring its integrity;
- Privatise ICSI post folio companies where appropriate;
- Privatise the Development Bank of Solomon Islands (DBSI);
- Work on reviving the projects:
  - SIPL
  - Gold Ridge Mining

PRODUCTIVE SECTOR

Agriculture

The following will be undertaken:

- Revive and reopen SIPL
- Encourage all forms of rice growing
- Assist farmers to establish source farms for domestic consumption as well as for export
- Provide assistance to rehabilitate cocoa and coffee projects and increase cocoa and coffee planting
- Accelerate the development of the Palm Oil Plantation on Vangunu, Western Province and the 'out-grower scheme
- Privatise the livestock industry - LDA
- Identify, diversify and encourage other cash crops for export
- Actively pursue the development of the Aluta Basin Palm Oil project

Lands

The Government will undertake the following in this sector:

- Introduce the Lands Titles Act Amendment Bill in Parliament

- Collect all outstanding land rentals and institute legal action against those who fail to pay up
- Return selected alienated land to identified rightful land-owners
- Complete work on peri-urban policy on TOL areas
- Immediate reviewing of land/s that have been properly and lawfully granted but have not been developed with a view to repossessing those lands
- Identify, acquire and allocate land for development in urban centers and rural areas

Forestry

The following will be undertaken:

- Encourage local and foreign logging companies that have suspended operations to restart their activities and issue licences to new ones.
- Expand domestic and export market for plantation and indigenous timber.
- Review and amend the relevant sections of the Forestry Act.
- Increase sustainable harvesting of plantations and natural forest timber strands.
- Continue to encourage the privatisation of the re-aforestation programs and projects.
- Encourage tree planting on smallholder basis throughout the country.

Fisheries

The following will be undertaken:

- Review fishing licence fee, charges and levies.
- Rehabilitate fisheries in rural areas and provide training and financial assistance to local fishermen to engage in more commercially based fishing activities.
- Rehabilitate giant clam farms and encourage the setting up of pearl/oyster, sea-weed, bech-de-mer farms and research and development projects of the above.
- Encourage a controlled and sustainable export of live reef fish.

Tourism

The following will be undertaken:

- Recruit under Technical Assistance the head of the Tourism Division.
- Recruit under Technical Assistance an advisor to the Solomon Islands Visitors Bureau [SIVB].
- Reduce through subsidy international airfares of Solomon Islands Airlines for a reasonable period.
- Dispatch a delegation to discuss with relevant countries which still place travel embargoes by advising their citizens not to travel Solomon Islands.
- Continue to aggressively promote Solomon Islands overseas as a safe (or an alternative) tourist destination.
- Rehabilitate tourism facilities and encourage credit line to set up Eco-tourism establishments especially in rural areas.

Infrastructure Development

Existing social and economic infrastructure are either affected by the effects of the ethnic conflict or in need of urgent maintenance. The rehabilitation of these infrastructure and building of new ones are essential to revitalise the economy. The Government is therefore committed to rehabilitate social and economic infrastructure and building new ones needed to facilitate halting of the current economic decline, stabilise and finally reverse it to achieve economic recovery.

Commerce Trade and Industries

The following will be undertaken:

- Review the operations and functions of CEMA with the view to divesting of its monopoly status.
- Approach the MSG member countries to understand Solomon Islands need to place tariffs on imports currently enjoyed as non-tariff under the MSG's Trade Agreement.
- In collaboration with the private sector, formulate a recovery program for industries and business ventures that have suffered from the ethnic conflict.
- Review or amend the Foreign Investment Act, Immigration Act, Employment Act and Passport Act.
- Formulate investment profiles and promote them to interested foreign investors and developers.
- Establish and declare 'duty-free zones' within the Country.
- Continue work on the Noro Industrial Township, Bina Harbour Industrial Port and Wairokai Indutrial Seaport;
- Establish work on Selwyn Bay Industrial seaport; and
- Establish work on Vanikoro Industrial Seaport.

GOVERNMENT FUNCTIONS

OFFICE OF THE PRIME MINISTER

- Coordination of Ministerial Functions
- Cabinet
- National Development Council
- National Parliamentary and Political Affairs
- Constitutional Affairs
- Information
- Honours and Awards
- National Security

STATUTORY AUTHORITY

- Solomon Islands Broadcasting Corporation
- Commission of inquiry
- Leadership Code Commission
- Ombudsman Commission
- Public Service Commission
- Judicial & Legal Service Commission

- Police and Prison Service Commission
- Teaching Service Commission
- National Education Commission (proposed)

MINISTRY OF HOME AND ECCLESIASTICAL AFFAIRS

- Citizenship
- Local Government - Honiara City
- Electoral Functions
- Ecclesiastical Affair
- Gaming and Lotteries
- Public Holidays
- Cinematography & Censorship
- National Archives
- National Disasters

STATUTORY AUTHORITY

- National Disaster Council
- Gaming and Lottery Board
- Honiara City Council
- Electoral Commission

MINISTRY OF FINANCE

- The Budget
- Banking
- Loans and Guarantees
- Statistics
- Treasury
- Internal Auditing Systems & Stock verification
- Aid Management (Bilateral & Multi-lateral)
- Inland Revenue
- Custom & Excise
- Insurance
- Price Control
- Central Tendering
- Financial Management & Accountability
- Macroeconomic Policy

STATUTORY AUTHORITY

- Central Bank of Solomon Islands
- Solomon Islands National Provident Fund
- Investment Corporation of Solomon Islands
- Development Bank of Solomon Islands
- Credit Union League
- Home of Finance Corporation

- Peoples Bank (Proposed)
- Solomon Islands Unit Trust (Proposed)
- Auditor General Office
- Central Tender Board

MINISTRY OF ECONOMIC REFORMS & STRUCTURAL ADJUSTMENTS

- Constitutional & Legislative Reforms
- Public Service Reforms
- Monetary & Fiscal Reforms
- Sectoral Reforms
- Institutional Reforms

MINISTRY OF RECONCILIATION PEACE AND NATIONAL UNITY

- Peace Process
- Reconciliation
- Rehabilitation

MINISTRY OF FOREIGN AFFAIRS

- Foreign Affairs
- Diplomatic Relations - Bilateral & Multilateral
- Consular matters and Relations
- Protocol -Ceremonials
- Representations- Overseas Missions
- Treaties and Conventions
- Trade Relations

MINISTRY OF FORESTRY, ENVIRONMENT & CONSERVATION

- Forestry
- Research
- Environment & Conservation
- Timber Marketing and Research
- Licensing

STATUTORY AUTHORITY

- Timber & Marketing Board (Proposed)

MINISTRY OF COMMERCE, EMPLOYMENT & TRADE

- Investment
- Local Entrepreneurship
- Immigration
- Labour
- Trade and Testing

- Industrial Development
- Trade-Internal & International
- Commerce

STATUTORY AUTHORITY

- Commodity Export Marketing Authority
- Solomon Islands Ports Authority
- Investment Board

MINISTRY OF LANDS & SURVEYS

- Lands
- Surveys
- Hydrography
- Housing
- Physical Planning
- Cartography
- Resettlement

MINISTRY OF NATIONAL PLANNING

- National Development Planning
- Manpower Planning
- Policy Evaluation and Monitoring
- Coordination and implementation of Programs
- Project Formulations, Appraisal & Funding
- Population Planning
- Micro Projects Unit

MINISTRY OF CULTURE, TOURISM & AVIATION

- Tourism Development
- Cultural Affairs
- Aviation
- Meteorology
- National Museum
- National Art Gallery & Cultural Center
- Relics, Monuments & Memorials

STATUTORY AUTHORITY

- Solomon Islands Visitors Bureau
- Civil Aviation Authority (Proposed)
- Air Transport Licensing Authority
- National Cultural Commission (Proposed)

MINISTRY OF PROVINCIAL GOVERNMENT AND RURAL DEVELOPMENT

- Provincial Government Development
- Provincial Budgets
- Rural Development
- Provincial Development Unit

MINISTRY OF TRANSPORT, WORKS & COMMUNICATIONS

- Infrastructure Development (Road & Bridges)
- Shipping and Maritime
- Communications
- Postal Services
- Spectrum
- Television
- Land Transport

STATUTORY AUTHORITY

- Postal Corporation
- Solomon Islands Television Board

MINISTRY OF HEALTH AND MEDICAL SERVICES

- Health & Medical Services
- Institutional Infrastructure Development
- Environmental Health
- Social Welfare
- Health Education
- Population Control

STATUTORY AUTHORITY

- Medical Board
- Dental Board
- Hospital Board
- Nursing Council
- Pharmaceutical Board
- Practitioners Board

MINISTRY OF POLICE NATIONAL SECURITY AND JUSTICE

- Law and Order
- Police Training
- Law enforcement and security
- Fire Service
- Vehicle Licensing and Registration
- Traffic

- Solomon Islands National Reconnaissance and Surveillance Force
- Law Reform
- Public Solicitor
- Director of Public Prosecution
- Attorney General Chambers
- Fire Arms Control & Licensing

MINISTRY OF MINES, ENERGY AND WATER RESOURCES

- Mining
- Mining Exploration
- Energy
- Water Resources
- Geology
- Licensing
- Hydrology

STATUTORY AUTHORITY

- Solomon Island Electricity Authority
- Solomon Islands Authority

MINISTRY OF EDUCATION AND TRAINING

- Institutional Infrastructure Development
- Education Policy
- Schools and Education Institutions
- Inspectorate
- Curriculum
- Selection and Guidance
- Informal Education
- Teaching Services
- Library Services
- Scholarship

STATUTORY AUTHORITY

- Solomon Islands College of Higher Education

MINISTRY OF WOMEN, YOUTH AND SPORTS DEVELOPMENT

- Youth Development
- Sports Development
- Women Development
- Parks

STATUTORY AUTHORITY

- National Council of Women
- National Youth Congress
- National Sports Council

MINISTRY OF AGRICULTURE AND LIVESTOCK

- Agriculture
- Quarantine
- Livestock
- Research
- Extension
- Farm Management and Development

STATUTORY AUTHORITY

- Livestock Development Authority

MINISTRY OF FISHERIES AND MARINE RESOURCES

- Fisheries Resources
- Marine Resources
- Fisheries Licensing
- Marine Conservation

OFFICE OF THE PRIME MINISTER

BACKGROUND

The office of the Prime Minister is fully responsible for the overall coordination of the government through the executive collective decisions of the Cabinet and Caucus.

FUNCTIONS OF THE OFFICE

(i) The following Portfolio subjects are formally assigned to this office:

- Coordination of Ministerial Functions;
- Cabinet;
- Public Service;
- National Policy Unit (NPU);
- National Parliamentary and Political Affairs;
- Constitutional Affairs and Development;
- Information;
- Honors and Awards; and
- National Security.

(ii) This Office is responsible and answerable for the following Statutory Authorities:

- Solomon Islands Broadcasting Corporation;
- Commission of Inquiry;
- Leadership Code Commission;
- Public Service Commission;
- Ombudsman Commission;
- Judicial & Legal Service Commission;
- Police and Prison Service Commission; and
- Teaching Service Commission.

3. POLICY OBJECTIVES
The Objectives of the Office are to:

- Coordinate the work of all Ministers and their Line Ministries;
- Progressively develop the National Constitution with a view to effect major Constitutional Reforms to change the form and system of Government form a Unitary Constitutional Monarchy to a sovereign Democratic Federal Republic with the Commonwealth of Nations;
- Effect political reforms to ensure political stability and participation of all citizens in the governance of the country;
- Strengthen the Government solidarity through full participation of the Government backbenchers;
- Develop an information delivery system that plays its role in the promotion of National development, unity and identity;
- Enhance Parliamentary Democracy through strengthening and developing of the National Parliament

  Infrastructure, Services and Parliamentary practices;

- Improve efficiency, productivity, cost effectiveness and service delivery of the Public Service;
- Introduce and implement a revised Reform and Structural Adjustment Program;
- Improve bilateral relations with selected countries; and
- Restoration of National Security.

4. DEVELOPMENT STRATEGIES
In pursuit of its objective this Office shall be guided by the following strategies:

- Establish a Policy, Security and Coordinating Unit;
- Establish a (Think Tank) within the Office of the Prime Minister;
- Recruit a legal advisor, economic and financial advisor to work in the Prime Ministers Office; and
- Take an active role in developing bilateral relationship with selected Asian countries.

5. PROGRAM TARGETS: 2002 - 2005
The Office shall pursue the following program targets:

- Appoint the Constitutional Council to rewrite the Constitution taking into account the report of the "State Government Task Force 2001";
- Establish a Policy Security and Coordinating Unit and a "Think Tank" within the Prime Minister's Office;
- Recruit legal, financial and economic advisors;
- Engage back-benchers as Board Chairpersons, Chairpersons of Parliamentary Standing Committees and on special assignments;
- Lead a business delegation to Malaysia, Singapore, Japan and Republic of China;
- To provide for political stability by reforming the Constitution to:
  - Provide for a Political Party with the majority after General Elections to form the Government;
  - Elected Members of Parliament who switch party membership after General Elections to automatically lose their seats and seek re-election.
- Review the Leadership Code (Further Provision Act) and Ombudsman Commission (Further Provisions Act);
- Introduce a revised Reform and Structural Adjustment Program;
- Review the Public Service Act taking into account the following:
  - Rightsizing of the Public Service;
  - Recruit suitable persons under Technical Assistance to head the Public Service;
  - Public Service Wage Structure;
  - All Senior Officers be required to sign "Performance Contracts" with the Public Service Commission;
  - NPF Scheme to replace Pensions Scheme;
  - In-service Training; and
  - Appropriate examinations to be set up for Public Service recruitment and promotions.
- Continue to put in place an Act of Parliament for the Terms and Conditions of Former Prime Ministers;
- Arrange Provincial visits by the Prime Minister;
- Coordinate and disseminate as widely as possible information on Government's development policies;
- Establish formally the National Security Council; and
- Set up a Commission of Inquiry into acquisition of land on Guadalcanal by non-Guadalcanal persons with a view to making findings and recommendations on the validity of land transactions prior to 1st October 1998.

MINISTRY OF HOME AND ECCLESIASTICAL AFFAIRS

1. BACKGROUND
The Ministry deals with the internal portfolio subjects. Its primary aims include the need to present and promote Solomon Islands' image and to instill nationalism, patriotism, pride and a sense of belonging and identity in our people.
2. FUNCTIONS OF THE MINISTRY
(i) The Portfolio subjects formally assigned to the Ministry are:

- Citizenship;
- Local Government-Honiara City and Territories;
- Births, Deaths and Marriages;
- Elections;
- Ecclesiastical Affairs;
- Gaming and Lotteries;
- Public Holidays;
- Civic Affairs;
- Cinematography and Censorship;
- National Archives;
- National Disasters; and
- National Symbols and Banners.

(ii) The Ministry is responsible and answerable for the following Statutory Authorities:

- Electoral Commission;
- Constituency Boundary Commission;
- Honiara City Council;
- National Disaster Council;
- Gaming and Lotteries Board; and
- Censorship Board.

3. POLICY OBJECTIVES:
The Objectives of the Ministry are to:

- Establish and promote more acceptable criteria for the acquisition of citizenship;
- Review and amend the Electoral Provisions Act and the National Constitution to provide for more efficient, participatory and representative democratic electoral process;
- Coordinate and promote more effectively ecclesiastical affairs of the people as provided for in the National Constitution for the freedom of association and worship;
- Promote the efficient and effective operations of the Honiara City Council and Territories which are directly administered by the National Government under the Federal System;
- Manage and promote disaster awareness including dissemination of information to the populace through out the Nation for the purposes of disaster preparedness and efficient deliveries of relief services to disaster stricken areas; and
- Foster National respect, identity and diversity in unity.

4. DEVELOPMENT STRATEGIES
The Ministry will be guided by the following strategies in pursuance of its objectives:

- Ensure fair and acceptable criteria for the acquisition of Solomon Islands citizenship;
- Keep the National Parliament Electoral Provisions Act and the National Constitution under close scrutiny and Examination to ensure the attainment of fair representative government at all Levels of Solomon Islands Society;
- Safeguard the ecclesiastical affairs of the People in the exercise of their basic rights and freedoms as provided for in the Constitution;
- Improve the administration of the Electoral Commission by providing proper and appropriate resources to carry out its functions;
- Continue to improve the work of the National Disaster Council for disaster preparedness and relief work;
- Foster a close working partnership with The Solomon Islands Christian Association (SICA) and Non-Governmental Organizations (NGO's);

5. PROGRAM TARGETS: 2002-2005
The following Program targets will be pursued:

- Review and amend the Citizenship Act. Dual Citizenship should be considered;
- Review the performance of the National Disaster Council with a view to enhancing its role and performance;
- Work on the adaptation of a national dress;
- Continue to assess the number and Boundaries of electoral constituencies;
- Review the Gaming and Lotteries Act and All licences issued to casinos;
- Establish a Church Trust Foundation;
- Provide schools throughout the country with the National Flag and establish a National Flag Day for schools;
- Draw up a policy on refugees and asylum seekers; and
- Work closely with SICA and NGO's; and
- Institute a 'Thanksgiving Week' each year for the reunion of families, clans, tribes, and for rendering gratitude to God for his great kindness in life.

MINISTRY OF FINANCE

1. BACKGROUND
The diagnosis of the Public sector expenditure over the past years has revealed the need for the Ministry of Finance to restructure its Public Sector expenditure. The Ministry will focus on six major issues:

- The serious institutional, procedural, and processing Problems of budgeting, investment planning and co-ordination.
- The accounting function is very weak, leading to poor control and non-existence of Auditing.
- Recurrent costs continue to be high.
- >Expenditure pattern does not reflect Government's priorities.

- Institutional and administrative capacity is both weak in the line Ministries and in the government statutory bodies.
- The public sector investment programs are too large for the Government's implementation capacity.

2. FUNCTIONS OF THE MINISTRY

(i) The Portfolio subjects formally assigned to the Ministry are:

- Budget;
- Banking;
- Treasury;
- Loans and Guarantees;
- Statistics;
- Internal Auditing, Systems and Verification;
- Aid Management (Bilateral & Multi-lateral);
- Inland Revenue;
- Customs & Excise;
- Insurance;
- Price Control;
- Central Tendering;
- Financial Management & Accountability; and
- Macro Economic Policy.

The Ministry is responsible for and answerable to the following Statutory Authorities:

- Central Bank of Solomon Islands;
- Development Bank of Solomon Islands;
- Solomon Island National Provident Fund;
- Investment Corporation of Solomon Islands and its Portfolio Companies;
- Solomon Island Credit Union League;
- Home Finance Corporation;
- Solomon Mutual Insurance (SMI);
- Merchant Bank (Proposed);
- Solomon Islands Unit Trust (Proposed);
- Auditor General's Office; and
- Central Tender Board.

3. POLICY OBJECTIVES

The objectives of the Ministry are to:

- Develop an efficient and effective fiscal and monetary policies;
- Develop and implement a Provincial funding system;
- Strengthen Ministerial staff through an appropriate training;
- Improve and strengthen the Revenue collection divisions;
- Further develop the 1979 Loans and Security Act;
- Reduce budget deficit;
- Improve budgetary discipline in all Ministries;

- Improve financial control and macro-economic management;
- Broaden the base of the financial system;
- Improve availability of credit facilities in rural areas;
- Maintain an interest rate regime conducive to the private sector;
- Reduce inflation rate; and
- Restore and protect foreign exchange reserve to satisfactory level.

4. DEVELOPMENT STRATEGIES

To pursue its objectives the Ministry will be guided by the following strategies:

- Make budget more transparent; prepare realistic financing plan for all domestic and external resources, investment and recurrent expenditure including debt services on a commitment basis;
- Introduce a program of budgetary and accrual accounting system into the budget;
- Improve tax administration and collection;
- Reduce the overall deficit to levels sustainable with the domestic financial system;
- Encourage the establishment of financial institutions to increase competition and improve available services;
- Maintain positive real interest rates and maintain a flexible interest rate policy;
- Apply sound monetary and fiscal policies to bring down and stabilize the rate of inflation; and
- Implement a review of tax and tariff structures to be consistent with macro-economic and policy objectives.

5. PROGRAM TARGETS: 2002-2005

These program targets will be undertaken:

- Privatization of ICSI portfolio companies;
- Budget preparation and implementation;
- Review of import and export duty;
- Vest the discretionary powers to grant duty and goods tax remissions in a Committee;
- Review and broaden tax basis;
- Review the Government Accounting system;
- Establish of a Public Enterprises Unit;
- Establishment of a Provincial Funding system;
- Enact legislation to merge current Goods and Sales Tax systems into a single VAT system;
- Introduce a fixed levy per cubic meter on all round logs exported.
- Establish and encourage credit facilities for rural resources owners to assist them develop their resources especially in these areas;
  - Tourism;
  - Cottage industries;
  - Small-scale Commercial fishing;
  - Mining;
  - Shipping;

    - Rural mini-hydro power plants; and
    - Honey, cocoa, rice, livestock;
- Transform DBSI into People's Bank;
- Review the NPF;
- In line with the policy of Home Improvement set up a Home Credit Facility;
- Review and revise banking and financial system legislation
- Review the CBSI Act;
- Undertake other programs which may be assigned by the responsible Minister and Cabinet; and
- Undertake and revive the following identified projects;
- Gold Ridge Mining;
- SIPL;
- Honiara Main Road Upgrading Project;
- Merchant Bank Establishment;
- People's Bank;
- Unit Trust Establishment;
- Munda International Airport;
- Fuel Storage relocation;
- Aluta Basin Oil Palm project;
- Guadalcanal Province Headquarters; and
- CEMA.

MINISTRY OF ECONOMIC REFORM & STRUCTURAL ADJUSTMENTS.

1. BACKGROUND

Solomon Islands have considerable potential to achieve balanced social and economic development. However, the prospects for a medium-term growth are shadowed by substantial fiscal imbalances, persistent inflation, inadequate economic infrastructure, shortage of skilled manpower, and low level of international reserves. While some real GDP growth has been maintained in recent years, the private sector continues to be squeezed by Government pre-emption of the domestic savings and the inflationary effect of the monetarizing huge budget deficits. This Ministry has been introduced to emphasize the commitment to economic and structural reforms.

2. FUNCTIONS OF THE MINISTRY

The portfolio subjects formally assigned to the Ministry are:

- Constitutional & Legislative Reform;
- Public Service Reforms;
- Monetary & Fiscal Reforms;
- Sectoral Reforms; and
- Institutional Reforms.

3. POLICY OBJECTIVES

The Objectives to be pursued are to:

- Restore and retain the economy onto a stable and sustainable level where investment is conducive so that the country is able to compete with the outside world;
- Continue to improve essential services and economic infrastructures;
- Effective utilization of external resources; and
- Effective planning and management of the Public investments.
-

4. DEVELOPMENT STRATEGIES

In pursuing its objectives the Ministry will adhere to these strategies:

- The stimulation and support of private sector Growth on a commercial and competitive base;
- Maintenance of an undistorted structure of key prices in the economy;
- The elimination of hidden subsidies interests, rents, wages, salaries and exchange rates;
- The provision of sites to facilitate access for investments;
- The streaming of investment approvals; and
- The continuation of improving manpower training, technology transfer and market development;
- Establish effective planning and budget making executive for public sector, recurrent and capital investment and management of external assistance;
- Reduce size and cost of Government through salaries, wages, retrench and restructuring of Provincial Government and Ministries within and along the changing roles and responsibilities;
- Reduce domestic borrowing through restraints placed on recurrent expenditures, reduce subsidies, and expand tax base and collect tax receipts;
- Re-structure the Government expenditures;
- Rehabilitation of Government Investments, human resources and improve efficiency and skills; and
- Continue commercialization and privatization.

5. PROGRAMME TARGETS

These proposed program targets will be undertaken.

5.1 Constitutional and Legislative Reforms

- Rewrite and amend the Constitution And amend other subsidiary legislation with the aim of removing duplication, inefficiency and other impediments that hinder development:
- Introduce new legislation to cope with Modern day development aspirations of Solomon Islanders;
- Enforce the various existing legislations and bring to justice all offenders.
- Scrutinize and amend as necessary the Following:
    - The National Constitution
    - Public Finance and Audit Act
    - Investment Act
    - Land and Titles Act

- Labor Act

5.2 Public Service Reforms

- Review Public Service functions and structures;
- Review Public Service Terms and conditions.
- Review of the Public Service Act and amend the existing General Orders to: Improve manpower training.

5.3 Fiscal and Monetary Reforms
Reviews would be carried out on these:

- Taxation;
- Exemptions and concessions;
- Expenditures restraints;
- Subsidies and transfers;
- Monetary & Credit Policy;
- International Reserves;
- Exchange Rate; and
- External Debt.

5.4 Institutional Reforms
These reforms will be undertaken:

- Public Sector investments;
- Strengthening of Financial Institution;
- Review of Social Sector expenditure; and
- Privatization & commercialization.

5.5 Sectoral Reforms

- Review of the Agricultural development;
- Promotion of Industrial development;
- Promotion of Tourism;
- Development of Human Resources;
- Forestry and Environmental issues; and
- Housing Development

5.6 Social impact of the Structural Adjustments
5.7 Foreign Financial requirement
5.8 Technical Assistance

MINISTRY OF RECONCILIATION, PEACE & NATIONAL UNITY.

1. BACKGROUND
This Ministry has been established to emphasize Government's commitment to pursue and restore peace and normalcy to the country.
2. FUNCTIONS OF THE MINISTRY
(i) The Portfolio subjects assigned to the Ministry are:

- National Reconciliation;
- Rehabilitation;
- National Unity; and
- Peace Process.

(ii) The Ministry is responsible and answerable for these bodies:

- Peace Monitoring Council (PMC); and
- International Peace Monitoring Team (IPMT)

3. POLICY OBJECTIVES

The objectives of the Ministry are to:

- Coordinate and implement the terms of the Townsville Peace Agreement (TPA)
- Ensure the Peace process is sustained and restored to the country;
- Carry out the process of rehabilitating ex-combatants;
- Ensure the process of National Reconciliation and Healing is achieved;
- Seek funding for and where appropriate, pay compensation to those who lost properties as stipulated in the TPA;and
- Implement the Amnesty Act.

4. DEVELOPMENT STRATEGIES

In pursuing its objectives the Ministry will be guided by these strategies:

- Reconvene Townsville Peace Agreement Review meetings between the Parties to the agreement;
- Activate the demobilization, re-integration and rehabilitation plans and programs;
- Continue to seek funding for rehabilitation of ex-combatants;
- Identify and create public works to engage ex-combatants;
- Improve the administration of disbursement of rehabilitation funds;
- Provide resources and strengthen the work of the Peace and Reconciliation Committee (PRC);
- Encourage Youth Groups, Women Groups, Churches and NGOs to participate actively in the Peace Process;and
- Engage the Brotherhood of the Church of Melanesia (Tasius) and other Church organizations to assist in the retrieval of illegal arms.

5. PROGRAM TARGETS: 2002 - 2005

The Ministry will pursue these program targets:

- Reconvene the TPA Review meetings by June 2002;
- Set a date for the return of arms and ammunitions as required by the Amnesty Acts;
- Engage the Tasius [Melanesian Brotherhood] to assist in the retrieval of arms;
- Continue to seek funding for rehabilitation as stipulated in the TPA;

- Initiate dialogue with renegade factions of the former Isatabu Freedom Movement so that they accept and be involved in the Peace process;
- Engage Youth, Women, Churches, NGOs and other Civil Society Groups to participate in the Peace process;
- Coordinate the implementation of the TPA; and
- Stop all new ethnic related claims.

MINISTRY OF FOREIGN AFFAIRS.

1. BACKGROUND
The Ministry's main task is to promote and safeguard the country's interests and good image overseas through maintaining and enhancing of friendly and cordial relation with states and International and Regional Organizations, especially those states with which it has formal diplomatic ties and organizations of which it is a member.
2. FUNCTIONS OF THE MINISTRY
(i) The Portfolio subjects formally assigned to the Ministry are:

- Foreign Affairs;
- Diplomatic Relations-Bilateral and Multi-lateral;
- Consular Relations and Consular matters;
- Protocol - Ceremonials;
- Overseas Missions Representation; and
- Treaties and Conventions.

3. POLICY OBJECTIVES
The Ministry is to pursue these objectives:

- Conduct its foreign relations based on reciprocal respect for and trust in the sovereignty of other states;
- Promote the interest of and maintain the sovereignty of Solomon Islands in the conduct of its bilateral and multi-lateral relations;
- Pursue a foreign aid policy based on selective Rationalization of aid development assistance and usage premised on the aspirations of the Nation;
- Maintain, support and assess the country's efforts of cooperation with other countries in the South Pacific region, the UN and Commonwealth;
- Assess the need and scope to establish SI resident representation in the Asian region;
- Continue reviewing and assessing initiatives for the peaceful resolution of the Bougainville conflict; and
- Continue staff training to ensure efficient and professional service in the Ministry's Management and operation.

4. DEVELOPMENT STRATEGIES
In pursuit of its objectives the Ministry shall pursue these strategies:

- Build confidence and trust with our development partners;

- Pursue the strengthening of trade relations and other functional cooperation with Pacific Rim countries;
- Draft a Foreign Relations Bill and ensure its passage in Parliament;
- Review Solomon Islands overseas representation with a view to achieving cost effectiveness and efficiency;
- Review and assess Solomon Islands relations with other states and membership of international and regional organizations to determine the extent of benefits derived from Those relationships and association;
- Continue to encourage the PNG Government and BRA leadership to maintain dialogue as a way to seek a negotiated peaceful solution to the Bougainville issue;
- Ensure cost-effective and efficient of Solomon Islands overseas diplomatic missions and consular offices;
- Continue to train and maintain a career diplomatic corps for the Ministry's home base and the country's overseas missions; and
- Enhance and strengthen Solomon Islands relations with others Forum Member countries as well as with the Melanesian Spearhead group Members.

5. PROGRAM TARGETS: 2002-2005
These proposed program targets shall be pursued:

- Actively engaged in dialogue with our development partners with a view to normalizing their sovereign risk rating of Solomon Islands;
- Dispatch a mission to the Melanesian Spearhead Group member countries to seek their agreement for Solomon Islands to temporarily place tariff on goods currently on exemption under the MSG Trade Agreement;
- Commission a study mission to the Pacific Rim countries;
- Carry out an evaluation of the Solomon Islands membership of International and Regional Organizations and institutions and report thereon to SIG;
- Formulate and enact a Foreign Relations Bill by the end of 2003;
- Undertake an evaluation report on Solomon Islands diplomatic relations with other states;
- Continue consultations with PNG Government and BRA leadership until there is a peaceful resolution to the Bougainville issue;
- Establish a resident mission, either diplomatic or consular in the ASEAN region;
- Establish a Diplomatic Training Corps and formulate a professional training program; and
- Appoint and assign Emissaries to the Asian region and the European Union.

MINISTRY OF FORESTRY, ENVIRONMENT & CONSERVATION.

1. BACKGROUND
This Ministry is responsible for the important portfolio subjects of Forestry Development, the Environment and Conservation. It is incumbent on the

Government to ensure that future generations of Solomon Islands can still enjoy and have experiences of our natural forests, the natural heritage of the country. The forest resources of the country is mostly located on customary lands and hence the Government will put in place policies that assist land owning groups to derive maximum benefit from the utilization of their resources as well as reforestation on already logged land. The forestry sector is a significant contributor in terms of revenue earner for the country and a major source of employment. However, this has been considerably affected by the recent ethnic tension especially on Guadalcanal. The Government puts priority on this productive sector, as its sustainable development will assist in the revitalization of the economy.

2. FUNCTIONS OF THE MINISTRY

(i) The portfolio subjects formally assigned to the Ministry are:

- Forestry;
- Research;
- Environmental and Conservation;
- Timber Marketing and Research; and
- Licensing.

(ii) The Ministry is responsible and answerable for these Statutory Authorities:

- North New Georgia Timber Corporation; and
- SI Timber Marketing Board (Proposed).

3. POLICY OBJECTIVES

The objectives of the Ministry are to:

- Ensure sound Forest Management and Land Conservation practices further developed and Maintained in perpetuity;
- Improve the efficiency of forest industry production, strengthen value-added processing facilities and maximize the market value of logs;
- Expand domestic and export marketing for plantation and indigenous timber;
- Support and promote the appropriate end-users of timbers;
- Involve Landowners in the ownership and operation of the timber industry.
- Maximize employment opportunities and undertake greater manpower planning, development and training;
- Promote public awareness to increase environmental, social and economic benefits of forests;
- Increase timber products other than log exports for domestic consumption and exports;

4. DEVELOPMENT STRATEGIES

The Ministry will be guided by these strategies in pursuit of its objectives:

- Review the Forestry and Environment Acts;

- Ensure sustainable harvesting of trees;
- Encourage foreign investors through provision of appropriate incentives to establish processing in veneer and plywood for export;
- Encourage processing through incentives so that round logs exports would be phased out;
- Emphasis is placed on enabling resources owners to harvest their own resources on a sustainable basis;
- Encourage and assist resources owners in processing and exporting their timber resources;
- Foreign investors and land owners will be required under the terms of their licenses to replant trees on logged land; and
- Under carbon sink programs, encourage youth and women and landowners to replant trees.

5. PROGRAM TARGETS: 2002 - 2005
These program targets will be pursued:

- Implement a program for policy development, administration and support services in these areas:
  - Management services;
  - Training and education;
  - Timber utilization, research and promotion; and
  - Civic-cultural research.
- Recruit a TA to head the Forestry Division;
- Encourage foreign and local companies in replanting by applying appropriate administrative and legislative measures;
- Establish a Timber Marketing Authority;
- Review the forestry export quota;
- Continue to encourage privatization of reforestation programs and projects;
- Monitor the shipment of export round logs;
- Assist youth and women grounds and landowners to plant one million trees by 2005;
- Continue research and inventory of timber resources, other plant species and wild life;
- Review the Forestry, Environment and Conservation Acts; and
- Publish a book of all Solomon Islands tree species and fauna for conservation purposes as well as for tourist and public information.

MINISTRY OF COMMERCE, EMPLOYMENT AND TRADE.

1. BACKGROUND
This Ministry covers the important Economic Sectors of Local and Foreign Investment, Trade, Employment, Commerce and Industrial Development.
The impact of the ethnic conflict had adversely affected almost all existing activities. In its effort to revitalize the economy, the Government is committed to putting together an economic and financial package which aims at assisting struggling businesses, encourage new investments in all provinces, and diversify the economic base.

2. FUNCTIONS OF THE MINISTRY
(i) The Portfolio subjects formally assigned to the Ministry are:

- Investment;
- Local Entrepreneur;
- Immigration;
- Labour;
- Trade and Testing;
- Industrial Development;
- Commerce; and
- Internal and External Trade.

(ii) The Ministry is responsible and answerable for these statutory authorities:

- Commodities Export Marketing Authority;
- Solomon Islands Ports Authority;
- Foreign Investment Board; and
- Registrar of Corporate Affairs.

3. POLICY OBJECTIVES
The objectives of the Ministry are to:

- Encourage more foreign investors to invest in the country;
- Encourage more indigenous people to participate in various investment and commercial activities;
- Diversify into new investment areas;
- Create more employment opportunities;
- Encourage foreign investment as a means of transferring skills;
- Encourage investment as a means of import substitution;
- Solomon Islands to invest in overseas countries through Unit Trust Development;
- Reduce trade and balance of payment imbalances;
- Seek better prices and quality supplies;
- Encourage re-export;
- Encourage Trading with other Pacific Countries;
- Maintain the growth of the Labour Force at a level that is compatible with the creation of employment opportunities;
- Improve Labour skills, performance and skill at work;
- Improve employees and employers relationship;
- Encourage improved commercial activities; and
- Encourage cottage industries as a further means of self-employment.

4. DEVELOPMENT STRATEGIES
In pursuing its objectives the Ministry will be guided by these strategies:

- Design an economic and financial package which aims at rehabilitating struggling businesses and encourage new investments;
- Repeal and replace the Foreign Investment Act;

- Establish necessary infrastructure;
- Provide land for various investments;
- Establish a one stop-shop to receive and decide on investment proposals;
- Reserve areas of investment opportunities for indigenous Solomon Islanders;
- In consultation with the Ministry of Finance, review the present tax regime both direct and indirect tax, to broaden the country's economic base;
- Set up trade consulars in selected overseas countries;
- Research into alternative sources of imports and encourage bulk purchase;
- Review the price Advisory Council with a view to providing it with a Secretariat and established membership;
- Create an investment climate which will yield more jobs through increased foreign investment and by providing more development opportunities in rural areas;
- Provide more financial assistance to local Solomon Islanders through the judicious use of its fiscal and monetary policies;
- Encourage more related and practical training to our local business people;
- Allocate available land for development purposes;
- Support and encourage trade delegations to other trading partner nations;
- Establish an Industrial Commission to promote fair-trading and arbitrate over unfair trading between businesses and corporations; and
- Liberalize CEMA.

5. PROGRAM TARGETS: 2002 - 2005

The Ministry will pursue these program targets:

- Design an economic and financial package to rehabilitate and assist struggling businesses and encourage new investments;
- Acquire new sites for industrial development;
- Identify and reserve areas of investment solely for Solomon Islanders;
- Review the existing Immigration Act;
- Review the existing Labour Act;
- Repeal and replace the Investment Act;
- Review the Trade Dispute Act;
- Identify and declare duty free zones;
- Review the Company Act;
- Reinstate Foreign and Local Investment Awards;
- Hold seminars with the private and the commercial sectors;
- Sponsor Overseas Trade Missions;
- Expand the Local Industrial activities;
- Prepare full investment packages for purposes of selling them to foreign investors;
- Promote local manufactured goods and Agricultural Commodities for export; and
- Allow multiple visa privileges and Business Immigration special fees to selected Foreign Investors who are involved in processing and

manufacturing industries and those who have long term business interest in the country;

5.1 PROJECTS:

- Coffee Processing Facility;
- Cargo vessels;
- Bina Habour and Noro Development;
- Duty free zones;
- Wairokai Industrial Sea Port;
- Suava Bay Fisheries Center;
- Ranadi and Henderson Industrial Estates; and
- Pineapple Juice processing facility;
- Selwyn Bay Industrial Seaport; and
- Vanikoro Industrial Seaport.

MINISTRY OF LANDS AND SURVEY.

1. BACKGROUND

Land is one of the underlying issues that has given rise to the ethnic tension which nearly brought the country to its knees. Hence, new emphasis is being placed on land resources in relation to its use, development and security. This is one of the priority and productive areas that will be attended to by the Government.

2. FUNCTIONS OF THE MINISTRY

(i) The portfolio subjects formally assigned to the Ministry are:

- Lands;
- Survey;
- Hydrograph;
- Cartography;
- Physical Planning; and
- Resettlement Scheme;

3. POLICY OBJECTIVES

The objectives of the Ministry are to:

- Distribute residential, civil and public land in urban and semi-urban areas according to need;
- Maximize the security of Government, freehold and customary land in the country with the view to increasing value per unit of land, security for investment and other usages of land;
- Return developed and undeveloped alienated and to original landholding groups or tribes either for resettlement on development;
- Activate and put in motion the 1995 Customary Recording Act;
- Establish a competent and efficient land management unit for the compilation and dissemination of the land use and development information;

- Reviews the Land Titles Act and other relevant legislation with a view to vesting the fiscal decision on customary land disputes in the Chiefs;
- Identity opportunity areas for proper development; and
- Identity and acquire land for resettlement of citizens whose low lying islands are threatened by rising sea level and other National Disaster

4. DEVELOPMENT STRATEGIES
The Ministry will be guided by these strategies:

- Immediately review lands that have been lawfully granted but have not been developed with a view to repossessing those lands;
- Put in motion measures to institutionalize land to increase land security in rural areas;
- Negotiate with landowners for purposes of an aggressive tourism industry;
- Regularize and standardize policies on urban, semi-urban and rural areas.

5. PROGRAM TARGETS: 2002 - 2005
The Ministry will pursue these program targets:

- Appoint, as soon as possible, a new Commissioner of Lands;
- Return Gizo and Alu Forestry projects to original land owners;
- Return selected alienated lands to original landowners;
- Finalize and recommend to the Prime Minister for purposes of appointment a Commission of Inquiry to inquire into acquisition of land on Guadalcanal as required by the Townsville Peace Agreement;
- Establish a Lands Trust Board;
- Continue to appoint and train land recording officers;
- Complete the work on semi-urban policy on TOL and other peripheral areas;
- Upgrade the computer system on land information;
- Table in Parliament the Lands Titles Amendment Bill;
- Reserve land for resettlement schemes;
- Carry out a pilot program on customary land reform; and
- Implement the Customary Land Recording Act.

MINISTRY OF NATIONAL PLANNING.

1. BACKGROUND
This Ministry is pivotal for the properly planning and coordination of development. From its position of responsibilities, it is able to have an overview of all sectoral and provincial planning activities and programmes. It, therefore, has to ensure that plans, programmes and projects are implemented, monitored and reviewed in line with approved policies and legislative provisions for which expenditure is authorized by Parliament through the Annual Budget Estimates and the National Development Plan. The Programme of Action contains the Guidelines for the formulation and implementation of projects for development in any given period within the time span of the National Development Plan which may range from five

to twenty years. The task of project identification, is the responsibility of the other ministries. For the purpose of this present Programme of Action, the chosen time span for the National Development is five years. As a matter of priority, the Ministry will redirect its resources towards post conflict reconstruction, restoration of Law and Order and the revitalization of the National Economy.

2. FUNCTIONS OF THE MINISTRY

(i) The Portfolio subjects formally assigned to the Ministry are:

- National Development Planning;
- Human Resources Development Planning;
- Policy Evaluation and Monitoring;
- Project Formulation, Appraisal and Funding;
- Programmes Implementation and Coordination; and
- Population Planning and monitoring.

3. POLICY OBJECTIVES

The overall objectives to be pursued are to:

- Redirect resources towards post conflict reconstruction, restoration of Law and Order and revitalization of the National Economy;
- Oversee, coordinate and monitor overall national development;
- Coordinate the implementation of the Programme of Action;
- Monitor and review sectoral programmes;
- Evaluate and monitor policies and programmes formulation and implementation; and
- Coordinate provincial development plans and programmes.

4. DEVELOPMENT STRATEGIES

The strategies to be pursued are:

- Redirecting of resources to address post conflict re-construction, restoration of Law and Order and the revitalization of the economy;
- Review all planning activities which had been undertaken during the past 22 years;
- Preparation of five years National Development Plan 2002 - 2005;
- Prepare short term and medium term plans and strategies for economic recovery;
- Preparation of the population plan;
- Coordination and monitoring of the program of action;
- Assess and coordinate development assistance programs from Development Partners;
- Assist provincial authorities with the training of their planning staff in view of constitutional changes that are to be effected;
- Re-organisation of the Ministry for effective and efficient performance and productive output;
- Further development of the role and work of the National Planning Consultative Committee; and
- Assisting and servicing of the National Development Council.

5. PROGRAM TARGETS: 2002 - 2005
The Ministry will pursue these program targets:

- Redirect resources to address post conflict reconstruction, restoration of Law and Order and economic recovery;
- Convene a National Economic summit;
- Prepare and complete the following plans:
  - The National Development Plan 2002 - 2005;
  - A Human Resources Plan 1995 - 2005; and
  - A Population Plan 2002 - 2005.
- Review Planning activities;
- Coordinate and monitor the implementation of the program of Action;
- Carry out policy evaluation and monitoring;
- Assess and coordinate foreign aid programs;
- Undertake courses for Provincial Planning Staff;
- Further develop the work of the National Planning Consultative Committee; and
- Participate in the servicing of the National Development Council.

MINISTRY OF CULTURE, TOURISM AND AVIATION.

1. BACKGROUND
As the biggest growing international industry, tourism can provide a major and expanding source of foreign exchange earnings for Solomon Islands. In the short-term to the medium term, the tourism sector appears to be best placed in terms of economic base diversification, contributing to the economic growth and employment generation. By nature the tourism industry is susceptible to conflict situations. This was exactly what happened to the industry in Solomon Islands at the height of the ethnic tension. Nonetheless, relative to other industries, it is also equally relevant that the industry is best placed to quickly bounce back and recover in the shortest time possible. The Ministry has been established to emphasize the Government determination to tap this industry in its commitment to revitalize the economy.
2. FUNCTION OF THE MINISTRY.
(i) The Portfolio subjects formally assigned to the Ministry are:

- Tourism Development
- Cultural Affairs
- Aviation
- Meteorology
- National Museum
- National Art Gallery and Cultural Center
- Relics, Monuments & Memorials

(ii) The Ministry is responsible for and answerable to the following Statutory Authorities:

- Solomon Islands Visitors Bureau
- Air Transport Licensing Authority (ATLA)

- Civil Aviation Authority (proposed)

3. POLICY OBJECTIVES.
The objectives of the Ministry in its sectors are:
(i) In the Tourism sector:

- Ensure that tourism development is in harmony with national development policies and development;
- Increase tourist arrivals through continued hotel development, improved runway and NAVAIDS;
- Build an international airport in the Western Province or elsewhere in the Solomon Islands;
- Increase the level of tourism awareness among local people and visitors to Solomon Islands;
- Ensure that adverse effects on local customs and cultures are avoided and the national cultures are enhanced; and
- Promote and develop eco-tourism and natural sites.

(ii) In the area of Culture the objectives are:

- Promote cultural programs in urban and rural areas;
- Establish an appropriate National Cultural Policy and Legislation; and
- Research into the establishment of National Council of Chiefs.

(iii) In aviation the objectives are:

- Continue to improve air services to the rural areas;
- Continue to provide and improve navigational facilities to local and international air services; and
- Establish additional weather station, widening the scope-observation of existing stations and improving the network of meteorology and rainfall observation.

4. DEVELOPMENT STRATEGIES
In pursuing its objectives the Ministry will be guided by these strategies:

- Recruit under Technical Assistance an
- Recruit under TA an advisor to assist the Visitors Bureau;
- Reduce Solomon Airlines international airfares through subsidy for a trial period of one month;
- Ensure that domestic operators maintain a high level of safety;
- Commission a delegation to seek dialogue with governments of countries that still placed high travel advisories to their citizens intending to travel to Solomon Islands as tourists;
- Government should utilize its taxation policy to entice investors to invest in the tourism sector;
- Local financial institutions will be encouraged to channel more financial resources to hotels and tourism related activities;

- Improve the internal transport and communication system;
- Adopt an 'open sky' policy and investigate the possibility of the introduction of competitive airlines to improve air services in terms of efficiency and costs;
- Up-date and improve air services and air navigational facilities in order to cope with changing technology;
- Review the Civil Aviation Act with a view to establishing a Civil Aviation Authority;
- Ensure that domestic operators maintain a high level of safety;
- Further development of electronic meteorological data processing in Honiara;
- Widening the scope of information services for specific needs of weather sensitive and industries in particular agriculture, transport, water resources and energy;
- Construction of Headquarters and Institutional residences; and
- Promote Cultural program in urban and rural areas.

5. PROGRAM TARGETS: 2002 -2005.
The Ministry will undertake these program targets:

- Recruit TA to head the Tourism Division;
- Recruit TA as advisor to SIVB;
- Reduce Solomon Airline international airfares for a trial period of one month;
- Commission a delegation to work on travel advisories imposed by overseas countries on their citizens travel to Solomon Islands;
- Review Solomon Islands Airline with the view to privatising the company;
- Improvement of existing airfields and constructing a number of new ones;
- Completion of Henderson Runway and upgrading of NAVAIDS;
- Establishment of Civil Aviation Authority;
- Construction of International Airport in the Western Province;
- Promotion of existing and new eco-Tourism sites;
- Identify and develop a niche market for Tourists;
- Meteorology services improvements and construction of its Headquarters;
- Upgrading of National Museum, National Art Gallery and Cultural Center;
- Establish appropriate National Cultural Policy and Legislation;
- Establish the Leili Island Tourism Site Development and Marketing;
- Build an International airport in Malaita Province;
- Build an International airport in Temotu Province.

MINISTRY OF PROVINCIAL GOVERMENT & RURAL DEVELOPMENT.

1. BACKGROUND
The Ministry is charged with the important responsibility of developing a Provincial Government system that provides for the devolution of powers and decentralization of functions to empower the majority of people in the provinces who are the custodians of natural resources to participate in the decision-making concerning matters which affect their lives. The other responsibility of the Ministry is to oversee the planning and coordination of orderly rural development.

2. FUNCTIONS OF THE MINISTRY
(i) The Portfolio subjects assigned to the Ministry are:

- Provincial Government Development;
- Rural Development;
- Provincial Elections;
- Provincial Development Units; and
- Provincial Budgets and Funding systems.

3. POLICY OBJECTIVES
The policy objectives of the Ministry are to:

- Develop a Provincial Government system consistent with the State Government Task Force Report 2001;
- Allocate and transfer certain percentages of state revenue to Provincial Governments;
- Ensure that Provincial Governments are fully accountable for functions devolved to them;
- Ensure that Provincial Governments are fully accountable for the finances allocated for their services; and
- Ensure the orderly development of rural areas;

4. DEVELOPMENT STRATEGIES
The Ministry will be guided by these strategies:

- Continue to work on developing a Provincial Government that is in line with the State Government Task Force Report 2001;
- Ensuring the availability of financial and manpower resources for the establishment of Provincial Governments;
- Put in place measures which would ensure that the provinces derive benefits from their resources; and
- Direct more emphasis on infrastructure development in provinces such as roads, wharves and bridges.

5. PROGRAM TARGETS: 2002 - 2005
These program targets will be undertaken:

- Continue work on developing a PGA system consistent with the State Government Task Force 2001;
- Table a special Provincial government Bill in Parliament to defer holding of elections for dissolved Provincial Assemblies;
- Introduce better funding systems for province;
- Convene premiers conferences;
- Arrange tour by Minister to all Provinces;
- Actively participate in rehabilitation and the peace; process;
- Work out and apply sharing of certain percentages of revenue for provinces; and
- Repeal the PGA 1997 at an appropriate time.

MINISTRY OF TRANSPORT, WORKS & COMMUNICATIONS.

1. BACKGROUND

Transport and Communications do play an important role in the overall development of the Solomon Islands economy. While reasonable development had been undertaken, in terms of infrastructure facilities, the continuing development and improvement of transportation to and communication with remote isolated islands, communities and areas with development potential will be given priority. Real efforts will be taken to ensure that the transport and communications systems do function in a cost-effective, efficient and integrated manner within a framework of a thoroughly considered and determined program. Priority will also be given to maintain and rebuild infrastructure facilities that have been destroyed during the ethnic conflict on Guadalcanal.

2. FUNCTIONS OF THE MINISTRY

(i) The Portfolio subjects formally assigned to the Ministry are:

- Infrastructure Development - Roads, Bridges and Wharves.
- Shipping and maritime;
- Communications;
- Postal Services Policies;
- Spectrum;
- Television; and
- Land Transport.

(ii) The Ministry is responsible and answerable for this Statutory Authority:

- Postal Corporation.

3. POLICY OBJECTIVES

(i) The overall objectives of the Ministry are to:

- Maintain and rebuild infrastructures destroyed during the ethnic conflict;
- Initiate public works as part and parcel of rehabilitating ex-combatants;
- Develop and provide an efficient network of transport services to all part of the country;
- Coordinate development so as to ensure a coherent and integrated approach;
- Continue research and the development of a more cost-effective means of transport;
- The Ministry's specific objectives in the main modes of transportation are:

3.1 Land Transport

The objectives in this sub-sector are:

- Maintain and rebuild infrastructures destroyed during the ethnic conflict;
- Construct the Malaita South Road;
- Put in place a development program for Guadalcanal Province which includes the following;
    - Aola-Marau road;

    - Marau-Kuma road;
    - Guadalcanal Trans-insular road;
    - Lambi-Tangarare road;
    - Wharves at Marau, Tetere, Variana, and Aola.
- Provide road access to isolated and rural areas of social and economic development;
- Improve and upgrade the major roads and bridges and adequately maintain them;
- Provide roads and bridges to support the diversification of production in primary industries;
- Bring about effective control and regulation of public transport system and ensure regular services at minimum costs while at the same time maintain safety and good quality of services.

3.2 Marine Transport
The objectives of this sub-sector are to:

- Rationalize inter-island shipping services and improve the quality of sea-borne transportation system;
- Develop and assist an efficient and cost-effective inter-island shipping service;
- Provide necessary marine transport facilities so as to provide logistics support for the primary production industries;
- Privatize the operation of the semi-government shipyard; and
- Introduce shipping services subsidize to operators serving uneconomical routes.

3.3 COMMUNICATIONS
The objectives in this sub-sector are to;

- Expand the postal services system as a network to contribute to overall national development;
- Extend and coordinate the telecommunications industry to improve its role in national development and unity;
- Provide a greater penetration of services especially to its rural areas and outer islands; and
- Introduce TV station.

4. DEVELOPMENT STRATEGIES
The ministry will be guided by these strategies:
4.1 LAND TRANSPORT

- Maintain and rebuild infrastructure destroyed during the ethnic conflict;
- Formulate a strategic Land Transport policy which should take into account the importance of a cost-effective transportation linkages system throughout the country;

- Designing and implementation of a progressive Land Transportation plan for a ten year period and;
- Ensuring official emphasis of professional, technical and dedicated workforce in the ministry while allowing for the participation of capable private sector companies in carrying out approved programs and projects.

4.2 MARINE TRANSPORT:

- The nationalization of inter-island shipping services and the improvement of the quality of the sea-borne transportation system;
- The development of an efficient and cost-effective inter-island shipping service;
- The provision of necessary marine transport facilities so as to provide logistical support for primary production industries;
- Privatize Sasape Marina Shipyard; and
- Subsidized uneconomic routes.

4.3 COMMUNICATIONS:

- The progressive expansion of the postal services system as a network for overall national development;
- The extension and coordination of the telecommunications network to improve its role in national development and unity;
- Provide a greater penetration of services and rural areas and outer islands;
- Activating the improvement of services in all areas of communications; and
- Establish a TV broadcasting station.

5. PROGRAM TARGETS: 2002 - 2005
The Ministry will pursue these program targets:
5.1 LAND TRANSPORT:

- Maintain or rebuild infrastructure destroyed during the ethnic conflict;
- Construct the Malaita-South road;
- Put in place a development program for Guadalcanal which include the following:

  Aola-Marau road;
  Marau-Kuma road;
  Guadalcanal Trans-insular road;
  Lambi-Tangarare road; and
  Wharves at Marau, Tetere, Variana and Aola.

- Construct new roads and maintain existing ones;
- Upgrade urban roads;

- Construct new bridges and upgrade existing ones in both rural areas and urban centers;
- Continue and complete the Munda-Noro road;
- Reactivate the Road Authority; and
- Introduce user-pay [road levies] on main roads in Honiara.

5.2 MARINE TRANSPORT:

- Establish an appropriate route licensing system to ensure that operators provide adequate services to all part of the country;
- Review the existing freight rates and subsidy to establish an appropriate tariff structure;
- Establish an appropriate ship financing scheme to encourage private sector operators to replace obsolete vessels;
- Privatize Sasape Marina Shipyard;
- Assist boat-building groups in Langga-Langga Lagoon, Malaita Province and other groups in other provinces to continue ship-building projects; and
- Maintain and improve rural maritime facilities.

5.3 COMMUNICATIONS:

- Continue the expansion of the postal services system and a network for overall national development;
- Continue the extension and coordination of the telecommunications network to improve its role in national development;
- Provide a greater penetration of services especially in rural areas and outer islands;
- Increase the automatic exchange capacity and opening of new automatic exchanges in Honiara and provincial centers;
- Relocate relay transmitters for Auki and Malaita Province;
- Further enhance the performance and output of the philatelic bureau;
- Develop new services such as the courier and electronic mail services;
- Establish a postal banking services;
- Review DOMSAT Network with a view for expansion to embrace government sub-centers;
- Review the existing joint venture arrangement;
- Establish a TV Broadcasting Station;
- Install legislation to deregulate and discourage monopoly by independent service providers thus allowing for greater and diverse participation in the telecommunications industry; and
- Revise the now obsolete 1971 Telecommunications Act.

MINISTRY OF HEALTH AND MEDICAL SERVICES.

1. BACKGROUND
Health is a right that needs to be protected for every citizen of the country. The Government adheres to the concept that "a healthy people make a healthy

nation". The Government places priority on the provision of basic health and medical services to its people throughout the country.

2. FUNCTIONS OF THE MINISTRY

(i) The Portfolio subjects formally assigned to the Ministry are:

- Health Services;
- Medical Services;
- Nursing Services;
- Hospital and Clinics;
- Public Health;
- Health Education;
- Traditional Medicine;
- Rural water supply and sanitation;
- Social welfare;
- Physiotherapy;
- Central Pharmacy; and
- Population control

(ii) The Ministry is responsible and answerable for these statutory authorities:

- Hospitals Board;
- Medical Board;
- Pharmacy Practitioners Board; and
- Nursing Council.

3. POLICY OBJECTIVES

The objectives of the Ministry are:

- Work towards the general acceptance of the primary Health Care Program to achieve the global aim of "Health for all by the year 2005";
- Strengthen preventive health services through the primary Health Care Program;
- Improve and strengthen hospitals, Area Health Centers and Clinic Services;
- Increase the training of medical and health personnel;
- Introduce a health policy emphasizing the need to improve health care in collaboration with churches, NGOs and other organizations;
- Ensure the attainment of a population growth rate at a level which is conducive to better, health standard of living;
- Ensure that there is a place for traditional medicine practitioners in the health and medical system;
- Ensure all communities have access to good clean water and proper sanitation; and
- Provide assistance to charitable organizations such as the Red Cross and the Disabled Association.

4. DEVELOPMENT STRATEGIES

The Ministry will be guided by the following strategies:

- Amend relevant legislations to update and provide efficient health and medical service;
- Improve the terms and conditions of health and medical workers; and
- Improve and strengthen hospital and clinic services.

5. PROGRAM TARGETS: 2002 - 2005

These program targets will be undertaken by the Ministry:

- Family planning and population control;
- Health manpower development;
- Primary health care;
- Urban and rural health and medical services;
- National bulk purchasing and distribution of drugs;
- Dental Services;
- Rehabilitate clinics destroyed during ethnic tension;
- Build clinics to meet pressure of people returning to Malaita as a result of the ethnic tension;
- Convene National Health Seminar;
- Carry out further research into tropical medicine;
- Amend relevant health legislation;
- Control of Malaria and other vector borne diseases;
- Increase intakes for:
    - Nurse Training;
    - Para-medical Training;
    - Doctors Training; and
    - Dentists Training.
    - Encourage more training in specialized fields;
    - Work on the third phase of the Central Hospital;
    - Increase financial allocations of Health Services grants to both private hospitals and clinics;
    - Research into herbal medicines;
    - Promote education awareness on environmental health and Aids and include these in school curriculum;
    - Upgrading of Provincial Hospitals including Church hospitals;
    - Encourage community participation in Health Services;
    - Enact legislation to regulate Private medical services; and
    -

MINISTRY OF POLICE, NATIONAL SECURITY & JUSTICE.

1. BACKGROUND

The 20th Century closed with occurrence of the worst social and political unrest the people of Solomon Islands have ever experienced. The nation and its people emerged into the 21st Century with total anxiety and uncertainty about the future surrounded by the near collapsed of Law and order and a National Economy meltdown. Hence, the restoration of Law and Order is crucial to the Government's commitment to return the country to full normalcy. In the immediate and short-term projection, Law and Order, Internal Security, provision of Justice and the Revitalization of the Economy will form the most important national priorities.

2. FUNCTIONS OF THE MINISTRY

(i) The Portfolio subjects formally assigned to the Ministry are:

- Law & Order;
- Police Training;
- Law enforcement and security;
- Fire Service;
- Vehicle Licensing and Registration;
- Traffic;
- Solomon Islands National Reconnaissance & Surveillance Force;
- Law Reform;
- Public Solicitor;
- Director of Public Prosecution;
- Attorney General;
- Firearms Control & Licensing; and
- Prison Service.

3. POLICY OBJECTIVES

The objectives of the Ministry are to:

- Restore Law and Order and ensure it is maintained and enforced;
- Enforce and maintain internal security;
- Execute court decisions;
- Continue Police and Prison Housing;
- Application of Justice to all citizens;
- Continue Law reforms;
- Coordinate legal matters and proper administration of courts;
- Review and establish improved framework for house of chiefs and Local Courts;
- Ensure Prison conditions meet internationally accepted standards;
- Develop an efficient and effective Fire Service;
- Protect the territorial integrity and sovereignty of Solomon Islands in time of emergency; and
- Engage the Police Force in Civil Works and assist in times of Natural Disasters.

4. DEVELOPMENT STRATEGIES

In pursuing its objectives the Ministry will be guided by these strategies:

- Actively involved in the Peace Process;
- Implement the Amnesty Acts;
- Continue the restructuring of the Police Force and Prison Service;
- Strengthen the Police through recruitment and provision of adequate logistics;
- More training for Police Paramilitary and Prison Service personnel;
- Build and improve Police and Prison Service housing;

- Reduce the number of special constables to a level required by the Police Force;
- Introduce or amend relevant legislation to provide for required changes which could ensure effective administration of justice, law and the courts; and
- Enforce discipline in the Police Force and Prison Service.

5. PROGRAM TARGETS 2002 - 2005
The Ministry will undertake these program targets:

- Restore Law and Order and ensure it is maintained by the Police Force;
- Actively involved in the Peace Process;
- Implement the Amnesty Acts;
- Enforce the return of illegal arms and stolen property;
- Reconstruct the Marau Police Station;
- Seek funding to complete the Central Prison at Rove;
- Continue to restructure the Police Force and Prison Service;
- Establish separate prison for young offenders;
- Amend the Police Act;
- Support the training of Lawyers and Magistrates and identify candidates to undergo legal training;
- Amend the Ombudsman (further provisions) Act;
- Implement the Customs Recognition Act;
- Reduce the number of special constables to a level required by the Police Force;
- Continue with the housing program for the Police Force and Prison Service;
- Implementation of village courts/local courts;
- Encourage more specialized training for lawyers and magistrates;
- Enforce discipline in the Police Force and Prison Service; and
- Introduce legislation to strengthen the Special Branch (SB).

MINISTRY OF MINES, ENERGY & WATER RESOURCES.

1. BACKGROUND
The Ministry is a priority productive sector in the Government's drive for revitalization of the economy following the ethnic conflict. All efforts will be made in consultation with stakeholders to reopen the Gold Ridge Mining Project. Further, most of the mineral and potential energy resources are located on customary land. Hence, policies and legislations have to be in place to ensure active participation of landowners. In so doing, they too can meaningfully benefit from the development of these resources.
2. FUNCTIONS OF THE MINISTRY
(i) The Portfolio subjects formally assigned to the Ministry are:

- Mining;
- Minerals;
- Energy;
- Geology;

- Water Resources;
- Licensing; and
- Hydrology

(ii) The Ministry is responsible and answerable for these Statutory Authorities:

- Solomon Islands Electricity Authority (SIEA);
- Mines and Minerals Board; and
- Solomon Islands Water Authority (SIWA).

3. POLICY OBJECTIVES
(i) The objectives for the development of the Mining sector are as follow:

- Develop a comprehensive mining industry for social and economic development by providing employment and diversifying the country's exports earnings. Internationally recognized environmental safeguards will have to be met before the opening of mines;
- Ensure development of mineral and hydro-carbon resources are done in such a way that the interest of landowners are fully catered for;
- Re-open Gold Ridge Mine and open another Gold Mine; and
- Open the Bugotu Nickel Mine.

(ii) The objectives for the development of the Energy sector are as follow:

- Develop potential energy resources to meet the increasing industrial needs of the country;
- Ensure that people have access to an integrated cost-effective and affordable power supply; and
- Review SIEA to immediately redress the chronic power failures currently being experienced.

4. DEVELOPMENT STRATEGIES
The Ministry will be guided by these strategies in the pursuit of its objectives:

- Identifying of potential mines and hydro carbon sites;
- Continue close consultation with stakeholders with a view to open the Gold Ridge Mine;
- Review and where necessary amend the Mines and Minerals Act;
- Continue to re-assess current licences on mineral prospecting that are attractive to potential mining companies. Once economical deposits of mineral are confirmed a maximum period of three years will be given to license holders and if mining operations do not start within this period the licence would to be deemed to have automatically expired;
- Negotiation with the Landowners who would pave the way for the establishment of mines;
- Continue identifying potential sources to be developed to meet the increasing energy needs of the country's industries;

- Re-assess and find potential funding for the Development of alternative energy;
- Strengthen the Energy Division to continue to identify Potential sources to be developed for alternative energy in rural areas;
- Review the SIEA with a view to transfer ownership on either BOT or BOOT basis; and
- Establish water systems and other infrastructures in Identified areas for integrated projects.

5. PROGRAM TARGETS: 2002 - 2005
These program targets will be pursued:

- Issue prospecting licence to companies interested in mining minerals and oil in the country;
- Re-open the Gold Ridge Mining Project;
- Open another Gold Mine;
- Open Bogotá Nickel Mine;
- Privatize SIEA on either BOT or BOOT basis;
- Establish a fuel farm;
- Find interested developer to fund and build the Lungga Hydro Scheme;
- Continue the program of surveying and evaluating mini-hydro and solar projects in certain suitable locations throughout the country especially government substation and rural areas; and
- Open a number of mini-hydro and solar energy projects in the rural areas.

MINISTRY OF EDUCATION AND TRAINING.

1. BACKGROUND
This Ministry is concerned with education as a right. As much as possible, all children should have access to schools. It is envisaged that the Ministry will be strengthened to provide central direction to and coordination of policies to produce an enlightened society as well as an educated manpower readily available for the country's development requirements and advancement into the 21st century.
2. FUNCTIONS OF THE MINISTRY
(i) The Portfolio subjects assigned to the Ministry are:

- Education;
- Pre-School Training;
- Scholarships;
- Curriculum Development;
- Teaching Service;
- Library Service;
- Research Control;
- Schools and Educational Institutions;
- Selection and Guidance; and
- Informal Education.

(ii) The Ministry is responsible and answerable for this statutory authority:

- Solomon Islands College of Higher Education/University of Solomon Islands (the latter is proposed).

3. POLICY OBJECTIVES

The objectives of the Ministry are to:

- Ensure that Education is a right to be enjoyed by all;
- Shift emphasis from the philosophy of "Education for What" to the philosophy of "Education for Living";
- Give equal opportunity to both males and females in schools and institutions of learning;
- Increase the percentage of secondary schools intakes;
- Formally adopt as policy the establishment of Vocational/Rural Training Centers;
- Put in place more literacy and community education opportunities;
- Increase more environmental, health, culture and tradition awareness in schools;
- Convert SICHE into a University; and
- Encourage certain private organizations to establish their own primary and secondary schools.

4. DEVELOPMENT STATEGIES

The Ministry will be guided by these strategies:

- Review the Education system with a view to:
  - Students not to sit elimination examinations until they reach Form 5;
  - Five years of attending secondary without school fees being paid; and
- Amend relevant sections of the 1978 Education Act to cater for changes which could assist in achieving the education policy objectives.

5. PROGRAM TARGETS 2002 - 2005

The Ministry will undertake these program targets:

- Review the education system with a view towards abolishing school fees until students reach Form 6, as well as removing elimination exams until Form 5;
- As a matter of policy, establish more Vocation/Rural Training Centers;
- Continue establishing more community high schools;
- Continue the allocation of grants to Secondary Schools;
- Continue to Introduce Forms 4 and 5 in some community high schools;
- Increase teacher training opportunities for both primary and secondary schools;
- Renovate and expand the National Library;
- Establish some senior secondary schools only, i.e., Forms 4 - 6;
- Rehabilitate schools destroyed as a result of the ethnic tension;
- Consider establishing separate classes/schools for boys and girls;

- Introduce in Parliament the amendment to the 1978 Education Act;
- Institute Flag raising in schools;
- Divert World Bank assistance to the strengthening and improvement of community high schools;
- SICHE to become University of Solomon Islands;
- Establish the National Education Commission;
- Place more local input and flavor into the curriculum contents;
- Recommence school broadcasts;
- Encourage individuals or groups of interested persons to establish institutes or opportunities of high learning;
- Phase out KGVI National Secondary School to become an exclusively Form 7 institution;
- Review the terms of conditions of employment of teachers;
- Develop sports and physical education in schools;
- Establish a scholarship schemes to which the private sector has direct access and give support to;
- Convert the National Training Unit (NTU) to a National Scholarship Selection Board (SSB) whose membership should be drawn from a wider community representation;
- Investigate the feasibility of establishing a Tertiary Students Scholarship Scheme; and
- Encourage the establishment of more pre-schools throughout the country.

MINISTRY OF YOUTH, SPORTS AND WOMEN.

1. BACKGROUND
Women and Youth play very important roles in the overall development of the country. In recognition of the importance of these roles and to enhance their full participation in nation building, a new Ministry is being established to coordinate policy and priorities in relation to their involvement.
2. FUNCTIONS OF THE MINISTRY

- The Portfolio subjects assigned to the ministry are:
- Women in Development;
- Youth Development;
- Sports Development;
- Development of Fine Arts; and
- Parks.

(ii) The Ministry is responsible and answerable for these statutory Authorities:

- National Council of Women;
- National Youth Congress; and
- National Sports Council;

3. POLICY OBJECTIVES:
The Objectives of the Ministry are:

- Encourage women to be equal partners in the political, economic social and cultural development of the country;
- Ensure that women and youth receive appropriate training and to acquire skills that enable them to play their roles fully in nation building;
- Engage youth in cultural, self employment schemes and civil programs and activities so that they become law abiding citizens of the country;
- Develop Solomon Islands into a sporting nation; and
- Develop Solomon Islands into a nation of Fine Arts.

4. DEVELOPMENT STRATEGIES:
The Ministry shall be guided by these strategies:

- Give special attention to and assist women and youth engaged in business and economic activities;
- Create opportunities for school push outs to engage in productive development and community work;
- Establish youth voluntary scheme;
- Set up a National Sports Institute;
- Develop and improve sporting facilities starting in the capital;
- Strengthen and coordinate women activities in overall nation building;
- Review the youth congress, the National Council of women and the National Sports Council;
- Upgrade the music unit at SICHE to embrace other Fine Arts; and
- Set aside scenic areas for parks and World Heritage sites.

5. PROGRAM TARGETS: 2002 - 2005
The Ministry will undertake these program targets:

- Establish a credit facility for women;
- In collaboration with Churches and other NGOs continue youth and Women Training Programs;
- Strengthen the National Youth Congress, the National Council of women and the National Sports Council;
- Established provincial women Councils;
- Build the National Sports Stadium;
- Establish the National Sports Institute;
- Provide overseas scholarships for deserving sportsmen and sportswomen;
- Introduce legislation for parks and youth voluntary schemes;
- Assist youth self-employment by establishment of a credit facility to kick start income generating projects;
- Upgrade the Music Unit at SICHE to include other Fine Arts;
- Introduce legislation to safeguard the "Rights of the Child," and
- Actively involve Women and Youth in the Peace process.

MINISTRY OF AGRICULTURE & LIVESTOCK.

1. BACKGROUND

The backbone of the country's economy is agriculturally based where 85% of the population, living in subsistence affluence, depend on agriculture for their livelihood as well derive their main source of income. Being a relatively well-endowed country with so far ample agricultural land, it is surprising that after more than 20 years of independence, the country continue to depend on certain overseas food which can be grown and raised in Solomon Islands. The country's agricultural exports production especially SIPL has been badly affected by the ethnic tension. Measures will be taken to revive this important sector. The Ministry has been mandated to revive and correct dislocations in priority productive sectors of the economy.

2. FUNCTIONS OF THE MINISTRY

(i) The Portfolio subjects assigned to the Ministry are:

- Agriculture;
- Quarantine;
- Livestock and Horticulture;
- Research;
- Extension Services; and
- Form Development and Management.

(ii) The Ministry is responsible for this Statutory Authority:

- Livestock Development Authority.

3. POLICY OBJECTIVES

The objectives of the Ministry are:

- Increase output and productivity in food gardening;
- Increase copra and coconut oil export;
- Increase cocoa and oil palm export;
- Increase spices development and export;
- Increase domestic coffee production;
- Continue beef development and increase domestic production for domestic market;
- Increase pig, chicken, meat and egg production;
- Research into and introduce pawpaw as an export commodity;
- Improve production and marketing of honey products;
- Improve the capacity for successful marketing of agriculture produce; and
- Strengthen institutional arrangements for all areas of agriculture.

4. DEVELOPMENT STRATEGIES

The Ministry will be guided by these strategies:

- Priority will be placed on:
    - Rehabilitating agriculture projects affected by the ethnic conflict;
    - Rural areas facing population and development pressures;
    - Areas that would provide food crops for urban markets;

    - Emphasis will be on increased training, extension, capital assistance, research, and demonstration and input supply for food production.

- Revitalize the Solomon Islands Plantation Limited;
- Encourage Sylvania Plantations to (SI) Ltd. To increase land under palm oil production and encouragement of an Out grower Scheme;
- Maximize production potential from existing coconut plantation including assisting small-holder farmers in production of high quality copra, replanting of senescent palms and control of pests diseases and marketing;
- Assist farmers through a guarantee credit facility to increase cocoa plantings, provision of drier parts and training and processing, provision of quality seeds, pest and disease control;
- Assist in the production of Nepalese Kaboke Chili for Domestic and exports markets as well as vanilla on suitable areas in the Provinces;
- Assist groups, individuals and schools venturing into rice production which will include extension and advice, in source instances infrastructure developments, seed shortage and processing facilities;
- Encourage Arabic and Robust Coffee plantings on Isabel and other highland areas for processing and marketing;
- Establish of an elite breeding herd for improve progressive and than distributing this to selected ranches designated breeding farms around the country;
- Assist farmers with breeding stock and facilitating the establishment of 250-300 sow units on a suitable central location by the private sector and provide assistance with downstream processing of pig products;
- Encourage commercial poultry operations around urban centers particularly in Honiara, and establish a dual purpose flock to supply stock to farmers with a view to improving village progeny;
- Distribute goats to farmers and promotion of leathering amongst small-holders farmers;
- Improve the quality of honey in the country and strengthen the Honey Producers Cooperative, and encourage farmers to have more hives;
- Priority would be in training and extension, research and management; and
- Accelerate research into pawpaw latex and develop for exports.

5. PROGRAM TARGETS: 2002-2005

The Ministry shall pursue these program targets:

- Identify landholding groups to open lands and develop the land for commercial tree crops and other farms of horticulture;
- Identify individuals or family groups around the perimeter of Honiara, Auki and Gizo, who own tillable land to encourage and assist them to develop source farms to supply tourism programs as well as the public;
- Identify landholding groups or individuals who are interested in cattle, chicken, meat, eggs, pig, coffee, goat and bee-keeping production or any other agricultural products to be assisted directly by the Government;

- Assist farmers through guarantee credit facility to do more cocoa plantings and rehabilitate their cocoa plots affected by the effects of the ethnic tension;
- Revitalize and develop the ex-Sol rice land on the Guadalcanal Plains in collaboration with the Guadalcanal Province and ROC;
- Establish a pineapple juice processing plant in Malaita Province and other provinces;
- Establish a central coffee processing plant on Isabel;
- Improve the National Vegetable Demonstration farm;
- Provide improved fruit trees and vegetable;
- Develop pawpaw latex for export;
- Provide assistance to farming groups on Individuals to
- establish vegetable farms to Supply urban centers starting with Honiara;
- Pursue oil palm 'out grower' schemes;
- Promote community rice production;
- Revitalize the cattle and livestock development program; and
- Enlarge the bee-keeping project.

MINISTRY OF FISHERIES & MARINE RESOURCES.

1. BACKGROUND
The Ministry has been established to emphasize the Government's commitment and drive to aggressively developed this productive sector to meet both domestic consumption and overseas export. Hence it contributes significantly to the revitalization of the economy.
2. FUNCTIONS OF THE MINISTRY
These Portfolio subjects are assigned to the Ministry:

- Fisheries and Marine Resources;
- Aquaculture;
- Research & Development; and
- Licensing.

3. POLICY OBJECTIVES
The objectives of the Ministry are:

- Coordinate all fisheries operations within the 200 miles economic zone of Solomon Islands to achieve better maximum benefit for the people of Solomon Islands;
- Improve current fishing facilities to encourage Local fishermen to effectively preserve and Market their fish and other perishable marine Products; and
- Ensure harvesting practices of Marine resources are properly coordinated and monitored to ensure that certain resources are not unnecessarily depleted.

4. DEVELOPMENT STRATEGIES
In pursuit of its objectives the Ministry will be guided by these Strategies:

- Encourage fisheries enterprises (full-time fishing on commercial basis) focusing on deep sea pelagic and net fishing;
- Improve and upgrade storage facilities and ice-making machines in Honiara and various fisheries center;
- Identify interested entrepreneurs and encourage them to develop more efficient aqua-culture projects;
- Encourage prawn farming in the provinces;
- Priority will be place on encouraging seaweed farming, giant clams and pearl farming; and
- Improve transportation of fish to urban markets.

5. PROGRAM TARGETS

The Ministry will pursue these programs targets:

- Establish giant clam shells, black lips, pearl and bech-de-mer farms in the Provinces and embark on the giant clam shell marine culture pilot project;
- Establish prawn farms in the Provinces;
- Privatize all rural fisheries centers;
- Identify and encourage fish farming;
- Provide training for local fishermen;
- Provide financial assistance to local fishing groups to acquire fishing gears and facilities;
- Commence pearl shell spot collection;
- Commission a fish transportation vessel;
- Increase the supply of fish for domestic and overseas markets;
- Increase the output growth of marine and aqua-culture;
- Increase the processing of raw tuna for export markets; and
- Encourage the establishment of base facilities for other companies.

TRAVEL TO SOLOMON ISLANDS

SOLOMON ISLANDS ... the eco-tourism destination of the Pacific. Here upon a thousand warm, colourful, tropical islands, you will find natures richness and beauty in the smiling company of a caring, friendly people.

Soaring, mist-enshrouded mountain peaks preside above dense, abundant, rainforests. Waterfalls and rivers cascade to an intricate coastline, Here, the villages lay scattered around lazy lagoons and sun soaked golden beaches bedecked with coconut palms beckon the likes of you and I.

As beautiful below as it above ... the warm sparkling clear waters hold a visual feast to delight the most fastidious diving enthusiast. Here mother nature weaves her watery spell amongst the sunken relics of World War 2. On the surface, sport fishermen can't believe their luck, boaties discover that this is truly one of the most enchanting cruising grounds in the world and locals use the sea as the highway between their villages and towns.

This is indeed and eco-tourism destination, an unspoiled, unhurried and totally unforgettable place to visit. Beyond Honiara with its comfortable hotels, a sprinkling of accommodation facilities of acceptable standard, can be found throughout the islands. Located in the most desirable of locations they offer friendly helpful service and intimate knowledge of their surroundings and local attractions. The unique charm of the islands is best expressed in this environment of relaxation and goodwill.

Go exploring here amongst a willing and friendly people. Experience their fascinating way of life, discover their history, learn of headhunters, of custom lands, of ancient traditions, marvel at their handicrafts and village life, be captivated by their music. It is here, away from the trappings of the conventional tourist trail, that you will discover the real charm of these magic islands and perhaps discover a little of yourself as well.

IMPORTANT INFORMATION

LOCATION

The Solomon Islands are a widespread archipelago of some 990 mountainous islands and low-lying coral atolls. They stretch approximately 1500 kilometres South-east from Papua New Guinea into the south-west Pacific and the Coral Sea. The subsidiary island groups of Santa Cruz, Lord Howe and Duff are administered by the Solomon Islands. The capital of Honiara is situated on the island of Guadalcanal.

POPULATION

Total population is a little over 320,000 people. Over 90% of the people are Melanesian. Polynesian and some Micronesians can be found mostly in the outlying islands. A small minority of European, Chinese and others inhabit the main centres and resort locations.

CLIMATE

Tropical with average daytime temperatures around 29 degrees and high humidity. Evenings may be as cool as 19 degrees. There are no defined seasons but November to May are wetter months and squalls and cyclones may occur.

LANGUAGE

There are approx. 87 different native languages, including Melanesian Pidgin English which is used predominantly. English is used and understood throughout.

DRESS

Informal light attire is appropriate for both day and evening wear. A sweater for the occasional cool evening. Bikinis and swimming briefs should be confined to the beaches and resort pool areas

CURRENCY/BANKING

The standard unit of currency is the Solomon Islands Dollar. $1 Australian dollar will buy approx. $2 Solomon Island dollars. Westpac, ANZ Bank and the National Bank of the Solomon Islands open Monday to Fridays 8.30am to 3.00pm and offer the best exchange rates. Credit cards and travellers cheques are not usually accepted beyond the main resort areas.

HEALTH

Like many other tropical countries, Malaria is also endemic in the Solomon Islands. Appropriate anti-malarial medication should be taken. It is wise to consult your doctor or chemist a few weeks before leaving home. Water is normally safe in the major resorts, but precautionary boiling is recommended in other areas. (If in doubt..ask)

ENTRY REQUIREMENTS

Commonwealth, U.S., and most E.E.C. visitors, do not need visas. Others may obtain visas through British Consulates. 7 day transit visas are available on arrival. All visitors must have a valid passport and return, or onward ticket. Persons intending to work, mast have a work permit.

CUSTOMS/DUTY FREE/ DEPARTURE TAX

200 cigarettes or 250 grams of tobacco. 2 litres of spirits, or equivalent. Electrical goods in excess of SI$40.00 are dutiable. Departure Tax is SI$30.00.

ELECRICITY

240 volts. Available in Honiara and major resort areas.

TELECOMMUNICATION

24 hour international telephone, fax, telex, and telegram service is available through TeleKom from Honiara and most major hotels and resorts.

TIME

11 hours ahead of Greenwich Mean Time.

TIPPING

Not expected and not encouraged.

The main port of entry into The Solomon Islands is at Henderson International Airport on the island of Guadalcanal, situated approx. 20 minutes drive from the capital of Honiara. The town is situated on the northern coastline and incorporates a small, picturesque sea port at Point Cruz.

SHOPPING

Honiara town centre is level, shady and interesting, with a bustling air and interesting shops, some specialising in local handicrafts, others in duty free goods. The range of products is however limited . Here also is the centre of commerce, banks, postal service, Telekom, restaurants, tourist information centre, local tour operators etc.

A wonderful opportunity to mix with the locals presents itself at the several colourful outdoor markets around the town. Here you will find an interesting array of local goods and produce, from fresh fish and vegetables, fruit, peanuts and betel nuts, to carvings, basketware, calico laplaps and shells.

RESTAURANTS

A good selection of restaurants offer a variety of different cuisines. Some hotel restaurants feature cultural nights with local musicians and groups performing traditional song and dance.

There are a number of Chinese restaurants and other that specialise in fresh local seafood such as Coconut Crab and Lobster. French, Japanese, Thai and Italian dishes can also be found on the menus of Honiara.

CLUBS

Both the Point Cruz Yacht Club and Guadalcanal Club are situated downtown and welcome overseas guests for drinks and light meals. Activities include regular dances, lawn bowls, tennis, snooker, film nights, sailing and boating. The Super Club Casino in Old Chinatown has an excellent restaurant and fully catered casino; whilst at the Honiara Casino on Point Cruz, players enjoy Baccarat, blackjack, Roulette and more.

WORTH VISITING

The Solomon Islands National Museum in the centre of Honiara. Featuring a display of custom houses and wonderful carvings which demonstrate the diversity of cultures throughout the country. In a natural amphitheatre the visitor is entertained with live performances of provincial dances and other culture related displays.

Santa Cruz Hill where Alvro de Mendana who discovered the islands, together with his advisers, named them "Solomon Islands". A perfect vantage point.

Solomon Islands Peace Memorial atop Mount Austin, with its four white monoliths inscribed "Rest in Peace". This simple but impressive structure was erected by a Japanese Veteran group as a memorial to all men who died during the bitter Guadalcanal campaign of World War 2. Good views.

A good paved road runs both east and west from Honiara. It provides the opportunity to view some of the scenic delights of the island.

East of the town you will find: Betikama High School, renowned for its wonderful selection of carvings, handicrafts and WWII relics; Red Beach and Tetere Bay, scene of the successful amphibious landing by the U.S. Marines; The Palm Oil plantations; local villages and finally Vulelua Island Resort. The road west takes you along the coast to Tambea Resort and Lambi Bay. The journey takes about an hour. Along the way stop at the Japanese War Memorial at Poha River; visit Vilu Village War Museum; see Bonegi Beach, a giant clam farm and coconut plantations; pass Cape Esperance, where 13,000 Japanese soldiers were evacuated and finally arrive in Tambea, where the resort provides an ideal stopping place for lunch.

Several guided walks and treks provide the opportunity to see local villages, tropical bush, unique flora and fauna, rivers and impressive waterfalls. Use a local guide or tour company to show you the way, or take a scenic flight if time is short.

WORLD WAR 2 BATTLE SITES

Some of the fiercest fighting of the War took place in and around Honiara. Names like Bloody Ridge, Red Beach, Skyline Ridge and Henderson Field will live long in the memories of both sides.

Here in 1942, World War Two's bloodiest and longest campaign saw the loss of nearly 3S,000 lives and the turning point of the war in the Pacific.

There are many battle sites and relics of the war to be found not only here, but throughout the islands. Ask locally for directions or better still, for an excellent commentary and to cover all points of interest, engage the services of a local tour guide.

GETTING AROUND IN HONIARA

BUSES: run along the main road, Mendana Avenue. A destination card is displayed in the front window. The fares are modest.

TAXIS: cannot be booked and do not have meters. They can be flagged down in the street and the fare should be negotiated before the journey commences. Taxis are always available outside the airport terminal. The normal fare from Henderson Airport to Honiara is around SI$20. (AU$10)

RENTAL CARS: Available from both Budget and Avis, who both operate and office in Honiara.

GETTING AROUND IN THE SOLOMON ISLANDS

The full Solomon Airlines (+677 20031) domestic network as of October 1999 is shown below.
Western Pacific Airlink (+677 36111) fly to some of these and others not shown on the map (see below).

Western Pacific Airlink (Tel: +677 36533 or 36111, Fax: +677 36476) fly a small (8-seater) Islander plane and service the following destinations:

- ***Kagau (Kaghau), south-east Choiseul***
- ***Geva, Vella Lavella Island, Western Province***
- ***Gizo, Western Province***
- ***Kukudu, Kolombangara Island, Western Province***
- ***Ringi, Kolombangara Island, Western Province***
- ***Munda, Western Province***
- ***Ramata, New Georgia, Western Province***
- ***Batuna (Mbatuna), Vangunu Island, Western Province***
- ***Gatokae (Nggatokae), Western Province***
- ***Kwailabesi, Malaita***
- ***Atoifi, Malaita***
- ***Afutara, Malaita***

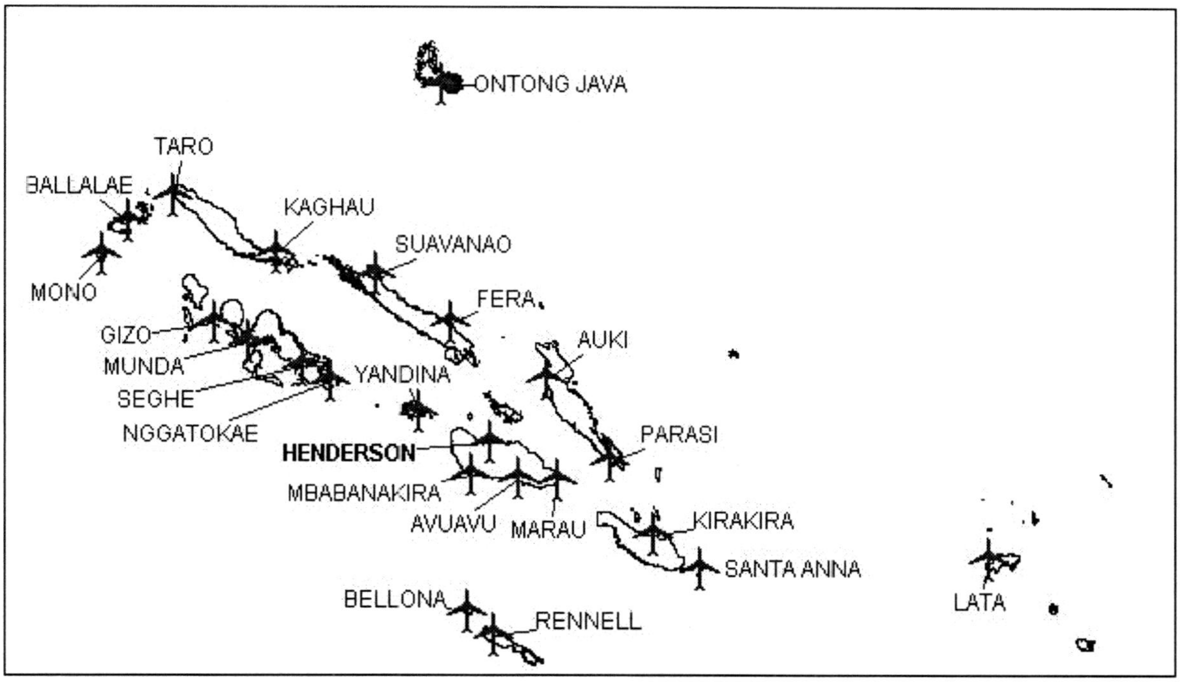

Maps courtesy of Bob Vincent, Eddie Kakai and Mick Saunders of The Map Factory, Census Office census@welkam.solomon.com.sb

INTER-ISLAND SHIPPING

Transwestern Shipping (Western Province)
Tel: +677 23186
M.V.Tomoko

Wings Shipping (Western Province)
Tel: +677 22811
M.V.Iuminao

Malaita Shipping Company (Malaita)
Tel: +677 23501
Fax: +677 23503
Ramos I,II,III

Isabel Development Corporation (Santa Isabel)
Tel: +677 22126
Fax: +677 22009
LIGOMO IV, M.V.FEARN

Temotu Development Authority (Temotu)
Tel: +677 53145
Fax: +677 53145
M.V.Eastern Trader

ACTIVITIES

Sports activities include golf, tennis, bush walking and a wide range of aquatic sports - swimming, sailing, surfing, windsurfing, waterskiing, snorkelling and game fishing.

The Solomons are renowned as a scuba diver's paradise with coral, shipwrecks, giant clams, tropical fish and game fish.

High quality craft work is available and includes ebony and 'kerosene' wood carvings, bowls with mother-of-pearl inlays, shell jewellery, baskets, bags, hats and mats woven from pandanus or coconut palm.

Although the only craft shops are in Honiara, you can buy work direct from craftsmen and women in the other islands.

Daily markets are held throughout the Solomons. The Central market in the capital of Honiara is the largest and most colourful.

FOOD

Major hotels have restaurants and there are international-style restaurants in Honiara. Hotels have beer gardens and bars and several private clubs welcome visitors. Island night barbecues are held regularly and are very popular.

SUPPLEMENTS

FOREIGN MISSIONS

NEW YORK	
Ambassador	HE Mr. Collin Beck
Postal Address	Solomon Islands Missions to the United Nation Suite 8008 800 2nd Avenue New York, N.Y. 10017-4709 United States of America Tel: 00 1 212 5996192/3 Fax: 00 1 212 6618925 Email: simny@solomons.com
BRUSSELS	
Ambassador	HE Mr. Joseph Ma'ahanua
Postal Address	Embassy of Solomon Islands Avenue Edouard Lacomble, 17 1040 Brussels Belgium Tel: 00 32 2 732 7085 Fax: 00 32 2 732 6885 Email: siembassy@compuserve.com
CANBERRA	
High Commissioner	HE Mr. Milner Tozaka
Postal Address	Solomon Islands High Commissioner 1st Floor JAA Building Unit 4/19 Napier Close Deakin P O Box 256 Deakin West ACT 2600 Canberra, Australia Tel: 00 61 26 282 7030 Fax: 006126 282 7040 Email: info@solomon.emb.gov.au
TAIPEI	
Ambassador	HE Mr. Beraki Jino
Postal Address	Embassy of Solomon Islands 7F, No.9, Lane 62 Tienmu W.Rd. Taipei 111, Taiwan Republic of China Tel: 886 2 2873 1168 (Chancery), 886 2 2877 2787 (Residence) Fax: 886 2 2873 5224 Email: solomon.embassy@msa.hinet.net
PORT MORESBY	
High Commissioner	HE Mr. Philip Kapini
Postal	Solomon Islands High Commission

Address	Unit 2, GB House Port Moresby Papau New Guinea Tel: 00 675 323 4333 Fax: 00 675 323 4334 Email:sihicomm@daltron.com.pg

SELECTED CONTACTS

GOVERNMENT

MINISTRY OF	DEPARTMENT OF	PERMANENT SECRETARIES	MINISTERS	EPS/PHONE
Office of the Prime Minister & Cabinet	Prime Minister's Office and Cabinet	Toswel Kaua [Secretary the PM and Cabinet] Tel: 28617	Sir Allan Kemakeza (PM) Tel: 22202	22202/21863
	Public Service Division	Mr. Fred Ganate	John Garo	24268/24275/ 28617
Finance, National Reform and Planning	National PLanning and aid co-ordination	Jane Waitara	Fred Fono	28608/38336
	Finance and Treasury	Shadrach Fanega Tel: 24102 Fax: 28619	Peter Boyers	28619/24102
Foreign Affairs, Commerce and Tourism	Foeign Affairs	Barnabas Anga Tel: 28614 Fax: 25084	Laurie Chan Tel: 25476	20351/28612
	Commerce, Industries and Employment	Jeffery Whickam Tel: 28614 Fax: 25084	Walton Naezon	22856
	Culture and Tourism	Luke Eta Tel: 28603	Trevor Olavae Tel: 26848	28603/26848
Agriculture and Lands	Agriculture and Lifestock	Edward Kingmele Tel: 28615	E.Kwanairara Tel:24426	28615/24426
	Lands and Survey	Donald Kudu Tel:28600 Fax:27298	Siriako Usa Tel: 26240	26240/22750
Provincial Government and Constituency Development	Provincial Government and Constituency Development	John Tuhaika Tel:28606	Stephen Paeni Tel: 21072	28606/21072
	Home Affaires	Ruth Liloqula Tel: 28601	Nelson Kile Tel/Fax: 25591	28601/25591

	National Reconciliation and Peace	Ethel Sigimanu Tel: 28616	James Tora Tel:28616	28616/23087
Health and Medical Services	Health and Medical Services	Dr.J Leafasia Tel: 28610 Fax: 20085	Johnson Koli Tel: 22376 Fax:20085	
Police, National Security and Justice	Police and National Security	George Hiele Tel: 28607		21049/22208
	Justice and Legal Affairs	James Remubatu	Augustine Taneko	21048
Infrastructure and Development	Infrastructure and Development	John Ta'aru Tel: 28605 Fax:28705	Bernard Giro Tel:25641	28605/25641
	Communication, Aviation and Meteorology	Nairie Alamu	Simeon Bouro Tel: 28620	28620/27751
Natural Resources	Forestry, Environment and Conservation	Steve Likaveke Tel: 28611	David Holosivi Tel:22453	28611/22453
	Fisheries and Marine Resources	Tione Bugotu Tel:28604/39143 Fax: 38730	Paul Maenu Tel:38774	28604/39143
	Mines and Energy	Don Tolia Tel: 28609	Basil Manelegua Tel: 25937	28609/25937
Education and Human Resources	Education and Human Resources Development	Dr.Derick Sikua Tel:28613	Snyder Rini Deputy Prime Minister Tel:28613	28613/26248

GOVERNMENT EMAIL DIRECTORY

Name	Contact Person	Email
Prime Minister's and Cabinet	Permanent Secretary: Toswell Kaua	pspm@pmc.gov.sb
Public Service Department	Permanent Secretary: Fred Ganate	pspsd@pmc.gov.sb
Department of National Reform and Planning	Permanent Secretary: Jane	psnrp@pmc.gov.sb
Department of Finance and Treasury, Customs, Statistics, IRD, ERU and BST	Permanent Secretary: Shadrach Fanega	psfinance@pmc.gov.sb
Department of Police National	Permanent	pspolice@pmc.gov.sb

Security	Secretary: George Hiele	
Department of Education and Human Resources Development	Permanent Secretary: Derick Sikua	pseducation@pmc.gov.sb
Department of Justice and Legal Affairs	Permanent Secretary: James Remubatu	psjustice@pmc.gov.sb
Department of Health and Medical Services, Referral Hospital, Stores, Simtr and HQ	Permanent Secretary: Dr. Judson Leafasia	pshealth@pmc.gov.sb
Department of Foreign Affairs	Permanent Secretary: Barnabas Anga	psfa@pmc.gov.sb
Department of Commerce, Industries and Employment	Permanent Secretary: Jeffery Wickam	pscommerce@pmc.gov.sb ps@commerce.gov.sb
"	Director of Trade: Heinz Vaekesa	trade@commerce.gov.sb
"	Director of Foreign Investment: Derick Ahaira	investment@commerce.gov.sb
"	Director of Business: Joe Heroau	business@commerce.gov.sb
"	Director of Labour:	labour@commerce.gov.sb
"	Director of Immigration:	immigration@commerce.gov.sb
"	Director of Industries: James Apato	idd@commerce.gov.sb
"	Director of Consumers: Oliver Jino	dir_consumers@yahoo.com.au
"	ICT Development Officer	commerce@commerce.gov.sb
"	Webmaster	moira@commerce.gov.sb
Department of Culture and Tourism	Permanent Secretary: Luke Eta	pstourism@pmc.gov.sb
Department of Agriculture and Livestock	Permanent Secretary: Edward Kingmele	psagriculture@pmc.gov.sb
Department of Lands and Survey	Permanent Secretary: Donald Kudu	pslands@pmc.gov.sb

Department of Infrastructure and Development	Permanent Secretary: John Ta'aru	psinfrastructure@pmc.gov.sb
Department of Communication, Aviation and Meteorology	Permanent Secretary: Nairie Alamu	pscommunication@pmc.gov.sb
Department of Forest, Environment and Conservation	Permanent Secretary: Steve Likaveke	psforestry@pmc.gov.sb
Department of Fisheries and Marine Resources	Permanent Secretary: Tione Bugotu	psfisheries@pmc.gov.sb
Department of Mines and Energy	Permanent Secretary: Don Tolia	psmines@pmc.gov.sb
Department of Home Affairs	Permanent Secretary: Ruth Lilogula	psha@pmc.gov.sb
Department of National Reconciliation and Peace	Permanent Secretary: Ethel Sigimanu	pspeace@pmc.gov.sb
Ministry of Provincial Government and Constituency Development www.peoplefirst.net.sb	Permanent Secretary: John. M.Tuhaika	psprovgov@pmc.gov.sb tuhaika@pipolfastaem.gov.sb
"	PFnet Cafe Manager: Randell Biliki	cafe.manager@pipolfastaem.gov.sb

BANKS

ANZ Banking Group Ltd
P.O.Box 10, Honiara, Solomon Islands
Tel: 21835
Fax: 22957 / 24463
Email: langstont@anz.com

Westpac Banking of Solomon Islands
P.O.Box 466, Honiara, Solomon Islands
Tel: 21222
Fax: 23419
Email: westpac@solomon.com.sb

NBSI National Bank of Solomon Islands
(commercial banking)
PO Box 37
Honiara
Solomon Islands
Tel: +677 21874
Fax: (International Dept.) +677 23478
Corresponding bank for US$: Bank of Hawaii, New York
SWIFT code: NBSISBSB

CBSI Central Bank of Solomon Islands
PO Box 634
Honiara
Solomon Islands
Tel: +677 21791
Fax: +677 23513
Email: Currency and Banking Manager
Jerry Pitisopa

DBSI Development Bank of Solomon Islands
PO Box 911
Honiara
Solomon Islands
Tel: +677 21595
Fax: +677 23715
Email: dbsi@solomon.com.sb

CHURCHES

Church of Melanesia
PO Box 19, Honiara, tel: +677 21892, Fax: +677 21098

Catholic Archdiocese of Honiara
PO Box 237, Honiara, tel: +677 21943, Fax: +677 22869
Catholic Church of the Solomon Islands web page
http://www.catholicnet.com/solomon.htm
http://www.catholicnet.com/solomon/katolika.htm

South Seas Evangelical Church
PO Box 16, Honiara, tel: +677 22388,

United Church of PNG and SI
PO Box 82, Munda, tel: +677 61125, Fax: +677 20453

SDA Seventh Day Adventist Mission
PO Box 63, Honiara, tel: +677 21191

Assemblies of God Church
PO Box 928, Honiara, tel: +677 25512, Fax +677 22786

Bahai Faith
PO Box 245, Honiara, tel: +677 22475 (after hours 22290) , Fax: +677 25368

Christian Outreach Centre
PO Box 1386, Honiara, tel: +677 24130

ACCOUNTANTS

Goh and Partners
PO Box 261, Victory Building, Mendana Avenue, Honiara, Solomon Islands.
Tel: +677 21654 Fax: +677 23726
Email: gohwtaeyi@solomon.com.sb
http://www.commerce.gov.sb/business_directories/advhpages/goh.htm

Pricewaterhouse Coopers
PO Box 70, Honiara, Solomon Islands
Tel: +677 21851 Fax: 23342

FPS Business Consultancy
PO Box 735, Honiara
Tel: 22989
Fax: 25707

MISI and Associates
PO Box 202, Honiara
Tel: 22621
Fax: 24326

LAWYERS

Sol-Law Barristers and Solicitors (commercial)
PO Box 498, Honiara
Tel: 23886
Fax: 20356
Email: sollaw@solomon.com.sb

Andrew Radclyffe (commercial)
PO Box 729, Honiara
Tel: 24095
Fax: 24096

Charles Ashley (commercial)
PO Box 111, Honiara
Tel: 23784

Public Solicitors Office
PO Box 553, Honiara Tel: 22769 (Head Office)
PO Box 44, Auki Tel: 40175 (Malaita Office)
PO Box 84, Gizo Tel: 60175 (Western Province Office)
PO Box 2, Kirakira Tel: 50160 (Makira Office)

Family Support Centre
PO Box 1725, Honiara
Tel: 26999
Fax: 20619
Email: fsc@solomon.com.sb

Bridge Lawyers, Barristers and Solicitors (environmental/logging/mining)
PO Box 821, Honiara
Tel: 24876

SHIPPING AGENTS

Sullivans (SI) Ltd.
PO Box 3, Honiara, Solomon Islands
Tel (677) 21643 Fax: (677) 23889
Email: shipserv@solomon.com.sb
http://www.commerce.gov.sb/Business_Directories/AdvHPages/sullivans_ltd.htm

Solomon Islands Ports Authority
PO Box 307, Honiara, Solomon Islands
Tel (677) 22646 Fax: (677) 23994

Malaita Shipping Company Limited
PO Box 584 Honiara
Tel: 23501 / 23502

Isabel Development Company (trading as Shipping and Port Services)
PO Box 92, Honiara
Tel: 22122 / 22126
Fax: 22009

TRAVEL AGENTS

Guadalcanal Travel Service
P.O.Box 114, Honiara, Solomon Islands
Phone : (677) 22586 Fax : 677 26184
Email : gts@solomon.com.sb
http://www.commerce.gov.sb/Business_Directories/AdvHPages/gts.htm

Business Directory
http://www.commerce.gov.sb/Business_Directories/serv03.htm

OTHERS

ATASI Alliance Training Association of Solomon Islands
PO Box 1702 Honiara
Tel: +677 21701
Fax: +677 23974
Director: Martin Hou

EEC (Delegation of the Commission of the European Communities in SI)
PO Box 844 Honiara
Tel: +677 22765
Fax: +677 23318
Email: ecsol@solomon.com.sb
Permanent Representative: Tom Leemans

SICUL Solomon Islands Credit Union League
PO Box 368
Honiara
Solomon Islands
Tel: +677 23564
Fax: +677 20131

Solomon Islands Association of Rural Training Centres SIARTC
PO Box 556
Honiara
Solomon Islands
Tel: +677 24253
Fax: +677 27295

Solomon Islands Honey Producers Cooperative Association Ltd.
PO Box R175
Honiara
Solomon Islands
Tel: +677 30067
Fax: +677 39041
Email: honey@solomon.com.sb

Solomon Islands Business Enterprise Centre
PO Box 972
Honiara
Solomon Islands
Tel: +677 26651
Fax: +677 26650
Email: simbec@solomon.com.sb

Willies Electrical Skills Centre and Electrical Contractor
PO Box R169
Honiara
Solomon Islands
Tel: +677 30477 / 30333
Fax: +677 30477 / 30543

National Museum
PO Box 313
Honiara
Tel/Fax: +677 23351
Director +677 22309

National Art Gallery
PO Box 1353
Honiara
Telfax: +677 24594

Solomon Islands Electricity Authority SIEA
PO Box 6
Honiara
Tel: +677 26666 / 21711 / 39422(engineering)
Fax: +677 21467

IMPORTANT BUSINESS CONTACTS

ACCOUNTANCY SERVICES

GOH & Partners
Web Page!
Certified Public Accountants
Commissioner for Oaths
Notary Public
PO Box 261,
Victory Building,
Mendana Avenue,
Honiara,
Solomon Islands
Tel (677) 21654 Fax: (677) 23726
Email:
gohwtaeyi@welkam.solomon.com.sb

BUTCHERS

Sullivans (SI) Ltd.
PO Box 3,
Honiara,
Solomon Islands
Tel (677) 21643 Fax: (677) 23889
Email:
shipserv@welkam.solomon.com.sb

CAR HIRE, SALES, SERVICING

Kosol Corporation Ltd.,

PO Box 89,
Honiara,
SOLOMON ISLANDS
Tel: +677 30703 / 30081
Fax: +677 30806
Email: kosol@solomon.com.sb

COURIER SERVICES

B.J.S Agencies Ltd.
P.O.Box 439
Honiara
Solomon Islands
Phone: 677 21394
Fax: 677 21027
Email: bjs@welkam.solomon.com.sb

CULTURAL & HISTORICAL TOURS

Gizo Historical and Cultural Museum
Cultural tours, bush walks
Wilson Hivu
Titiana Village
Gizo
Western Province
Solomon Islands
c/o Steven Roni, IDD Officer
Tel/Fax:(677) 60076
or c/o Telekom Fax 60128

Guadalcanal Travel Service

Tours, *WW2, Bushwalks, Travel*
P.O.Box 114
Honiara
Solomon Islands
Phone : (677) 22586
Fax : 677 26184
Email : gts@welkam.solomon.com.sb

Solomon Charters
Web Page!
PO Box 132
Gizo
Solomon Islands
Ph ++677 60324
Fax ++677 60321
Email: solchar@solomon.com.sb
Website:
http://www.solomoncharters.com

FISHING, SPORT

Ramata Riches Fishing,
Mavo Guest House, Marovo
Eco-resort, Game Fishing, etc.
North New Georgia
Western Province
Solomon Islands
Tel:(677) 20481 / 24951
Email : SI Visitors Bureau

Solomon Charters
PO Box 132
Gizo
Solomon Islands
Ph ++677 60324
Fax ++677 60321
Email: solchar@solomon.com.sb
Website:http://www.solomoncharters.co
m

FORESTRY

Kolombangara Forest Products Limited
P. O. Box 382
Honiara
Solomon Islands
Phone: 677 60230
Fax: 677 60020
Email: kfpl@welkam.solomon.com.sb

HANDICRAFT & ART

B.J.S Agencies Ltd.
P.O.Box 439
Honiara
Solomon Islands
Phone: 677 21394
Fax: 677 21027
Email: bjs@welkam.solomon.com.sb

MANUFACTURING AND PROCESSING

Fielders Industries (SI) Ltd.
P. O. Box 502
Honiara
Solomon Island
Phone : 677 30146
Fax : 677 30399
Email:
fielders@welkam.solomon.com.sb

MUSEUMS AND CULTURE

Gizo Historical and Cultural Museum
Cultural tours, bush walks
Wilson Hivu
Titiana Village
Gizo
Western Province
Solomon Islands
c/o Steven Roni, IDD Officer
Tel/Fax:(677) 60076
or c/o Telekom Fax 60128

PHILATELIC SERVICES

Solomon Islands Philatelic Bureau
Web Page!
PO Box 1930
Honiara
Solomon Islands
Tel: (677) 22108 Fax: (677) 20440 / 21472

SCRAP METAL

B.J.S Agencies Ltd. ***Web Page!***
P.O.Box 439

Honiara
Solomon Islands
Phone: 677 21394
Fax: 677 21027
Email: bjs@welkam.solomon.com.sb

SHIPPING

Sullivans (SI) Ltd. *Web Page!*
PO Box 3,
Honiara,
Solomon Islands
Tel (677) 21643 Fax: (677) 23889
Email:
shipserv@welkam.solomon.com.sb

TOURISM & TRAVEL

Guadalcanal Travel Service
Web Page!
Tours, *WW2, Bushwalks, Travel*
P.O.Box 114
Honiara
Solomon Islands
Phone : (677) 22586
Fax : 677 26184
Email : gts@welkam.solomon.com.sb

Paeloge Surfing Lodge
Eco-resort with good surfing
John Wesly
c/o Steven Roni,
IDD Officer,
Gizo,
Western Province
Solomon Islands
c/o Steven Roni, IDD Officer
Tel/Fax:(677) 60076
or c/o Telekom Fax 60128

Travel Industry Services
International & Domestic Flights
P.O.Box 114
Honiara
Solomon Islands
Phone : 677 20336
Fax : 677 26184
Email : gts@welkam.solomon.com.sb

Serere Fringing Reef Lodge
Eco-Resort
P.O.Box 1417
Honiara,
Solomon Islands
Tel: (+677) 39708
Email: serere@welkam.solomon.com.sb

Rogosakena Lodge *Web Page!*
Eco-resort
Ralph Tenapiko,
Mbatuna Postal Agency,
Marovo Lagoon,
Western Province,
Solomon Islands
destsolo@welkam.solomon.com.sb

Phoebe's Rest House *Web Page!*
Guest house, backpackers
Phoebe Pitisopa,
P.O.Box 61,
Gizo,
Solomon Islands
Tel:(677) 60161 Fax: 60035

Nello's Villa *Web Page!*
Guest house, backpackers
Gizo,
Solomon Islands
Fax: c/o Telekom (677) 60128

Mavo Guest House *Web Page!*
Eco-resort, Game Fishing, etc.
PO Box 1384
Honiara
Solomon Islands
Tel:(677) 24951 / 20481
Email : SI Visitors Bureau

Gizo Historical and Cultural Museum
Cultural tours, bush walks
Wilson Hivu
Titiana Village
Gizo
Western Province
Solomon Islands
c/o Steven Roni, IDD Officer
Tel/Fax:(677) 60076
or c/o Telekom Fax 60128

Babanga Island Eco Resort
Gilbertese Eco-resort
Osia Ta'asi
Gizo
Western Province
Solomon Islands
c/o Steven Roni, IDD Officer
Tel/Fax:(677) 60076
or c/o Telekom Fax 60128

Jeanna Resort *Web Page!*
Eco-resort
PO Box 36
Gizo
Western Province
Solomon Islands
Tel: +677 60046
Fax: c/o Telekom 60128

Kosol Corporation Ltd.,
Car Hire/Rental, Sales/Servicing
PO Box 89,
Honiara,
SOLOMON ISLANDS
Tel: +677 30703 / 30081
Fax: +677 30806
Email: kosol@solomon.com.sb

Mono Eco-Lodge
Eco lodge, Shortland Islands
c/o Mono Postal Agency
Stirling Island
Shortland Islands
Western Province
Solomon Islands

Auki Lodge
Auki's Premier Hotel
PO Box 170Auki
Malaita
Solomon Islands
Tel: +677 40131
Fax: +677 40044

Kopik Guest House
Town Guest House and backpackers
PO Box 25
Gizo
Western Province
Solomon Islands
Tel: +677 60374
Fax: c/o Gizo Telekom (please allow for delays) +677 60128

The wilderness Lodge
Western Province
Solomon Islands

TRADING, WHOLESALERS, IMPORTS & EXPORTS

Chamber of Commerce and Employer
General Secretary
P.O Box 650
Honiara
Solomon Island
Tel/Fax: 22907
Email:chamberc@welkam.solomon.com.sb

Sullivans (SI) Ltd.
PO Box 3,
Honiara,
Solomon Islands
Tel (677) 21643 Fax: (677) 23889
Email:
shipserv@welkam.solomon.com.sb

B.J.S Agencies Ltd.
P.O.Box 439
Honiara
Solomon Islands
Phone: +677 21394
Fax: +677 21027
Email: bjs@welkam.solomon.com.sb

SOLOMON ISLANDS - EUROPEAN COMMUNITY

COUNTRY STRATEGY PAPER

AND NATIONAL INDICATIVE PROGRAMME

for the period 2002 - 2007

I:\CSP\Sol\CSS27septRev.gm.doc

TABLE OF CONTENTS

SOLOMON ISLANDS

Country Strategy Paper

The Government of the Solomon Islands and the European Commission hereby agree as follows:

(1) The Government of Solomon Islands, represented by (name and title), and the European Commission, represented by (name and title), hereinafter referred to as the Parties, held discussions in Honiara on ....2002 with a view to determining the general orientations for co-operation for the period 2002 - 2007. The European Investment Bank was represented at these discussions by (name and title)

During these discussions, the Country Strategy Paper and an Indicative Programme of Community Aid in favour of Solomon Islands were drawn up in accordance with the provisions of Articles 2 and 4 of Annex IV to the ACP-EC Partnership Agreement, signed in Cotonou on 23 June 2000. These discussions complete the programming process in Solomon Islands.

The Country Strategy Paper and the Indicative Programme are annexed to the present document.

(2) As regards the indicative programmable financial resources which the Community envisages to make available to Solomon Islands for the period 2002-2007, an amount of € 6.7 million is foreseen for the allocation referred to in Article 3.2 (a) of Annex IV of the ACP-EC Partnership Agreement (A-allocation) and of € 7.8 million for the allocation referred to in Article 3.2 (b) (B-allocation). These allocations are not entitlements and may be revised by the Community, following the completion of mid-term and end-of-term reviews, in accordance with Article 5.7 of Annex IV of the ACP-EC Agreement.

(3) The A-allocation is destined to cover macroeconomic support, sectoral policies, programmes and projects in support of the focal or non-focal areas of Community Assistance. The Indicative Programme under Chapter VI concerns the resources of the A-allocation. It also takes into consideration financing from which Solomon Islands benefits or could benefit under other Community resources. It does not pre-empt financing decisions by the Commission.

(4) The B-allocation is destined to cover unforeseen needs such as emergency assistance where such support cannot be financed from the EU budget, contributions to internationally agreed debt relief initiatives and support to mitigate adverse effects of instability in export earnings. The B-allocation shall be triggered according to specific mechanisms and procedures and does therefore not yet constitute a part of the Indicative Programme.

(5) Pending the entry into force of the Financial Protocol of the ACP-EC Partnership Agreement and within the framework of the present Country Strategy Paper and Indicative Programme, financing decisions for projects and programmes can be taken by the Commission at the request of the Government of Solomon Islands, within the limits of the A- and B-allocations referred to in this document and under the condition that sufficient resources are available in the general reserve of the eighth EDF. The respective projects and programmes shall be implemented according to the rules and procedures of the eighth EDF until entry into force of the Financial Protocol for the Ninth European Development Fund

(6) The European Investment Bank may contribute to the implementation of the present Country Strategy Paper by operations financed from the Investment Facility and/or from its own resources, in accordance with Articles 3 (a) and 4 of the Financial Protocol of the ACP-EC Partnership Agreement (see Chapter 6 for further details).

(7) In accordance with Article 5 of Annex IV to the ACP-EC Partnership Agreement, the National Authorising Officer and the Head of Delegation shall annually undertake an operational review of the Indicative Programme and undertake a mid-term review and an end-of-term review of the Country Support Strategy and the Indicative Programme in the light of current needs and performance.

The mid-term review shall be undertaken within two years and the end-of-term review shall be undertaken within four years from the date of signature of the Country Support Strategy and the National Indicative Programme. Following the completion of the mid- and end-of-term reviews, the Community may revise the resource allocation in light of current needs and performance.

The agreement of the two parties on this Country Strategy Paper and the National Indicative Programme, subject to the ratification and entry into force of the ACP-EC Partnership Agreement, will be regarded as definitive within eight weeks of the date of the signature, unless either party communicate the contrary before the end of this period.

Signatures

For the Government of Solomon Islands   For the Commission

....

Date,

PART A : SOLOMON ISLANDS : Country Strategy Paper

EXECUTIVE SUMMARY

The main objective of the Country Strategy Paper is to define, on the basis of a comprehensive analysis of the economic, social and political situation, a response strategy for EC support under the 9th EDF, taking into account the current economic crisis and the on-going and planned activities of Government and other development partners.

Solomon Islands in located in the Pacific Ocean east of PNG and has a landmass of 27 990 sq km with a population of 409 000. GDP per capita has fallen from € 810 In 1998 to € 440 in 2001. The country is confronted with a serious economic and social crisis in the aftermath of a two-year ethnic tension. Poor governance and mis-management of public funds have compounded the crisis. Solomon Islands has valuable natural resources which, if managed properly, could allow for improved economic and social development. These resources could contribute to poverty alleviation and reduced vulnerability to outside influences. Furthermore, development contributes to reduce the possibility of ethnic tension and other civil strife.
Thus the medium term challenges of Solomon Islands are to:

- Re-build the country's economy after two years of ethnic conflict.
- Restore good governance.
- Attract investors and re-invigorate exports.
- Promote economic activities at village level.
- Address the demands for de-centralisation towards the provinces in a realistic and equitable way.
- Find a balance between respect for traditional values and modernity in such a way that economic changes can be accommodated without creating distortions to the social fabric.

Sustainable Rural Development has been selected for EC support as is corresponds very well to four of the medium-challenges mentioned above and takes into account other areas already covered by other interventions. The mechanism selected for delivering this assistance is the Micro-Projects concept which has already proven its success in Solomon Islands under the 8th EDF and which responds very well to the current administrative weaknesses of Central and Provincial Governments.

85% of envelope A, or € 5.7 million is earmarked for Sustainable Rural Development and 15 % or € 1.0 million will be allocated directly to Non-State Actors in particular for capacity building.

1. ACP/EU CO-OPERATION OBJECTIVES

In accordance with Article 177 of the Treaty Establishing the European Community, community policy in the sphere of development co-operation shall foster:

- The sustainable economic and social development of the developing countries, and more particularly the most disadvantaged among them;
- The smooth and gradual integration of the developing countries into the world economy;
- The campaign against poverty in the developing countries.

These objectives have been confirmed and reinforced in Article 1 of the ACP-EC Partnership Agreement, signed in Cotonou on 23 June 2000, which puts main emphasis on the objective of reducing and eventually eradicating poverty. Co-operation between the Community and Solomon Islands shall pursue these objectives, taking into account fundamental principles laid down in Article 2 of the Agreement – especially the principle of encouragement of the development strategies by the countries and populations concerned - and essential and fundamental elements as defined in Article 9.

In their Statement on the European Community's Development Policy of 10 November 2000, the Council of the European Union and the European Commission determined a limited number of areas selected on the basis of their contribution towards reducing poverty and for which Community action provides added value: link between trade and development; support for regional integration and co-operation; support for macro-economic policies; transport; food security and sustainable rural development; institutional capacity-building, particularly in the area of good governance and the rule of law. The Statement also specifies that in line with the macro-economic framework, the Community must also continue its support in the social sectors (health and education), particularly with a view to ensuring equitable access to social services.

The Treaty establishing the European Community foresees that the Community and the Member States shall co-ordinate their policies on development co-operation and shall consult each other on their aid programmes, including in international organisations and during international conferences. Efforts must be made to ensure that Community development policy objectives are taken into account in the formulation and implementation of other policies affecting the developing countries. Furthermore, as laid down in Article 20 of the Agreement, systematic account shall be taken in mainstreaming into all areas of co-operation the following thematic or cross-cutting themes: gender issues, environmental issues and institutional development and capacity building.

The above objectives and principles and the national policy agenda presented in the next chapter constitute the starting point for the formulation of the present Country Strategy Paper, in accordance with the principle of national ownership of development strategies.

In its communication on conflict prevention (April 2001), the Commission has announced its intention to focus more clearly its co-operation on addressing root causes of conflict in an integrated way. In this context, the Commission will seek to incorporate specific conflict prevention (or resolution) measures into its various sectoral programmes.

2. NATIONAL DEVELOPMENT STRATEGY

Before the outbreak of the ethnic conflict in June 1999, the Government of Solomon Islands appeared to be on track with many of the reforms and areas of development as contained in its Medium Term Development strategy (MTDS) – see Annex 6. The conflict has derailed the process although Government remains formally committed to the principles of the MTDS, but this of little more than academic value at this juncture.

In fact, Government lacks, at present, a clear strategy for economic recovery from the ethnic tensions. Available finance (obtained largely from Taiwan) is being used to provide compensation payments so as to consolidate peace, in accordance with Melanesian tradition. Unfortunately, some unscrupulous politicians are exploiting the situation for their own short term gains. Remissions of taxes on imports of beer and sigarettesand on the export of logs are given freely by the Minister of Finance. Government has in fact yet to come to terms with economic reality. Once it does so, a major intervention by the BWIs will be necessary for reconstruction of the national economy.

3. ANALYSIS OF POLITICAL, ECONOMIC AND SOCIAL SITUATION

3.1. Introduction

Solomon Islands is situated to the east of Papua New Guinea and the north east of Australia. The country is made up of six large and several hundred small islands, most of them populated, with a total land area of 27 990 km² and an ocean area within an exclusive economic zone of 1.34 million km². The population of 409 000 is growing at 2.8% per year. 42% of the total population is under the age of 15. In the age range 5-14 years, 57% attended school during 1999. 15% of the population live in urban areas, with Honiara the capital being by far the largest urban centre (pop. 49 000). Only 23% of the population of 14 years of age and over are involved in paid work. This highlights the importance of the subsistence sector (agriculture and fishing) in the economy of the Solomon Islands.

Real GDP has dropped between 1996 and 1999 by 2.5% with a further decline in 2000 of an estimated 18%. GDP per capita in 2000 was estimated at € 580 and has probably dropped to € 440 in 2001.

The country is amongst the least economically developed in the Pacific. The country's main natural resources include timber, fish, gold, copra, cocoa and oil palm. Agriculture accounts for about 25% of GDP. Solomon Islands is ranked 123 in terms of its UN Human Development Index. There is no poverty line established but with a UN-Human Poverty Index of 49.1 Solomon Islands is among the poorer ACP countries. The country is prone to natural hazards, in particular cyclones. Solomon Islands is culturally rich and diversified and is amongst the most traditional societies in the Pacific. The country has, however, come to a crossroads regarding the model to adopt to make the transition from a traditional to a modern society. The ethnic conflict (1998 – 2000) is in some ways an illustration of the difficulties faced in the transition process.

3.2. Political situation

The country is a constitutional monarchy with the British sovereign as head of state, represented by a governor-general, who must be a Solomon Islander. Executive power is in the hands of a Cabinet headed by the Prime Minister. The legislature is the unicameral 50-seat National Parliament, elected for four-year terms by universal adult suffrage. There are 9 provinces, each with a provincial government headed by a Premier.
Since Independence in 1978, governments in Solomon Islands have had an average life span of two to three years. Policy objectives have not always been oriented towards sustainable development and have not necessarily been consistent from one government to the next one.

Since early 1999, the Solomon Islands has gone through a period of turmoil caused by ethnic tension on Guadalcanal -the main Island- between the original inhabitants and immigrants from the neighbouring province of Malaita. The immigrants came in over the past decades, first as labourers but later established themselves successfully as (small) traders and commercial farmers, taking up land apparently not in use by the local population at that time. The tensions have been brewing for a number of years but were aggravated in early 1999 by the emergence of the Guadalcanal Isatabu Freedom Movement (IFM) and the rival Malaita Eagle Force (MEF). In June 1999 the situation came to a head with increased violence, and subsequently an estimated 20,000 Malaitians and other non-Guadalcanal citizens left the island.

The tension culminated in a complete taking over of power in Honiara by the Malaita Eagle Force, assisted by a faction of the Police Force, on 5 June 2000. The Prime Minister was taken into custody. The move was negatively received by the international and donor community. The event happened during the visit of a ACP/EU Joint Assembly Mission to Solomons. Two days later, Government and the MEF agreed to seek a "constitutional" solution to the problem, the Prime Minister was released and it was agreed to discuss the issue during a special session of Parliament on 15 June.

Under duress, Prime Minister Ulufa'alu (from Malaita) resigned to make place for a new Prime Minister and Government which is supposed to be in a better position to restore law and order and to bring the militias together. Parliament (itself elected in free and fair elections in August 1997) elected on 30 June 2000 opposition leader Hon. Manasseh Sogavare, as next Prime Minister. In the procedure the constitutional and democratic process was followed and the new Government was recognised by the Commission and other donors as legitimate.

The new Government put efforts to restore peace as the only major point on its agenda. A cease fire was eventually signed on 5 August 2000, followed by a comprehensive Peace Agreement concluded in Townsville, Australia on 15 October 2000. Major elements are restoration of the police force, surrender of arms in exchange for amnesty, return of stolen property, more autonomy for the provinces, rehabilitation programmes. The arms surrender process is monitored by a small unarmed team from a number of Commonwealth counties. It appears, however, that the surrender of arms and restoration of law and order has not progressed as anticipated. Lack of proper financial crisis management and financial hand-outs by government to the Militias as 'compensations' is depleting the financial resources of Government to the detriment of their normal functions (health and education). It is a fact that the Townsville Peace Agreement appears to hold well, although armed militias are still around in parts of Guadalcanal causing a security problem.

General elections have taken place on 7 December 2001. All major bilateral donors provided financial and technical assistance to the electoral process and sent international observers. The elections took place in a peaceful atmosphere and were generally regarded as free and transparent. A new Government under Prime Minister Sir Allan Kemakeza was sworn in on 19 December 2001.

In the restoration of peace, and in bringing about transparency in political and good governance issues, Non-State Actors play an important role. Their position has been strengthened during and after the ethnic conflict.

Human Rights organisations have at times expressed concerns about violations of human rights including brutal killings by militant movements, and police brutality. Amnesty International heavily criticised the Townsville Peace Agreement to grant amnesty for crimes directly related to the ethnic tension. Various aid organisations, including the EU, provided humanitarian type of aid to internally displaced people during the height of the tension. With the gradual return to normalcy, respect for human rights in Solomon Islands restored.

3.3. Economic and social situation

3.3.1. Recent economic developments

The collapse in law and order in June 2000, and an escalation of the ethnic violence between the two warring groups had disastrous effects on the service and manufacturing companies operating in Honiara and elsewhere, many of which are still closed. The situation was further

aggravated by a mass evacuation of foreign nationals, for fear of their safety and lives. These foreign nationals have been the driving force in private sector development particularly in the primary and services industries.
According to the Central Bank of the Solomon Islands exports fell by over 50% in 2000, partly due to either the closure of a number of companies or the suspension of activities and partly due to a drop in world prices. This impacted negatively on the Government's financial situation with revised revenue estimates for 2000 being more than 30% lower than the original budget. The year 2000 budget was essentially abandoned and replaced by short-term mini-budgets. Government called on donors to provide massive budget support to key sectors such as education, health and law and order. Government's cash problems were compounded by tax remissions given to selected companies as well as selected individuals and by additional expenditure, particularly in relation to peace dividend or 'compensation' claims.

The effects of the ethnic tension on the economy have been particularly severe in Guadalcanal. Solomon Islands Plantation Limited (SIPL) has been closed since June 1999, resulting in the cessation of palm oil exports (formerly this constituted around 20% of total exports, about 1800 jobs). It is highly unlikely whether the company will open again and it would take at least 24 months from restart before full production can be achieved.

In June 2000 gold exports (25% of exports in 1999) also ceased following the destruction of plant and equipment at Gold Ridge Mine (550 jobs were lost). Production for the first six months of 2000 had been high (50 000 ounces of gold and 20 000 ounces of silver). If the owners decide to resume production it will take at least 6 months from restart for production to begin again. Assets from both SIPL and Gold Ridge have been damaged through theft, vandalism and neglect and landowners have made demands to renegotiate contract terms.

Other traditional sectors as well as activities in other provinces have also been affected. Fish exports (about 21% of total exports in 1999) have fallen by over 20% due to a combination of poor world tuna prices and the ethnic unrest. National Fisheries Development in Central Province closed in December 1999 and Solomon Taiyo in Western Province suspended operations, following tension related incidents, in July 2000 (about 2500 jobs were lost). Copra and coconut oil exports have also been affected by a combination of low world prices and mis-management of the marketing agency (CEMA), which is technically bankrupt. Tourism in the country has effectively ceased. Exports of logs was temporarily affected with the evacuation of most of the foreign nationals working in the country. However, Government has been active in trying to fast track new deals with foreign companies in the logging industry in order to boost urgently needed foreign reserves. Similarly, the government agreed on a fisheries agreement with Taiwan to issue licences for one year to up to 40 pure-seiners at a cost per licence of USD 8,000. The deal also included income for the government as a percentage of the catch. Actual revenue figures have not been publicised and the deal has been criticised as being too unfavourable f or Solomon Islands.

Total imports have fallen by about 35% and are expected to remain depressed for the rest of the year. In early 2001, foreign exchange reserves had declined to only slightly more than one-month of imports (approximately € 20 million).

In its 2001 Peace budget amounting to € 140 million the government projected (optimistically) € 44 million of foreign loans and € 44 million cash grants from donors. Domestic revenue estimates, mainly trade and income taxes, amounted to € 53 million as compared to € 82 million for the 2000 budget prior to the coup. The 2001 budget figure represents a 30% increase over the pre-coup 2000 budget. Essentially a large financing gap remains to be filled.

3.3.2. Economic structural characteristics

A rapid population increase on certain islands represents a real challenge to maintaining the standards of living. Constraints on the use of land represent another major obstacle to development. Various investment proposals and existing investments have been abandoned or hampered because of refusals by land owners and/or because of land disputes. Most land in Solomon Islands is owned by clans or tribes with ownership rules differing from island to island (e.g. patrilinear in some, matrilinear in other). Very little land has been formally surveyed and registered. Existing traditional and more so legal procedures to settle land issues are tedious and lengthy. There is generally awareness that land problems represent an obstacle to development but concrete steps to address them have yet to be taken by the government in close collaboration with the traditional leaders and land owners or their representatives.

Many of the smaller populated islands are located several hundreds of miles from the nearest larger island. Few ships call in at these remote islands on a regular basis. The economy on these small islands is by and large subsistence oriented and only few basic services (education and health) are being provided by the government. Maintaining transport links with the remote islands, by air or by sea, is essential for nation building and from a social point of view even though it may be uneconomic.

The limited revenue generating capacity of the country, as a result of a small productive basis, economic mismanagement combined with the ever growing need for education and health services, public infrastructure, result in an unhealthy dependence on outside financial support. During the recent years, the full public investment budget and part of the recurrent budget have been financed by donors.

3.3.3. Consequence of Recent Economic Events on Society

An estimated 5000 people (or 15% of formal employment) are unemployed as a direct result of key industries closing down on Guadalcanal and Western Province, and Government placed some 1000 public servants on unpaid leave.

The financial crisis due to the tension has had a severe impact on basic social services such as health and education. Shortage of trained medical staff and medicines has been felt in most rural and urban clinics. As many medical and teaching staff cannot be paid regularly, half of the schools and clinics throughout the country remain closed. Some clinics have re-opened owing to assistance by Australia in providing essential drugs. Assistance in providing teaching materials has helped a number of secondary schools. The migration of Malaitians has created overcrowding of the social infrastructure on Malaita Island. The situation in the capital Honiara is not much better than in the countryside: the Central Hospital in Honiara can only provide the most essential services and this even not on a continuous basis. The College of Higher Education in Honiara was also confronted with a financial problem which prevents it from functioning.

3.3.4. Social structural characteristics

Female school enrolment is 36% for primary level and 18% for secondary level. About 64% of the people have access to safe water and 18% to sanitation. Although WHO has provided assistance to reduce malaria incidence, the disease remains a major health threat throughout the Solomon Islands, especially to young children and elderly persons. An estimated fifty street children have made their appearance in Honiara.

At 2.8% per year population growth rate is high at international level and too high when related to the growth rates of the past year of social and economic infrastructures. The 1999 census data reveal that 41.5% of the total population is under 15 years of age.

The high population growth has contributed to problems of malnutrition, low levels of primary education, poor health standards and overpopulation of certain islands. Additional population pressures are due to the displacement of over 20,000 people due to the ethnic tension.

Qualified and competent people are scarce in both government and the private sector. Women are clearly disadvantaged if not discriminated against. Few women have become provincial or national leaders. Despite the difficulties confronting individuals, women's groups are nevertheless establishing themselves as an important pillar of civil society. Women are important in agriculture and in small trading of agricultural produce and consumer goods. An issue is the general problem of wife beating, a practice which meets increasing resentment from Civil Society organisations.

Analytical, managerial and technical skills are insufficient and impact negatively on the government's performance, on economic output, on social and political stability and on good governance.

Solomon Islands remains one of the most traditional societies amongst ACP countries. Monetisation is limited and goods and services are usually obtained through barter together with own-production. While the larger part of these systems are all Melanesian, the other being Polynesian and Micronesian, there is a wide diversity of social rules and structures, languages and rituals. The ethnic tension illustrates the extremely volatile and tense relations in the country between the various islands and within one island between different tribal groups. By contrast, the *wantok* system of intra clan economic and social support and protection safeguards most individuals from poverty and social hardship.

3.3.5. Environment

Solomon Islands enjoy relatively unspoilt but extremely fragile ecological systems. These include the marine systems (fish, plants and reefs) and the remaining primary and secondary forests. Unsustainable logging and fishing represent real threats to these delicate systems. Although policy makers usually adhere in words to the principles of equitable and sustainable exploitation reality is often different. Successive governments have exploited the resources for quick revenue generation rather than for the sustainable economic development of the country. In addition, the human and technical capacity to design, manage and monitor properly the use of the country's natural resources, including mining, is currently hardly available in the Solomon Islands.

The Forestry Bill, submitted to Parliament by the previous Government, is currently under review. Although the Bill contains the first steps to come to a sustainable management of the Forestry resources, it still requires translation into more detailed and quantified measures and targets. Before the Bill, harvest rates were 2.5 to 3 times the sustainable level, but these had begun to come down due to lower foreign demand and improving forestry practices. Recently, however, harvest rates have started to rise rapidly and monitoring of forestry activity has weakened considerably.

Fishing rights were granted early in 2001 to Taiwanese ships against rates regarded as well below the real value. Lack of Government control in the Post-Conflict situation gives cause for concern as it could lead to abandonment of sustainability principles in the exploitation of fisheries and forestry resources.

3.3.6. Status and role of non-state actors

Civil society is gradually assuming a more important role in Solomon Islands, and especially in the Post-Conflict situation. The various organisations are not necessarily consulted systematically by the government on major policy matters but there is growing awareness amongst civic society groups of the need to develop a lobbying capacity.

There has been substantial mobilisation of civic society groups (NGOs, National Council for Women, Church groups, Youth groups, Amnesty International) during the ethnic tension. Several of the groups have approached donors for capacity building and have received a positive response. A number of NGOs have received support from European NGOs but there is room for longer term support to transfer know-how to local NGOs. It is recognised that more efforts are needed to promote closer collaboration between local NGOs.

Trade unions are operational and are capable of mobilising their members in the government and in the private sector. They have been pressurising the government in the aftermath of the tension to allow government workers sent on unpaid leave to return to their jobs or to for the workers to receive severance packages. Eventually, all workers were allowed to return to work and receive a salary.

3.3.7. External Environment

Regional Integration

In order to foster the smooth and gradual integration of ACP States into the world economy, economic and trade co-operation under the **Cotonou Agreement** aims at concluding new WTO compatible trading arrangements, removing progressively barrier to trade and enhancing co-operation in all areas relevant to trade. Economic Partnership Agreements shall be negotiated as from September 2002, taking into account regional integration among ACP States.

The Solomon Islands is a member of the Pacific Island Forum. At their meeting in Nauru in August 2001, the Leaders of the Pacific Island Forum approved and signed: (1) an Umbrella Agreement including Australia and New Zealand, called "Pacific Agreement on Closer Economic Relations", (PACER) for future economic co-operation amongst Forum members; and (2) a free trade area amongst the 14 ACP Forum Island Countries (FICs) called "Pacific Island Countries Trade Agreement" (PICTA), without Australia and New Zealand.

PACER provides for the establishment of subsidiary agreements for free trade areas, notably PICTA, as well as negotiations of Forum-wide free trade areas including Australia and New Zealand. The free trade area among the ACP Forum Island Countries (PICTA), which will enter into force after six countries have ratified it, provides for liberalisation within 8 years up to 2010, and until 2012 for the Small Island States and LDCs. However, sensitive industries will be protected through a negative list that will only be eliminated by 2016.

Solomon Islands has been a member of the Melanesia Spearhead Group (MSG) since 1993. The Group which comprises Solomon Islands, Papua New Guinea, Vanuatu, Fiji and the Kanaks of New Caledonia, has a free trade arrangement, covering some 240 listed products. Products such as tobacco and alcohol are not included on the list.

Although MSG has contributed to an increase in regional imports to Solomon Islands, there is a feeling that MSG does not provide any incentive for the growth of the Solomon Island industrial sector. The other three member countries already had a well established manufacturing industry before MSG came into effect and the level playing field caused by MSG means that Solomon Islands now has no comparative advantage in attracting investment in industry. The only produce that Solomon Islands currently exports regionally are handicrafts and beer, which are not covered by MSG.

Solomon Islands have also been involved in the early negotiations of the legal text for a Pacific Regional Trade Arrangement (PaRTA) to include the 14 Forum Island Countries (less New Zealand and Australia).

The Solomon Islands are a member of WTO.

Trade

In 1999 the Solomon Islands exported most to Japan, which accounted for more than one third of total Solomon Islands exports. The Solomon Islands imported most from Australia, almost 40% of total imports. The EC accounted for 14% of total Solomon Islands exports and 6% of Solomon Islands imports.
In the year 2000, exports from the Solomon Islands to the EU dropped to € 13 m., down from € 35 m. in 1998 and € 28 m. in 1999. Imports from the EU fell from € 10 m. in 1999 to less than € 3 m. in 2000. Thus, in 2000 both exports to and imports from the EU fell to their lowest levels for a decade (1990-2000).

In 2000 the Solomon Islands exported to the EU mainly prepared or preserved fish (62% of total exports to the EU) and products such as coconut "copra" (25%), while imports consisted in large part of machinery (for more than one third of imports from the EU).

The Solomon Island benefits, or can potentially benefit, from a number of preferential trade agreements and arrangements. These are:

- Lomé Convention/Cotonou Agreement;
- The EU's "Everything But Arms" regulation (February 2001), which extended duty- and quota-free access to all products originating in least-developed countries;
- SPARTECA: This agreement with Pacific Islands and Australia/New Zealand provides duty free access for agricultural products into the Australian/New Zealand markets
- Melanesian Spearhead Group (MSG) bilateral trade agreements.

3.4. Medium term challenges

(a) Macro-economic stability programme, mobilisation of donor resources

A programme to achieve macro-economic stability has to be implemented consistently. This programme in combination with a revitalisation of the main industries would allow to gradually re-build the tax-base, increase foreign exchange reserves and meet government's debt servicing commitments. Fiscal policy would have to be consistent with macroeconomic stability. Measures to increase revenue and control expenditure would have to be enforced strictly.

In view of the catastrophic state of the economy and government finances, the BWIs will eventually have to provide a significant financial injection in support of a stabilisation programme.

(b) Attract investors, re-invigorate exports

The few major businesses that generated exports, employment and revenue nearly all closed as a result of the ethnic tension. The re-opening of some or all of these companies is necessary to re-establish local as well as overseas investors' confidence in Solomon Islands and to spur life into the economy . The government will have to follow consistently, i.e. without policy reversals, an economic policy which strengthens this confidence and allows for economic growth. This requires strong and visionary economic management capacity. This capacity is available in a limited amount and should be increased through better education of the next generations and specific training and capacity building for the current one.

(c) Promote value adding activities at village level

Dependency in the rural areas on copra as a cash earner could be reduced by promoting low cost value adding activities for coconut tree based products (e.g. ropes, mats, artifacts, coconut oil as fuel and for making soap, coconut water). Coastal Fishing is another activity with strong prospects for growth. Development at village level represents part of the answer to the problems accompanying growth of urban centres including youth unemployment and urban poverty.

(d) Capacity building

General shortage of trained and skilled local personnel in the private sector as well as in government departments is a major impediment to development. A major investment into increasing education standards as well as institutional capacity building is generally recognised as urgent.

(e) Address the demands for de-centralisation towards the provinces in a realistic and equitable way

The demands from provinces for more decision-making power have been accepted by the central government. The success of the de-centralisation process is conditional upon well focussed, transparent and equitable management of financial and other resources.

(f) Tradition versus modernity

Solomon Islands is generally considered one of the most traditional societies in the Pacific. The country has, however, come to a crossroads regarding the model to adopt to make the transition from a traditional to a modern society. A compromise will have to be found between adapting (not abandoning) Solomon islanders' traditions to the internal and external pressures to move towards a modern society. Despite a number of serious structural impediments the country has considerable potential for development from its human resources, abundant natural resources, areas of magnificent natural beauty and a rich cultural history and traditions.

4. PAST AND ONGOING EC CO-OPERATION : RESULTS, LESSONS AND EXPERIENCE

4.1. Summary of ongoing EDF actions

EC support in the past has focussed on the transport sector (roads and sea) and rural development including agriculture, fishing and forestry. Support has been provided to the health and education sectors (formal and non-formal) and for capacity building within government. A structural adjustment programme in support of economic reforms (€ 4.2 mn.) was carried out in the context of a larger IMF, World Bank and Asian Development Bank supported programme. Assistance has been given to civic society and to the media during the tension and as part of the peace process.

Efforts have been made to gradually re-focus the ongoing programme to three areas. In each of these areas EDF is in financial terms a major player. The first is the education sector in the wider sense, i.e. including institutional capacity building and on-the-job training. The second sector is transport with interventions in both physical infrastructure as well as institutional capacity building and sectoral reforms. The third main area is support to grassroots development through the micro-projects programme.

The funds for the various interventions originated mainly from programmable resources through the National Indicative Programme (€ 20.9 million for 7th EDF, € 19 million for 8th EDF), structural adjustment funds (€ 4.2 million) and from Stabex allocations (€ 41.8 million in 1998, € 29 million in 1999). Budget resources have been used for forestry programmes and ethnic tension related rehabilitation (€ 2 million). The European Investment Bank provided three loans to the Development Bank of Solomon Islands (total € 4.0 million) but the last intervention encountered difficulties as DBSI was not able to meet its commitments. A number of actions have been supported by the CDE. Finally, Solomon Islands benefited from the regional indicative programme in the areas of aviation, forestry and fishing including support to the Forum Fisheries Agency which is based in Honiara.

Education and capacity building

The objectives for the education sector are essentially twofold. The first one is to address the market needs, i.e. government and the private sector, for professionals. The Solomon Islands College of Higher Education, the National Institute of Public Administration and possibly other institutions require financial resources as well as management and accounting training. Similarly, the formal education system is being reformed so as to meet the future needs of the country. Finally the non-formal education sector, through the Rural Training Centres, provides education to those young people which have not been able to pursue their education in the formal schooling system. Similar to the transport sector, a start has been made to fundamentally revise the education sector policy. Stabex 1999 funds have been entirely targeted to these efforts. The EDF assistance in the education sector is particularly recognised as the pre-condition and basis for specific donor interventions with the EU being the lead donor in the sector.

Transport and communication
The objectives of the interventions in the transport sectors are to improve the economic infrastructure in the short-term whilst at the same time building capacity to maintain and further improve this infrastructure. Past interventions, however, have been somewhat disconnected from one another. The need for concentration of efforts on road maintenance as opposed to road construction and on improving the marine sector in general was recognised and resulted in a series of actions aimed at establishing a general transport sector policy. This policy includes re-defining the role of government and of the private sector in the transport sector. More than 60% of the Stabex 1998 funds are being used to support these major structural reforms in addition to NIP funds. About 60% of 8th EDF funds are directed towards the transport sector. The EU is considered the lead donor with other donors consulting closely with the EU before engaging in specific interventions.

Microprojects
The micro-projects programme (€ 3.0 million) is particularly well suited to Solomon Islands because such projects provide an appropriate response to village needs in a flexible format. Microprojects also promote self-determination and active participation in development issues by grassroots groups. Microprojects indeed contribute to capacity building of grassroots groups as important members of Civil Society.

Small enterprises
The activities include setting up in a sustainable way rural fisheries centres, supporting capacity building in the eco-tourism sub-sector, revitalising credit sector for small businesses through the Development Bank of Solomon Islands.

A summary table the interventions under the 6th, 7th and 8th EDF is annexed (Annex 7).

4.2. Lessons and experience

Evaluations (Rural Fisheries, RTCs, Stabex and MRIP) and reviews conclude that, by and large, past EDF projects have had positive and lasting impact more at the micro rather than at the macro level. A number of ministries and other institutions, clinics and schools, villages, farming communities and individuals have benefited from a wide variety of interventions.

Many times projects prospered during the first phase of implementation but ran into difficulties once they were handed over to the government or to the direct beneficiaries. Project design may have taken insufficient account of the relatively weak technical and managerial capacity of local beneficiaries or institutions and underestimated the need for long-term, rather than medium-term, training and other capacity building requirements. These requirements can only be addressed in a sustainable way by improving education standards, from primary to tertiary levels and including vocational training.

Over and above the difficulties at project level is the need to have a stable political and financial environment as well as government departments responsible for the project actually performing their duties and fulfilling their initial commitments. The EDF funded projects did not suffer as much in their implementation as expected initially. This is mainly due to the substantial input in Technical Assistance and the funding of running costs for project management. In terms of capacity building this approach is, of course, not sustainable in the long term and will have to be revisited when the situation returns to normal.

4.3. Other donor programmes

Donors are involved in a wide range of activities and as indicated above are expected to provide additional assistance to help the country cope with the devastating impact of the ethnic crisis.

The details of donor involvement, as at mid-2001, are shown in the donor matrix in Annex 2. This matrix covers the pre-conflict situation and was projected for the period 2000-2002. Many of the programmes are now off-track although commitments have not been withdrawn.

The social sectors receive substantial bilateral and multilateral support with the health sector receiving the larger part of bilateral assistance with additional involvement from the World Bank. The education sector is covered by various donors with the larger part being provided by the EC. Other donors indeed consider the EC's support to the sector as the foundation for their own targeted support.

The transport sector, mainly road construction and/or maintenance, benefits from multilateral assistance from ADB, Kuwait and the EC. The EC in addition provides substantial support to policy reforms in the sector and capacity building in particular.

Donors provide support for post-conflict stabilisation and rehabilitation in various sectors. Microprojects are funded by Australia, Taiwan and the EC.

The agricultural sector continues to receive support from the Republic of China with New Zealand and the EC have downscaled their inputs in absence of a long-term policy for reforms in the sector (including reform of CEMA). The EC's input focuses microproject type of interventions in the sector in the context of the post-conflict stabilisation programme.
Various capacity building actions are ongoing in the Ministries of Finance, Planning, Public Works, Health and Education. These are financed by Australia, the EC and the World Bank.

5. RESPONSE STRATEGY

5.1. Steps taken immediately after the ethnic crisis

The national policy responses to the crisis include in the short-term consolidation of the peace process and implementation of a macro-economic stabilisation programme.

In the aftermath of the ethnic tension, the short-term donor response has been to finance a post-conflict rehabilitation programme. Areas of concentration included the health and education sectors, micro projects or similar, infrastructure, police, water and electricity supply, peace process related activities, and actions aimed at de-centralisation of national responsibilities to the provinces. Under the Rehabilitation Budget Line, the Commission provided in 2000 a € 0.5 million programme for assistance to the displaced persons. Displaced persons will receive further assistance through a € 12.6 million Post-Conflict Rehabilitation package, agreed in July 2001 and funded from existing NIP and Stabex resources, which also includes emergency assistance to the education sector and the December 2001 elections.

In order to provide the basis for renewed economic and social development there is now an urgent need for a macro-economic stabilisation programme with essential support of the BWIs.

5.2. Possible focal sectors for EC support

Sectors, which are expected to remain a priority for the government for the medium term and which currently benefit from donor support are:

- health
- human resources development (education and capacity building)
- transport and communication
- rural development and community development
- development of natural resources
- small businesses and tourism
- police, judiciary

The above sectors have all benefited from EDF support in the past and a number of projects are still ongoing. A number of sectors (e.g. health, agriculture) continue receiving substantial support from other donors. The EDF is therefore no longer directly involved in these sectors.

Human resources development and to a somewhat lesser extent, the transport and communication sector, are arguably amongst the most essential areas to respond in a sustainable way to the immediate and medium term challenges facing Solomon Islands. The availability of sufficient managerial and technical capacity, obtained through good quality training and from formal as well as non-formal education, is a prerequisite for proper decision making at all levels and for economic, social, political and cultural development.

The improvement of education levels (primary, secondary, tertiary) and the strengthening of capacity is necessarily complemented by physical investments in order to accelerate economic and social returns on both the software (development of human resources) and the hardware (e.g infrastructure).

This has been the view of the Government and the European Commission when allocating the Stabex 99 resources (€ 29 million) for the larger part (90%) to capacity building operations and education. Stabex 98 has been earmarked largely for transport infrastructure.

Small businesses support is, under the present circumstances, not an immediate priority but could become important once the situation has returned to normal.

The focal sector selected for our intervention under the 9th EDF is **Sustainable Rural Development and Community Development,** an area where EDF assistance has been forthcoming since several years. In order to assist further grassroots development beyond what is done through the existing Micro Projects programme (ending in 2003) it is proposed to allocate 85 % of Envelope A or € 5.7 million of the amount to a micro projects phase II. This activity will be given an equitable nation-wide distribution.

There are strong reasons for the selection of this sector:

1. It takes into account other areas already covered by other interventions (see the chapter above)
2. The apparent demand for Micro Projects as demonstrated under Phase I (see Annex 5).
3. The sector responds very well to four of the six Medium Term Challenges as mentioned in Chapter 4.3 by bringing development without rudely disturbing the traditional rural

environment, promoting value added activities at village level, capacity building and promoting the process of decentralisation.

4. In term of planning and implementation the approach takes fully into account the administrative weakness of central and provincial Governments, which have been aggravated as a result of the ethnic conflict.
5. It gives full scope for the strengthening of Non-State Actors.
6. The Micro Project concept includes a local contribution component which fosters ownership of the individual projects.

Micro projects will contribute to the development of the village economy through the construction and operation of education, health, agriculture and other facilities as well as building capacity to develop and maintain social and economic infrastructure by government and communities. Micro-projects is a proven means to ensuring the alleviation of rural poverty. A feature of the micro-projects approach which helps encourage beneficiaries to maintain infrastructure is community ownership of the projects and the inclusion of their own contribution to the project costs.

Quality village based education and village services are an important means of strengthening the village economy. The strategic direction for the village economy will be to encourage greater production in the agriculture sector and the establishment of more village-based industries and services that will result in employment creation.

A successful intervention in this sector depends on high quality management in its implementation and conducive policy environment. Around 140 interventions can be foreseen. It is anticipated that around 20% of therural population of Solomon Islands will benefit directly or indirectly from the Programme.

Outside the focal sector, 15 % of envelope A or € 1.0 million will be directly allocated to Non-State Actors. Capacity building of Non-State Actors will be an important element in the Programme. Following earlier positive experiences under the 8th EDF Micro-Projects Programme, it is also envisaged that Non-State Actors will be important vehicles for the implementation of individual projects within the focal sector.

5.3. Consistency with Government Policy

The proposal reflects one of government's policy priorities to improve living conditions in the rural communities. This would be done through community initiated and owned building or rehabilitation of basic rural infrastructure and income generating projects. This will in turn contribute to alleviating poverty. Women groups have been a beneficiary of the microprojects phase I and will continue to be.

The proposed intervention is coherent and complementary with existing EDF activities aimed at capacity building and upgrading of economic infrastructure.

The proposed microprojects intervention and further capacity strengthening assistance is furthermore in line with the principles outlined in the Cotonou Agreement to assist in the sustainable eradication of poverty in Solomon Islands.

5.4. Complementarity with other donors

Australia and Taiwan are involved in medium/long term grassroots projects, but only in a limited extent.

There has been and is close co-ordination between the various donors (Australia,, Japan, New Zealand, Taiwan, United Kingdom, Asian Development Bank, International Monetary Fund, UNDP, World Bank).

Mechanisms such as regular meetings between donors will be maintained to ensure close co-ordination and optimal and complementary impact of donor support.

5.5. Involvement of non-state actors

Consultation with representatives of the non-state sector have confirmed the need for further support to the rural communities.

NGO and Community based organisations currently benefit from EDF support through the existing micro-projects programme. A number of them indeed act as an intermediary between communities and the NAO. These organisations will continue benefiting from EDF support to strengthen their project initiation and management capacity. In addition, in accordance with the Cotonou Agreement, Non-State Actors will be granted a direct financial allocation from the 9th EDF Financial Envelope A, amounting to 15 % or € 1.0 million, in particular for capacity building support in critical areas to reinforce their capabilities.

5.6. Other instruments available

Solomon Islands is expected to continue benefiting from EIB and CDE support, albeit for relatively smaller interventions. Finally, Solomon Islands is anticipating increased support from the regional indicative programme.

Solomon Islands reaffirms its commitment to the Regional Integration objectives of the Regional Indicative Programme and will play its full role to ensure that these are realised. NIP resources may be used to complement regional resources in this regard especially in building trade analysis capacity.

5.7. Coherence with Community policies

There are obvious linkages between the proposed response strategy for Solomon Islands and development policies advocated by the Community. First, the strategy is consistent with Article 177 of the EU Treaty. Two of its principal objectives are poverty eradication and sustainable development.
In fisheries, the EC will ensure coherence between its commercial interests in harvesting tuna from the Pacific, and the developmental imperatives of equitable returns, promotion of onshore fish processing and coastal fisheries, transparency in providing accurate information on fishing effort and catch, and strict adherence to the principles of resource conservation and sustainability.

PART B : SOLOMON ISLANDS NATIONAL INDICATIVE PROGRAMME

6. NATIONAL INDICATIVE PROGRAMME

6.1 Introduction

Within the general framework of the present Country strategy paper, the Parties have agreed on the main priorities for their co-operation and on the sector(s) on which the support of the Community will be concentrated. A detailed Indicative Programme including a set of tables on commitments and disbursement forecasts as well as a preliminary chronogramme is presented hereunder. It is based on the resources of the A-allocation.

6.2.

The EC Country Support Strategy for Solomon Islands will be financed through different instruments with following indicative allocations:

(a) **9th EDF A-envelope** (€ 6.7 million). This amount shall serve to cover long term development operations within the framework of the Support Strategy. It is to be divided as follows:

- Sustainable Rural Development (85%)
- Direct Support to Non-State Actors (15%)

(b) **9th EDF B-envelope** (€ 7.8 million.). This will be mobilised to provide additional support when this becomes necessary as a result of external factors.

Apart from the above-mentioned financial instruments, of which the A-envelope is the main programmable basis for the Indicative Programme, the 9th EDF also includes the "Investment Facility" as a financing instrument managed by the European Investment bank (see Part A, chapter 5). The Investment facility does not form part of the Indicative Programme.

Specific action could be financed via budget lines, especially in the areas of decentralised co-operation, NGO financing, human rights and democracy. These are subject to specific rules and regulations and depend on availability of funds. Solomon Islandscan also benefit from the Regional Indicative Programme or from trade specific operations, according to needs and availability of funds. More details will be discussed in the framework of the 9th EDF regional programming for the Pacific Island States.

6.3. Areas of Concentration

Within the general framework of the present Country strategy paper, the Parties have agreed on the main priorities for their co-operation (see previous chapter) and on the sector(s) on which the support of the Community will be concentrated. It is based on the resources of the A-allocation.

Amounts mentioned in this chapter indicate the global repartition of funds between the focal sector and other programmes. This repartition can be modified in the context of operational, performance or ad hoc reviews.

The Focal Sector is **Sustainable Rural Development.** The overall objective is to reduce poverty, social inequality and dependence on state intervention. The following specific objective shall be pursued: to respond to expressed needs of rural communities for social and socio-economic development within their socio-cultural context.

85 % of envelope A or € 5.7 million shall be reserved for this sector.

The major interventions foreseen are:

Successful completion of about 140 microprojects over a period of 4 to 5 years in the rural areas to contribute to:

- access to improved and/or extended social services (education, health, support to women and youth) and public utilities
- increased employment and income within target groups
- access to improved and/or extended economic infrastructure
- better organised and more self-reliant communities

From envelope A, the balance of 15 % or € 1.0 million will be directly allocated to Non-State Actors, in particular for capacity building projects. Non-State Actors will also perform a major role in the implementation of the individual projects.

6.4. Macroeconomic support

The Indicative programme does not foresee macroeconomic support. However, in the light of changing circumstances, it may be decided to reallocate funds from other headings in the Indicative programme to this type of support. Such a decision may be taken by specific agreement between the Chief Authorising Officer and the National Authorising Officer or in the context of an operational, performance or ad hoc review.

6.5. 9th EDF Indicative Programme: Intervention framework in Rural Development

	Performance indicators	Sources of verification	Assumptions
Long-term national sector targets: Social and Socio-economic development of rural communities	Increased number of people having access to education, health, water and income generating activities.	Reports and statistics of Ministries of Planning, Health and Education.	
Intervention objectives: Improved access to education, health and water facilities.	Number of well functioning classrooms, health centres, water supply systems, income generating activities	Reports and statistics of Ministries of Planning, Education, Health.	Rural Development remains a priority for Government policy
Results: (1) 140 projects completed to create and rehabilitate social end economic infrastructure facilities. (2) Community contribution 25% to develop sense of ownership. (3) Improved Community skills to plan and implement projects.	Number of projects successfully completed Full community contribution and participation Quality of community management	Project reports Mid-term review Final evaluation Delegation reports	Good quality of Project Implementation
			High quality management Communities have the cash or other resources to contribute to project costs

6.6. ACTIVITY PIPELINE CHRONOGRAMME

Titles	Amounts (in € million)	Identification	Appraisal	Financing decision
Rural Development programme	5.7	2001/2	2002/1	2002/2
Support to NSAs	1.0	2002/1	2001/1	2002/2

6.7. Tentative forecast of estimated commitments of 9th EDF resources (€ million)

		Cumulative commitments										
	Indicative total	2001/2	2002/1	2002/2	2003/1	2003/2	2004/1	2004/2	2005/1	2005/2	2006/1	2006/2
Rural Development programme			-	5.7	5.7	5.7	5.7	5.7	5.7	5.7	5.7	5.7
Support to NSAs				1.0	1.0	1.0	1.0	1.0	1.0	1.0	1.0	1.0
TOTAL (cumulated)		**-**	**-**	**6.7**	**6.7**	**6.7**	**6.7**	**6.7**	**6.7**	**6.7**	**6.7**	**6.7**

6.8. Tentative forecasts of estimated payments of 9th EDF resources

(in € million)

		Cumulative payments										
	Indicative total	**2001/2**	**2002/1**	**2002/2**	**2003/1**	**2003/2**	**2004/1**	**2004/2**	**2005/1**	**2005/2**	**2006/1**	**2006/2**
Rural Development programme				1.5	2.9	4.2	5.2	5.7	5.7	5.7	5.7	5.7
Support to NSAs				0.1	0.4	0.6	0.8	1.0	1.0	1.0	1.0	1.0
TOTAL				**1.6**	**3.3**	**4.8**	**6.0**	**6.7**	**6.7**	**6.7**	**6.7**	**6.7**

ANNEX 1: Donor Matrix - period 2000-2002

Solomon Island Government Development Strategy				
	Economic development	Social development	Productivity sector	Post-conflict rehabilitation
Government	Export / Industrial development in accordance with Townsville Peace Agreement	Education (scholarships), Rural Community development		Support to peace process
Non-state actors (NGOs, churches)		Non-formal education, village development, promotion of gender equality		Support to peace process
European Commission	Transport	Education, Micro-projects	Farmer support	
Republic of China (Taiwan)	Transport	Up-grading of Central Hospital, Micro-projects (Rural Constituency Development Fund)	Rice farming	Compensation for lost properties as a result of ethnic tension.
Australia	Strengthening of Ministry of Finance (financial management, customs)	Health, Education, Support to Police		Support to peace process, Community peace and restoration fund
Asian Development Bank				Infrastructure rehabilitation (schools, roads, bridges, water supply systems, clinics, prisons)
World Bank		Health, Education, Population planning		
United Kingdom		Primary Education		Emergency budgetary support (primary education)
Other	Honiara road up-grading (Kuwait)	Education (NZ), micro-projects (NZ), support to Police (NZ), Health (UN), Sports infrastructure (FIFA)		Emergency support to health sector (WHO)

ANNEX 2: Description of the programming process in Solomon Islands

The ethnic tension has resulted in the collapse of the economic reform programme which had been in place from 1998 onwards. Medium term policies had to be abandoned in favour of short-term conflict resolution actions. People's minds, including staff in various government departments, were not oriented towards medium term planning but focused on the day-to-day crisis confronting the country. A revised medium term policy document formally adopted by Parliament or Cabinet and reflecting the new economic and social priorities and actions was not available.

In absence of these formal new policy guidelines the existing Medium Term development Strategy 1999-2001 was used as starting point for the present country support strategy even though it had been put aside. The assumption that the larger part of the MTDS would still hold once the ethnic tension would be resolved was verified with and confirmed by the NAO.

The programming process was furthermore hampered by the absence of up-to-date sectoral assessments and reliable economic and social statistics.

In order to overcome the existing handicaps in terms of availability of formal policy and other documentation a series of meetings were held with government officials and sectoral experts (transport, education, finance, agriculture, fisheries, microprojects,...) to provide an updated assessment of the status and main problems confronting the country's development. Inputs were also taken from IMF/World Bank assessments and reports and from regular co-ordination meetings with other donors.

The High Commission of the United Kingdom, the only EU Member State present in Solomon Islands was invited and commented on the draft. The draft strategy paper was reviewed with the NAO and staff of the Ministries of Finance, Planning, Transport and Education.

Non-state actors were informed of the strategy during a meeting organised jointly by the European Commission and the NAO. They were consulted on an ad-hoc basis during the process. They are expected to continue to play an important role in the implementation of the NIP as the micro projects concept id ideally suited to the type of assistance they can provide.

Selected macro-economic indicators **ANNEX 3**

Nominal GDP (1999) USD 359 million
GDP/capita (1999) USD 879

	1996	1997	1998	1999	2000 proj	2001 proj
Real GDP growth rate (%)	3,5	-2,3	1,1	-1,3	-14,0	3,4
Consumer prices (end-of-period)	N/A	10,4	10,3	8,0	6,0	N/A
Government accounts in million USD						
Government revenue and grants	34,7	29	35,5	38,6	29,5	37,5
Government expenditure	38,6	33,2	37,1	41,3	34	39,3
Overall balance	-3,9	-4,1	-1,6	-2,7	-4,5	-1,8
Domestic borrowing	0,9	3,4	-1,7	-0,7	5	0,6
Foreign borrowing	1,6	0,7	3,2	1,7	-0,5	1,2
Privatisation	1,4	0	0	1,6	0	0
Money and credit (annual percent change)						
Net foreign assets	152,4	41,9	48,6	9	-37,8	11,6
Net domestic assets	-4,3	-6,3	-19,8	0,5	62,8	5,6
credit to government	-1,2	1	-20,6	-0,1	41	3,3
credit to private sector	5,1	10,1	25,3	8,3	7,7	12,8
Broad Money	15	6,7	4,8	4,9	9,5	7,4
Balance of payments in million USD						
Exports, FOB	162,4	173,9	140,8	149,7	105,9	118,6
of which timber	98,4	83	40,7	46,2	45	51,2
fish	29,7	48,9	40,3	32,9	21,9	24,1
gold	0,1	0,1	14,1	37,2	18,2	20
other	34,3	41,9	45,6	33,4	20,8	23,4
Imports, CIF	-151,2	-209,4	-146,9	-140,1	-119,3	-134,2
Current account	12	-37,9	16,4	35,1	7,1	21,6
Percent of GDP	2,9	-8,7	4,6	9,8	2,5	7,4
Grants	53,5	40	56,3	56,3	28,6	51,2
Capital account	-2,6	31,9	3,7	-33,3	-24,6	-21
Overall balance	9,4	-6	20,1	1,8	-17,5	-0,6
Gross official reserves (million USD)	32,2	31,7	47,9	50,6	33,4	34
In months of imports	1,6	1,3	2,8	2,7	2,4	2,2
Government gross debt as a % of GDP (end-of-period)	49,7	53,4	55,4	58,9	75	71,2
domestic	23,9	22	22,1	21,4	29,3	27,7
foreign	25,8	31,3	33,2	37,5	45,7	43,5
in million of USD	104,2	106,4	118,1	128,3	126,7	130,2
Exchange rate SBD/USD, end-of-period	3,62	4,75	4,86	5,08	5,09	-

Source :
1) IMF Staff report for the 2000 Article IV consultation, January 5, 2001
2) IMF "Recent economic developments", January 5, 2001

GDP by sector of origin (in %) **in million SBD dollars**

estimates in 1992 prices	1996	1997	1998	1999	1996	1997	1998	1999
primary sector	173,5	175,6	161,1	154,6	17,8	18,5	16,7	16,3
of which agriculture	46,3	51	49,1	37,6	4,8	5,4	5,1	4,0
forestry	69,5	64,9	44,7	52	7,1	6,8	4,6	5,5
fishing	57,7	59,7	67,3	65	5,9	6,3	7,0	6,8
secondary sector	102,9	88,2	93	113,8	10,6	9,3	9,7	12,0
mining and exploration	0,2	0,2	16,7	41,1	0,0	0,0	1,7	4,3
manufacturing	37,9	38,3	39,6	39,6	3,9	4,0	4,1	4,2
electricity and water	17,5	18,8	19,8	20,9	1,8	2,0	2,1	2,2
construction	47,3	30,9	16,9	12,2	4,9	3,2	1,8	1,3
Tertiary	397,5	386,3	400,7	368,7	40,8	40,6	41,7	38,8
retail and wholesale trade	94,1	93,9	102,4	95,9	9,7	9,9	10,6	10,1
transportation and communication	45	41,7	52,3	37,2	4,6	4,4	5,4	3,9
finance	113,4	105,3	91,2	85,5	11,6	11,1	9,5	9,0
other services	145	145,4	154,8	150,1	14,9	15,3	16,1	15,8
Monetary GDP at factor cost	673,9	650,2	654,9	637,1	69,2	68,3	68,1	67,1
Non-monetary GDP at factor cost	166,2	170,6	175,1	182	17,1	17,9	18,2	19,2
Real GDP at factor cost	840,2	820,8	830	819,1	86,3	86,3	86,3	86,3
Taxes less subsidies	133,6	130,5	131,9	130,2	13,7	13,7	13,7	13,7
Real GDP at market prices	973,8	951,4	961,9	949,3	100,0	100,0	100,0	100,0
Nominal GDP at current market prices	1461	1612	1728	1739	-	-	-	-

Source:
1) IMF Staff report for the 2000 Article IV consultation, January 5, 2001
2) IMF "Recent economic developments", January 5 2001

Basic population statistics 1999 population census data

1. Total Population	1970	160,998
	1976	196,823
	1986	285,176
	1999	409,042
2. Annual Rate of increase, 1986 – 99		2.8%
3. Sex Ratio, males per 100 females		107
4. Life expectancy at birth	Males Females	62.2 years 65.3 years
5. Age groups, 1999	0 – 14 15 – 24 25 – 59 60+	42% 21% 32% 5%
6. (provisional) infant mortality, per 1000 live births		28
7. (provisional) Total fertility rate, children per woman at child-bearing age		4.5 children
8. Children 5 – 14 years attending school		57 per cent
9. Literacy rate (15 years and over)	Total Male Female	76% 83% 68%
10. Economic Activities		
Population in paid work		57,472 (23% of Population greater than 14 years of age)
Population in unpaid work		111,905 (45% of population greater than 14 years of age)
Population looking for paid employment		28,000 persons
11. Percentage of households with the following facilities available		
Access to piped drinking water		52%
Modern toilet facility		23%
Electricity		16%
Working radio		41%
Bed-net		80%
12. Average household size, persons per household		6.3 persons

ANNEX 4

Sector of Concentration - Sustainable Rural Development

The activities under the sector of concentration will be undertaken within the framework of the Micro Projects concept. The experiences with the Micro Projects implemented under the 8th EDF are summarised hereunder.

The Micro Projects Programme in Solomon Islands (€ 3 million) commenced on 1 November 2000. The team consists of a Project Manager, Technical Adviser, locally recruited Engineer and a Secretary/Clerk.
During the set up period the team put together guidelines for the Programme and an application format which were available for distribution to interested parties. Procedures were developed for the Office and the appraisal and implementation of Projects. Standard forms were designed for appraisals and reporting, and for recording of receipts and payments and community contribution. Provincial centres were visited and the provincial planners and technical officers were briefed on the Programme. Six individuals were approached to serve on the Steering Committee which would meet monthly and these included a Director of an NGO and the President of the National Council of Women.

The Annual Work Programme commenced on 1 March 2001 and the team began to appraise the applications which had already been submitted. Since the terms of reference covered over eight different sectors and the funds had to be allocated over nine provinces a basis of distribution was established to allocate the annual budget to each province and then to each sector.
A preliminary appraisal form is completed for each application and reference is made to cost, number of beneficiaries and the risk and sustainability of the project. This form is then checked by another member of the team and a decision made as to whether to reject the application, obtain more details or recommend a site visit. During the site visit a meeting will be held with the community to confirm their agreement with the project and their willingness to meet the community contribution. Specific questions will be raised with the women of the community to ensure the gender issue has been addressed. If the results of the site visit are satisfactory a formal appraisal is carried out by the Project Manager and Technical Advisor and this is presented with the project proposal to the Steering Committee with their recommendations. At each meeting a list is also submitted of those projects which have been rejected and the reasons why.

Up to May 2001 five project proposals have been approved with a total funding value of € 110.000. One is a water supply project to complete over 40 village water projects in all provinces, there is a women's skills and business training project, a Provincial Ward Development and Strategic Planning Workshop (including Project Cycle Management), a school water supply project and the supply of an oil screw press for a rural training centre. With the return of normalcy following the ethnic conflict it is expected that project submissions will increase. There are several projects in the pipeline. Standard designs are now been produced for clinics, classrooms and staff houses together with material and labour costing and it is hoped and these will accelerate implementation

ANNEX 5

Medium Term Development Strategy

The initial period of the MTDS (conceive in the pre-conflict period) covered the three years from 1999 to 2001 but the implementation of the strategy was originally expected to go several years beyond 2001. Below is an extract from the MTDS with comments.

The overall goal of the MTDS is the attainment of a higher and sustainable level of economic growth consistent with a more equitable distribution of the benefits from economic development, amongst all Solomon Islanders.

1. Macroeconomic and general policy reforms

The areas of concentration include the public finance and budget reforms, public sector reform, reforms of state-owned enterprises and facilitating private sector development.

Major progress was made between early January 1998 and early 2000 in each of the four above areas. The coup of June 5th, the change of government and the priority being put on obtaining peace resulted in the reform agenda being interrupted. In early 2001 the government announced the creation of the Ministry of Economic Reform and Structural Adjustment, the mandate of which is to revitalise the economic reform programme, including privatisation of State Owned Enterprises. No progress has been achieved to date.

2. Sectoral strategies

The priority areas for the sectoral strategies include human resource development, improvement of physical infrastructure and natural resource development and environment and finally development of tourism, small businesses and foreign investments and trade.

Education
The objective of reform in education is to redirect resources to the majority of the population at the primary, secondary school and community education levels. Higher education will continue, but the level of public funding will be drastically reduced and redirected at the lower reaches of the education system.
Education has been and remains a priority for the government. This applies to secondary education and in the aftermath of the coup the government has recognised the need also to strengthen considerably primary level education.

Health
In the medium term, health reform will aim to shift resources towards preventive healthcare and encourage the public to meet the resource shortfall in curative health through user pay and other cost recovery schemes.
Similar to the education system health services have deteriorated, at national and provincial level, as a direct result of government's major financial difficulties after the ethnic tension. The sector is also considered a priority by the government.

Women and youth
Government will encourage a greater balance in gender roles, by creating more equal opportunities for females in all fields including education, employment and in decision-

making. Gender based violence towards women and children is recognised a as possible problem which is studied by UNPFA. The important role of the women in the Peace Process in Solomon Islands is widely recognised.
Policy will aim to harness the potential of the young through education, training and involving them in specific social and economic development programs at the community level.

Transport and communication
Substantial new investment was to be injected into the transport and communication sector for the construction of new roads and bridges, the rehabilitation and upgrading of existing roads and their maintenance. Marine transport and air navigation will also be improved."
Substantial investments were to be made to upgrade roads in Guadalcanal and Malaita as about 90% of all road traffic is located in those 2 provinces. The government was committed to improve its maintenance capacity considerably, with donor assistance. Likewise, the government intends to improve marine infrastructure and domestic shipping services. Various initiatives were identified after the ethnic tension to employ jobless youths and ex-militants in labour based road and bridge maintenance programmes.

Natural Resource Development (agriculture, forestry, fisheries)
Key actions in the agricultural sector include promotion of rural development by increasing food production and improving living standards. Research and extension services should be provided to replace shifting cultivation by more intensive farming through technology transfer and better farm management. A second action is to promote expansion of plantation agriculture. Minimisation of land disputes through a faster registration of land will be pursued. Thirdly, policy action will be taken to improve tax collection from agricultural exports. Finally, the privatisation of State Owned Enterprises (SIPL, CEMA) will continue.
Relatively little progress has been made in implementing the above policy. A major reform programme was being identified with donor assistance but was put on hold during the ethnic tension.

Policy in the Forestry sector would aim to restore the logging rate to sustainable levels and strengthen sustainable management capacity.
Until early 2000 substantial efforts were underway to improve management of the forestry resources. A new and progressive forestry act was part of this policy. The results were partly undone during the tension but the government, keen to increase export revenue after the tension, intended to strengthen monitoring of logging and exports. Exploitation of the country's forest resources in a sustainable way is a major and essential issue, and has given rise to concern in the past, which continues in the present, equally in terms of the Government's cash crisis and loans from Taiwan. Existing forestry legislation has to be translated into practical measures.

Policy reform in the commercial fishery sector will be directed at inducing more foreign investment (capital, management, technology and marketing expertise) in the sector; developing more inshore facilities and reducing government ownership of companies in the sector. In fact Government's ownership of Solomon Taiyo has increased. Care is to be taken to ensure that the commercial exploitation remains sustainable In the artisanal fishery sector most of the 31 fish centres established throughout the Solomon Islands have failed, largely because provincial administrations could not manage them. In the medium term, consideration will be given to privatising these fish centres or injecting more investment to build up management capacity. The artisanal fisheries sector is of importance for the creation of rural income and have great value as a protein source in the local diet.

Similarly to the forestry sector there is a need for a long-term strategic plan to improve management of the country's vast fisheries resources and ensure their sustainable harvesting.

Tourism and small businesses

The government will support the development of tourism by ensuring that there is political and macroeconomic stability in the country. Offering appropriate incentives will encourage foreign and domestic investment (including indigenous Solomon Islands) to enter into the eco-tourism sector. Training will also be provided at all levels of the industry, including marketing and promotion, in order to raise the quality and international competitiveness of the tourism service.

The tourism sector was hard hit by the ethnic tension with tourist levels reduced to a minimum. In order to generate export revenues and jobs the government is committed in the longer term to revitalise the eco-tourism sector.

Solomon Islands - EDF and bucgetlines commitments and disbursements (OLAS Sheets) ANNEX 6

	Primary commitments				Secondary commitments				Disbursements		
NIP (total)	**Before 1999**	**1999**	**2000**	**Total**	**Before 1999**	**1999**	**2000**	**Total**	**1998**	**1999**	**2000**
6th EDF (16,000,0(	15.276.905	0	150.000	15.426.905	14.953.386	-3.050	458	14.950.794	14.708.379	45.956	-5.835
7th EDF (20,900,0(	16.562.701	1.203.778	2.798.534	20.565.013	12.175.948	3.181.338	2.604.618	17.961.905	8.425.076	3.074.586	3.480.860
8th EDF (19,000,0(	0	1.953.000	11.044.000	12.997.000	0	0	2.446.200	2.446.200	0	0	629.347
Sub-total	*31.839.606*	*3.156.778*	*13.992.534*	*48.988.918*	*27.129.334*	*3.178.288*	*5.051.276*	*35.358.899*	*23.133.455*	*3.120.542*	*4.104.373*
SAP	**Before 1999**	**1999**	**2000**	**Total**	**1998**	**1999**	**2000**	**Total**	**1998**	**1999**	**2000**
8th EDF	0	3.700.000	500.000	4.200.000	0	1.800.000	389.000	2.189.000	0	1.800.000	0
Sub-total	*0*	*3.700.000*	*500.000*	*4.200.000*	*0*	*1.800.000*	*389.000*	*2.189.000*	*0*	*1.800.000*	*0*

	Commitmen-s				Commitments (same as primary one)				Disbursements to joint account EU/ACI		
STABEX	**Before 1999**	**1999**	**2000**	**Total**	**Before 1999**	**1999**	**2000**	**Total**	**Before 1999**	**1999**	**2000**
6th EDF	31.268.105	0	0	31.268.105	31.268.105	0	0	31.268.105	31.268.105	0	0
7th EDF	8.097.193	0	0	8.097.193	8.097.193	0	0	8.097.193	8.097.193	0	0
8th EDF	182.989	41.820.222	0	42.003.211	182.989	41.820.222	0	42.003.211	182.989	0	41.820.222
Sub-total	*39.548.287*	*41.820.222*	*0*	*81.368.509*	*39.548.287*	*41.820.222*	*0*	*81.368.509*	*39.548.287*	*0*	*41.820.222*

	Commitments				Commitments (same as primary one)				Disbursements		
EIB	**Before 1999**	**1999**	**2000**	**Total**	**Before 1999**	**1999**	**2000**	**Total**	**Before 1999**	**1999**	**2000**
6th EDF	0	0	0	0	0	0	0	0	0	0	0
7th EDF	2.000.000	0	0	2.000.000	2.000.000	0	0	2.000.000	648.275	651.225	0
8th EDF	0	0	0	0	0	0	0	0	0	0	0
Sub-total	*2.000.000*	*0*	*0*	*2.000.000*	*2.000.000*	*0*	*0*	*2.000.000*	*648.275*	*651.225*	*0*

	Commitments				Commitments (same as primary one)				Disbursements		
	Before 1999	**1999**	**2000**		**Before 1999**	**1999**	**2000**		**Before 1999**	**1999**	**2000**
Budget lines	450.000	0	1.316.620	1.766.620	450.000	0	1.316.620	1.766.620	450.000	0	1.316.620
Sub-total	*450.000*	*0*	*1.316.620*	*1.766.620*	*450.000*	*0*	*1.316.620*	*1.766.620*	*450.000*	*0*	*1.316.620*

OVERALL TOTAL	***73.837.893***	***48.677.000***	***15.809.154***	***138.324.047***	***69.127.621***	***46.798.510***	***6.756.896***	***122.683.028***	***63.780.017***	***5.571.767***	***47.241.215***

Actual payments for STABEX projects

	before 1999	**1999**	**2000**	
EDF 6 and 7	31.268.105	1.800.000	1.500.000	balance of FMO 86-93 and 94-95
EDF 8	0	0	0	FMO signed end 2000

(b) In the case of a Corporation, its corporate name and registered or principal place of business;

(x) with respect to the Secretary or where there are joint secretaries, with respect to each of them.

(a) In the case of an individual, his present Christian name and surname, any former Christian name and surname and usual residential address and

(b) In the case of a corporation, its corporate name and registered office.

Registrar of Companies
Ministry of Justice
P O Box 404
Honiara
SOLOMON ISLANDS

3. *FEES*

(i) Statement of particulars . $ 25.00

(ii) Notice of change . $ 20.00

(iii) Cessation of Business . $ 10.00

(iv) Notice of happening of event . $10.00

(v) Inquiry whether a proposed name be registered . $ 10.00

(vi) Certificate of Registration $ 20.00

(vii) Application to lodge a statement of particulars or notice of change out of time $5.00

(viii) Company incorporation application fee . $ 50.00

(ix) Incorporation fee $250.00

For further details contact:-

Registrar of Companies
Ministry of Justice
P O Box 404
Honiara
SOLOMON ISLANDS

Tel: (677) 22227/20465 Fax: (677) 20786
E-mail : investment@commerce.gov.sb
www.commerce.gov.sb

INVESTMENT DIVISION

DEPARTMENT OF COMMERCE, EMPLOYMENT & TRADE

SOLOMON ISLANDS

BUSINESS INCORPORATION & FEES.

BUSINESS INCORPORATION

1. TYPES OF BUSINESS.

In Solomon Islands, a business may be carried on in any one of the following forms:

(i) By an individual operating as a sole proprietorship;

(ii) By two or more persons in partnership;

(iii) By a community group as a co-operative entity;

(iv) By a locally incorporated company or a foreign company registered under the provisions of the Companies Act.

Under the business names Act 1971, any business name, other than the surnames and initials of the partners in the firm of surname and initials of the sole partners, or corporate names of all which are partners must be registered with the Registrar of Companies or form (Form B/N2). Completion of this should entitled you to carry on business activities in Solomon Islands.

There are at least four (4) common types of companies required under the provisions of Companies Act. The are:-

(i) Companies limited by shares;

(ii) Companies limited by guarantee;

(iii) Companies limited by both shares and guarantee;

(iv) And unlimited company.

2. COMPANY INCORPORATION

When incorporating a company either as a business name other than your own name, a company or a foreign owned company you shall be required to meet followings:-

2.1 Registration of Business Name.

The followings should be included in your application with an appropriate fee;

(a) (i) promoter names, addresses, citizenship and % shareholdings,

(ii) nature and scale of operations;

(iii) certificate of approval from Investment Division;

(iv) authorized capital;

(b) The application is then forwarded to the Honourable Minister of Commerce & Tourism for further recommendation and approval.

(c) Application and recommendation is returned to the Registrar of Companies.

(d) Your company is then registered.

2.2 Registration of Company.

The registration of a company as a limited liability should also follow steps 2.1(a)-(d) above as well as lodgement of these documents for incorporation.

(i) articles of association;

(ii) memorandum of association;

(iii) declaration of compliance with the requirements of the Companies Act (Form 3 - companies);

(iv) notice of situation of registered office (Form 25 - companies);

(v) particulars of directors or secretary (Form 32 - companies);

2.3 Registration of a foreign company.

Applying for registration of an overseas company is covered in part III of the Companies Act (Cap. 66).

An overseas company incorporated outside Solomon Islands and establishes a place of business within the country shall within one month of the establishment of the place of business deliver to the Registrar of Companies for registration of the followings:

(i) a certified copy of the charter, statutes or Memorandum and Articles of the company or other instrument constituting or defining the constitution of the company;

(ii) a list of the Directors and Secretary of the company with the following particulars;

(iii) name and address of one or more persons who live in Honiara and are authorized to accept services of notice and legal processes on behalf of the company. The person appointed must sign a statement to say he/she accept such an appointment;

(ix) with respect to each director:

(a) In the case of an individual, his present Christian name and surname, and any former Christian name or surname, his/her usual residential address, his/her nationality and his/her business occupation, if any or if he/she has no business occupation but holds any other directorship or directorships, particulars of such directorship or of some one of those directorship; and

Table A1: Summary of the Asian Development Bank's Strategy

ITEM	OBJECTIVE: Provide Transportation Infrastructure and Services	OBJECTIVE: Create an Enabling Business Environment
Strategic Focus / Key Result Areas	• To rehabilitate and maintain physical infrastructure in locations of major economic activity, ADB will assist the Solomon Islands Government to sustainably develop, fund, and manage a national transport plan (NTP). • To facilitate improved availability and efficiency of interisland transport services, ADB will assist the Government to implement a franchise scheme for uneconomic routes.	• To improve the policy and institutional framework for business development, ADB will assist the Government to strengthen the legal and regulatory environment for business investment. • To enhance the efficiency and effectiveness of state-owned enterprises (SOEs) and encourage public-private partnerships, ADB will support the conduct of SOE reform exercises
Ongoing / Proposed Loans	• Loan 1823-SOL: Post-Conflict Emergency Rehabilitation Project (approved in 2000 for US$10 million)	None proposed in this period
Ongoing / Proposed Technical Assistance	• Institutional Strengthening for the Ministry of Infrastructure Development (MID) (2004) • Diagnostic Study of Interisland Transport (2004) • Implementation of Interisland Transport Reforms (2005) • MID reform program (2006)	• SOE Reforms and Private Sector Participation (2004) • Business Environment Reforms (2005) • Economic Development Report (2005) • Supporting Transformation of SOEs (2005, standby) • Private Sector Participation Program (2006) • Secured Transaction Reforms (2006)
Other Assistance	• Regional TA for Civil Aviation Safety and Security (2003) • Regional TA for Pacific Regional Transport Analysis (2003) • Economic Report (PIER) for the Solomon Islands (2005 - jointly planned with the World Bank)	• Regional TA for Improving the Legal Business Environment in the Pacific (2003) • Regional TA for the Development of Secured Transactions Framework (2004) • Economic Report (PIER) for the Solomon Islands (2005, jointly planned with the World Bank)
Target Outcomes	• Current infrastructure stock (roads, wharves, airstrips) operates to design standards (to be specified in the NTP) • Air and sea transport service frequencies to all provinces meet an agreed upon minimum standard (to be specified in the NTP)	• Increased private sector investment, production, and employment • Reduced fiscal allocations to and contingent liabilities from SOEs • Enhanced corporate governance and improved financial and service delivery performance of retained SOEs
Performance Indicators	• NTP approved by end- 2004 and updated every 2 years • NTP funding channels and mechanisms, including Transport Development Trust Fund, operating efficiently by end- 2005 • MID contract management systems in place by end- 2005 • Transport agreement(s) for uneconomic routes signed between the Government and operators, in accordance with due process	• Legal and regulatory reform action plan approved by end-2004 and implemented by June 2007 • Increased number of new businesses registered • Increased credit provision to private businesses • Agreed-upon list of SOEs privatized or otherwise transformed by 2007 • Remaining SOE portfolio restructured as appropriate, and meeting accounting and reporting requirements

COUNTRY AND PORTFOLIO INDICATORS, AND ASSISTANCE PIPELINE

Table A2.1: Progress Toward the Millennium Development Goals and Targets

Goals and Targets	1990	1995	Latest Year	
Goal 1. Eradicate Extreme Poverty and Hunger				
Target 1: Reduce incidence of extreme poverty by half from 1990 to 2015				
1. Proportion of population below US$1 per day (PPP-values) (%)	—	—	—	
2. Poverty gap ratio	—	—	—	
3. Share of poorest quintile in national consumption (%)	—	—	—	
Target 2: Reduce the proportion of people who suffer from hunger by half from 1990 to 2015				
4. Prevalence of child malnutrition (% of children under 5)	23.0 (1989)	12.6	11.0	(2000)
5. Proportion of population below minimum level of dietary energy consumption (%)	—	—	—	
Goal 2. Achieve Universal Primary Education				
Target 3: Attain 100 percent primary school enrolment by 2015				
6. Net enrolment ratio in primary education (%)	83.3[a]	93.0[b] (1994)	66.0	(2001)
7. Proportion of pupils starting Grade 1 who reach Grade 5	84.9[a]	81.0[c] (1996)	—	
8. Literacy rate of 15-24 year olds (%)	—	—	—	
Goal 3. Promote Gender Equality and Empower Women				
Target 4: Eliminate gender disparities in primary and secondary education by 2005 and to all levels of education no later than 2015				
9. Ratio of girls to boys in (%)				
Primary education	80.0[a]	81.0[e] (1994)	88.0[c]	(1998)
Secondary education	58.0[d]	60.0[e] (1994)	60.0[c]	(1998)
10. Ratio of young literate females to males (% of age group 15-24)	—	—	—	
11. Share of women in wage employment in the non agriculture sector	33.3[a]	—	—	
12. Proportion of seats held by women in national parliament	0.0[f] (1991)	2.0[f]	0.0[f]	(2003)
Goal 4. Reduce Child Mortality				
Target 5: Reduce infant and child mortality by two-thirds from 1990 to 2015				
13. Under-5 mortality rate (per '000 live births)	36.0[a]	30.0[a]	24.0[a]	(2002)
14. Infant mortality rate (per '000 live births)	29.0[a]	25.0[a]	20.0[a]	(2002)
15. Proportion of 1-year-old children immunized against measles	70.0[g] (1989-1990)	68.0[c]	78.0[a]	(2002)

Goals and Targets	1990	1995	Latest Year	
Goal 5. Improve Maternal Health				
Target 6: Reduce maternal mortality rate by three quarters between 1990 and 2015				
16. Maternal mortality ratio (per 100,000 live births)	550.0 (1992)	209.0 (1997)	130.0[a]	(2000)
17. Births attended by skilled health staff (% of live births)	85.0[g] (1990-1991)	87.0[b] (1995-1997)	85.0[a]	(1995-2002)
Goal 6. Combat HIV/AIDS, Malaria, and Other Diseases				
Target 7: Have halted by 2015, and begun to reverse the spread of HIV/AIDS				
18. HIV prevalence rate among pregnant women 15-24 years old pregnant women	Nil	Nil	Nil	
19. Contraceptive prevalence rate (% of women aged 15-49)	—	5.8	7.0	(1999)
20. Number of children orphaned by HIV/AIDS	—	—	—	
Target 8: Have halted by 2015, and begun to reverse the incidence of malaria and other major diseases				
21. Malaria:				
Prevalence rate (per 100,000 people)	44,000[h] (1992)	—	15,172[a,b]	(2000)
Death rate (per 100,000 people)	—	—	8.0[a,b]	(2000)
22. Proportion of population in malaria risk areas using effective malaria prevention and treatment measures [i]	—	—	53.0	(1999)
23. Tuberculosis (TB):				
Prevalence rate (per 100,000 people)	—	57.0[a] (2000)	52.0[b]	(2001)
Death rate (per 100,000 people)	—	8.0[a] (2000)	12.0[b]	(2001)
24. Proportion of TB cases:				
DOTS detection rate (%)	—	57.0[a] (1996)	67.0[a,b]	(2001)
DOTS treatment success (%)	—	65.0[a]	81.0[a,b]	(2000)
Goal 7. Ensure Environmental Sustainability				
Target 9: Integrate the principles of sustainable development into country policies and programs and reverse the loss of environmental resources				
25. Forest area (% of total land area)	90.3[a,b]	—	88.8[a,b]	(2000)
26. Nationally protected areas (% of total land area)	—	0.3[a] (1997)	0.1[j]	(2003)
27. GDP per unit of energy use (PPP$ per kg oil equivalent)	—	—	—	
28. Carbon dioxide emissions (per capita metric tons)	0.506[a]	0.431[a]	0.389[a]	(1999)

Goals and Targets	1990	1995	Latest Year	
Target 10: Halve, by 2015, the proportion of people without sustainable access to safe drinking water				
29. Access to an improved water source (% of population)				
Total	—	64.0[b] (1995-1997)	71.0[a,l]	(2000)
Urban	82.0[k]	—	94.0[a,l]	
Rural	58.0[k]	—	65.0[a,l]	
Target 11: By 2010, to have achieved a significant improvement in the lives of at least 100 million slum dwellers				
30. Access to improved sanitation (% of population)				
Total	—	16.0[b] (1995-1997)	34.0[a,l]	(2000)
Urban	73.0[k]	—	98.0[a,l]	
Rural	2.0[k]	—	18.0[a,l]	
31. Access to secure tenure (% of population)	—	—	—	

— no data available.
DOTS = directly observed treatment, short course; GDP = gross domestic product; HIV/AIDS = Human Immunodeficiency Virus/Acquired Immune Deficiency Syndrome; kg = kilogram; PPP = purchasing power parity.

[a] United Nations Statistics Division (UNSD), Millennium Indicator Database (2003) (http://millenniumindicators.un.org)
[b] UNDP Human Development Report 2003; UNDP Pacific Human Development Report 1999.
[c] Asian Development Bank Key Indicators 2003.
[d] United Nations Economic and Social Commission for Asia and the Pacific (UNESCAP)/UNDP2003 Promoting the Millennium Development Goals in Asia and the Pacific: Meeting the Challenges of Poverty Reduction .
[e] United Nations Educational, Scientific and Cultural Organization (UNESCO), Institute for Statistics. (http://www.uis.unesco.org)
[f] Inter-Parliamentary Union (IPU), Information on National Parliaments (http://www.ipu.org)
[g] UNESCAP, Economic and Social Survey of Asia and the Pacific 2002
[h] ADB, Discussion Paper on Poverty Assessment (2001), under regional technical assistance (RETA) 5907: Poverty Assessment in Pacific Developing Member Countries.
[i] Figure refers to proportion of population using bed nets.
[j] World Resources Institute, Earth Trends 2003. (http://earthtrends.wri.org)
[k] World Health Organization (WHO)/United Nations Children's Fund (UNICEF), Joint Monitoring Programme for Water Supply and Sanitation, Coverage Estimates 1980-2000 (http://www.unicef.org/programme/wes)
[l] WHO/UNICEF/Water Supply and Sanitation Collaborative Council, Global Water Supply and Sanitation Assessment 2000 Report.

Sources: Unless otherwise specified, data are from the (i) Government of Solomon Islands/United Nations Development Program (UNDP), Solomon Islands Human Development Report 2002: Building a Nation, and the (ii) United Nations, Common Country Assessment Solomon Islands (Final Draft, 23 March 2002).

Table A2.2: Country Economic Indicators

Item	Fiscal Year 1999	2000	2001	2002	2003
A. Income and Growth					
1. GDP per Capita (US$, current)	755	692	646	503	470
2. GDP Growth (%, in constant prices)	(0.9)	(13.3)	(10.1)	(4.0)	3.8
a. Agriculture	(4.0)	(43.0)	(12.6)		
b. Industry	22.2	(49.2)	(33.2)		
c. Services	(8.0)	(26.0)	(4.6)		
B. Savings and Investment (current market prices)			**(% of GDP)**		
1. Gross Domestic Investment	—	—	—	—	—
2. Gross Domestic Saving	—	—	—	—	—
C. Money and Inflation			**(annual % change)**		
1. Consumer Price Index[a]	8.0	7.3	6.8	7.3	8.3
2. Total Liquidity (M2)	4.5	0.4	(13.3)	4.0	19.4
D. Government Finance			**(% of GDP)**		
1. Total Revenue and Grants	46.8	35.5	22.5	25.0	16.1
2. Total Expenditure and Onlending	51.1	39.7	34.0	36.1	15.3
3. Overall Fiscal Surplus / Deficit ( )	(4.3)	(4.2)	(11.5)	(11.1)	0.9
E. Balance of Payments					
1. Merchandise Trade Balance (% of GDP)	12.9	(7.9)	(12.3)	(8.5)	(2.9)
2. Current Account Balance (% of GDP)	25.5	0.0	(5.2)	(5.2)	0.4
3. Merchandise Export (US$) growth (annual % change)	6.5	(53.8)	(32.6)	13.5	20.2
4. Merchandise Import (US$) growth (annual % change)	(25.1)	(16.0)	(12.4)	(11.0)	(2.8)
F. External Payments Indicators					
1. Gross Official Reserves (US$ million, end of period)	50.6	31.4	21.2	12.9	29.8
Months of imports	3.7	2.7	1.8	1.3	
2. External Debt Service (% of exports of goods & services)	4.5	8.2	0.8		
3. External Debt (% of GDP)	42.0	42.7	51.2	73.7	73.4
G. Memorandum Items:					
1. GDP (current market prices, million local currency)	1523.0	1480.0	1479.0	1516.0	1592.0
2. Exchange Rate (SI$ per US dollar, annual average)	4.9	5.1	5.3	6.8	7.4
3. Population (million)	0.409	0.420	0.432	0.444	0.457

— not available

GDP = gross domestic product.

[a] period average

Sources: Department of National Reform and Planning, National Economic Recovery, Reform, and Development Plan 2003-2006, October 2003; Central Bank of Solomon Islands; International Monetary Fund; ADB staff estimates.

Table A2.3: Poverty Indicators

Item	1990	1995	Latest Year	
1. Development Progress Indices				
Human Development Index (HDI)				
Pacific HDI		0.191[a] (1994)	0.371[a]	(1998)
PDMC Rank (out of 12 PDMCs)		9	11	
Global HDI			0.632[b]	(2001)
Global Rank (out of 175 countries)			123	
Human Poverty Index (HPI)	—	49.1[a] (1998)	23.2	(1999)
PDMC Rank (out of 12 PDMCs)	—	11	—	
Composite Vulnerability Index	—	—	8.398[c]	(1998)
PDMC Rank (out of 7 PDMCs)	—	—	4	
Gender-Related Development Index	—	—	0.596	(1999)
Global Rank	—	—	—	
2. Poverty Indicators				
Head Count Index (% poor of total households)	—	—	—	
Poverty Severity Index (%)	—	—	—	
3. Inequality Indicators				
Gini Coefficient	—	—	—	
Household Income (% of total)				
National[d]				
Rural[e]				
Honiara[f]				
Income Ratio (H20/L20)	—	—	—	

— = no data available; H20/L20 = ratio of share in total income of the highest income quintile group to the lowest income quintile group; PDMC = Pacific developing member country.

[a] UNDP *Pacific Human Development Report* 1994, 1999.

[b] UNDP *Human Development Report 2003.*

[c] Asian Development Bank, Discussion Paper on Poverty Assessment (2001), under regional technical assistance (RETA) 5907: *Poverty Assessment in PDMCs*

[d] Rural Areas Household Income and Expenditure Survey (HIES) in 1993 and the Honiara Income Distribution Survey in 1995 showed that the bottom 93% of households received 22% of total incomes, while the top 1% of households received 52% of total incomes.

[e] The 1993 Rural Areas HIES reported that the bottom 84% of rural households accounted for just one half of 1% of total household incomes in rural areas.

[f] In the 1991 Honiara HIES, the top 10% of Honiara households were reported to have received over 50% of total income in Honiara.

Sources: Unless otherwise specified, data are from the Government of Solomon Islands/United Nations Development Program (UNDP), *Solomon Islands Human Development Report 2002: Building a Nation.*

Table A2.4: Social Indicators

Item	1990	1995	Latest Year	
1. Demographic Indicators				
Total Population ('000)	315.0[a]	366.0[a]	457.0[a]	(2003 est.)
Annual Population Growth Rate (% change)	3.0	3.2	2.9	
Dependency Ratio (% of dependents to working age)	102.4 (1986)	81.6 (1999)	85.2[b]	(2001 est.)
Total Fertility Rate (births per woman)	6.1 (1986)	5.4[c] (1995) 4.8 (1999)	4.4[b]	(2000-05 projection)
Ave. Household Size	6.5 (1986)	—	6.3	(1999)
2. Health				
Life Expectancy at Birth (years)	54.6 (1986)	61.1 (1999)	65.4[d]	(2002)
Male	54.3 (1986)	60.6 (1999)	63.6[d]	(2002)
Female	55.0 (1986)	61.6 (1999)	67.4[d]	(2002)
Population with Access to Health Services (%)	—	38.2[e]	74.7	(1999 est.)
Urban	—	—	100.0	(1999)
Rural	—	—	70.0	(1999)
Population per Doctor	—	6,355[c,f]	9,513	(1999)
Government Expenditure on Health				
As % of Total Government Spending	12.6 (1991)	13.5 (1994)	14.9	(2001)
As % of GDP	3.7 (1991)	3.8 (1994)	5.9	(2001)
3. Education				
Adult Literacy Rate (%) [g]	22.0[f] (1991)	30.0[f] (1994)	76.6	(1999)
Male	27.0[f] (1991)	—	83.7	(1999)
Female	17.0[f] (1991)	—	69.0	(1999)
Combined Gross School Enrollment Ratio (% of aged 5-19 years)	34.8 (1986)	—	56.3	(1999)
Male	38.0[b] (1986)	—	58.1	(1999)
Female	31.0[b] (1986)	—	54.3	(1999)
Gross Primary Enrollment (% of aged 5-14 years)	39.0[b] (1986)	75.0[c] (1996)	76.5	(1999)
Male	41.0[b] (1986)	78.0[c] (1996)	78.2	(1999)
Female	36.0[b] (1986)	70.0[c] (1996)	74.6	(1999)

Table A2.5: Environment Indicators

Item	1990	Latest Year	
1. Energy Efficiency of Emissions			
Traditional Fuel Use (% of total energy use)	—	50.0	(1996)
2. Water Pollution			
Water Bodies Exceeding Contact Recreation Standards			
Biological Oxygen Demand (BOD)	—	—	
Chemical Oxygen Demand (COD)	—	—	
3. Air Pollution			
Carbon Dioxide (CO_2) Emissions			
Total ('000 metric tons)	161.3	165.0	(1999)
Per unit of GDP (kg/PPP$ GDP)	—	—	
Sulfur Dioxide (SO_2) Emissions			
Total ('000 metric tons)	—	1.0	(1995)
4. Land Use and Deforestation			
Total Land Area (km^2)	28,370	28,370	(2003)
Average Annual Deforestation			
Area (remaining km^2)	—	24,860	(2000)
% change	0.2 (1990-95)	0.2	(1990-2000)
Arable Land (% of total land)	1.0 (1993)	4.0	(2001)
Cropland, Permanent (% of total land)	1.0 (1993)		
Pastures, Permanent (% of total land)	1.0 (1993)		
Population Density, Rural (people per km^2)	787 (1998)	911	(2002)
5. Biodiversity and Protected Areas			
Nationally Protected Area(s)			
Area (km^2)	—	20	(2003)
Number	—	7	(2003)
Mammals (number of threatened species)	20 (1998)	20	(2002)
Birds (number of threatened species)	18 (1998)	23	(2002)
Higher Plants (number of threatened species)	—	16	(2002)
Reptiles (number of threatened species)	—	4	(2002)
Amphibians (number of threatened species)	—	—	
6. Urban Areas			
Urban Population			
% of total population	13.0 (1986)	20.8	(2002)
Per Capita Water Use (liters/day)	—	—	
Wastewater Treated (%)	—	—	
Solid Waste Generated per Capita (kg/day)	—	—	

— = no data available GDP = gross domestic product kg = kilogram km^2 = square kilometer PPP = purchasing power parity

Sources: Central Intelligence Agency (CIA), *The World Factbook* (2001-2003). (http://www.cia.gov); Secretariat of the Pacific Community (SPC), Demography/Population Programme *Oceania Population 2000 & 2003.* (http://www.spc.int/demog); United Nations Development Programme (UNDP), *Human Development Report* (2000-2003); United Nations Statistics Division (UNSD), Millennium Indicator Database 2003 (http://milleniumindicators.un.org); World Bank, *The Little Green Data Book* (2000-2004); World Resources Institute, Earth Trends 2003 (http://earthtrends.wri.org)

Table A2.6: Development Coordination Matrix

Sector/Thematic/Area	ADB Strategy/Activities	Other Development Partners' Strategy/Activities
A. Law, Economic Management, and Public Policy	• State-Owned Enterprise Reforms and Private Sector Participation (2004) • Economic Development Report (2005) • Standby: Supporting Transformation of State-Owned Enterprises (2005)	• Community Peace and Restoration Fund (AusAID) • Governance and Reform Assistance (AusAID) • Capacity Building and Institutional Strengthening for Customs and Excise (AusAID) • Provincial Grants Facility (AusAID) • Land Administration and Management - Institutional Strengthening Project (AusAID) • National Disaster Management Office (AusAID) • Law and Justice Institutional Strengthening Programme (AusAID) • Department of National Planning Capacity and Institutional Strengthening (EU) • National Authorising Officer Programme Management Unit Phase II (EU) • Police Commissioner Office Support (EU) • TA for Department of Provincial Government (EU) • Demobilisation of Special Constables (EU) • Capacity Building Project (NZAID) • National Peace Council (NZAID) • Provincial Offices Reconstruction (Taipei,China) • Visit Solomons Campaign (Taipei,China) • Police Housing (Taipei,China) • Isabel Provincial Government Office (UNDP)
B. Industry and Trade	• Business Environment Reforms (2005) • Private Sector Participation Program (2006)	• Small Business Programme (NZAID) • Ecotourism Development (NZAID) • Rural Tourism Development (Taipei,China)
C. Finance	• Secured Transactions Reforms (2006)	• Ministry of Finance Strengthening Programme (AusAID) • Support to Central Bank of SI (WB)
D. Education	• No programmed activity in this sector	• Australian Training and Education Awards (AusAID) • Australian Development Scholarships (AusAID) • Preparatory Studies, Restructuring, and Support for Ministry of Education (EU) • Educational Materials (EU) • Assistance to SICHE (EU) • School Infrastructure Rehabilitation (EU) • European Union Tertiary Scholarships (EU) • Emergency Support for Secondary Education (EU) • Rural Training Centers Phase IV (EU) • School Rehabilitation and Construction Project (JICA) • Scholarships for Studying in Japan (JICA)

Sector/Thematic/Area	ADB Strategy/Activities	Other Development Partners' Strategy/Activities
		• Education Sector Investment and Reform Programme (NZAID and EU) • Tertiary Training and Education Awards (NZAID) • SI Training and Education Awards Scheme (NZAID) • Regional and In-Country Scholarships (Taipei,China) • Basic School Supplies Project (Taipei,China) • Post graduate Scholarships (UK)
E. Health, Nutrition, & Social Protection	• No programmed activity in this sector	• Institutional Strengthening Project (AusAID) • Health Sector Support Trust Fund (AusAID) • Global Fund Against TB, AIDS, Malaria County Program • Extended Immunization Program (JICA) • Clinic Renovations (JICA) • Provincial Hospital Upgrades (JICA) • Support for SICHE Nursing School (JICA) • Red Cross Capacity Building (NZAID) • Upgrading of National Referral Hospital (Taipei,China) • Strengthening of Primary Health Care (Taipei,China) • HIV/AIDS Programme (SPC) • Reproductive Health and Family Planning (UNFPA) • Integrated Management of Childhood Illnesses (UNICEF) • Health Sector Development Projects (WB) • WHO Solomon Islands (WHO) • Support for a Peaceful Civil Society Fund (AusAID) • Funds for Save the Children (AusAID) • Support for Kastom Garden (AusAID) • Human Rights Small Grants for Women (AusAID) • Micro Projects Scheme Phase II (EU) • Assistance to Non state Actors (EU) • Community-Based Grass Roots Projects (JICA) • Civil Society Leadership Development (NZAID) • Rural Constituency Development Fund (Taipei,China) • Small Grants Scheme (UK) • Youth Development Program (UK) • Women, Peace, and Security (UNIFEM)
F. Transport and Communication	• Post-Conflict Emergency Rehabilitation Project (2000) • Institutional Strengthening for Ministry of Infrastructure Development (2004) • Diagnostic Study of Interisland Transport (2004) • Implementation of Inter island Transport Reforms (2005)	• Inter island Shipping Facility (EU) • Marine Infrastructure Program (EU) • Honiara International Airport Development (JICA) • Wharves Repair Project (JICA) • Rural Communication Improvement Project (JICA)

Sector/Thematic/Area	ADB Strategy/Activities	Other Development Partners' Strategy/Activities
	• Ministry of Infrastructure Development Reform Program (2006)	• Completion of Gizo Road (Taipei,China) • Provincial Airfields Development (Taipei,China) • Provincial Shipping (Taipei,China) • Munda – Noro Road (Taipei,China) • Port Handling Equipment Replacement (Taipei,China)
G. Energy	• No programmed activity in this sector	• Assistance to Solomon Islands Electricity Authority (AusAID) • Generator parts to Lunga power station (JICA) • Rural Electrification (Taipei,China)
H. Water Supply, Sanitation, and Waste Management	• No programmed activity in this sector	• Support for Solomon Islands Water Authority (JICA) • Rural Urban Water Supply Rehabilitation (JICA) • Micro Water Projects (JICA) • Renbel Micro Water Supply (JICA) • Reducing Vulnerability in Solomon Islands (SOPAC)
I. Agriculture and Natural Resources	• No programmed activity in this sector	• Regional Initiatives on Genetic Resources (AusAID) • National Biodiversity Strategy and Action Plan (GEF) • National Bio-Safety Framework (GEF) • International Waters Programme (GEF) • National Capacity Self Assessment Project (GEF) • National Action Plan on Land Degradation (GEF) • Forest Management Program (AusAID) • Rural Fisheries Enterprises Phase III (EU) • Land and Marine Tenure Strategy (EU) • Rehabilitation of Copra and Cocoa Industry (EU) • Agriculture Sector Survey (EU) • Charcoal Burner Support to Organic Farming (JICA) • Honeybee Industry Development Support (NZAID) • Rice Production and Marketing (Taipei,China)

AusAID = Australian Agency for International Development; EIB = European Investment Bank; EU = European Union, GEF = Global Environment Facility; HIV/AIDS=Human Immunodeficiency Virus/Acquired Immune Deficiency Syndrome; JICA = Japan International Cooperation Agency; NZAID = New Zealand Agency for International Development, REG = regional; RETA = regional technical assistance, SICHE = Solomon Islands College of Higher Education; SIG = Solomon Islands Government; SOE = state-owned enterprises; SOPAC = South Pacific Applied Geoscience Commission; SPC = Secretariat of the Pacific Community; UK = United Kingdom; UNDP = United Nations Development Programme; UNFPA = United Nations Population Fund; UNICEF = United Nations Children's Fund; UNIFEM = United Nations Women's Fund, WB = World Bank, WHO = World Health Organization.

Table A2.7: Portfolio Indicators - Portfolio Amounts and Ratings
(public sector loans, as of 31 December 2003)

Sector	Net Loan Amount		Total		Rating [a]											
					Highly Satisfactory		Satisfactory		Partly Satisfactory		Unsatisfactory		Potential Problem [b]		At Risk [c]	
	$ million	%	no.	%	no.	%	no.	%	no.	%	no.	%	no.	%	no.	%
Agriculture and Natural Resources	-	-	-	-	-	-	-	-	-	-	-	-	-	-	-	-
Energy	-	-	-	-	-	-	-	-	-	-	-	-	-	-	-	-
Finance	-	-	-	-	-	-	-	-	-	-	-	-	-	-	-	-
Industry and Trade	-	-	-	-	-	-	-	-	-	-	-	-	-	-	-	-
Multisector	-	-	-	-	-	-	-	-	-	-	-	-	-	-	-	-
Others	12.6	100.0	2	100.0	-	-	-	-	-	-	2	100.0	-	-	2	100.0
Transport and Communication	-	-	-	-	-	-	-	-	-	-	-	-	-	-	-	-
Total	**12.6**	**100.0**	**2**	**100.0**	-	-	-	-	-	-	**2**	**100.0**	-	-	**2**	**100.0**

[a] One rating for implementation progress and development objectives, based on the lower rating of either.
[b] Potential problem loans are satisfactory loans, but have four or more risk factors associated with partly satisfactory or unsatisfactory performance.
[c] A loan is "at risk" if it is rated as partly satisfactory, as unsatisfactory, or as a potential problem.

Table A2.8: Portfolio Indicators - Disbursements and Net Transfers of Resources
(public sector loans, as of 31 December 2003)

Disbursements and Transfers	OCR	ADF	Total
Disbursements			
Total Funds Available for Withdrawal ($ mn)	-	12.6	12.6
Disbursed Amount ($/mn, cumulative)	-	1.0	1.0
Percentage Disbursed (disbursed amount/total available)	-	8.0	8.0
Disbursements ($/mn, latest year)	-	0.2	0.2
Disbursement Ratio (%) [a]	-	2.1	2.1
Net Transfer of Resources ($ mn)			
1999	-	(1.0)	(1.0)
2000	-	(0.5)	(0.5)
2001	-	(0.8)	(0.8)
2002	-	-	-
2003	-	(3.0)	(3.0)

ADF = Asian Development Fund, OCR = ordinary capital resources.
[a] Ratio of disbursements during the year over the undisbursed net loan balance at the beginning of the year less cancellations during the year. Effective loans during the year have also been added to the beginning balance of undisbursed loans.

Table A2.9: Portfolio Indicators - Evaluation Rating by Sector
(as of 31 January 2004)

	GS/HS/S		PS		US		Total	
Sector	**No.**	**%**	**No.**	**%**	**No.**	**%**	**No.**	**%**
Agriculture and Natural Resources	0	0.0	0	0.0	2	100.0	2	100.0
Energy	0	0.0	1	100.0	0	0.0	1	100.0
Industry and Trade	0	-	0	-	0	-	0	-
Transport and Communications	1	100.0	0	0.0	0	0.0	1	100.0
Water Supply, Sanitation and Work Management	0	0.0	1	100.0	0	0.0	1	100.0
Finance	0	0.0	1	50.0	1	50.0	2	100.0
Multisector	0	-	0	-	0	-	0	-
Others	0	-	0	-	0	-	0	-
Total	1	14.3	3	42.9	3	42.9	7	100.0

GS=generally successful HS=highly successful, PS=partly successful, S=successful, US=unsuccessful.

Source: Operations Evaluation Department / Post Evaluation Information System.

Table A2.10: Portfolio Implementation Status
(public sector loans, as of 31 December 2003)

Sector	Loan No.	Loan Seg	Title	Net Loan Amount OCR ($mn)	Net Loan Amount ADF ($mn)	Approval Date	Effectivity Date	Closing Date Original	Closing Date Revised	Progress (%complete)	Cumulative Contracts /Commitments ($ millions	Cumulative Disbursements ($ million)	Rating IP	Rating DO	Potential Problem[b]	At Risk[a]
MS	1628	(SF)	Privatization of State-Owned Enterprises		1.0	27 Aug 98	24 Nov 28	31 Dec 2000	31 Jan 2002	80%	0.9	1.0	U	U	Yes	Yes
MS	1823	(SF)	Post-Conflict Emergency Rehabilitation Project[c]		11.5	21 Dec 2000	19 Mar 01	30 Jun 2004	-	4%	1.0	0.0	U	U	No	Yes
			Total		**12.6**						**1.9**	**1.0**				

ADF=Asian Development Fund, DO-development objective, IP=implementation progress, OCR=ordinary capital resources, OTH=others, Seg=segment (pertaining to loans with more than one withdrawal authority), U=unsatisfactory

[a] "Yes" for loans with four or more risk factors associated with partly satisfactory or unsatisfactory performance.

[b] A loan is considered "at risk" if it is rated as "PS" or "U" in either implementation progress or development objectives, or if it is a potential problem loan.

[c] Suspended as of 31 December 2003.

Table A2.11: Assistance Pipeline for Nonlending Products and Services, 2005–2006

Sector Assistance Name	Responsible Division	Assistance Type	Sources of Funding: ADB Source	ADB Amount ($'000)	Others Source	Others Amount ($'000)	Total ($'000)
2005							
Transport and Communications							
1. Implementation of Interisland Transport Reforms	PAHQ	ETSW	JSF	500.00	TBD	300.00	800.00
Law, Economic Management, and Public Policy							
2. Business Environment Reforms	PAHQ	ETSW	TASF	400.00	TBD	200.00	600.00
3. Economic Development Report	PAHQ	ETSW	TASF	300.00	TBD	300.00	600.00
Total				**1,200.00**		**800.00**	**2,000.00**
Standby: Supporting Transformation of State-owned Enterprises	PAHQ	ETSW	TBD	300.00		0	300.00
2006							
Transport and Communication							
1. Ministry of Infrastructure Development Reform Program	PAHQ	LD	TASF	400.00	TBD	200.00	600.00
Law, Economic Management, and Public Policy							
2. Private Sector Participation Program	PAHQ	ETSW	TASF	400.00	TBD	300.00	700.00
3. Secured Transactions Reforms	PAHQ	ETSW	TASF	700.00	TBD	0.00	700.00
Total				**1,500.00**		**500.00**	**2,000.00**
Total				**2,700.00**		**1,300.00**	**4,000.00**

AO = advisory and operational, ADB = Asian Development Bank, AUS = Australian Grant, PAHQ = Pacific Operations Division, TASF = Technical Assistance Special Fund.

Source: Asian Development Bank staff estimates.

CONCEPT PAPERS FOR NONLENDING PRODUCTS AND SERVICES

This appendix contains the concept papers for the following nonlending products:

(i) Table A3.1: Implementation of Interisland Transport Reforms
(ii) Table A3.2: Business Environment Reforms
(iii) Table A3.3: Economic Development Report
(iv) Table A3.4: Supporting Transformation of SOEs (standby)
(v) Table A3.5: Ministry of Infrastructure Development Reform Program
(vi) Table A3.6: Private Sector Participation Program
(vii) Table A3.7: Secured Transactions Reforms

Table A3.1: Implementation of Interisland Transport Reforms

1. Type/modality of assistance

- ☐ Lending
  - ☐ Project loan
  - ☐ Program loan
  - ☐ Sector loan
  - ☐ Sector development program loan
  - ☐ Other:
- ☒ Nonlending
  - ☐ Project preparatory
  - ☒ Other than project preparatory
    - ☒ Economic, thematic, and sector work
    - ☐ Institutional development
    - ☐ Other:

2. Assistance Focus

a. If assistance focuses on a particular sector or subsector, specify the
Sector(s): Transportation and Communication
Subsector(s): Civil Aviation; Ports, waterways and shipping

b. For project preparatory and lending, classification
- ☐ Core poverty intervention
- ☐ Poverty intervention
- ☐ Other

c. Key thematic area(s)
- ☒ Sustainable economic growth
- ☐ Inclusive social development
- ☐ Governance
- ☐ Gender and development
- ☐ Environmental sustainability
- ☐ Regional cooperation
- ☒ Private sector development

3. Coverage

☒ Country ☐ Subregional ☐ Interregional
☐ Internal policy development

4. Responsible division/department: PAHQ, Pacific Department

5. Responsible ADB officer(s): Robert Guild, Transport Specialist

6. Description of assistance(s)

a. Background/linkage to country/regional strategy:

Interisland water transport in Solomon Islands is provided mostly through quasi-public provincial shipping services, supplemented by a few private operators on a minority of routes. Air transport is provided solely by the government-owned airline. There is little real competition in service provision anywhere. Due to a dispersed and very poor population, interisland services mostly run at a loss. The few private shipping operators are supported by erratic public subsidies, while the domestic air routes are cross-subsidized by international operations. As a result, the shipping fleet is poorly maintained and unsafe; the domestic aviation fleet is down to two very old aircraft; and both water and air transport are chronically unreliable. Rural people therefore cannot regularly access markets for their produce or access social services, with consequent negative impacts on growth and poverty.

Related activities by ADB and other development partners commenced in 2004, including development of a National Transport Plan, creation of a Transport Development Fund, and diagnostic assessment of inter island transport that is expected to develop options for sector reform.

The ADB Solomon Islands CSPU 2005—2006 supports the National Economic Recovery, Reform and Development Plan, 2003—2006 (NERRDP) by aiming to achieve rapid, pro-poor, private sector-led economic growth through support to the Government in (i) providing transportation infrastructure and services, and (ii) strengthening the enabling environment for private sector development. The proposed TA will directly support the first objective, and is consistent with ADB's Private Sector Strategy and Pacific Strategy for the New Millennium.

b. Goal and purpose:

The goal of the TA is to assist in developing more efficient and effective interisland shipping and air services. The purpose is to assist the Ministry of Infrastructure Development (MID) in carrying out reforms of its Marine and Civil Aviation Departments to implement the recommendations expected from the diagnostic study of interisland transport in 2004, including support for reform of service providers in both sub-sectors.

c. Components and outputs:

The components and outputs of the proposed TA will depend on the output of the previous year's diagnostic assessment of the sector, which will produce a reform road map. The TA will then help implement the road map, as appropriate.

d. Expected results and deliverables:

In response to the earlier diagnostic assessment, it is likely that the TA will include activities for facilitating the development of private sector shipping operators, support for development of concession agreements for domestic aviation, design of a transparent and contestable franchise scheme for uneconomic air and sea routes, and capacity building for the Marine and Civil Aviation Departments.

e. Social or environmental issues or concerns:

Reform of interisland transport is expected to have significant social benefits through increased access to markets for rural produce and increased access to social services including health and education, both contributing significantly to poverty reduction.

f. Plans for disseminating results/deliverables:

A related TA for institutional strengthening of MID that is programmed for 2004 will use extensive stakeholder involvement and participatory methods to facilitate a "whole of government" approach in support of institutional reform and national transportation planning, including creation of a Transportation Policy and Planning Unit. It is expected that implementation of this TA would be incorporated in those mechanisms.

7. Proposed executing/implementing agency: Ministry of Infrastructure Development

8. Nature/extent of government/beneficiary involvement in identifying or conceptualizing the assistance:

During the 2004 Country Programming Mission and during fact-finding for related TAs the proposed TA was discussed with stakeholders in the Government and key development partners involved in the transport sector, all of which agreed on a high priority on reforming domestic transport. Reform of interisland transport was identified as a priority in a National Transportation Strategy Workshop held in February 2004.

9. Timetable for assistance design, processing, and implementation

a. Year included in CSP Update: 2004

b. Expected date of submission for approval
Lending:
Nonlending (project preparatory):
Nonlending (other than project preparatory): 2005

c. Period and duration of assistance:
Lending:
Nonlending: 2005—2006

10. Financing Plan

a. For lending
- ☐ Ordinary capital resources:
- ☐ Asian Development Fund:
- ☐ Other:

If cofinancing is required, indicate amount and sources sought: $____, from ____________.
If known, provide cost estimates and financing arrangements.

Source	Amount ($)
ADB Financing	
Government Financing	
Other Financing	
Total Cost	

Source:

b. For nonlending
- ☐ No resources required, other than ADB staff
- ☐ ADB's administrative budget:
- ☒ Grant TA funds: $500,000
- ☐ Other: $300,000

If cofinancing is required, indicate amount and sources sought: $300,000 from bilateral trust funds

If known, provide cost estimates and financing arrangements.

Source	Amount ($)
ADB Financing	
Government Financing	
Other Financing	
Total Cost	

Source:

ADB = Asian Development Bank; CSP = country strategy and program; PAHQ = Pacific Operations Division; PARD = Pacific Department; PPTA = project preparatory technical assistance, TA = technical assistance

Table A3.2: Business Environment Reforms

1. Type/modality of assistance

- ☐ Lending
  - ☐ Project loan
  - ☐ Program loan
  - ☐ Sector loan
  - ☐ Sector development program loan
  - ☐ Other:
- ☒ Nonlending
  - ☐ Project preparatory
  - ☒ Other than project preparatory
    - ☒ Economic, thematic, and sector work
    - ☐ Institutional development
    - ☐ Other:
- ☐ Activities financed by JFICT or JFPR

2. Assistance Focus

a. If assistance focuses on a particular sector or subsector, specify the
Sector(s): Law, Economic Management, and Public Policy
Subsector(s): Economic Management, National government administration

b. For project preparatory and lending, classification
- ☐ Core poverty intervention
- ☐ Poverty intervention
- ☐ Other

c. Key thematic area(s)
- ☒ Sustainable economic growth
- ☐ Inclusive social development
- ☐ Governance
- ☐ Gender and development
- ☐ Environmental sustainability
- ☐ Regional cooperation
- ☒ Private sector development

3. Coverage

☒ Country ☐ Subregional ☐ Interregional
☐ Internal policy development

4. Responsible division/department: PAHQ, Pacific Department

5. Responsible ADB officer(s): W. Wicklein, PSD Specialist

6. Description of assistance(s)

a. **Background/linkage to country/regional strategy:**

In Solomon Islands, business laws and regulations and supporting legal institutions are often ineffective, because they tend to be outdated, flawed in design, not fitting to the country's setting and business environment, or often simply not applied properly. As a result, related transaction costs for businesses are high, exacerbating the impediments caused by the country's historically unfriendly business environment, and adding to the high cost environment for the private sector.

The Government has recognized the vital role the private sector must play in rehabilitating the economy. The RAMSI-led process has been providing a window of opportunity for the private sector, as well as for reforms to improve the enabling environment for businesses. The Government is in the process of establishing an Economic Reform Unit to oversee, coordinate, and implement private sector regulatory reforms; infrastructure policy and regulation; state-owned enterprise reform and privatization; financial sector reforms; provincial economic development; statistical collection service reforms; and specific sectoral policy reforms to promote new investments in potential growth areas.

This unit will have a major role in implementing the outcomes of this proposed TA.

The ADB Solomon Islands CSPU 2005-2006 supports the National Economic Recovery, Reform and Development Plan, 2003-2006 (NERRDP) by aiming to achieve rapid, pro-poor, private sector-led economic growth through support to the Government in (i) providing transportation infrastructure and services, and (ii) strengthening the enabling environment for private sector development. The proposed TA will directly support the second objective, and is consistent with ADB's Private Sector Strategy and Pacific Strategy for the New Millennium.

b. Goal and purpose:

The proposed TA will support the Government in improving the legal and regulatory frameworks governing private business activity. The efficiency of the country's legal and regulatory business environment will be improved with a view to reducing risk, uncertainty, and transaction costs for private businesses, improving corporate and public governance, and increasing productivity and investment. This will include reforms of commercial laws, regulations, and supporting legal institutions.

As part of regional TA 6162-REG: Improving the Legal Business Environment in the Pacific, ADB is assisting the Government to help formulate a relevant reform agenda. This proposed country-specific TA will complement these efforts by helping implement the reform agenda once established by the regional TA.

c. Components and outputs:

Components and outputs of this proposed TA will depend on the output of TA6162-REG, which will produce a detailed reform road map for the improvement of the legal business environment. The proposed TA will then help implement the road map, as appropriate.

d. Expected results and deliverables:

The results and deliverables will largely depend on the output of TA 6162-REG, which is likely to include new or amended business laws and regulations, as appropriate.

e. Social or environmental issues or concerns:

None.

f. Plans for disseminating results/deliverables:

Due to the linkage of the TA to a regional exercise (TA 6162), the results are to be widely distributed not only country wide (through the Chamber of Commerce), but also regionally through mechanisms associated with the Forum Secretariat (especially the annual Forum Economic Ministers Meetings).

7. Proposed executing/implementing agencies: Ministry of Finance, National Reform, and Planning (Economic Reform Unit) and Ministry of Commerce, Industries and Employment.

8. Nature/extent of government/beneficiary involvement in identifying or conceptualizing the assistance:

The private sector, through the Chamber of Commerce and similar private sector organizations, will be involved in the process of the diagnostic study (TA 6162), and hence will have a direct and significant input in the design of the proposed TA.

9. Timetable for assistance design, processing, and implementation

a. Year included in CSP update: 2004

b. Expected date of submission for approval
   Lending:
   Nonlending (project preparatory):
   Nonlending (other than project preparatory): 2005
   Activities financed by JFICT or JFPR:

c. Period and duration of assistance

Lending:
Nonlending: 2005—2006

10. Financing Plan

a. For lending
- ☐ Ordinary capital resources:
- ☐ Asian Development Fund:
- ☐ Other:

If cofinancing is required, indicate amount and sources sought: $____, from ____________.
If known, provide cost estimates and financing arrangements.

Source	Amount ($)
ADB Financing	
Government Financing	
Other Financing	
Total Cost	

Source:

b. For nonlending
- ☐ No resources required, other than ADB staff
- ☐ ADB's administrative budget:
- ☒ Grant TA funds: $400,000
- ☐ Other: $200,000

If cofinancing is required, indicate amount and sources sought: $200,000 from bilateral trust funds

If known, provide cost estimates and financing arrangements.

Source	Amount ($)
ADB Financing	
Government Financing	
Other Financing	
Total Cost	

Source:

ADB = Asian Development Bank CSP = country strategy and program; PAHQ = Pacific Operations Division; PARD = Pacific Department; RAMSI = Regional Assistance Mission to Solomon Islands, TA = technical assistance

Table A3.3: Economic Development Report

1. Type/modality of assistance

- ☐ Lending
  - ☐ Project loan
  - ☐ Program loan
  - ☐ Sector loan
  - ☐ Sector development program loan
  - ☐ Other:
- ☐ Nonlending
  - ☐ Project preparatory
  - ☐ Other than project preparatory
    - ☒ Economic, thematic, and sector work
    - ☐ Institutional development
    - ☐ Other:

2. Assistance Focus

a. If assistance focuses on a particular sector or subsector, specify the
Sector(s): Law, Economic Management, and Public Policy
Subsector(s): Economic Management, National government administration

b. For project preparatory and lending, classification
- ☐ Core poverty intervention
- ☐ Poverty intervention
- ☐ Other

c. Key thematic area(s)
- ☒ Sustainable economic growth
- ☐ Inclusive social development
- ☒ Governance
- ☐ Gender and development
- ☐ Environmental sustainability
- ☐ Regional cooperation
- ☒ Private sector development

3. Coverage

☒ Country ☐ Subregional ☐ Interregional
☐ Internal policy development

4. Responsible division/department: PAHQ, Pacific Department

5. Responsible ADB officer(s): Robert Guild, Transport Specialist

6. Description of assistance(s)

a. Background/linkage to country/regional strategy:

ADB programming for Pacific developing member countries is founded on a subregional cooperation strategy and program (SCSP), the Pacific Strategy for the New Millennium 2000, in combination with national Country Strategy and Program Updates (CSPUs). In-depth analytical work is often accomplished through the Pacific Islands Economic Report (PIER) series of ADB, but a report has not been prepared for Solomon Islands. The proposed TA will prepare a new economic report to allow comprehensive assessment of conditions and priorities for development.

The Solomon Islands economy faces deep and long-standing problems, including historically weak employment growth and, more recently, employment contraction, low levels of private investment, poorly performing public investments and enterprises, and an inflexible land tenure system. These challenges have been exacerbated by the ethnic tension and conflict that led to destruction of the country's few export-oriented industries and the near-collapse of the economy. All have contributed to widespread poverty that may be worsening.

Economic reform and recovery will be possible provided appropriate actions are taken along with prudent policies.

There is a need to explore new productive opportunities as well as revive and reform traditional productive activities and services. Copra and cocoa appear to have the potential for higher income earnings, and crop diversification should be pursued. Reviving the palm oil, mining, and fishing industries is a longer-term prospect. Fiscal and macroeconomic stability, and reform of the business environment, are required. Meanwhile, the poor performance of state-owned enterprises including electricity, water, air and sea transport, and others are creating constraints to increased productivity and market access.

The report will assess these opportunities and constraints in the national economy and contribute to the formulation of development strategies and policies. It will strengthen linkages between the Government's National Economic Recovery, Reform and Development Plan 2003-2006 (NERRDP) and ADB's proposed country strategy, which aims to promote rapid, pro-poor, and private sector-led economic growth. The proposed TA will provide fundamental information to support strategic activities in (i) providing transportation infrastructure and services; and (ii) strengthening the enabling environment for the private sector, including SOE reform, and will lay the foundation for future programming.

b. Goal and purpose:

The goal of the economic development report is to contribute to the sustainable economic development of Solomon Islands. The TA will study the economy's past development, current issues, and future prospects to identify development opportunities, constraints, and policy options.

c. Components and outputs:

The study will cover macroeconomic, sectoral, and thematic areas to help shape the policy dialogue between Solomon Islands and its development partners including ADB. The report will review and analyze the macroeconomic performance of the economy in the recent past with a view to capturing underlying trends and future prospects. It will also review and analyze major productive sectors of the economy with a view to identifying development opportunities, constraints, and policy options. Special attention will be paid to long-term problems, new challenges, and sectors offering new opportunities.

The report will focus on policies and practices in need of reform, particularly of state-owned enterprises (SOEs), to identify opportunities to relieve capacity constraints and increase the efficiency of basic infrastructure and services. An area of special concern is the existing legislative and regulatory environment governing SOEs, and the public sector's capacity to exercise the necessary oversight. Other development partners, including the World Bank, AusAID, and the European Union, have indicated particular interest in contributing to the analysis in these areas.

d. Expected results and deliverables:

The report will publish information on key constraints and opportunities for the Solomon Islands economy and make it available to all stakeholders in the development of the country, particularly the Government and ADB. The report will result in improved awareness by government officials, development partners, the private sector, and civil society of current economic issues and prospects. All aspects of the report will inform future preparation of the country strategy and program update (CSPU).

e. Social or environmental issues or concerns: None

f. Plans for disseminating results/deliverables:

The report will be published and widely distributed under the Pacific Studies Series of ADB. Its main audience will be government officials and staff of funding and aid agencies. The business community, academics, students, and others interested in the development of Solomon Islands will also use the report. The report will support economic growth, public sector reform, private sector development, and poverty reduction, in line with the regional and country strategy. The report will be developed through workshops and seminars, which will help disseminate information within the country while the report is being prepared.

7. Proposed executing/implementing agency: Ministry of Finance, National Reform, and Planning

8. Nature/extent of government/beneficiary involvement in identifying or conceptualizing the assistance:

The proposed TA was discussed during the 2004 Country Programming Mission, and during fact-finding for other programmed TAs, with stakeholders in the Government and key development partners. A PIER is typically prepared through a participatory process involving widespread consultations, workshops and seminars involving the Government, the private sector, and civil society. It concludes with the publication, distribution, and dissemination of the report as widely as possible.

9. Timetable for assistance design, processing, and implementation

a. Year included in CSP Update: 2004

b. Expected date of submission for approval
Lending:
Nonlending (project preparatory):
Nonlending (other than project preparatory):2005

c. Period and duration of assistance
Lending:
Nonlending: 2005

10. Financing Plan

a. For lending
☐ Ordinary capital resources:
☐ Asian Development Fund:
☐ Other:

If cofinancing is required, indicate amount and sources sought: $____, from ____________.
If known, provide cost estimates and financing arrangements.

Source	Amount ($)
ADB Financing	
Government Financing	
Other Financing	
Total Cost	

Source:

b. For nonlending
☐ No resources required, other than ADB staff
☐ ADB's administrative budget
☒ Grant TA funds: $300,000
☐ Other: $300,000

If cofinancing is required, indicate amount and sources sought: $300,000 from partner agencies contributing to the report

If known, provide cost estimates and financing arrangements.

Source	Amount ($)
ADB Financing	
Government Financing	
Other Financing	
Total Cost	

Source:

ADB = Asian Development Bank, AusAID = Australian Agency for International Development, CSP = country strategy and program, CSPU = country strategy and program update, PAHQ = Pacific Operations Division, PIER = Pacific Islands Economic Report, SCSP = subregional cooperation strategy and program, TA = technical assistance

Table A3.4: Supporting Transformation of SOEs (standby)

1. Type/modality of assistance

- ☐ Lending
  - ☐ Project loan
  - ☐ Program loan
  - ☐ Sector loan
  - ☐ Sector development program loan
  - ☐ Other:
- ☐ Nonlending
  - ☐ Project preparatory
  - ☐ Other than project preparatory
    - ☒ Economic, thematic, and sector work
    - ☐ Institutional development
    - ☐ Other:

2. Assistance Focus

a. If assistance focuses on a particular sector or subsector, specify the
Sector(s): Law, Economic Management, and Public Policy
Subsector(s): Economic Management, National government administration

b. For project preparatory and lending, classification
- ☐ Core poverty intervention
- ☐ Poverty intervention
- ☐ Other

c. Key thematic area(s)
- ☒ Sustainable economic growth
- ☐ Inclusive social development
- ☐ Governance
- ☐ Gender and development
- ☐ Environmental sustainability
- ☐ Regional cooperation
- ☒ Private sector development

3. Coverage

☒ Country ☐ Subregional ☐ Interregional
☐ Internal policy development

4. Responsible division/department: PAHQ, Pacific Department

5. Responsible ADB officer(s): W. Wicklein, PSD Specialist

6. Description of assistance(s)

a. Background/linkage to country/regional strategy:

Solomon Islands has of 17 SOEs including statutory authorities; air transport services; telecoms; resource-based enterprises in forestry, fishing, and agricultural production; and service providers in ship repair, printing, tourism, and export marketing. ADB supported a public sector reform project begun in 1998 (now closed) and expects to carry out additional TA for SOE reform and private sector participation in 2004. The proposed TA will assist the Government in implementing the recommendations developed through these activities.

The experience of Solomon Islands shows that government and inadequately regulated monopolies produce services usually of low quality and unnecessarily high costs. These SOEs have created numerous problems for the economy, due to (i) partial crowding out of the private sector through unfair competition; (ii) higher cost of inputs to private enterprises; (iii) inconsistent and unreliable service delivery and quality; (iv) appointment of board members as political favors, resulting in governance problems; and (v) the mixing of regulatory and commercial functions, resulting in SOE mismanagement and poor governance.

The focus of SOE-related reform efforts should be on increased efficiency and productivity, and improved service delivery at reasonable prices. Appropriate strategies and options need to be assessed on a case-by-case basis and may include corporatization, commercialization, licenses, concessions, and sale of shares to private investors and strategic partners that bring advanced technology and management skill, access to new market channels, and industry knowledge. Special consideration needs to be given to transport infrastructure, as the very poor state of road transport, unreliable interisland shipping services, and the perennial problems of Solomon Airlines pose considerable barriers to market access. The privatization process as envisaged under the public sector reform project requires continued commitment, considering the significant challenges in this area.

The ADB Solomon Islands CSPU 2005-2006 supports the National Economic Recovery, Reform and Development Plan, 2003-2006 (NERRDP) by aiming to achieve rapid, pro-poor, private sector-led economic growth through support to the Government in (i) providing transportation infrastructure and services, and (ii) strengthening the enabling environment for private sector development. The proposed TA will directly support the second objective, and is consistent with ADB's Private Sector Strategy and Pacific Strategy for the New Millennium.

b. Goal and purpose:

The goal of the TA is improved efficiency and effectiveness and increased private sector participation in areas of existing monopoly service provision. The purpose is to continue assisting the Ministry of Finance, National Reform, and Planning in carrying out reforms begun in 1998 and the recommendations expected from a related TA in 2004.

c. Components and outputs:

The components and outputs of this TA will depend on the output of the previous year's assessment of SOE reform options, which will produce a reform road map. The proposed TA will then help implement the road map.

d. Expected results and deliverables:

In response to the 2004 assessment, it is likely that the TA will include activities for transforming SOEs, facilitating the development of private sector service providers, updating the relevant regulatory and legislative environments, and capacity building for the various agencies of government expected to supervise the providers.

e. Social or environmental issues or concerns:

Because reform of SOEs could affect the prices paid for basic services, recommendations should include measures for mitigating any negative impacts on poor people.

f. Plans for disseminating results / deliverables:

Related national and regional TAs are planned in several areas of economic reform that involve consultations with the private sector and civil society. This TA will be included in these consultations. Since private sector participation is an emerging issue in the Pacific development agenda, dissemination of the results, both nationally and regionally, will be accorded high priority.

7. Proposed executing/implementing agency or agencies: Ministry of Finance, National Reform, and Planning

8. Nature/extent of government/beneficiary involvement in identifying or conceptualizing the assistance:

The proposed TA was discussed during the 2004 Country Programming Mission with stakeholders in the Government and key development partners. As the main TA counterpart, the Economic Reform Unit of the Ministry of Finance, National Reform, and Planning will be closely involved in TA design.

9. Timetable for assistance design, processing, and implementation

a. Year included in CSP Update: 2004

b. Expected date of submission for approval
Lending:
Nonlending (project preparatory):
Nonlending (other than project preparatory):

c. Period and duration of assistance
Lending:
Nonlending: 2005-2006

10. Financing Plan

a. For lending
- ☐ Ordinary capital resources:
- ☐ Asian Development Fund:
- ☐ Other:

If cofinancing is required, indicate amount and sources sought: $____, from ____________.
If known, provide cost estimates and financing arrangements.

Source	Amount ($)
ADB Financing	
Government Financing	
Other Financing	
Total Cost	

Source:

b. For nonlending
- ☐ No resources required, other than ADB staff
- ☐ ADB's administrative budget
- ☒ Grant TA funds: $300,000
- ☐ Other:

If cofinancing is required, indicate amount and sources sought:
If known, provide cost estimates and financing arrangements.

Source	Amount ($)
ADB Financing	
Government Financing	
Other Financing	
Total Cost	

Source:

ADB = Asian Development Bank; CSP = country strategy and program, PAHQ = Pacific Operations Division, SCSP = subregional cooperation strategy and program; SOE = State-Owned Enterprise, TA = technical assistance

Table A3.5: Ministry of Infrastructure Development Reform Program

1. Type/modality of assistance

- ☐ Lending
  - ☐ Project loan
  - ☐ Program loan
  - ☐ Sector loan
  - ☐ Sector development program loan
  - ☐ Other:
- ☒ Nonlending
  - ☐ Project preparatory
  - ☒ Other than project preparatory
    - ☐ Economic, thematic, and sector work
    - ☒ Institutional development
    - ☐ Other:
- ☐ Activities financed by JFICT or JFPR

2. Assistance Focus

a. If assistance focuses on a particular sector or subsector, specify the
   Sector: Transportation and Communication
   Subsector: Multi-modal transport and sector development

b. For project preparatory and lending, classification
- ☐ Core poverty intervention
- ☐ Poverty intervention
- ☐ Other

c. Key thematic area(s)
- ☒ Sustainable economic growth
- ☐ Inclusive social development
- ☐ Governance
- ☐ Gender and development
- ☐ Environmental sustainability
- ☐ Regional cooperation
- ☒ Private sector development

3. Coverage

☒ Country ☐ Subregional ☐ Interregional
☐ Internal policy development

4. Responsible division/department: PAHQ, Pacific Department

5. Responsible ADB officer(s): Robert Guild, Transport Specialist

6. Description of assistance(s)

a. Background/linkage to country/regional strategy:

Solomon Islands recently emerged from several years of conflict and is facing a long period of recovery and rehabilitation of essential infrastructure and services that have been destroyed or become derelict through lack of maintenance. Significant external resources are becoming available to implement major capital works and fund comprehensive maintenance programs. However, the Ministry of Infrastructure Development (MID) has limited capacity to plan and manage the necessary activities. The proposed TA will help MID restructure and implement the necessary reforms to assert and maintain control of the planning and development process.

Related activities by ADB and other development partners commenced in 2004, including development of a National Transport Plan, creation of a Transport Development Fund, and creation of a Transport Policy and Planning Unit. Additional activities include promotion of a private sector contracting industry and development of tender procedures. It will be necessary to institutionalize these processes and integrate them with the Government's wider processes for development and recurrent budgets, regulation, and policy analysis, facilitated by the expected creation of an

Economic Reform Unit that will drive reforms in these areas.

The ADB Solomon Islands CSPU 2005-2006 supports the National Economic Recovery, Reform and Development Plan, 2003-2006 (NERRDP) by aiming to achieve rapid, pro-poor, private sector-led economic growth through support to the Government in (i) providing transportation infrastructure and services, and (ii) strengthening the enabling environment for private sector development. The proposed TA will directly support the second objective, and is consistent with ADB's Private Sector Strategy and Pacific Strategy for the New Millennium.

b. Goal and purpose:

The TA will consolidate MID's capacity to plan and coordinate infrastructure development through policy, regulation, finance, and asset management as well as promote private sector involvement in infrastructure development. The purpose is to assist MID in implementing the recommendations expected from TAs that will begin in 2004.

c. Components and outputs:

The components and outputs of this TA will depend on the output of the previous year's diagnostic assessment of the sector, which will produce a reform road map. The proposed TA will then help implement the road map, as appropriate. It is expected that a "twinning" arrangement begun in 2004, in which a more developed infrastructure agency from the region will act as an institutional mentor to MID, will be reassessed and adjusted.

d. Expected results and deliverables:

The TA will result in updated and completed procedural and regulatory systems that will allow MID to change from provider to manager of the nation's infrastructure, and continue supporting its provision through the private sector.

e. Social or environmental issues or concerns:

Improved provision of infrastructure is expected to have significant social benefits through increased access to markets for rural produce and increased access to social services including health and education, both contributing significantly to poverty reduction.

f. Plans for disseminating results/deliverables:

The process used by the TA will require extensive stakeholder involvement and participatory methods to facilitate a "whole of government" approach to support of institutional reform in MID.

7. Proposed executing/implementing agency: Ministry of Infrastructure Development

8. Nature/extent of government/beneficiary involvement in identifying or conceptualizing the assistance:

As the main counterparts, the Ministry of Finance National Reform, and Planning and the Ministry of Infrastructure Development have corresponded regularly on this TA through a series of missions in late 2003 and early 2004. Key development partners were consulted during country programming in 2004.

9. Timetable for assistance design, processing, and implementation

a. Year included in CSP update: 2004

b. Expected date of submission for approval
   Lending:
   Nonlending (project preparatory):
   Nonlending (other than project preparatory): 2006
   Activities financed by JFICT or JFPR:

c. Period and duration of assistance
   Lending:
   Nonlending: 2006-2007

10. Financing Plan

a. For lending
- ☐ Ordinary capital resources:
- ☐ Asian Development Fund:
- ☐ Other:

If cofinancing is required, indicate amount and sources sought: $____, from ____________.
If known, provide cost estimates and financing arrangements.

Source	**Amount** ($)
ADB Financing	
Government Financing	
Other Financing	
Total Cost	

Source:

b. For nonlending
- ☐ No resources required, other than ADB staff
- ☐ ADB's administrative budget
- ☒ Grant TA funds: $400,000
- ☐ Other: 200,000

If cofinancing is required, indicate amount and sources sought: $200,000 from bilateral trust funds

If known, provide cost estimates and financing arrangements.

Source	**Amount** ($)
ADB Financing	
Government Financing	
Other Financing	
Total Cost	

Source:

ADB = Asian Development Bank CSP = country strategy and program, PAHQ = Pacific Operations Division; TA = technical assistance

Table A3.6: Private Sector Participation Program

1. Type/modality of assistance

☐ Lending
- ☐ Project loan
- ☐ Program loan
- ☐ Sector loan
- ☐ Sector development program loan
- ☐ Other:

☒ Nonlending
- ☐ Project preparatory
- ☒ Other than project preparatory
  - ☒ Economic, thematic, and sector work
  - ☐ Institutional development
  - ☐ Other:

☐ Activities financed by JFICT or JFPR

2. Assistance Focus

a. If assistance focuses on a particular sector or subsector, specify the
Sector(s): Law, Economic Management, and Public Policy
Subsector(s): Economic Management

b. b. For project preparatory and lending, classification
- ☐ Core poverty intervention
- ☐ Poverty intervention
- ☐ Other

c. Key thematic area(s)
- ☒ Sustainable economic growth
- ☐ Inclusive social development
- ☐ Governance
- ☐ Gender and development
- ☐ Environmental sustainability
- ☐ Regional cooperation
- ☒ Private sector development

3. Coverage

☒ Country ☐ Subregional ☐ Interregional
☐ Internal policy development

4. Responsible division/department: PAHQ, Pacific Department

5. Responsible ADB officer(s): W. Wicklein, PSD Specialist

6. Description of assistance(s)

a. Background/linkage to country/regional strategy:

Extensive government involvement in the economy, combined with weak and heavily politicized regulatory regimes for providing services, pose a heavy burden on public finances, businesses, and consumers alike. While it is recognized that the per unit cost of producing public goods on a relatively small scale is high, the experience of Solomon Islands as well as that of most nations, strongly suggests that governments and inadequately regulated monopolies produce services of low quality and unnecessarily high costs.

Reform of Solomon Islands extensive SOEs is overdue and is being carried out under related TAs. These SOEs have created numerous problems for the private sector due to (i) partial crowding out through unfair competition (ii) higher cost of inputs due to lack of competition (iii) and inconsistent and unreliable service delivery and quality, among others.

The focus of SOE-related reform efforts is on increased efficiency and productivity, and improved service delivery at reasonable prices. These goals can best be attained through private sector participation in the SOE sector. Related TA will assess appropriate strategies and options including corporatization, commercialization, licenses, concessions, and sale of shares to private investors and strategic partners that will bring advanced technology and management skill, access to new market channels, and industry knowledge in addition to capital.

ADB's country strategy for Solomon Islands directly supports the Government's National Economic Recovery, Reform and Development Plan, 2003-2006 (NERRDP). The goal of the strategy is rapid, pro-poor and private sector-led economic growth through (i) providing transportation infrastructure and services, and (ii) strengthening the enabling environment for the private sector. The proposed TA directly supports the strategy's second objective and indirectly the former.

b. Goal and purpose:

The proposed TA will help increase efficiency and productivity, and improve service delivery at reasonable prices by assisting the Government in promoting private sector participation in the SOE sector. The TA will identify and help implement appropriate strategies toward this end, including corporatization, commercialization, licenses, concessions, and disposal of state assets to the private sector.

d. Components and outputs:

The proposed TA will complement the outputs of the related 2004 TA in this area. Hence, specifics as to the components and outputs of the proposed TA will be determined at a later stage.

d. Expected results and deliverables:

Results and specific deliverables will be determined during fact finding.

e. Social or environmental issues or concerns:

None anticipated.

f. Plans for disseminating results/deliverables:

Since private sector participation is an emerging issue in the Pacific development agenda, due consideration will be given to the dissemination of the results, both nationally and regionally.

7. Proposed executing/implementing agency: Ministry of Finance, National Reform, and Planning

8. Nature/extent of government/beneficiary involvement in identifying or conceptualizing the assistance:

The private sector will be involved in the project design to ensure that there is interest in increased private sector participation. As the main TA counterpart, the Economic Reform Unit, Ministry of Finance, will be closely involved in the TA design.

9. Timetable for assistance design, processing, and implementation

a. Year included in CSP update: 2004

b. Expected date of submission for approval
Lending:
Nonlending (project preparatory):
Nonlending (other than project preparatory): 2006
Activities financed by JFICT or JFPR:

c. Period and duration of assistance
Lending:
Nonlending: 2006-2007

10. Financing Plan

a. For lending

- ☐ Ordinary capital resources:
- ☐ Asian Development Fund:
- ☐ Other:

If cofinancing is required, indicate amount and sources sought: $____, from ____________.
If known, provide cost estimates and financing arrangements.

Source	Amount ($)
ADB Financing	
Government Financing	
Other Financing	
Total Cost	

Source:

b. For nonlending
- ☐ No resources required, other than ADB staff
- ☐ ADB's administrative budget
- ☒ Grant TA funds: $400,000
- ☐ Other: $300,000

If cofinancing is required, indicate amount and sources sought: $300,000, from bilateral trust funds

If known, provide cost estimates and financing arrangements.

Source	Amount ($)
ADB Financing	
Government Financing	
Other Financing	
Total Cost	

Source:

ADB = Asian Development Bank; CSP = country strategy and program; PAHQ = Pacific Operations Division; SOE = State-Owned Enterprise, TA = technical assistance.

Table A3.7: Secured Transactions Reforms

1. Type/modality of assistance

- ☐ Lending
  - ☐ Project loan
  - ☐ Program loan
  - ☐ Sector loan
  - ☐ Sector development program loan
  - ☐ Other:
- ☒ Nonlending
  - ☐ Project preparatory
  - ☒ Other than project preparatory
    - ☒ Economic, thematic, and sector work
    - ☐ Institutional development
    - ☐ Other:

2. Assistance Focus

a. If assistance focuses on a particular sector or subsector, specify the
Sector(s): Law, Economic Management, and Public Policy
Subsector(s): Economic Management, National government administration

b. For project preparatory and lending, classification
- ☐ Core poverty intervention
- ☐ Poverty intervention
- ☐ Other

c. Key thematic area(s)
- ☒ Sustainable economic growth
- ☐ Inclusive social development
- ☐ Governance
- ☐ Gender and development
- ☐ Environmental sustainability
- ☐ Regional cooperation
- ☒ Private sector development

3. Coverage

☒ Country ☐ Subregional ☐ Interregional
☐ Internal policy development

4. Responsible division/department: PAHQ, Pacific Department

5. Responsible ADB officer(s): W. Wicklein, PSD Specialist

6. Description of assistance(s)

a. Background/linkage to country/regional strategy:

The Government has recognized the vital role the private sector must play in rehabilitating the economy. The RAMSI-led process has opened a window of opportunity for the private sector, as well as for reforms to improve the enabling environment for businesses. The Government is in the process of establishing an Economic Reform Unit to oversee, coordinate, and implement private sector regulatory reforms, policy on and regulation of infrastructure service provision, state-owned enterprise reform and privatization, financial sector reforms, provincial economic development, statistical collection service reform, and specific sectoral policy reforms to promote new investments in potential growth areas. This unit will have a major role in driving the implementation of the proposed TA.

In the National Economic Recovery, Reform and Development Plan (NERRDP) strategic area of revitalizing the productive sector and rebuilding supporting infrastructure, it is acknowledged that the enabling private sector environment must be enhanced by improving both physical and institutional infrastructure, including the legal and regulatory framework.

Banking institutions provide few services, seldom reach beyond urban areas, and have high collateral requirements. In particular, the inadequate framework for collateralizing debt denies access to credit to many, largely because of land tenure issues and the apparent lack of a functioning secured-transactions framework. While it is possible currently to use some forms of collateral, the process is costly, inefficient, and risky to lenders. A sound legal framework for secured transactions would permit farmers, consumers, and businesses to use movable property as collateral for loans. The proposed TA will support the Government in improving the secured transactions framework.

ADB's proposed country strategy to Solomon Islands will directly support NERRDP. The strategy aims to achieve rapid, pro-poor, and private sector-led economic growth through support in (i) providing transportation infrastructure and services, and (ii) strengthening the enabling environment for the private sector. The proposed TA will directly support the second objective, and is consistent with ADB's Private Sector Strategy and the ADB strategy for the Pacific.

As part of a regional TA for Secured Transactions Reforms in the Pacific, proposed for 2004, ADB is assisting the Government of Solomon Islands in formulating a relevant reform agenda. The proposed country-specific TA will complement these efforts by helping to implement the reform agenda as established under the regional TA.

b. Goal and purpose:

The goal of the proposed TA is to increase and broaden access to credit in Solomon Islands and thus the rate of investment by businesses and individuals, to improve economic growth prospects for the country. The purpose is to assist the Government in establishing a well-functioning secured transactions framework. Toward this end, the TA will improve the legal, regulatory, and technical framework for secured transactions.

e. Components and outputs:

The TA will be based on the in-depth analytical study of the legal framework for secured transactions to be produced under the proposed RETA for Secured Transactions Reforms in the Pacific (proposed for 2004). Based on the RETA findings, the TA outputs will include a legal and regulatory framework for secured lending; an Internet-based notice filing archive, supplied on a turnkey basis; technical and administrative regulations governing the Internet-based notice filing archive for security interests; and a supplemental program for capacity building, public awareness building, and monitoring support.

d. Expected results and deliverables:

Deliverables include consultant reports delivered on time; draft laws delivered and passed by Parliament; filing archive established; legal practitioners, lenders, and filing archive operators trained; and initial operation of filing archive supported.

e. Social or environmental issues or concerns:

None.

f. Plans for disseminating results/deliverables:

Due to the linkage of the TA to a regional exercise (RETA), it is expected that the results will be widely distributed not only nationally, but also regionally.

7. Proposed executing/implementing agencies: Ministry of Finance, National Reform, and Planning (Economic Reforms Unit); Attorney General's Office.

8. Nature/extent of government/beneficiary involvement in identifying or conceptualizing the assistance:

The private sector, through the Chamber of Commerce, financial sector institutions, and legal practitioners will be closely involved at the project design stage, as will the Ministry of Finance, National Reform, and Planning and the Attorney General's Office.

9. Timetable for assistance design, processing, and implementation

a. Year included in CSP update: 2004

b. Expected date of submission for approval
Lending:
Nonlending (project preparatory):
Nonlending (other than project preparatory): 2006

c. Period and duration of assistance
Lending:
Nonlending: 2006-2007

10. Financing Plan

a. For lending
- ☐ Ordinary capital resources:
- ☐ Asian Development Fund:
- ☐ Other:

If cofinancing is required, indicate amount and sources sought: $____, from ____________.
If known, provide cost estimates and financing arrangements.

Source	Amount ($)
ADB Financing	
Government Financing	
Other Financing	
Total Cost	

Source:

b. For nonlending
- ☐ No resources required, other than ADB staff
- ☐ ADB's administrative budget
- ☒ Grant TA funds: $700,000
- ☐ Other:

If cofinancing is required, indicate amount and sources sought:
If known, provide cost estimates and financing arrangements.

Source	Amount ($)
ADB Financing	
Government Financing	
Other Financing	
Total Cost	

Source:

ADB = Asian Development Bank, CSP = country strategy and program; PAHQ = Pacific Operations Division; RAMSI = Regional Assistance Mission to Solomon Islands, RETA = regional technical assistance, TA = technical assistance.

Assistance Program for 2004

Table A4.1: Assistance Program for Nonlending Products and Services, 2004

Sector Assistance Name	Responsible Division	Assistance Type	Sources of Funding: ADB Source	ADB Amount ($'000)	Others Source	Others Amount ($'000)	Total ($'000)
Transport and Communications							
1. Diagnostic Assessment of Interisland Transport	PAHQ	AO	TASF	150.00	AUS	150.00	300.00
2. Institutional Strengthening for the Ministry of Infrastructure and Development	PAHQ	AO	TASF	700.00			700.00
Law, Economic Management, and Public Policy							
3. State-owned Enterprise Reforms and Private Sector Participation	PAHQ	AO	TASF	300.00	AUS	500.00	800.00
Total				**1,150.00**		**650.00**	**1,800.00**

AO = advisory and operational, ADB = Asian Development Bank, AUS = Australian Grant, PAHQ = Pacific Operations Division, TASF = Technical Assistance Special Fund.
Source: Asian Development Bank staff estimates.

GLOBAL BUSINESS & INVESTMENT LIBRARY

PRICE $149.95

Ultimate directories for export-import, investment, government and

- GLOBAL LAW FIRMS DIRECTORY — ISBN 0739767089
- GLOBAL BUSINESS CONTACTS DIRECTORY — ISBN 073976702X
- GLOBAL CHAMBERS OF WORLD — ISBN 0739767054
- GLOBAL CHAMBERS OF COMMERCE USA — ISBN 0739767046
- GLOBAL SLAVIC LIBRARIES DIRECTORY — ISBN 0739767100
- GLOBAL BUSINESS AND INDUSTRIAL DIRECTORIES PUBLISHERS DIRECTORY — ISBN 073967003
- AFRICA UNIVERSITY LIBRARIES — ISBN 073900936
- UNITED KINGDOM UNIVERSITY DIRECTORY — ISBN 0739700928
- GLOBAL OFFSHORE INVESTMENT & BUSINESS — ISBN 0739767097
- GLOBAL BUSINESS ASSOCIATIONS DIRECTORY — ISBN 0739767011
- GLOBAL TAX GUIDE EUROPE — ISBN 0739767119
- GLOBAL INVESTMENT FUNDS DIRECTORY — ISBN 0739767070
- GLOBAL US ECONOMIC — ISBN 0739767143
- GLOBAL WORLD TRADE — ISBN 073976716X
- WORLD TRADE ORGANIZATION — ISBN 0739707426
- KOREA UNIFICATION HANDBOOK — ISBN 0739700936
- GLOBAL OFFSHORE INVESTMENT & BUSINESS — ISBN 0739767097
- GLOBAL OFFSHORE BUSINESS CONTACTS — ISBN 0739739336
- GLOBAL TAX GUIDE ASIA — ISBN 0739767127
- GLOBAL OFFSHORE BUSINESS LAW HANDBOOK — ISBN 0739739344
- GLOBAL OFFSHORE TAX HANDBOOK — ISBN 0739739352
- GLOBAL TRANSPORTATION BUSINESS CONTACTS — ISBN 073970091X
- UNITED STATES TV BROADCASTIN — ISBN 0739707442
- PORTUGAL TELECOM INDUSTRY INVESTMENT & BUSINESS GUIDE — ISBN 0739707434

US REGIONAL INVESTMENT & BUSINESS LIBRARY-2000

Investment and Business are available for the following states and cities

Price: $99.95 each

ALASKA INVESTMENT & BUSINESS GUIDE

1.Alabama
2.Alaska
3.Arizona
4.Arkansas
5.Atlanta
6.Boston
7.California
8.Chicago
9.Colorado
10.Connecticut
11.Dallas
12.District of Columbia
13.Florida
15.Hawaii
16.Idaho
17.Illinois
18.Indiana
19.Iowa
20.Kansas
21.Kentucky
22.Los Angeles
23.Louisiana
24.Maine
25.Marylamd
26.Massachusetts
27.Miami
28.Michigan
29.Minnesota
30.Mississippi
31.Missouri
32.Montana
33.Nebraska
34.Nevada
35.New Hampshire
36.New Jersey
38.New York City
39.New York
40.North Carolina
41.North Dakota
42.Ohio
43.Oklahoma
44.Oregon
45.Pennsylvania
46.Philadelphia
47.Rhode Island
48.San Francisco
49.South Carolina
50.South Dakota
51.Tennessee
52.Texas
53.Utah
54.Vermont
55.Virginia
56.Washington
56.West Virginia
57.Wisconsin
58.Wyoming

- GLOBAL ECONOMIC, FINANCIAL DEVELOPMENT ORGANIZATIONS — ISBN 0739767062 — Intl economic development agencies and investment funds in over 100 countries
- GLOBAL CENTRAL BANK — ISBN 0739767038 — Central banks in about 100 countries
- GLOBAL INTERNATIONAL HUMANITARIAN ORGANIZATIONS DIRECTORY — ISBN 0739767186 — International organizations worldwide

WORLD EXPORT-IMPORT & BUSINESS LIBRARY

Ultimate directories for conducting export-import operations in the country. Largest exporters and

Directories are available for the following countries

RUSSIAN Export-Import BUSINESS DIRECTORY

Armenia
Austria
Azerbaijan
Belarus
Belgium
Czech Rep
Denmark
Estonia
France
Georgia
Germany
Greece
Ireland
Israel
Italy
Kazakhstan
Kyrgyzstan
Latvia
Liechtenstein
Lithuania
Luxemburg
Moldova
Netherlands
Pakistan
Portugal
Russia
Spain
Switzerland
Tajikistan
Turkmenistan
Ukraine
UK
USA
Uzbekistan

Price: $99.95 each

Please contact International Business Publications, USA for ISBN numbers
Please send your order to International Business Publications, USA.
P. O. Box 15343, Washington, DC 20003
Phone: (202) 546-2103. Fax: (202) 546-3255. E-mail: rusric@erols.com
Selected guides are available in electronic format on CD-ROM
Global Markets on Line: http://world.mirhouse.com

2006
WORLD INTERNATIONAL ORGANIZATIONS BUSINESS AND DEVELOPMENT LIBRARY

1. Abu Dhabi Fund for Development Handbook
2. African Development Bank Group(AfDB) Handbook
3. African Development Fund (AfDF) Handbook
4. Nigeria Trust Fund (NTF) Handbook
5. African Export-Import Bank (AFREXIMBANK) Handbook
6. Andean Community General Secretariat Handbook
7. Andean Development Corporation (CAF) Handbook
8. Arab Authority for Agricultural Investment and Development (AAAID) Handbook
9. Arab Bank for Economic Development in Africa (BADEA) Handbook
10. Arab Fund for Economic and Social Development (AFESD) Handbook
11. Arab Gulf Programme for United Nations Development Organizations (AGFUND) Handbook
12. Arab Maghreb Union (AMU) Handbook
13. Arab Monetary Fund (AMF) Handbook
14. Arab Organization for Agricultural Development (AOAD) Handbook
15. Arab Planning Institute - Kuwait Handbook
16. Arab Trade Financing Program (ATFP) Handbook
17. Asia-Pacific Economic Cooperation (APEC) Handbook
18. Asian and Pacific Coconut Community (APCC) Handbook
19. Asian Clearing Union (ACU) Handbook
20. Asian Development Bank (AsDB) Handbook
21. Association of Natural Rubber Producing Countries (ANRPC) Handbook
22. Association of South East Asian Nations (ASEAN) Handbook
23. Baltic Council of Ministers Handbook
24. Bank for International Settlements (BIS) Handbook
25. Bank of Central African States (BEAC) Handbook
26. Black Sea Trade and Development Bank (BSTDB) Handbook
27. Caribbean Centre for Monetary Studies (CCMS) Handbook
28. Caribbean Community (CARICOM) Handbook
29. Caribbean Development Bank (CDB) Handbook
30. Caribbean Regional Technical Assistance Centre (CARTAC) Handbook
31. Center for Latin American Monetary Studies (CEMLA) Handbook
32. Center for Marketing Information and Advisory Services for Fishery Products in Latin America and the Caribbean (INFOPESCA) Handbook
33. Central American Bank for Economic Integration (CABEI) Handbook
34. Central American Monetary Council (CAMC) Handbook
35. Central Bank of West African States (BCEAO) Handbook
36. Colombo Plan for Co-operative Economic and Social Development in Asia and the Pacific Handbook
37. Colombo Plan Staff College for Technician Education Handbook

38. Common Fund for Commodities Handbook
39. Common Market for Eastern and Southern Africa (COMESA) Handbook
40. Cooperation Council for the Arab States of the Gulf (GCC) Handbook
41. Council of the Baltic Sea States (CBSS) Handbook
42. Council of Europe Development Bank (CEB) Handbook
43. East African Development Bank (EADB) Handbook
44. Eastern Caribbean Central Bank (ECCB) Handbook
45. Economic Community of West African States (ECOWAS) Handbook
46. Economic Cooperation Organization (ECO) Handbook
47. European Bank for Reconstruction and Development (EBRD) Handbook
48. European Central Bank (ECB) Handbook
49. European Free Trade Association (EFTA) Handbook
50. European Investment Bank (EIB) Handbook
51. European Investment Fund (EIF) Handbook
52. European Union, The (EC) Handbook
53. Financial Fund for the Development of the River Plate Basin (FONPLATA) Handbook
54. Food and Agriculture Organization of the United Nations (FAO) Handbook
55. Fund for Co-operation, Compensation and Development (ECOWAS Fund) Handbook
56. Inter-American Development Bank (IDB) Handbook
57. Inter-American Institute for Cooperation on Agriculture (IICA) Handbook
58. Inter-Arab Investment Guarantee Corporation (IAIGC) Handbook
59. International Atomic Energy Agency (IAEA) Handbook
60. International Civil Aviation Organization (ICAO) Handbook
61. International Cocoa Organization (ICCO) Handbook
62. International Coffee Organization (ICO) Handbook
63. International Confederation of Free Trade Unions (ICFTU) Handbook
64. International Cotton Advisory Committee (ICAC) Handbook
65. International Fund for Agricultural Development (IFAD) Handbook
66. International Grains Council Handbook
67. International Labour Organization (ILO) Handbook
68. International Lead and Zinc Study Group Handbook
69. International Monetary Fund (IMF) Handbook
70. International Olive Oil Council (IOOC) Handbook
71. International Rubber Study Group Handbook
72. International Sugar Organization (ISO) Handbook
73. International Telecommunications Union (ITU) Handbook
74. International Tropical Timber Organization (ITTO) Handbook
75. Islamic Development Bank Group (IsDB) Handbook
76. Islamic Research and Training Institute (IRTI) Handbook
77. Joint Vienna Institute (JVI) Handbook
78. Kuwait Fund for Arab Economic Development Handbook
79. Lake Chad Basin Commission (LCBC) Handbook
80. Latin American Association of Development Financing Institutions (ALIDE) Handbook
81. Latin American Economic System (SELA) Handbook
82. Latin American Energy Organization (OLADE) Handbook
83. Latin American Export Bank (BLADEX) Handbook
84. Latin American Integration Association (ALADI) Handbook
85. Latin American Reserve Fund (LARF) Handbook
86. League of Arab States Handbook
87. Mekong River Commission (MRC) Handbook
88. Nordic Development Fund (NDF) Handbook

89. Nordic Investment Bank (NIB) Handbook
90. OPEC Fund for International Development Handbook
91. Organisation for Economic Co-operation and Development (OECD) Handbook
92. Organisation of Eastern Caribbean States (OECS) Handbook
93. Organization of American States (OAS) Handbook
94. Organization of Arab Petroleum Exporting Countries (OAPEC) Handbook
95. Organization of the Petroleum Exporting Countries (OPEC) Handbook
96. Pacific Financial Technical Assistance Centre Handbook
97. Pacific Islands Forum Secretariat Handbook
98. Pan American Health Organization (PAHO) Handbook
99. Regional Association of Oil and Natural Gas Companies in Latin America and the Caribbean (ARPEL) Handbook
100. Regional Electrical Integration Commission (CIER) Handbook
101. Saudi Fund for Development (SFD) Handbook
102. Secretariat for Central American Economic Integration (SIECA) Handbook
103. Secretariat of the Pacific Community Handbook
104. Sectorial Commission for the Common Market of the South (MERCOSUR) - Uruguay Handbook
105. South Asian Association for Regional Cooperation (SAARC) Handbook
106. South-East Asian Central Banks (SEACEN) Research and Training Centre Handbook
107. Training Centre for Regional Integration (CEFIR) Handbook
108. United Nations African Institute for Economic Development and Planning (IDEP) Handbook
109. United Nations Conference on Trade and Development (UNCTAD) Handbook
110. United Nations Development Program (UNDP) Handbook
111. United Nations Economic and Social Commission for Asia and the Pacific (ESCAP) Handbook
112. Asian and Pacific Centre for Transfer of Technology (APCTT) Handbook
113. Regional Coordination Centre for Research and Development of Coarse Grains, Pulses, Roots and Tuber Crops in the Humid Tropics of Asia and the Pacific (ESCAP CGPRT Centre) Handbook
114. Statistical Institute for Asia and the Pacific (SIAP) Handbook
115. United Nations Economic and Social Commission for Western Asia (ESCWA) Handbook
116. United Nations Economic Commission for Africa (UNECA) Handbook
117. United Nations Economic Commission for Europe (UN/ECE) Handbook
118. United Nations Economic Commission for Latin America and the Caribbean (ECLAC) Handbook
119. United Nations Educational, Scientific and Cultural Organization (UNESCO) Handbook
120. United Nations Industrial Development Organization (UNIDO) Handbook
121. United Nations Latin American and Caribbean Institute for Economic and Social Planning (ILPES) Handbook
122. Universal Postal Union (UPU) Handbook
123. West African Development Bank (BOAD) Handbook
124. West Africa Economic and Monetary Union Handbook
125. World Bank Group Handbook
126. World Food Program (WFP) Handbook
127. World Health Organization (WHO) Handbook
128. World Trade Organization (WTO) Handbook

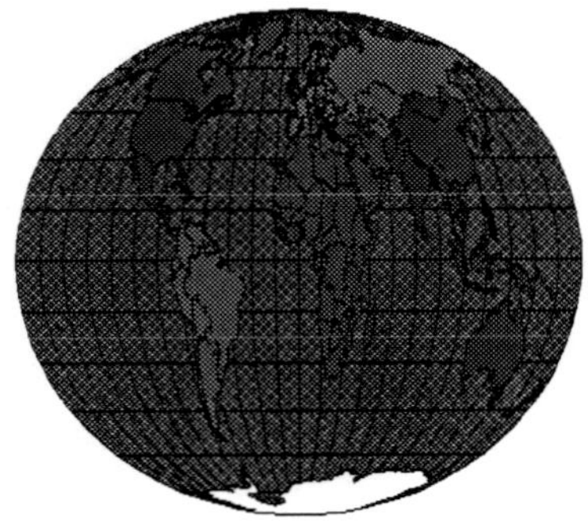

WORLD MINERAL & MINING SECTOR INVESTMENT & BUSINESS GUIDE LIBRARY

Price: $99.95 Each

1.	Afghanistan Mineral & Mining Sector Investment and Business Guide
2.	Albania Mineral & Mining Sector Investment and Business Guide
3.	Algeria Mineral & Mining Sector Investment and Business Guide
4.	Angola Mineral & Mining Sector Investment and Business Guide
5.	Argentina Mineral & Mining Sector Investment and Business Guide
6.	Armenia Mineral & Mining Sector Investment and Business Guide
7.	Australia Mineral & Mining Sector Investment and Business Guide
8.	Austria Mineral & Mining Sector Investment and Business Guide
9.	Azerbaijan Mineral & Mining Sector Investment and Business Guide
10.	Bahrain Mineral & Mining Sector Investment and Business Guide
11.	Bangladesh Mineral & Mining Sector Investment and Business Guide
12.	Belarus Mineral & Mining Sector Investment and Business Guide
13.	Belgium Mineral & Mining Sector Investment and Business Guide
14.	Benin Mineral & Mining Sector Investment and Business Guide
15.	Bolivia Mineral & Mining Sector Investment and Business Guide
16.	Bosnia and Herzegovina Mineral & Mining Sector Investment and Business Guide
17.	Botswana Mineral & Mining Sector Investment and Business Guide
18.	Brazil Mineral & Mining Sector Investment and Business Guide
19.	Brunei Mineral & Mining Sector Investment and Business Guide
20.	Bulgaria Mineral & Mining Sector Investment and Business Guide
21.	Burkina Faso Mineral & Mining Sector Investment and Business Guide
22.	Burundi Mineral & Mining Sector Investment and Business Guide
23.	Cambodia Mineral & Mining Sector Investment and Business Guide
24.	Cameroon Mineral & Mining Sector Investment and Business Guide
25.	Canada Mineral & Mining Sector Investment and Business Guide
26.	Cape Verde Mineral & Mining Sector Investment and Business Guide
27.	Cayman Islands Investment & Business Guide
28.	Central African Republic Mineral & Mining Sector Investment and Business Guide

For additional analytical, business and investment opportunities information, please contact Global Investment & Business Center, USA at (202) 546-2103. Fax: (202) 546-3275. E-mail: rusric@erols.com

29. Chad Mineral & Mining Sector Investment and Business Guide
30. Chile Mineral & Mining Sector Investment and Business Guide
31. China Mineral & Mining Sector Investment and Business Guide
32. Colombia Mineral & Mining Sector Investment and Business Guide
33. Comoros Mineral & Mining Sector Investment and Business Guide
34. Congo Mineral & Mining Sector Investment and Business Guide
35. Congo, Dem. Republic Mineral & Mining Sector Investment and Business Guide
36. Cook Islands Mineral & Mining Sector Investment and Business Guide
37. Costa Rica Mineral & Mining Sector Investment and Business Guide
38. Cote d'Ivoire Mineral & Mining Sector Investment and Business Guide
39. Croatia Mineral & Mining Sector Investment and Business Guide
40. Cuba Mineral & Mining Sector Investment and Business Guide
41. Czech Republic Mineral & Mining Sector Investment and Business Guide
42. Denmark Mineral & Mining Sector Investment and Business Guide
43. Djibouti Mineral & Mining Sector Investment and Business Guide
44. Dominican Republic Mineral & Mining Sector Investment and Business Guide
45. Dubai Mineral & Mining Sector Investment and Business Guide
46. Ecuador Mineral & Mining Sector Investment and Business Guide
47. Egypt Mineral & Mining Sector Investment and Business Guide
48. El Salvador Mineral & Mining Sector Investment and Business Guide
49. Equatorial Guinea Mineral & Mining Sector Investment and Business Guide
50. Eritrea Mineral & Mining Sector Investment and Business Guide
51. Estonia Mineral & Mining Sector Investment and Business Guide
52. Ethiopia Mineral & Mining Sector Investment and Business Guide
53. Fiji Mineral & Mining Sector Investment and Business Guide
54. Finland Mineral & Mining Sector Investment and Business Guide
55. France Mineral & Mining Sector Investment and Business Guide
56. Gabon Mineral & Mining Sector Investment and Business Guide
57. Gambia Mineral & Mining Sector Investment and Business Guide
58. Georgia Mineral & Mining Sector Investment and Business Guide
59. Germany Mineral & Mining Sector Investment and Business Guide
60. Ghana Mineral & Mining Sector Investment and Business Guide
61. Greece Mineral & Mining Sector Investment and Business Guide
62. Guatemala Mineral & Mining Sector Investment and Business Guide
63. Guinea Mineral & Mining Sector Investment and Business Guide
64. Guinea-Bissau Mineral & Mining Sector Investment and Business Guide
65. Guyana Mineral & Mining Sector Investment and Business Guide
66. Haiti Mineral & Mining Sector Investment and Business Guide
67. Honduras Mineral & Mining Sector Investment and Business Guide
68. Hungary Mineral & Mining Sector Investment and Business Guide
69. Iceland Mineral & Mining Sector Investment and Business Guide
70. India Mineral & Mining Sector Investment and Business Guide
71. Indonesia Mineral & Mining Sector Investment and Business Guide

For additional analytical, business and investment opportunities information, please contact Global Investment & Business Center, USA at (202) 546-2103. Fax: (202) 546-3275. E-mail: rusric@erols.com

72. Iran Mineral & Mining Sector Investment and Business Guide
73. Iraq Mineral & Mining Sector Investment and Business Guide
74. Ireland Mineral & Mining Sector Investment and Business Guide
75. Israel Mineral & Mining Sector Investment and Business Guide
76. Italy Mineral & Mining Sector Investment and Business Guide
77. Jamaica Mineral & Mining Sector Investment and Business Guide
78. Japan Mineral & Mining Sector Investment and Business Guide
79. Jordan Mineral & Mining Sector Investment and Business Guide
80. Kazakhstan Mineral & Mining Sector Investment and Business Guide
81. Kenya Mineral & Mining Sector Investment and Business Guide
82. Korea, North Mineral & Mining Sector Investment and Business Guide
83. Korea, South Mineral & Mining Sector Investment and Business Guide
84. Kuwait Mineral & Mining Sector Investment and Business Guide
85. Kyrgyzstan Mineral & Mining Sector Investment and Business Guide
86. Laos Mineral & Mining Sector Investment and Business Guide
87. Latvia Mineral & Mining Sector Investment and Business Guide
88. Lesotho Mineral & Mining Sector Investment and Business Guide
89. Liberia Mineral & Mining Sector Investment and Business Guide
90. Libya Mineral & Mining Sector Investment and Business Guide
91. Lithuania Mineral & Mining Sector Investment and Business Guide
92. Macedonia Republic Mineral & Mining Sector Investment and Business Guide
93. Madagascar Mineral & Mining Sector Investment and Business Guide
94. Malawi Mineral & Mining Sector Investment and Business Guide
95. Malaysia Mineral & Mining Sector Investment and Business Guide
96. Mali Mineral & Mining Sector Investment and Business Guide
97. Mauritania Mineral & Mining Sector Investment and Business Guide
98. Mauritius Mineral & Mining Sector Investment and Business Guide
99. Mayotte Investment & Business Guide
100. Mexico Mineral & Mining Sector Investment and Business Guide
101. Micronesia Mineral & Mining Sector Investment and Business Guide
102. Moldova Mineral & Mining Sector Investment and Business Guide
103. Mongolia Mineral & Mining Sector Investment and Business Guide
104. Morocco Mineral & Mining Sector Investment and Business Guide
105. Mozambique Mineral & Mining Sector Investment and Business Guide
106. Myanmar Mineral & Mining Sector Investment and Business Guide
107. Namibia Mineral & Mining Sector Investment and Business Guide
108. Nepal Mineral & Mining Sector Investment and Business Guide
109. Netherlands Mineral & Mining Sector Investment and Business Guide
110. New Zealand Mineral & Mining Sector Investment and Business Guide
111. Nicaragua Mineral & Mining Sector Investment and Business Guide
112. Niger Mineral & Mining Sector Investment and Business Guide
113. Nigeria Mineral & Mining Sector Investment and Business Guide
114. Norway Mineral & Mining Sector Investment and Business Guide

115.Oman Mineral & Mining Sector Investment and Business Guide
116.Pakistan Mineral & Mining Sector Investment and Business Guide
117.Papua New Guinea Mineral & Mining Sector Investment and Business Guide
118.Paraguay Mineral & Mining Sector Investment and Business Guide
119.Peru Mineral & Mining Sector Investment and Business Guide
120.Philippines Mineral & Mining Sector Investment and Business Guide
121.Poland Mineral & Mining Sector Investment and Business Guide
122.Portugal Mineral & Mining Sector Investment and Business Guide
123.Qatar Mineral & Mining Sector Investment and Business Guide
124.Romania Mineral & Mining Sector Investment and Business Guide
125.Russia Mineral & Mining Sector Investment and Business Guide
126.Rwanda Mineral & Mining Sector Investment and Business Guide
127.Sao Tome and Principe Mineral & Mining Sector Investment and Business Guide
128.Saudi Arabia Mineral & Mining Sector Investment and Business Guide
129.Scotland Mineral & Mining Sector Investment and Business Guide
130.Senegal Mineral & Mining Sector Investment and Business Guide
131.Sierra Leone Mineral & Mining Sector Investment and Business Guide
132.Slovakia Mineral & Mining Sector Investment and Business Guide
133.Slovenia Mineral & Mining Sector Investment and Business Guide
134.Somalia Mineral & Mining Sector Investment and Business Guide
135.South Africa Mineral & Mining Sector Investment and Business Guide
136.Spain Mineral & Mining Sector Investment and Business Guide
137.Sri Lanka Mineral & Mining Sector Investment and Business Guide
138.Sudan Mineral & Mining Sector Investment and Business Guide
139.Suriname Mineral & Mining Sector Investment and Business Guide
140.Swaziland Mineral & Mining Sector Investment and Business Guide
141.Sweden Mineral & Mining Sector Investment and Business Guide
142.Syria Mineral & Mining Sector Investment and Business Guide
143.Taiwan Mineral & Mining Sector Investment and Business Guide
144.Tajikistan Mineral & Mining Sector Investment and Business Guide
145.Tanzania Mineral & Mining Sector Investment and Business Guide
146.Thailand Mineral & Mining Sector Investment and Business Guide
147.Togo Mineral & Mining Sector Investment and Business Guide
148.Trinidad and Tobago Mineral & Mining Sector Investment and Business Guide
149.Tunisia Mineral & Mining Sector Investment and Business Guide
150.Turkey Mineral & Mining Sector Investment and Business Guide
151.Turkmenistan Mineral & Mining Sector Investment and Business Guide
152.Uganda Mineral & Mining Sector Investment and Business Guide
153.Ukraine Mineral & Mining Sector Investment and Business Guide
154.United Arab Emirates Mineral & Mining Sector Investment and Business Guide
155.United Kingdom Mineral & Mining Sector Investment and Business Guide
156.United States Mineral & Mining Sector Investment and Business Guide
157.Uruguay Mineral & Mining Sector Investment and Business Guide

158.Uzbekistan Mineral & Mining Sector Investment and Business Guide
159.Venezuela Mineral & Mining Sector Investment and Business Guide
160.Vietnam Mineral & Mining Sector Investment and Business Guide
161.Yemen Mineral & Mining Sector Investment and Business Guide
162.Yugoslavia Mineral & Mining Sector Investment and Business Guide
163.Zambia Mineral & Mining Sector Investment and Business Guide
164.Zimbabwe Mineral & Mining Sector Investment and Business Guide
165.Baltic Countries Mining and Mineral Industry Handbook
166.North America Mining and Mineral Industry Handbook
167.Pacific Countries Mining and Mineral Industry Handbook
168.Russia and NIS Mining and Mineral Industry Handbook
169.Africa – West Mining and Mineral Industry Handbook
170.Caribbean Countries Mining and Mineral Industry Handbook
171.Central Europe Mining and Mineral Industry Handbook
172.Middle East Mining and Mineral Industry Handbook
173.South America Mining and Mineral Industry Handbook
174.EU Mining and Mineral Policy Handbook

Breinigsville, PA USA
24 March 2011
258307BV00003B/2/A